# AN
# INVALUABLE
# TREASURE
## A HISTORY OF THE
# TSB

# AN
# INVALUABLE
# TREASURE
## A HISTORY OF THE
# TSB

MICHAEL MOSS AND IAIN RUSSELL

WEIDENFELD AND NICOLSON · LONDON

FRONTISPIECE: a section of the cover of the
prospectus for the flotation of the TSB, 1986.

# CONTENTS

# PREFACE AND ACKNOWLEDGEMENTS

I was brought up in the Cotswolds and then in Brislington on the outskirts of Bristol where savings banks were few and far between. We spent our holidays with my grandmother in Northumberland, at Tynemouth. It was here that I came to learn how important savings banks were in the culture of the north of England and Scotland. Every week, in her Sunday-go-to-meeting clothes, my grandmother, behatted, visited the Tynemouth Savings Bank (established 1836) to draw her housekeeping and talk over any problems with the actuary or one of the tellers. After the death of my grandfather at the Western Front in the closing days of the First World War, the savings bank, with its friendly welcome, gave my grandmother, along with other war widows, the confidence to manage her affairs. The ideals of thrift and temperance it promoted made it possible for her to send both her daughters to university.

This book is the story of how many savings banks, scattered up and down the country and playing a vital role in their communities, came together to form TSB Group plc, which was floated with such spectacular success in October 1986. It shows how the trustee savings banks have had to modify their objectives to match the changing expectations of their customers, without losing touch with their commitment to saving and investment for the future. As in any movement with such a long history, there have been good and bad times and internal disputes and disagreements, but there was always the conviction that placing cash in the bank is preferable to putting it in a sock under the bed and that wise financial management will bring domestic happiness. Although TSB Group plc in the 1990s is a far cry from the tiny savings bank opened in Ruthwell, Dumfriesshire, in 1810, the principle of the founding fathers – that people and their problems matter – remains true.

I would like to thank Sir Nicholas Goodison, the chairman, and Philip Charlton, until 1990 chief executive, and their colleagues for inviting me to write this book. They have been a source of perceptive advice and wise counsel. I am very indebted to John Whittall, an old TSB hand, and now managing director of Hill Samuel Mortgage Services Ltd, who has been my chief contact with the bank. At the Head Office in Milk Street, I have been regularly helped by Henry Stephens, the deputy secretary, who has rummaged through basements in the quest for important documents and unlocked many doors elsewhere in the United Kingdom. Until he retired in 1990, I received unstinting support from the Group's archivist, Colin Barlow, who had the task of arranging for the deposit of the TSB's huge holdings of archives in the custody of local authority record offices throughout England and Wales. Through the foresight of Richard Ellis and Iain Macdonald in Scotland, a comprehensive archive had been established through the heroic efforts of John McLintock, who now works in the Scottish Record Office.

I owe very special thanks to Iain Russell, who has worked closely with me on the project and whose name deservedly appears on the title page. He has been a constant mine of information, source of advice, critic, and friend over many years. He has relentlessly tracked down books, articles in obscure journals, missing archives and, most importantly for a book of this kind, illustrations. He has never taken no for an answer from hapless archivists years behind with their listing, from bankers who regarded our enquiries as bizarre, or from me when I obdurately refused to change what I had written. Together we have corresponded with and spoken to a great many people connected with the savings bank movement.

Iain Russell and I have visited many local record offices throughout the United Kingdom and the Republic of Ireland; we thank them all for allowing us free access to collections of records deposited by the TSB. We wish to thank the staff at the Mitchell Library, Glasgow; Glasgow University Library; the National Library of Scotland; the Public Record Office; the British Newspaper Library, Colindale; TSB, Ingram Street, Glasgow; and the Business Record Centre, Glasgow.

MICHAEL MOSS
*Glasgow, July 1993*

The illustrations are all drawn from the TSB archive, unless otherwise stated. We would like to thank the following for permission to reproduce illustrations:

Birmingham Central Library: 156, 162, 168, 196, 199; Bodleian Library: 35, 115, 154 *left*, 179; Bristol Libraries: 39 *right*; Chester City Record Office: 41; Clwyd Record Office: 72; Cork Savings Bank: 36, 138; Documentary Photography Archive, Manchester: 39 *left*, 43, 114 *right* and *below*, 140, 152, 159, 207, 219; Express Newspapers plc: 227; *Financial Times*: 308, 312; Glasgow Museums and Art Galleries, People's Palace: 125; *Glasgow Herald*: 303; Glasgow University Archives: 10, 76, 108, 124, 131, 142, 153, 154 *right*; Glasgow University Library: 11, 47; Greater London Record Office: 51; Grosvenor Museum, Chester: 68; Hugh Murray: 139; Hull City Record Office: 55, 66, 174; Hull Museum & Art Galleries: 103; *Independent*: 311; Liverpool City Archives: 24; Manchester Central Library: 38; *Manchester Evening News*: 269; Mary Evans Picture Library: 18; National Archives, Dublin: 53; National Railway Museum: 114 *above*; Norwich Castle Museum: 15; Public Record Office: 137, 141, 186, 191, 192, 197, 198, 201, 203, 204, 206, 208, 211, 212, 214, 215, 223, 226 *left*, 232; *Punch*: 85; Tyne & Wear Archive Services: 52; J. Walter Thompson: 258, 263, 264, 267, 280, 281, 285, 286, 288, 290; York City Archives: 234

# CHAPTER ONE

# AN

# INVALUABLE

# TREASURE

## *to 1817*

Saving money in the modern world is an enormous business with banks, insurance companies, investment trusts, building societies, friendly societies and government all competing vigorously with one another to win the custom of individuals by offering marginally higher interest rates and slightly 'better' services. It was not always so.

In the medieval world for those few who could afford to save, saving and salvation marched together. Money and valuables could be used not just to meet the vicissitudes of an earthly life, but also as importantly to pay for a better life in the world to come through oblations to the Church which in turn distributed alms to the poor and needy. After the Reformation in the sixteenth century, which emphasised the redemption of the individual through personal faith and works, the old order was replaced by more pragmatic attitudes. With the abolition of the religious houses which had provided the principal agencies for medieval charity, the focus for poor relief switched to the parish. It was the Christian duty of every individual with sufficient resources to give to the poor and the parish was the vehicle for ensuring equitable distribution.

At a time when many people were paid in kind, only the better-off artisans and professional people could contemplate saving to tide themselves and their families through times of hardship. In medieval times each town had guilds and societies of craftsmen and merchants which not only regulated local industry and commerce but also provided for members and their families in periods of sickness and distress and in old age. Most of these guilds and societies enjoyed the patronage and protection of the Church. As a result they were swept away at the Reformation only to re-emerge as secular societies with precisely the same objectives. With growing prosperity they flourished, often extending their membership beyond the bounds of their original trade or craft. New types of association were also formed purely to provide mutual assistance to members. These were often known at first as box clubs, so called because subscriptions were collected in boxes, and, from the seventeenth century, as friendly societies. As the economy developed these societies and trade associations came to invest their funds in everything from property to government stock.

Such practical responses to poverty, disability and old age were reinforced by the persistent need for the State to prevent unemployment, as idle hands could provide a usurper with easily motivated followers. The State adopted a combination of paternal and repressive policies making provision for the destitute and encouraging education and vocational training on the one hand, whilst on the other whipping vagrants and beggars who were perceived to be the potential catalyst of civil disorder. Throughout the country poor relief could be provided only by the parish in which a person qualified for 'settlement', i.e. place of birth. In England and Wales under the Poor Law Act passed in 1601, two years before Queen Elizabeth's death, care for the 'impotent' poor was provided in poorhouses, the able-bodied poor were given work, usually hemp picking, in 'houses of correction', and children apprenticed to a trade. The cost of such relief was covered out of rates assessed by each parish. In Scotland the emphasis was different. Indoor relief was provided only for the indigent and 'impotent', commonly met from the voluntary contributions of congregations; there was no provision for the able-bodied. Despite regular reports from throughout the United Kingdom of venality and corruption amongst the parish officials responsible for its administration, the Poor Law worked tolerably well except during periods of crisis like the harvest failures at the very end of the seventeenth century. Central to the system was the implicit assumption that the population remained relatively stable and that people maintained an affinity with their place of birth. These expectations became increasingly unrealistic during the eighteenth century as the population grew and people sought work far from home in the new factories and workshops spawned by the quickening pace of industrial development.

The population of Great Britain is estimated to have risen from around 6.25 million people in 1750 to 10 million in 1800. In many places the advance was so marked as to attract contemporary comment. The Church of Scotland ministers who contributed to Sir John Sinclair's *Statistical Account of Scotland*, published between 1791 and 1799, regularly referred to the soaring population even in remote areas. This increase in population was difficult for people at the time to explain, but was almost certainly due to a combination of better farming practices, widespread vaccination against smallpox and good weather in the 1760s and 1770s. It was not so much that there were more births, but that more children survived their early years. Industrial and commercial progress provided not only job opportunities but also firmly established the monetised economy – people were no longer paid partly in kind but entirely in cash, which they used to buy goods and services. The number of new jobs, most of which were to be found in the London area, in the fast-expanding towns in the Midlands and north of England, and in Scotland's central belt, did not keep pace with the growth of population. As a result the administration of the Poor Law began to strain at the seams. In England and Wales magistrates and church wardens who were responsible for administering the Poor Law generously interpreted the rules of the Elizabethan Poor Law Act of 1601 to meet the crisis, particularly providing outdoor relief for whole families at times of serious hardship following harvest failures. As a result of this assistance, according to a Berkshire magistrate, many poor people 'had been saved from an ignominious end, and many an innocent family from the most poignant distress'. Outdoor relief was encouraged by Thomas Gilbert's reforming Poor Law Amendment Act of 1782, which also allowed parishes to combine to build Union workhouses.

The industrial revolution in Britain in the second half of the eighteenth century was the outcome of a complex interaction of advantageous conditions: favourable geography, easily worked raw materials, government protection, an open society, a spirit of scientific inquiry, a developed financial infrastructure, improved transportation, and so on. Throughout the period the conditions that made for industrial and commercial growth were continually reinforced by a process of mutual interaction. The tangible signs of economic advance, apart from the sprawling industrial towns and factory villages, were canals linking most of central England to

the sea, and joining the Firths of Clyde and Forth in Scotland, improved turnpike roads, and marked changes in agricultural practice. Rapid progress challenged existing interpretations of economic behaviour, stimulating members of the new business élite and scholars to question whether State regulation and protection of trade was more of a hindrance than a help.

The most influential and widely read of the new thinkers was Adam Smith, professor of moral philosophy at the University of Glasgow and the author of *An Inquiry into the Nature and Causes of the Wealth of Nations* (1776). Central to his argument was that lasting growth could be achieved only by dismantling all barriers to trade, such as customs and excise duties, concessionary payments to domestic producers, tolls and a

Adam Smith (1723–90),
author of *The Wealth of Nations*
and advocate of free trade.

variety of customary taxes. The new world of free trade would foster economic growth and at the same time act as a spur to industrial and commercial efficiency. As a figure of the great intellectual revival of the late eighteenth century, known as the European Enlightenment, Adam Smith's concerns stretched beyond the world of business to the whole of society. Although he stipulated that there were limitations to his free market approach, many of those who were swayed by his ideas came to believe that he endorsed the principles of voluntary giving so long enshrined in the Scottish Poor Law as opposed to the compulsory rating system of England and Wales. The voluntary ideal, combined with free market attitudes, led to a belief that the poor should do more to help themselves. This was music to the ears of many property-owners who, in the times of poor harvests and recession in the 1780s, found the increasing burden of poor rates and voluntary contributions intolerable.

The concept of self-determination was rooted in a conviction that the poor could avoid becoming a burden on the parish if they saved some of their income during times of prosperity. To support this argument social reformers pointed to huge increases in consumption of gin and other spirits and widespread gambling. Saving, it was averred, would then achieve two socially desirable goals: poverty would be eradicated and the evils of drunkenness and gambling reduced, if not extinguished. Even before Adam Smith articulated his theory, commentators on the Poor Law had proposed the extension of friendly societies to every community providing a convenient avenue for saving. Enthusiasm for friendly societies and the

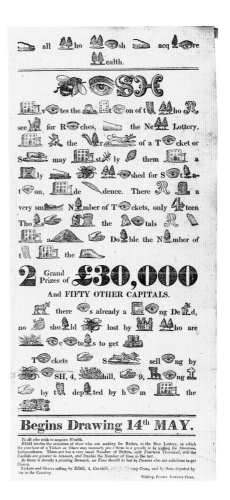

A lottery ticket, and a lottery agent's advertisement. A rage for Government lotteries developed during the late nineteenth century. They were abolished in 1826, in the face of criticism that this method of raising revenue encouraged profligacy among those who could least afford to gamble.

services they provided derived in part from the first actuarial investigations into mortality rates in the 1760s. This allowed friendly societies to offer improved benefits, principally through annuities, to a wider clientele.

Dr Richard Price, a radical Nonconformist minister in Old Jewry in London and himself an early actuary, published in 1771 a scheme for a national friendly society 'which would probably thrive', based on his experience as one of the co-founders in 1762 of the Equitable Assurance on Lives & Survivorships. Two years later, with the help of Mr Baron Maseres, he suggested, in his 'Proposal for Establishing Life Annuities in Parishes for the benefit of the Industrial Poor', a compulsory old age pension administered in England and Wales by church wardens. A Bill was introduced into Parliament which clearly stated that 'journeymen and handicraft traders and likewise household servants, labourers and divers other persons get more money as the wages of their labour and service than is sufficient for their present maintenance and might easily, if they were so minded, lay by, out of their said gettings, a sufficient sum to provide for their old age'. Although the Bill was rejected by the House of Lords, it stimulated widespread enthusiasm in every locality for the formation of friendly societies with not dissimilar objectives. It has been estimated that between 1760 and 1780 the pace of new creations accelerated rapidly and from 1780 to 1790 climbed sharply. By the end of the century there were over 7,000 friendly societies in England and Wales with nearly three-quarters of a million members meeting usually in club rooms of inns and taverns, perhaps once a month. The barriers to enrolment were high. There were entry fines (membership fees), annual subscriptions, penalties for non-attendance at meetings and non-payment of subscriptions when they fell due, and in many societies the additional cost of evenings of conviviality. Membership was usually restricted to either individual religious denominations or churches, or different professions or trades, or particular places of birth. Such regulations and the absence of legal registration gave the impression that friendly societies were exclusive secret associations.

The members of these societies, mostly craftsmen and professional men, greeted the outbreak of the French Revolution in 1789 with excitement, and as events unfolded the authorities became anxious that popular protest might spread across the English Channel. Suspicion turned on the friendly societies that might act as seedbeds for revolution because of their seemingly clandestine or hidden existence and the known radical sympathies of many of their leaders. After the execution of Louis XVI in 1793 and Britain's subsequent declaration of war on revolutionary France, the authorities took stern measures which culminated two years later in legislation to outlaw meetings of more than fifty people without permission of the magistrates and widened the definition of treason. Although many radical societies had members and sometimes titles in common with friendly societies, the government was, nevertheless, concerned to encourage genuine associations whose objectives were to provide benefit for the sick and infirm. This in turn would reduce the burden on the parishes, critical at a time when war expenditure was set to increase the National Debt.

George Rose, Secretary to the Treasury and MP for Christchurch in Dorset, took swift action to prevent friendly societies being engulfed by repressive measures against other associations. In 1793 he successfully piloted an Act through Parliament providing for voluntary registration which endowed societies with a legal status, allowing them to protect their funds in the courts. His purpose was as much to promote self-determination and the formation of new societies as to defend the existing organisations. Under the Act a friendly society was defined broadly as an association 'for raising, by voluntary subscriptions of the members thereof, separate funds for the mutual relief and maintenance of the said members in sickness, old age and infirmity'. The rules and regulations had to be approved by the Justices of the Peace and all the officers had to submit the names of two sureties and sign a bond. Rose was convinced that his Act was 'likely to be attended with very beneficial effects by promoting the happiness of individuals and at the same time diminishing the public burthen'. The Act more than fulfilled these expectations. After overtly political clubs were suppressed in 1795 and the activities of trade unions or combinations were circumscribed four years later, the energies of the more active artisans and professional people were directed towards the establishment and development of friendly societies. By the turn of the century there were just over 5,000 registered societies and when some 2,200 unregistered associations were allowed for, an estimated 7,200, with a total of 648,000 members. The majority of these were formed with the active support of local clergy, landowners and men of business. At the same time the system of providing outdoor relief to the poor was given formal expression in the so-called Speenhamland System (named after the Berkshire village where it was devised) which linked the amount of relief on a sliding scale to wages, family size and the price of wheat. Approved by the Berkshire quarter sessions in 1795 it was rapidly adopted, often in a modified form, in other parts of the country.

This spread of outdoor relief and accompanying growth in friendly societies took place against a background of intense inquiry into the nature of society. On a practical level medical men, social reformers and churchmen campaigned for improvements on a diversity of issues such as public health, prison conditions, the Poor Law and the abolition of slavery. The principal organisations concerned with the investigation of poverty were known as 'Societies for Bettering the Condition and Increasing the Comforts of the Poor'. These were established in a number of towns and cities in the United Kingdom on the model of the first, which was founded in London in 1796 by Sir Thomas Bernard, the Bishop of Durham and the great social reformer William Wilberforce. Although the founders of such societies believed that the burden of the poor on the rates must be reduced, they were not convinced that the poor should entirely help themselves. They were committed to a programme of 'the prevention of vice and contagion, the promotion of virtue and industry; and the general diffusion of moral and religious education'. Practical policies included well-constructed cottages for the poor, gardens, ground to keep cows and the provision of village shops. Laudable as such ambitions were, they were cast almost exclusively in a rural mode and were inappropriate in the context of the rapidly growing industrial towns of the Midlands, the north of England and Scotland, where poverty was acute.

Theorists, who considered the problem of poverty from an urban perspective, inspired or alarmed by the political economist Thomas Malthus, held up the spectre that if the population continued to grow unchecked, it would soon outstrip 'the power in the earth to produce subsistence for men'. Echoing Adam Smith, Malthus, in his *Essay on the Principle of Population* (1798; revised 1803), inveighed against the Poor Law as likely to militate against self-restraint and independence, the principal weapons – apart from disease – in holding down population growth. The Poor Law, it was argued – at least in England and Wales – may fulfil immediate needs, but in the long run did more harm than good. He used as evidence the example of Scotland where, in his opinion, the limited benefits provided by a voluntary system and the social stigma derived from their acceptance, caused ordinary people 'to make very considerable exertions to avoid the necessity of applying for such a scanty and precarious relief'.

Malthus encouraged the poor to save in times of prosperity to meet future periods of austerity, and proposed the foundation of Country Banks 'where the smallest sums would be received and a fair interest granted for them'. With no regard to practical banking problems, he advocated that deposits were to be available at call. Although such advice begged the question as to whether the worst off had money to save, there were plenty of social commentators, vicars and ratepayers who shared this opinion. Their problem was how to implement the suggestions advanced by Malthus.

Throughout the country many looked to the friendly societies to provide the means for thrift, while a few experimented with alternative local organisations for saving. In 1798 Mrs Priscilla Wakefield established a Female Benefit Club incorporating a Children's Bank in the parish of Tottenham, to the north of London. Anybody could open an account for a child, making regular monthly contributions of a penny or more. Three years later, in 1801, Martin Frederick Barss published his *Grand Universal Economical Union Plan for Providing Against Old Age, Indigence, Calamity, Sickness or Superannuation*. Barss claimed that his scheme would 'in the course of a few years wonderfully lessen the poor rates of the several parishes in the Kingdom' by providing a form of health and social security scheme. Nothing came of the proposal but others were keen to take up the idea, notably the merchant, public servant and social commentator, Patrick Colquhoun.

Born in Dumbarton in the west of Scotland in 1745, Colquhoun made a fortune in the tobacco trade between the Clyde and North America. When Glasgow was pitched into an economic crisis following the outbreak of the American War of Independence, he established the first Chamber of Commerce in the United Kingdom in an effort to develop other trading opportunities for the city. He moved to London in 1787 to establish the Scottish Commercial Agency, becoming one of the first stipendiary magistrates in the metropolis three years later. Appalled by the extent of habitual criminality on the streets of the capital, he published in 1796

The remarkable Mrs Priscilla Wakefield (1750–1832), the Quaker author, philanthropist
and founder of the first British savings bank, with her husband Edward and her sister
Catherine Bell. Painted about 1774 by Francis Wheatley.

*A Treatise on the Police of the Metropolis* in which he painted a grim picture of the conditions in
the capital. Colquhoun expounded the surprising theory that the root of the problem lay in
overspending, a reflection of the higher wages available to artisans and clerks in London: 'the
improvident and even the luxurious living which prevails too generally among various classes
of the lower ranks of people in the metropolis leads to much misery and many crimes'.
Accustomed to the frugality of life in Scotland, he condemned particularly the consumption
by those who could not afford it 'of expensive food in its season' and 'the habit of spending a
great deal of valuable time as well as money unnecessarily in public houses' in London.
Estimating that labouring people spent £3 million a year in public houses, he urged the poor
'to exercise the utmost economy in their preparation and consumption of food'. However, he
offered no practical advice as to how the money saved should be invested.

The following year Colquhoun's friend, the political scientist, Jeremy Bentham, suggested
the establishment of 'Frugality Banks' or savings banks paying interest on deposits, not unlike

the Benefit Club at Tottenham, within 'Houses of Industry' to be built and managed by a proposed National Charity Company. This was an ambitious scheme to 'privatise' poor relief. Although these proposals remained unrealised, Bentham had endorsed in more general terms Malthus's idea of a bank for savings. This was a concept very different from the English private banks which existed solely for the benefit of commerce, industry and large landowners. The commercial banks held cash balances for customers in current accounts, but paid no interest as their principal function was to discount bills of exchange, the principal means of paying for raw materials and manufactured products. During 1797 the first practical national life insurance office, the Pelican Life Office, was formed, using as its outlet the agencies controlled by its sister organisation, the Phoenix Fire Office.

At the time Bentham made his suggestion, Pitt's government was committed to taking more direct repressive measures to counter the threat of revolution and growing lawlessness. By the end of the year the danger was acute. The coming to power of Napoleon Bonaparte as First Consul of France in November 1799 coincided with a disastrous harvest in the United Kingdom. Food riots were commonplace, particularly in the Midlands and the North, and a census of the poor conducted in 1803 revealed that over a million people were regularly in receipt of poor relief. It was during this period of mounting concern about the condition of the poor that Priscilla Wakefield converted her Female Benefit Club into a Benefit Bank, recognised at the time 'as the first distinct Bank for Savings publicly set on foot for the benefit of the lower classes'. The bank was open only on the first Monday of the month 'for receipts and payments'. Interest was paid at 5 per cent on every £1 that remained on deposit for twelve months. Depositors were free to recall their investments on demand on any day the books were opened. A trustee was appointed for every £100 that were held by the bank. The bank soon reported remarkable feats of saving, allowing, it was claimed, depositors to become capitalists in their own right. One nurse was reported as depositing the huge sum of £140, and a servant saving enough to purchase five houses which brought him an income of £50 per annum.

During 1804 George Rose, then Vice-President of the Board of Trade and Joint Paymaster General, wrote his *Observations on the Poor Law* calling for ideas to help solve the intractable problem of poverty. Within a year John Bone had published a widely circulated reply, condemning the existing compulsory Poor Law system: 'Instead of being a provision for the poor and a boon granted to solace the last days of infirmity and age, under the pressure of misfortune, we behold it wringing away the earnings of the frugal and industrious, to bestow them upon the idle and profligate, and after having deceived the poor with delusive hopes, granting them nothing more than one mode of wretchedness in exchange for another.' He proposed that by removing the cushion of relief the 'vicious' would no longer have any reason 'to dissipate their youth and strength in indolence and carelessness'. To supplement the voluntary contributions of the better-off, he proposed a scheme similar to that of Barss with a retreat for the aged and infirm financed by subscriptions. In addition he advised 'that a Bank should be opened to receive the small savings of the youth of both sexes, who have no dependence but their labour and economy, and to return them on the day of their marriage with the interest and premiums proportioned to the amount'. He had no doubt that 'the future of our young people would be materially improved by the possession of a small number of pounds at their outset in life, for the want of which they are prevented from entering upon small houses'.

The debate was given added impetus in 1805 by a further sharp rise in prices, making the lot of the poor even more acute. Colquhoun developed his views in two pamphlets, published in 1806: 'A Treatise on Indigence; exhibiting a general view of the national resources for productive labour; with propositions for ameliorating the condition of the poor, and improving the moral habits and increasing the comforts of the labouring people, particularly the rising generation', and 'A new and appropriate system of education for the labouring people'. In the first he reviewed the development of thinking about the relief of poverty since Adam Smith published his *Wealth of Nations* in 1776. He reflected that the 'bad management and heavy burdens of the poor' that troubled him were as nothing to current conditions with an annual expenditure in England and Wales of over £4 million. Despite their success he was convinced that friendly societies addressed only a small fraction of the population. Elaborating the ideas of Bentham and Bone, he proposed a National Deposit Bank for Parochial Societies, managed by the government. Unlike friendly societies with their fixed subscription rates, members would be free to pay from 1s to 10s a month. However, like friendly societies, the failure to pay a monthly subscription would result in all previous deposits being forfeited, unless the member was able to make up any arrears. The funds collected would be invested by the National Deposit Bank in government securities. The funds would be guaranteed by the government and the expenses of operating the bank would be met out of a proportion of the interest. After the first year the parochial offices would be open daily from 9.00 a.m. to 6.00 p.m. 'for the purpose of receiving and registering the claims of members who are afflicted with sickness, or who may conceive themselves entitled under any of the contingency secured to them, to receive money'. Well aware that this scheme might be criticised on the grounds that people lacked the wherewithal to save, Colquhoun went to great pains to demonstrate that, despite evidence to the contrary, disposable incomes had increased out of all recognition with falling prices of basic foodstuffs and a doubling of wages. He argued that it was this new-found prosperity that had led to an increase in criminality. He pointed out that there was no less than one public house to every thirty-seven families in London. In a recession, with no savings, the poor turned to pawnbrokers – 'so rooted is this habit of trusting to the pawnbroker's shop for assistance, while an article of furniture or a rag remains, upon which money can be raised, that a dependence on this resource often deadens the stimulus to forethought, . . . yet in so great a degree has it become a habit, that if these modes of raising money were not accessible, or were suddenly taken away, thousands would unavoidably perish in the streets'. The National Deposit Bank would be a powerful force for social change and 'unquestionably give a new and more provident character to menial servants and thereby rescue many females from the walks of prostitution'.

Characterised by his contemporaries as 'pompous and domineering in his manners', Colquhoun was not the man to persuade politicians to put such a project into action. Bone, whose ideas did not require government action to be realised, determined to launch an experimental 'retreat' for the 'aged and infirm'. Suitably christened Tranquillity, the institution was established in 1806 by the voluntary contributions of the 'nobility, gentry etc., who choose to become subscribers with a view to recommend such poor persons as may be thought proper objects'. Apart from providing a retreat for the elderly and the infirm, Tranquillity was also to provide temporary accommodation for families and individuals coming to town, to care for and educate orphans, and last but not least 'provide baths to which all itinerant dealers, wandering persons and others may resort to wash themselves, and where conveniences shall be

A pawnbroker's shop, as portrayed by George Cruikshank for Charles
Dickens's *Sketches by Boz*. According to Patrick Colquhoun, in 1806
there were 240 licensed pawnbrokers in London alone.
He complained that 'the dependence on this resource often
deadens the stimulus to forethought'.

provided for washing and drying their clothes'. The Court of Directors, in addition to those elected by members subscribing more than £5 per annum, was a roll-call of the great and the good from the Archbishop of Canterbury to the Governor of the Bank of England.

Despite Bone's grandiose and fanciful ambitions, the method of subscribing to Tranquillity through the aptly named Economical Bank bore a distinct resemblance to Colquhoun's scheme, with variable contributions, anything from 6d to £600, to appeal to every class of investor. There were to be no fines for the failure to meet subscriptions when they fell due. Funds were to be invested at compound rates of interest to be paid to the subscriber 'at the period of age in a proportionate annuity for the remainder of his life'. Those who failed to subscribe a sufficient sum to produce an adequate annuity were to be helped out of the voluntary contributions of the better-off. An annuity did not require the recipient necessarily to live in the Tranquillity retreat. Accounts could be opened by married men, single women and children and youths. Facilities were also to be provided for soldiers and sailors who were not well supplied with friendly societies. Five 'respectable gentlemen, wholly unconnected with the contrivance of the plan', were appointed as Trustees of the funds. John Bone went to considerable trouble to design a ticket or rudimentary passbook, which was referenced to the relevant page in the institution's receipt book. It was left to the customer to ensure that monies deposited with the Economical Bank were entered correctly in the receipt book, 'otherwise the sum will never be acknowledged to his credit, but will be forfeited to the Extra Fund'. Directly Tranquillity was well established the directors were to apply to Parliament to allow those members who paid poor rates to contract out.

Within less than a year of the launch of Tranquillity, Samuel Whitbread, the reforming MP for Bedford, decided to introduce a Bill into Parliament which would sanction a simplified bank based on post offices. Borrowing his ideas directly from the proposals put forward by John Bone and Patrick Colquhoun, Whitbread's plan allowed investors to deposit not more than £20 a year or £200 in total with post offices. Deposits were to be invested in government annuities and administered by Commissioners for a newly established Poor's Fund. Investors could make withdrawals on demand when they would receive the market price of their stock plus any accrued interest. Administrative costs were to be met out of a levy of one penny in the pound on all deposits and interest on unclaimed deposits, supported, if need be, by the Consolidated Fund. With Parliament preoccupied with the measure to abolish the slave trade, the Bill failed to attract support and was allowed to lapse. Bone reacted violently to Whitbread's scheme accusing him of undermining public confidence in Tranquillity. He condemned the role ascribed to the State by Whitbread, fearing it would be a deterrent to would-be savers distrustful of government motives.

From his experience in operating Tranquillity, Bone also cast doubt on the confident assumption he had shared with Colquhoun that the poor had money to save. By analysing household budgets, he explained in a pamphlet *Wants of the People* (1807) that only by the most prudent economy could the majority of the population prevent themselves falling into debt or resorting to crime. Amongst many examples, he quoted the instance of a young man aged twenty-four who had sought his advice at the Economical Bank:

> He said that he worked from six o'clock in the morning till six o'clock at night, and received sixteen shillings per week wages and had been so employed one year. I endeavoured to preach economy to him, upon the ground stated in everything that I have written upon the subject … It was not without some surprise that I found him so perfectly systematic, as to be ready to assure me, that, though he is wholly unencumbered, his wages, apparently ample for a single man, were scarcely sufficient to keep him in life and health, even with most rigid care. His expenses were regulated as follows: His lodging cost him two shillings and sixpence weekly and he breakfasted upon bread and butter and milk and water, to save the expense of tea. His dinner consisted of half a pound of meat and a pint of porter; he could afford nothing to eat or drink between dinner and supper; but he supped also upon bread and butter, with the addition of a pint of porter. Amongst the items of his expense was one shilling paid weekly to his landlady, for cooking for him at her fire, and in consideration of supplying him with salt and pepper, and a small quantity of soap, to wash himself with; and another item was fivepence per week for washing and mending. In addition to these regular expenses, he had purchased two coarse shirts, for seven shillings each, and two handkerchiefs, for two shillings each; two pairs of worsted stockings had cost him five shillings; and five pairs of shoes, at seven shillings per pair, had cost him one pound fifteen shillings; which, with the expense of mending the old ones, being seven shillings and sixpence more, amounted to two pounds two shillings and sixpence. He had not debited himself with a single farthing for any of those nameless wants or idle extravagancies, which the poor are supposed to indulge in; and yet he had only one pound nine shillings and tenpence, remaining at the end of the year, after paying his daily expenses. The thing appeared incredible at first sight, but he accounted for it in the most satisfactory manner.

In direct opposition to Colquhoun, Bone believed the rising tide of criminality to be the outcome not of prosperity but of grinding poverty which condemned 'many of the honest and hard-worked people of England … to crawl over the soil for a few years, without ever once gasping a single breeze of pleasure, or being regarded with any greater degree of complacency than the reptiles which crawl over it also'. After such an admission it is hardly surprising that his Economical Bank had closed its doors by the end of June 1807 as too few subscribers had come forward.

The Provident Institute of London, founded at the same time as Tranquillity in 1806, remained open with an established clientele. Its objectives had been less ambitious: to provide old age pensions for artisans and clerks. It was based largely on Baron Maseres's ideas. Over 10,000 leaflets had been distributed, attracting a steady flow of customers for deferred annuities for old age. These had been purchased 'chiefly by the better-off servant, and occasionally their masters for them; also by comedians, music masters, and others whose incomes are now liberal, but will certainly fail when they become old'. As its promoter Barber Beaumont freely conceded, it had failed to win the support of 'the artisan and labourer for whom the plan was deemed to be peculiarly suited, and [for] whom it has been strongly recommended, . . . and THEY ARE RIGHT'. He attributed the cause to their need for as much cash as possible in the middle years of life to support a family rather than in a doubtful old age.

Despite such misgivings, faced with mounting poor rates there were others who were keen to experiment with local savings schemes. Expenditure on poor relief continued to grow inexorably and could be expected to increase even further following Napoleon's economic blockade of Britain under his Continental System imposed in 1807. In October of that year the Revd John Mackersy established the West Calder Friendly Bank at West Calder in Midlothian not far from Edinburgh. Like its predecessors, its purpose was 'to preserve the savings of the industrious to a time when sickness, old age, or any other causes, should make them useful'. Meetings were held at the same time as those of a flourishing friendly society set up some years before. The minimum subscription was 2s 6d a quarter. There were fines for non-payment. Subscriptions at this level, combined with fines, suggest that the bank was aimed at artisans and domestic servants, who enjoyed more or less continuous employment and higher wages than the majority of rural labourers whose work was largely seasonal. All deposits with the new bank were placed with two of Edinburgh's commercial banks which, unlike their English counterparts, were accustomed to paying interest on cash placed on deposit by customers. At the opposite end of the country at Bath in Somerset, a society was formed the following year to attract the savings of servants. There were no lower limits on individual deposits, but directly an account contained £50 the sum had to be withdrawn.

These are only two examples of the local thrift organisations initiated in these years which persuaded Dr Joseph Adams, a public health pioneer, to formulate his 'Plan for a Bank for Savings' in 1808. This offered practical advice on how a national bank should be constituted, emphasising that the rules and regulations should be simple and easily comprehended by members. He recommended that there should be no limit on the size of deposits and no fines for non-payment. He suggested that financial muscle could be given to the new bank through a guarantee fund by 'one hundred rich persons' depositing £1,000 each in the bank's funds, which were to be held by the Bank of England. A year later Horace Twiss, a London barrister, proposed a similar scheme but instead of a central bank he advocated the formation of local savings associations with deposits invested in government stock as in Whitbread's scheme. There was by now an emerging consensus that the funds of a savings bank should be invested with the government at a fixed rate of interest, with an allowance to cover expenses. As far as practical deposits of any denomination were to be accepted and, to set a bank apart from a friendly society, there should be no fines for non-payment.

With the Continental System, which prevented imports into most of mainland Europe,

The Revd Henry Duncan (1774–1846),
'Father of the Savings Banks'.

already damaging British trade and manufacturing industry, the economic problems of the country were compounded by harvest failures in Scotland in 1808 and in the United Kingdom as a whole in the next four seasons. The grim harbinger of this spell of bad weather was a great snowstorm in Scotland and the north of England in May 1808 which destroyed trees and shrubs, brought on by a mild spring. When wheat prices soared in 1810 food riots were reported from every part of the country, which in industrial centres spilled over into attacks on new machinery blamed for rising unemployment.

In the parish of Ruthwell in Dumfriesshire in south-west Scotland, the minister, the Revd Henry Duncan, had no doubt local thrift organisations on a modest scale were an essential component in the campaign against poverty, if the Scottish principle of voluntary giving was not to be abandoned in favour of compulsory rates on the English model. A well-educated man of thirty-six, Duncan began to explore the literature on the subject of savings, particularly the writings of John Bone, loaned to him by his friend Colonel Erskine.

Although he reckoned that 'The Principles and Regulations of Tranquillity' were 'too complicated for general adoption', he was struck with Bone's concept of an Economical Bank as a vehicle for raising funds. He quickly concluded that such a bank 'might be attended with the most important results to the labouring classes' providing the prospect of 'a means of ameliorisation dependent on no begrudged and degrading poor law subsidies – not even on the Christian charities of the rich and benevolent – but on the prudent forethought and economy of the people themselves'. He also hoped that a bank would not only avoid the necessity of raising compulsory rates but also do away with the current practice in Scotland of parishes licensing the poor to beg. Throughout the spring of 1810 the whole subject of the poor had been actively debated in the *Dumfries & Galloway Courier* in response to a series of articles written by Duncan himself, using the pseudonym Philopennes. He had ready access to the newspaper's columns as he had established it the year before, with assistance from relatives in Liverpool. On 1 May he outlined his proposal for 'utilising parish banks'; castigating poor rates 'as a bribe to the industrious to become idle', he advocated the establishment of an 'economical bank, for the reception of the small savings of industrious tradesmen, servants, and labourers'. Disregarding Bone's experience, he argued that there were 'many individuals in this rank of life, who thoughtlessly spend more than two shillings in the week at the alehouse, or in purchasing finer clothes than their station requires for no other reason than the want of a convenient place for laying up their savings. To such as these a Parish Bank must be an invaluable treasure.' He proposed four simple rules. The banks were to have two funds, one to receive the deposits 'of those who are to be benefited by it', and the other to consist of 'charitable contributors'. The remaining three regulations dealt with the day-to-day management of the banks which were to be supervised by a governor, five directors and a treasurer. Deposits were to be lodged with a commercial bank, yielding current rates of interest.

This was not simply speculation. A son of the manse, with ten years of experience of the

The premises of Arthur Heywood, Sons & Co, Castle Street, Liverpool,
1787. Duncan worked in the bank from 1790 until 1793.

parochial ministry, Duncan was well placed to put his ideas into practice. He was born at Lochrutton in Kirkcudbrightshire in 1774 and educated at Dumfries Academy. At the age of fourteen he had been sent to the University of St Andrews. During the summer vacation at the end of Duncan's second year in 1790, Dr James Currie, a family friend, offered him the opportunity of taking a junior post with the Liverpool bankers, Arthur Heywood, Sons & Co. As his two brothers were already working in the town, Henry Duncan leapt at the chance – only to be quickly disillusioned. His employers complained that he devoted too much of his time to literary and intellectual pursuits rather than mastering the rudiments of trade and commerce. Chastened, Duncan resigned his position in 1793 and returned to Scotland bent on following his father into the Church. He immediately resumed his academic studies, being much influenced by the jurist John Miller at Glasgow and the moral philosopher Dugald Stewart at Edinburgh with his commitment to the common-sense school of philosophy. He thrived in the heady atmosphere of Edinburgh University's Speculative Society where he met and debated with some of the finest young minds of his generation. Although, like many of his contemporaries, he neglected to graduate, he left Edinburgh with a broadly based liberal education, greatly struck with the emphasis placed on self-reliance by his philosophy teachers.

Henry Duncan returned to Lochrutton in the spring of 1798 and was licensed to preach by the presbytery of Dumfries. While awaiting a call to a parish, he spent some months as a tutor to the sons of Colonel Erskine. He was offered three parishes in the spring of 1799: two in Dumfriesshire by the Earl of Mansfield and one in Ireland. Henry Duncan chose Ruthwell, a small country parish on the shore of the Solway Firth, which he believed would be not too demanding and would afford him leisure to indulge his own intellectual curiosity.

Inducted by the presbytery in 1799, the new minister quickly found that there was far more to do than he expected. The bad harvest of that year took its toll on the population, many being forced to seek relief from the parish funds collected at the church door each Sunday. Holding fast to his belief in self-determination, even in the face of such hardship, he took practical steps to provide aid. He arranged with his brothers in Liverpool to ship a cargo of Indian corn which he sold to the needy at cost price. In subsequent years in times of scarcity he obtained supplies of good-quality seed potatoes to distribute. He encouraged the womenfolk of the parish to take up spinning to supplement the family income and he employed jobless parishioners on agricultural improvement schemes on the glebe lands surrounding the manse.

Recognising that such measures offered only partial solutions to the problems of poverty, he turned at first to revitalising the local friendly society which had been founded in 1795 but had become moribund. According to Duncan 'it soon appeared that the Articles of the Society, as at first drawn up, were inadequate for the purpose for which they were intended ... many of the laws were expressed in a manner so vague and obscure that they served rather to encourage a contentious disposition, than to promote that spirit of order and harmony which ... is the only means of securing the respectability, and contributing to the success of the Institution'. Under his direction new rules and regulations were drawn up and the management of the society improved. It quickly became so popular that Duncan established another, specifically for women. Soon more than a quarter of the entire population of the parish, over 300 people, were friendly society members. From 1808 Duncan tried to inculcate ideals of thrift by writing a series of improving tracts, published under the auspices of Scotch Cheap Repository Tracts. The largest of these and the most widely circulated was *The Cottage Fireside*. As a contemporary article in the *Dumfries & Galloway Courier* stated, 'its chief object [was] to point out and remedy the common abuses which take place in the education of children, particularly amongst the Scottish peasantry'. The tract was divided into sections, each with its own moral lesson; for example, the obedience of children to their parents.

Despite this success Henry Duncan was not convinced that friendly societies provided the best vehicle for gathering the uncertain savings of the poor, thus prompting him to make his proposal for the opening of savings banks in every parish in Scotland. By way of example the Ruthwell Savings Bank opened its doors in May 1810 in the Friendly Society's rooms in the village. The trustees were members of the Kirk Session with Henry Duncan as Governor and the village schoolmaster as Treasurer. The Lord Lieutenant, the Deputy Lieutenant, and the Sheriff of the County, along with the local Member of Parliament, were all *ex officio* members of the Court of Directors, but the real work was done by elected representatives of the ordinary depositors with a minimum balance of £1 in their account. As he originally proposed there were also extraordinary members who were required to subscribe 5s a year and pay an entry fine of £2. In addition there were honorary members who subscribed a guinea a year and paid £5 on joining. The extraordinary and honorary members were also represented on the Court of Directors. The Annual General Meeting was able to veto any of the decisions of the Court and those of the Standing Committee of fifteen members. Customers could deposit between 1s and £10 and there was a fine of 1s for anyone who failed to invest more than 4s a year. This was a heavy imposition at a time when an agricultural labourer could not expect to earn more than 10s a week. To secure legal recognition, the bank was registered as a friendly society with the Dumfries quarter sessions. From the outset he made it plain that the purpose of the bank was to attract long-term deposits. Withdrawal was difficult as customers could take out their investment only at the quarterly meeting of the committee. This obstacle was offset by the inducement of a higher rate of interest (5 per cent instead of the standard 4 per cent) for depositors of more than three years' standing. Bonuses were also paid to regular savers from the

The cash box in which the funds of the Ruthwell Parish
Bank were locked away for safe keeping, until they
could be transferred to the local office of the British Linen
Company, the forerunner of the British Linen Bank.

auxiliary fund composed of the entry fines of the extraordinary and honorary members. Interest was earned by placing the savings on deposit with a local commercial bank, a practice familiar to Scottish bankers with their long-established commitment to private client interest-bearing deposit accounts.

Henry Duncan's scheme was not without its critics, on the grounds that it was, in effect, a friendly society and not a proper savings bank: 'No one should be made dependent upon any other contingency, for either the time or the amount of his payments: therefore no attempt should be made to enforce regularity of payments by fines or forfeitures of any sort.' Nevertheless, Duncan remained convinced of the propriety of his experiment. Like Priscilla Wakefield he was soon reporting astonishing achievements in personal saving. One case he quoted was of the young man who had invested his allowance for service in the local militia; he then began to save regularly and within four years had £14 to his credit. So convinced was Duncan of the utility of savings banks that he regularly used shining examples such as this to encourage their formation elsewhere.

Apparently independent of Henry Duncan's initiative, John Hay Forbes, a distinguished lawyer and son of the celebrated Edinburgh commercial banker Sir William Forbes, promoted a savings bank as a branch of the Society for the Suppression of Beggars in the city in December 1813. This was a winter of severe food shortages with many parts of rural Scotland gripped by famine. Whisky distilling was banned as barley was urgently required for making bread. Despite the gravity of the food crisis and exorbitant prices, Forbes believed passionately that savings by 'prudent economy' in better times could provide a cushion against wholly-to-be-expected harvest failures. The rules of the bank were straightforward, lacking the threefold classification of depositors at Ruthwell, but with broadly similar objectives. Coming from a banking background, Forbes conceived the new venture as effectively a commercial deposit bank on a small scale observing his father's strict rules of financial orthodoxy. The bank accepted deposits of anything above 1s, which were repayable on demand. Interest was payable at 4 per cent on every 12s 6d deposited. When £10 had been deposited in an account it was transferred to the commercial bank of Sir William Forbes & Co. Within nine months the bank had 106 subscribers, had received £221 and repaid £101. By October 1815 a further 643 contributors had been enlisted and John Forbes had no doubt that 'the poor man is now enabled to meet the payments of his half-yearly rent by PRECEDING SAVINGS, instead of FUTURE ANTICIPATIONS and the winter store is now laid up and paid for with ready money.'

In England the Liverpool Mechanics, Servants & Labourers Fund, founded in 1812, and the Bristol Savings Bank, founded the following year, had the same origins in the Liverpool Society for Bettering the Conditions of the Poor and the Bristol Prudent Man's Friendly Society respectively. Both these banks, however, approximated more closely to Henry Duncan's more charitable ideals than the strict commercial logic of John Forbes. By the time this generation of banks was established there was a clear prospect of peace after almost two decades of warfare. In the Peninsular Campaign during the summer, the Duke of Wellington had advanced towards the French border and in October Napoleon was convincingly defeated by the allies at the Battle of Leipzig. Early in 1814 the allies invaded France, capturing Paris in March and driving Napoleon into exile.

The coming of peace was a mixed blessing. It brought to an end the French Revolutionary Wars which had provided the catalyst to the whole debate about poverty as government urgently searched for ways of preventing political agitation at home, but on the other hand some 300,000 men, some very undesirable, would be discharged from the army and navy. The process of demobilisation was delayed by the slow progress of the Congress of Vienna to settle the terms of peace and Napoleon's subsequent escape from captivity on the island of Elba in March 1815, followed by his crushing defeat at the Battle of Waterloo in June. Only the home-based volunteer militia had been completely disbanded by the end of 1815. As a result there was time for politicians and economists to contemplate the possible effect of returning unemployed servicemen on an economy reeling from the sudden cessation of government war expenditure. William Cobbett, the radical journalist, forecast social and economic catastrophe: 'Were the whole army and navy to be reduced to that number which has hitherto been considered sufficient for a peace establishment, the country would be overrun with idle people, who would have no other means of subsistence but by plunder, as there would not be employment for them, and there are already more paupers than the country is able to support … soldiers having been so much accustomed during their campaigns in other countries, to put forth their hands and help themselves it might be attended with great danger … for to a soldier, when hungry, it makes but little difference whether he fills his belly at the expense of his friends or his enemies.' The economy rapidly slipped into recession and expenditure on poor relief climbed to unprecedented levels. There were reports of privation and hardship from almost every part of the country. Savings banks appeared to some to offer a means of preventing social disturbance.

As early as 1814 the Highland Society of Scotland – concerned with a part of the United Kingdom where distress was very pronounced because so much marginal land (hill pastures and wet lands) had been pressed into service to provide badly needed food during the war – appointed a committee to 'consider what is the best mode of forming institutions of the nature of savings banks for receiving the deposit of labourers and others'. Reporting in November the committee endorsed the establishment of savings banks on the Ruthwell and Edinburgh models as a practical way of helping the poor avoid resorting, at the first signs of distress, to the ubiquitous pawnbrokers. The committee was less than encouraged by friendly societies, and the peculiarly Scottish institution of a 'Menage', a savings club 'usually established for his own advantage by some retailer of those articles which persons in the situation of labourers have occasion to purchase very often by the keeper of tippling houses, and the result is that the members often spend four shillings when they deposit two; they are usually induced to accept of goods, or the money is often spent by the collector, and not unfrequently they get nothing at all'. Although the report offered little practical advice as to how a bank could be set up, its publication in 1815 coincided with that of an essay by Henry Duncan, *On the Nature and Advantages of Parish Banks Together with a Corrected Copy of the Rules and Regulations of the Parent Institution in Ruthwell*, providing a blueprint for ministers and heritors (landowners) who wished to launch a similar undertaking. Not long afterwards, John Forbes published a *Short Account of the Edinburgh Savings Bank* incorporating rules and book-keeping advice. This literature was widely distributed, resulting in turn in the setting up of savings banks or provident institutions not just in Scotland but also south of the border, stimulating the publication of similar pamphlets.

# BALANCE SHEET
### OF
# The Ruthwell Parish Bank,
### FOR THE YEAR ENDING 31st MAY, 1817,
##### THE FOLIO OF EACH ACCOUNT IN THE LEDGER BEING SUBSTITUTED FOR THE DEPOSITOR'S NAME.

| Folio | Interest to 1st June, 1817. | Balance transferred to New Account. | Fines. | | Folio | Interest to 1st June, 1817. | Balance transferred to New Account. | Fines. |
|---|---|---|---|---|---|---|---|---|
| | | | | Brought forward... | 110 | £62 14 7 | £1289 5 5 | £0 17 0 |
| 32 | £0 9 3½ | £5 17 4½ | £0 0 0 | | 110 | 0 15 5 | 16 15 5 | 0 0 0 |
| 34 | 0 1 10½ | 2 1 10½ | 0 0 0 | | 111 | 0 0 0 | 0 9 6½ | 0 0 0 |
| 35 | 0 1 3 | 0 3 3½ | 0 0 0 | | 112 | 0 12 5 | 20 12 5 | 0 0 0 |
| 36 | 0 2 0 | 2 16 4 | 0 1 0 | | 113 | 0 3 7 | 3 4 0 | 0 0 0 |
| 37 | 0 5 10½ | 8 5 10½ | 0 0 0 | | 114 | 0 3 7 | 4 9 8 | 0 0 0 |
| 38 | 0 2 0 | 2 9 10 | 0 1 0 | | 115 | 0 2 8 | 3 3 7 | 0 0 0 |
| 39 | 0 0 9 | 1 4 6 | 0 0 0 | | 116 | 0 4 5½ | 5 4 8 | 0 0 0 |
| 40 | 0 4 0 | 8 17 6 | 0 0 0 | | 117 | 0 0 0 | 0 3 0 | 0 0 0 |
| 41 | 0 3 0 | 3 4 9 | 0 1 0 | | 118 | 0 2 8 | 1 3 2 | 0 0 0 |
| 42 | 0 7 0 | 4 1 7½ | 0 0 0 | | 119 | 0 1 9½ | 2 3 9½ | 0 0 0 |
| 43 | 0 5 5½ | 6 12 0½ | 0 0 0 | | 120 | 0 0 10½ | 1 1 10½ | 0 0 0 |
| 44 | 0 2 4 | 3 7 1 | 0 0 0 | | 121 | 0 1 9½ | 2 3 9½ | 0 0 0 |
| 45 | 0 16 10 | 19 6 4 | 0 0 0 | | 122 | 0 3 7 | 4 3 7 | 0 0 0 |
| 46 | 1 1 4 | 25 19 8½ | 0 0 0 | | 123 | 0 2 8 | 3 2 8 | 0 0 0 |
| 47 | 1 8 3 | 31 10 1½ | 0 0 0 | | 124 | 0 1 9½ | 2 19 4 | 0 0 0 |
| 48 | 0 0 0 | 0 7 0 | 0 0 0 | | 125 | 0 1 6 | 0 2 3 | 0 0 0 |
| 49 | 0 15 11 | 14 16 0½ | 0 0 0 | | 126 | 0 2 7 | 2 2 7 | 0 0 0 |
| 50 | 0 1 0 | 1 3 7½ | 0 0 0 | | 127 | 0 5 0½ | 6 7 0½ | 0 0 0 |
| 52 | 0 3 9 | 0 4 8 | 0 0 0 | | 128 | 0 4 5½ | 5 4 5½ | 0 0 0 |
| 53 | 0 10 4 | 45 15 7 | 0 0 0 | | 129 | 0 1 11½ | 3 5 1½ | 0 0 0 |
| Male Friendly Society, 54 | 23 9 8½ | 491 9 8½ | 0 0 0 | | 130 | 0 3 10½ | 5 8 10½ | 0 0 0 |
| 55 | 0 4 0 | 4 13 1 | 0 1 0 | | 131 | 0 3 6 | 5 3 10 | 0 0 0 |
| 56 | 0 8 0 | 8 18 4 | 0 1 0 | | 132 | 0 1 6 | 2 1 6 | 0 0 0 |
| 57 | 0 0 2½ | 1 3 2½ | 0 0 0 | | 133 | 0 0 9 | 1 0 9 | 0 0 0 |
| 58 | 0 4 5 | 5 16 11½ | 0 0 0 | | 134 | 0 0 9 | 1 10 1 | 0 0 0 |
| 59 | 0 2 1½ | 2 4 1 | 0 0 0 | | 135 | 0 0 0 | 0 11 6 | 0 0 0 |
| Female Society, 60 | 8 2 4½ | 50 5 8 | 0 0 0 | | 136 | 0 1 6 | 2 13 10 | 0 0 0 |
| 61 | 0 3 6 | 3 8 7 | 0 0 0 | | 138 | 0 0 0 | 0 10 0 | 0 0 0 |
| 62 | 0 3 0 | 3 9 1½ | 0 0 0 | | 139 | 0 0 10½ | 1 12 3 | 0 0 0 |
| 63 | 0 6 10½ | 7 7 2½ | 0 0 0 | | 140 | 0 2 0 | 3 2 0 | 0 0 0 |
| 64 | 0 12 0 | 12 15 2 | 0 1 0 | | 141 | 0 0 6 | 1 0 6 | 0 0 0 |
| 65 | 0 1 10 | 3 2 2 | 0 0 0 | | 142 | 0 1 5 | 1 1 5 | 0 0 0 |
| 66 | 0 1 0 | 1 9 7 | 0 1 0 | | 144 | 0 0 11 | 2 2 11 | 0 0 0 |
| 67 | 0 8 11 | 10 0 0 | 0 0 0 | | 145 | 0 0 10 | 1 6 8 | 0 0 0 |
| 68 | 0 14 1½ | 1 3 1½ | 0 0 0 | | 146 | 0 0 6 | 2 0 6 | 0 0 0 |
| 70 | 1 10 4 | 32 14 7 | 0 0 0 | | 147 | 0 0 6 | 2 0 6 | 0 0 0 |
| 71 | 0 11 10 | 12 11 11 | 0 0 0 | | 148 | 0 0 6 | 2 0 6 | 0 0 0 |
| 72 | 1 15 0 | 36 19 2 | 0 1 0 | | 149 | 0 0 6 | 2 0 6 | 0 0 0 |
| 73 | 1 6 11 | 37 3 5½ | 0 0 0 | | 150 | 0 0 6 | 2 0 6 | 0 0 0 |
| 76 | 0 8 3 | 12 19 8 | 0 0 0 | | 151 | 0 0 1 | 1 1 1 | 0 0 0 |
| 77 | 0 15 8½ | 16 10 4 | 0 0 0 | | 153 | 0 0 0 | 0 1 0 | 0 0 0 |
| 78 | 0 11 0 | 12 8 6 | 0 0 0 | | 154 | 0 0 0 | 0 3 8 | 0 0 0 |
| 80 | 0 4 9 | 7 2 1½ | 0 0 0 | | 155 | 0 0 0 | 0 14 0 | 0 0 0 |
| 81 | 0 4 1 | 5 9 2½ | 0 0 0 | | 157 | 0 0 0 | 0 18 2 | 0 0 0 |
| 82 | 0 2 0 | 2 16 9 | 0 0 0 | | 158 | 1 2 11 | 31 2 11 | 0 0 0 |
| 84 | 0 2 0 | 4 4 8 | 0 1 0 | | 159 | 1 1 4½ | 38 16 4½ | 0 0 0 |
| 85 | 0 4 6½ | 4 13 11½ | 0 0 0 | | 160 | 0 1 1 | 2 1 1 | 0 0 0 |
| 86 | 0 11 0 | 12 0 9 | 0 0 0 | | 161 | 0 0 6½ | 1 1 6½ | 0 0 0 |
| 87 | 0 0 3 | 5 10 4½ | 0 0 0 | | 163 | 0 1 1½ | 2 1 1½ | 0 0 0 |
| 88 | 1 1 8½ | 23 18 8½ | 0 0 0 | | 164 | 0 10 3½ | 21 10 3½ | 0 0 0 |
| 89 | 0 0 6 | 1 4 6 | 0 0 0 | | 167 | 0 0 10 | 1 16 7 | 0 0 0 |
| 90 | 0 4 0 | 4 15 10 | 0 0 0 | | 169 | 0 0 10 | 1 14 10 | 0 0 0 |
| 91 | 0 3 0 | 3 4 11½ | 0 1 0 | | 170 | 0 1 6 | 5 2 5 | 0 0 0 |
| 92 | 0 12 6 | 14 12 10½ | 0 0 0 | | 171 | 0 0 10 | 1 2 3 | 0 0 0 |
| 93 | 0 16 10½ | 18 3 4½ | 0 0 0 | | 172 | 0 0 10 | 1 6 7 | 0 0 0 |
| 94 | 0 3 0 | 3 16 9½ | 0 0 0 | | 173 | 0 0 10 | 1 1 0 | 0 0 0 |
| 95 | 4 3 5½ | 113 5 4 | 0 0 0 | | 177 | 0 0 0 | 0 9 5 | 0 0 0 |
| 96 | 0 0 9½ | 4 1 1½ | 0 0 0 | | 178 | 0 0 0 | 0 6 6 | 0 0 0 |
| 97 | 0 6 4½ | 6 13 11½ | 0 0 0 | | 179 | 0 0 0 | 0 1 0 | 0 0 0 |
| 98 | 0 0 1½ | 3 4 8½ | 0 0 0 | | Interest on settled accounts, folios 79, 143, 165, 166, 168, | | 0 8 1 | |
| 99 | 1 11 6 | 33 1 2 | 0 1 0 | | | | | |
| 100 | 0 3 10 | 4 4 11 | 0 0 0 | | Amounts, | £70 19 6 | £1531 6 10 | £0 17 0 |
| 101 | 0 12 9 | 13 12 9 | 0 0 0 | | Surplus fund—balance of interest in favour of Parish Bank, | 2 19 10 | 2 19 10 | |
| 102 | 0 10 0 | 6 3 3 | 0 0 0 | | | | | |
| 103 | 0 3 0 | 3 17 1 | 0 1 0 | | Surplus fund—fines, | | 0 17 0 | |
| 104 | 0 6 0 | 6 7 6 | 0 0 0 | | | | | |
| 105 | 0 1 0 | 1 1 5½ | 0 1 0 | | Balance in British Linen Company's Office, | £73 19 4 | £1535 3 8 | |
| 106 | 0 10 2 | 12 14 8 | 0 0 0 | | | | | |
| 107 | 0 5 0 | 5 7 10½ | 0 1 0 | | | | | |
| 108 | 0 1 0 | 1 0 1 | 0 1 0 | | | | | |
| 109 | 0 7 0 | 7 12 10 | 0 1 0 | | | | | |
| Carried forward... | £62 14 7 | £1289 5 5 | £0 17 0 | | | | | |

The GENERAL MEETING of the RUTHWELL PARISH BANK takes place at Ruthwell Church, on the first Saturday of July, at three o'clock in the afternoon, when it is expected that there will be a full attendance, to receive new Vouchers, elect Office-bearers for the ensuing year, &c.

Dumfries:—Printed at the Dumfries and Galloway Courier Office.

This balance sheet shows that, in 1817, the Ruthwell Parish Bank was attracting mainly small deposits. Note that seventeen of the depositors were fined that year for failing to meet their minimum saving target of 4 shillings per annum.

During 1815 savings banks were founded at Bath, Bishop Auckland, Dumfries (by Henry Duncan's brother Thomas Tudor Duncan), Dundee, Ettrick Forest, Glasgow, Hawick, Kelso, and Kinross. The promoters of these banks drew heavily on the rhetoric of not only Henry Duncan but also Patrick Colquhoun and other observers of the changing urban scene. The Scottish banks deposited their takings with commercial banks on the model of Ruthwell and Edinburgh. In England, where there was no tradition of interest-bearing deposit banking, the new savings banks tended to use government stocks to provide a secure investment and guaranteed income.

Despite the worsening economic conditions, enthusiasm for founding new banks increased in 1816, with more than seventy formations in England. Amongst these was the Provident Institution for the Western Part of the Metropolis which numbered Patrick Colquhoun, William Wilberforce and Horace Twiss, the Revd Malthus and George Rose amongst its managers. Elsewhere in London other banks were set up, including the London Provident Bank under the presidency of Sir Thomas Baring, the doyen of private banking of the period, and the Southampton Row (Bloomsbury) Bank. Outside the capital there were other important initiatives that helped shape policy. The Devon & Exeter Savings Bank, chaired by Bishop Pelham with an illustrious board of managers, from the outset sought to provide a countywide service by appointing receivers to accept deposits in as many parishes as possible. The banks in Hampshire, at Portsmouth and Portsea, Southampton and Winchester, owed their initial success to the energy of George Rose who was still MP for Christchurch in the county. The principal advocate of savings banks in England, his *Observations on Banks for Savings* (1816) ran rapidly into several editions.

Unaware, or perhaps wilfully ignorant of the nature of Henry Duncan's Ruthwell Bank, George Rose wrote it off as a menage and singled out Edinburgh as an example to follow. Though he recognised that depositing funds with a commercial bank was not practical in the south of England 'where failures have unhappily occurred in the country banks of the highest credit' – a reference to a recent spate of failures – Rose was convinced that investment in government funds was the only practical expedient, spelling out the system he had recently designed for the Southampton bank. Taking heed of John Bone's experience in Tranquillity, he did not believe that daily labourers with young families could save anything, but he was certain that apprentices, unmarried journeymen and domestic servants all had money to save which many habitually spent on 'drunkenness and dissipation of the worst kind'. He argued that savings would prevent young craftsmen resorting to extortionate pawnbrokers in 'hard times', and becoming a burden on the parish. He also thought less convincingly that thrift would act as a deterrent against 'early and improvident marriages', thus preventing Malthus's haunting spectre of over-population becoming a reality. These opinions were echoed by Barber Beaumont, the managing director of the Provident Institute of London and sponsor of the St Paul's (Covent Garden) Bank, in *An Essay on Provident or Parish Banks for the Security and*

An early savings bank painted by Sir George Harvey.

*Improvement of the Savings of Tradesmen, Artificers, Servants, etc* that appeared at the same time. He had no doubt that young, single men and women had more to spend than ever before, much of which was wasted on drink and clothing.

By the time he wrote his pamphlet, Rose had already come to the conclusion that new legislation was needed to protect savings banks, incorporating safeguards not available through existing friendly society provision. After about six months' negotiation with the Treasury, a tentative Bill was introduced in Parliament in May 1816 but was rapidly withdrawn as inadequate. William Cobbett, an arch opponent of Rose, was quick to repeat his criticism of the whole concept of savings banks, declaring unequivocally in his periodical, the *Register*, that the poor did not earn enough to pay for the daily necessities of life let alone to save. Persuasive as such arguments were, there was mounting evidence from the newly formed savings banks that they were meeting a need, at least from some sections of the community, who did not have sufficient funds to deposit with a commercial bank or who did not wish to be bound entirely by the rules and regulations of friendly societies. During 1816 the Bristol Savings Bank took over £5,600 in deposit, the Salisbury Savings Bank over £4,700 from 183 depositors, and the Edinburgh Savings Bank nearly £4,700 from 215 depositors. With average family incomes then of less than £100, these were relatively large receipts from a small number of depositors.

Reflecting on such figures, the managers of savings banks were in two minds as to whether

ANNO QUINQUAGESIMO SEPTIMO

# GEORGII III. REGIS.

✳✳✳✳✳✳✳✳✳✳✳✳✳✳✳✳✳✳✳✳✳✳✳✳✳✳✳✳✳✳✳✳✳✳✳✳✳✳✳✳✳✳✳

*L.C.Pßh. 40.*

## C A P. CXXX.

An Act to encourage the Establishment of Banks for Savings in *England*. [12th *July* 1817.]

WHEREAS certain Provident Institutions or Banks for Savings have been established in *England*, for the safe Custody and Increase of small Savings belonging to the industrious Classes of His Majesty's Subjects; and it is expedient to give Protection to such Institutions and the Funds thereby established, and to afford Encouragement to others to form the like Institutions: May it therefore please Your Majesty that it may be enacted, and be it enacted by the King's most Excellent Majesty, by and with the Advice and Consent of the Lords Spiritual and Temporal, and Commons, in this present Parliament assembled, and by the Authority of the same, That if any Number of Persons who have formed or shall form any Society in any Part of *England*, for the Purpose of establishing and maintaining any Institution in the Nature of a Bank, to receive Deposits of Money for the Benefit of the Persons depositing the same, and to accumulate the Produce of so much thereof as shall not be required by the Depositors, their Executors or Administrators, to be paid in the Nature of Compound Interest, and to return the whole or any Part of such Deposit and the Produce thereof to the Depositors, their Executors or Administrators, deducting only out of such Produce so much as shall be required to be so retained for the Purpose of paying and discharging the necessary Expences attending the Management of such Institution, according to such Rules, Orders, and Regulations as shall have been or shall be established for that Purpose, but deriving no Benefit whatsoever from any such Deposit or the Produce thereof, shall be desirous of having the Benefit of the Provisions of this Act, such Persons shall cause the Rules, Orders, and Regulations established or to be established for the Management of such

*Persons forming Societies according to the Provisions herein prescribed, entitled to the Benefit of this Act.*

12 D                                                            Institution

The first page of the 1817 Savings Bank Act.

depositors were in fact being attracted from amongst those accustomed to seek poor relief at times of crises. The Berwick-upon-Tweed managers reported grateful customers remarking, 'Had it not been for the Savings Bank we should, in all probability, have been forced to apply to the parish for relief.' The Revd T. Lloyd of the Hertford Savings Bank had no doubts from his experience that 'these institutions, if properly attended to, will in the course of a very short time tend very materially to amend the present degraded character of the lower orders, and so memorialise them as to bring them back to their once state of independence'. Henry Duncan's brother Thomas at Dumfries shared his impression: 'Many have been relieved from their embarrassment by their little stores in the Parish Bank, who have candidly confessed that without the assistance of the Institution they must have been reduced to want.' Others were sceptical. William Davies of the successful Bath Provident Institution, with deposits of £17,000 by 1817, confessed that for the most part these had been invested by 'prudent servants who long have been in the commendable practice of saving'. The Wellington Provident Bank, also in Somerset, was an acknowledged failure due, according to the managers, to the effects of the recession in the economy. With such confused signals coming from the banks themselves, William Cobbett pressed his attack, but George Rose was not to be deflected.

At the beginning of February 1817 George Rose introduced a revised Bill which, imaginatively, provided that all deposits of savings banks in England and Wales should be placed on account with the Commissioners of the National Debt. Under its terms the Commissioners would pay interest at just over 4.5 per cent per annum, a substantial premium on the prevailing rate available on government stock, to attract investors. Deposits were to be held by the Bank of England in a separate fund for the banks for savings. Individuals were allowed to invest £100 in the first year and £50 a year thereafter for an unlimited time. There were no restrictions on deposits by friendly societies. The timing was propitious. Lord Liverpool's government was badly frightened by the prospect of revolution following disturbances at huge political meetings at Spa Fields in Islington in November and December 1816. As a result the government was willing to sponsor any measure at the same time that might encourage good citizenship and reduce the crippling burden of poor relief. Against a worsening political background which saw the Habeas Corpus Act suspended in March, George Rose steered his measure through Parliament, arguing that 'savings banks would gradually do away with the evils of the system of poor laws'. When pressed he admitted that the effect would be gradual and that he offered no panacea. Henry Duncan, himself, came to London to offer his personal support and advice. Despite the misgivings of some Members, the Bill, with some modifications, became law in July and was quickly followed by similar legislation for Ireland but not for Scotland, which remained keen to retain flexibility to invest.

After almost half a century of debate and experiment, savings banks were recognised legal entities. However their utility had yet to be demonstrated in practice and it remained to be seen if Henry Duncan's success in rural Ruthwell could be matched in fast-expanding industrial towns.

# CHAPTER TWO

# TO

# BANISH POVERTY

# AND WRETCHEDNESS

## *1817–61*

Wen George Rose's Act for the Protection and Encouragement of Banks for Savings in England became law in 1817, the United Kingdom was in the grip of a recession of unparalleled severity as Continental markets struggled to recover from the disruption caused by Napoleon's Continental System which had excluded British goods from most European markets. Unprepared for protracted economic difficulties with attendant unemployment and political agitation, the government of Lord Liverpool became increasingly concerned about the mounting cost of poor relief and what was perceived to be a moral decline in the country, manifest in apparent increased drunkenness, gambling and lawlessness. The government attacked the symptoms rather than the cause, only toying with direct intervention in the economy despite the huge wartime expenditure which had done much to stimulate the growth of industry. A Select Committee was appointed early in the year to examine the whole working of the Poor Laws, taking evidence between February and June 1817. The report, completed expeditiously by the first week in July – a week before George Rose's Act passed on to the statute book – broadly supported the attitudes of the protagonists of savings banks, condemning the poor law for 'diminishing' the 'natural impulse by which men are instigated to industry and good conduct by superseding the necessity of providing in the season of health and vigour for the wants of sickness and old age, and by making poverty and misery the conditions on which relief is to be obtained ... this system is perpetually encouraging and increasing the amount of misery it was designed to alleviate'. The Committee's sympathies were with the voluntary provision for the poor, characteristic of most Scottish parishes, and as a result had high hopes for the fledgeling savings banks 'not only in affording to the industrious poor a secure deposit for their savings, but in familiarising them with a practice of which the advantage will be daily more apparent'. This was music to the ears of hard-pressed ratepayers in both urban and rural parishes throughout the country at a time when the cost of provision of poor relief in England and Wales alone was still climbing towards a peak of nearly £8 million in 1818.

With readily available guidance on the practicalities of forming and operating a savings bank in now numerous pamphlets, there was widespread enthusiasm for establishing new banks up and down the country. In the expectation that the savings banks would lead in the long term to a reduction in rates, community leaders, usually urged into action by the clergy,

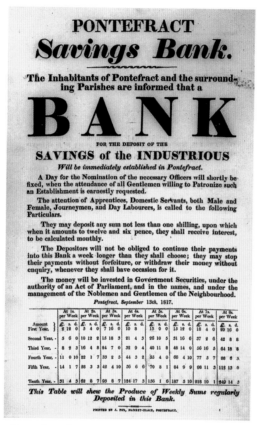

The Pontefract Savings Bank in Yorkshire was established
shortly after the 1817 Act became law.

contributed generously to the cost of getting banks started and often placed sums on deposit to provide initial liquidity. As in the previous two years, early success in winning deposits from tradesmen, artisans, shopworkers and domestic servants seemed to justify the optimism of the sponsors. The savings bank at Watford opened in August 1817 and within three months had taken over £4,700 in deposits without making a single repayment. Such experiences were not uncommon. Everywhere promoters were at pains to emphasise that they did not wish to undermine the popularity of friendly societies, which were enjoying a resurgence with the

The Cork Savings Bank established in 1817. This handsome
building was erected in 1842.

rapid growth in the number of the lodges or affiliated societies of what became national organisations, such as the Oddfellows, the Druids and the Shepherds. Apart from their social function, lodges usually provided sickness and funeral benefits to members.

By the end of December 1817, 101 savings banks in England and Wales had opened accounts with the Bank of England, which administered the Savings Bank Fund, and transmitted over £250,000 in deposits. The majority of these banks opened for only a few hours a week, such as Liverpool Savings Bank which transacted business only from 11 a.m. to 12 noon on the first Friday of every month. Others had more generous opening hours – Glasgow Provident Bank from 7 p.m. to 9 p.m. every Saturday evening and York Savings Bank from 11 a.m. to 12 noon each Saturday. Much of the work was undertaken voluntarily by the directors or managers. The books were kept by a paid actuary or secretary who was required to provide a surety bond in case he was tempted to embezzle the funds. New banks required little in the way of equipment and only a room to begin business. Hull Savings Bank rented a room in the town's Corn Exchange for £12 a year and purchased a ledger of 1,000 folios, a cash book, committee book, journal, a book for a numerical list of subscriptions, a director's table, a desk with railing, three chairs and an iron chest.

So impressed was the reformer and politician Sir Francis Burdett with the early achievement of the movement that he set about compiling an *Annals of Banks for Savings* (1818), which traced the origins of the concept, brought together the literature on their purposes and management, and provided a compendium of banks in existence in all parts of the United Kingdom. Although he succeeded in compiling what was, by the standards of the time, an objective account touching at times on the debate about the ability of the poor to save, he approached his task from the perspective of one who had no doubts of their utility. Saluting Henry Duncan as having founded the first successful savings bank, Burdett quoted him at length in his introduction, fully supporting his vision of a future Utopia, with savings banks at the centre ensuring an absence of poverty. Burdett had good cause to be enthusiastic. New banks continued to be established almost daily. During 1818, for example, 125 savings banks were established the length and breadth of England and Wales, from Aberystwyth to Great Yarmouth and from Carlisle to Penzance. The *Sheffield Mercury*, echoing Burdett, reflected on this achievement at the close of the year: 'We consider the establishment of these banks as one of the great improvements which distinguish modern times ... the establishment of Savings Banks may ultimately tend to banish poverty and wretchedness from society.' The momentum of the movement continued into 1819 with a further thirty formations and then flagged. By the end of that year, total deposits with the Savings Bank Fund exceeded £2.8 million. Almost uniformly, these early investors were drawn from the ranks of shopkeepers, skilled craftsmen, domestic servants, school-teachers, farmers, their wives and children – groups which were most represented amongst the subscribers to both national and local friendly societies. This early experience confirmed that there was a real gap in the market for the savings of regular wage earners who did not wish to be bound by the monthly deposits demanded by friendly societies. Yet it also corroborated the opinion of those commentators such as William Cobbett, who believed that savings banks would do nothing to reduce expenditure on poor relief as those families most likely to claim had nothing to save. Such an outcome did not dishearten the advocates of the new banks.

Ironically, the motive that inspired the cause of the savings banks was as much fear of the consequences of political reform championed by Sir Francis Burdett as by a desire to hold down poor rates. It was argued that personal savings, particularly if deposits were held by the government, would make men and women much less likely to support popular protests, which might destroy the capital they had worked so hard to put by. This line of reasoning was given added strength by the high level of participation of skilled craftsmen, who were also most prominent in the radical cause. Radical demands for the reform of Parliament through the widening of the franchise and redistribution of seats in favour of the new industrial towns in the Midlands and the north of England reached a crescendo in 1819, culminating in a great mass meeting of over 60,000 at Peter's Fields in Manchester in August. Alarmed at the size of the turnout, the authorities panicked, ordering the yeomanry to disperse the crowd at sabre point. In the ensuing riot, eleven men were killed – an event quickly dubbed the 'Peterloo

Peterloo was the culmination of a period of intense agitation for political reform, after the end of the wars with France. It was during this period, when the old social order appeared to be under serious threat, that most of Britain's greatest savings banks were established.

Massacre'. Without pausing to consider whether the yeomanry may have acted over-hastily, the government reacted swiftly with a package of repressive measures aimed at preventing insurrection by suppressing radicalism. Nine of the participants were hanged and almost a thousand transported. Early in the new year, Sir Francis Burdett was arrested on political charges and imprisoned. The genuine fear of total anarchy that gripped society was epitomised by the anonymous Edinburgh author of a pamphlet *On the Use and Abuse of Charity*, which advocated that charity should be given only as a reward for thrifty industry:

> Over a large mass of the community the dawn of revolution is spreading her bloody mantle.
> Whatever has been formerly held honourable is now lightly esteemed; and what was once
> reckoned sacred, is now despised. Royalty is openly derided, rank vilified, property considered
> as usurpation, patriotism held as false, virtue looked on with contempt, the Bible attacked as
> falsehood, and Christianity itself proscribed as a religion inconsistent with the person of man.

Political disturbance persisted during the next two years. However, with a steady improvement in the economy, encouraged by reductions in customs and excise duties, the bite had gone out of radical demands for reforms. Expenditure on poor relief retreated from the peak in 1818 falling to below £6 million in 1822, making discussions about the need to reform the Poor Law and to persuade the poor to help themselves in times of adversity less immediate. New savings banks continued to be formed, but at a much slower rate than before. Nevertheless, despite the changing public mood, the deposits held in the Savings Bank Fund on behalf of investors everywhere in the United Kingdom, apart from Scotland, went on growing, exceeding £6.5 million by 1822. This notable achievement was the outcome of rising real wages of many

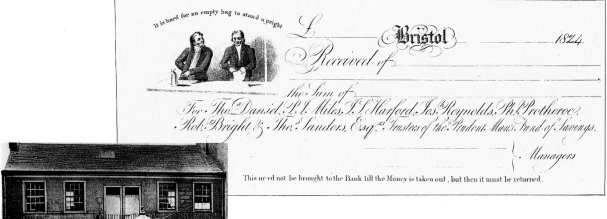

A deposit receipt for the Bristol Prudent Man's Fund of Savings, 1824.

LEFT Most of the early savings banks opened in public buildings, in rooms 'borrowed' for a few hours each week.

groups of skilled workers and the diligence of trustees in promoting the facilities of the savings banks, particularly amongst their own domestic servants. Customers were attracted by the competitive rates of interest and the flexibility of having cash available at all times to meet the exigencies of daily life. Uninterrupted growth continued until 1825 as the economy boomed in the second phase of industrialisation which saw the widespread introduction of steam power in the textile industry, further mechanisation, and the development of the steamship and the steam locomotive.

The habit of thrift inculcated by the savings banks and friendly societies had a profound effect on the outlook and disposition of those sections of society which had been the principal beneficiaries of industrialisation. This was evident in attitudes to alcoholic drink. Drunkenness, which had been tolerated in the eighteenth century throughout society, became unacceptable. During the early 1820s, sobriety, even total abstinence, was embraced by the 'respectable classes' as a virtue, allowing more of the family income to be saved. For the factory master, temperance had an essentially practical advantage as it was dangerous to operate the new machinery under the influence of drink and over-indulgence could seriously damage productivity. Since the culture of friendly societies was intimately associated with the conviviality of the public house, the savings banks at first profited from this fundamental change in opinion. The beginning of the temperance movement was part and parcel of growing acceptance by 'the aristocracy of labour' of a gospel of individual help which had originally been directed at the very bottom of the social scale. This gained ready credibility from the obvious opportunities for self-advancement offered by industrial expansion. In every community there were examples of men, and sometimes women, who had come from humble origins and by hard work and application had succeeded in establishing their own enterprises. In the popular perception it was success that counted, failure was overlooked or blamed on personal shortcomings. Hardly surprisingly, this shift in point of view by the leaders of the workforce reinforced the arguments of those who wished to restructure the Poor Law by making it more difficult to claim benefit and so reduce the burden on the rates.

Increasingly, protagonists of change in the Poor Law were committed to the deterrent of indoor relief in the workhouse. The leading advocate of this view was George Nicholls, who established a workhouse at Southwell in Nottinghamshire in 1827 and in a short time cut the poor rate to a fraction of its previous level. However, he believed that the poor had to be offered an alternative to the horror of the workhouse, which was to be provided by thrift and prudence – the handmaids of temperance. Three years earlier he had himself established the savings bank at Southwell for this very purpose. Without considering whether those at the bottom of the social scale could afford either to save or drink, thrift was to be encouraged amongst the poor and their children by the churches, particularly through Sunday Schools and later by temperance and abstinence societies.

Characteristically, it was in Scotland, with its long-standing commitment to the voluntary approach to the Poor Law that the Sunday School and abstinence movements blossomed. The first Sunday Schools were set up in Glasgow in 1815/16 and by the end of the following year 1,200 children were attending in the Tron parish alone. The first temperance society was formed in Greenock in 1829 after four years of debate. Within a year the first issue of the magazine the *Temperance Record* had appeared. Both Sunday Schools and temperance societies rapidly became popular throughout the United Kingdom. The advocates of self-denial and thrift were encouraged by what appeared to be inexorable growth in savings bank deposits which, by 1825, totalled more than £13.5 million. There was still a radical voice that questioned all these assumptions, arguing that taxation, particularly income tax used to raise revenue during the war and then abolished, should be employed to redistribute wealth in society. However

Will and Ned, recruited by Chester Savings Bank's Hawarden branch,
about 1880, to illustrate the advantages of opening an account.
Typically, the fortunes of the thrifty man are contrasted with those
of the beer-shop habitué.

# SAVINGS' BANK.

## WILL and NED. Two Labourers.

*WILL.* Well, Ned, and where are you going?

*NED.* Why, I'm going to the Black Bull, just to get a pint of beer, or so.—And where do you think *you* are going, William?

*W.* Why, I'm going to the *Saving Bank*, just to put in a Shilling or so.

*N.* Why what do you go *there* for?

*W.* I'll tell you, if you'll tell me first what you go to the Black Bull for.

*N.* Nay, I hardly know what I go for.—I go just for to pass the time. You know I am a single man,—and have no wife nor family,—and so I can afford to spend a trifle,— and so I do. I don't spend so much there as many. At first, I stinted myself to a Shilling in a week, and then somehow it got on to Eighteen-pence, and then to Two Shillings, and now I commonly spend about Half-a-Crown a week,—but I mean to stop there.

*W.* O, you do, do you?—Now, if I might guess, you'll *not* stop there. You see how wicked habits come creeping on by degrees. One Shilling—One-and-Sixpence—Two Shillings—Two-and-Sixpence.—How much money hast thou in thy purse, Master Neddy?

*N.* Purse.—Why what's the use of a purse to a poor man? A labouring man has no great need of a purse.

*W.* Well, I think I can partly see all the good you get by going to the Alehouse: and, as I know what you go there for, I must tell you now what I go to the *Saving Bank* for.

*N.* Well, what for?

*W.* Why, I thought a little ready money was a handy thing, and I knew many people that went to the Alehouse, early and late, and I never yet heard any of them say that they had the luck to find a purse of money there in all their lives.

*N.* Well, and did you find one at the Saving Bank?

*W.* Why yes, I did, as I may say, all the same. I've put into the Saving Bank now for five years. And I've got together between *Thirty and Forty Pounds*.

*W.* Well, but how much a week did you put in to get all that money?

*W.* Just Half-a-Crown,—just as much as you put into the Black Bull's mouth. You know I'm a single man, like you; but, if I go on putting into the Bank five more years, I shall be getting on towards *Eighty Pounds*, and I can marry then, when I've got something to marry with.

*N.* But what do you earn, William?

*W.* Why just the same as you do.

*N.* What a wonderful difference there is between a wise man and a fool! I see who's the fool. O Neddy! Neddy! Where are thy poor brains gone?—I doubt thy wits have been a wool-gathering for these last five years.

*W.* What, are you talking to yourself a bit Ned?

*N.* I'll tell you what Will, I think my eyes are beginning to open a little; and I think I can see that these Saving Banks, that one hears so much of now-a-days, are the most capital things that ever were invented. A man puts in his shillings there, and they seem to grow, and come out again, a great many more shillings,—just as a potatoe, when you put it into the ground, brings you such a lot more potatoes,—if the soil be good.

*W.* Yes, it's just the same. A Saving Bank is a rare soil to dib your money in. You can put in a Shilling a week, or two, or three, or whatever you can spare. They'll grow to Pounds, if you'll give 'em time.—There's good interest there.

*N.* And can you have a part of it out, any time when you happen to want it?

*W.* O yes, part, or all, just when you like. I take care, however, to keep mine *in* as long as I can, because, when its *out*, it has done growing,—like your potatoe. If, however, I am forced, any how, to lose a day's or a week's work, I need not go sneaking to the parish, like a beggar; but I can hold up my head, and help myself,—like a man.

*N.* I say, William?

*W.* What do you say?

*N.* I'll go with *you*, my lad. I'll to the right about. Good bye, Mister Black Bull. You may roar; but you sha'n't roar me out of any more of my money:—and so—*your servant Sir.*

*Youngman, Printer, Walden.*

well argued, such an approach was not popular with either the better-off, who controlled the political structure, or the emerging middle class, who represented the bulk of savings bank deposits.

The first test of confidence in the new savings banks came in the winter of 1825 with a swift downturn in the economy, signalled by a rapid acceleration in the rate of bankruptcies. At the beginning of December the commercial banks were gripped with panic. Customers hastily withdrew funds, fearing a breakdown of the financial system. After a fortnight of confusion and uncertainty, the banking house of Sir Peter Pole & Co collapsed on 17 December. By the evening of that day, the Bank of England had run out of £5 and £10 notes and the Mint was feverishly producing gold sovereigns in time for Monday opening. In the ensuing turmoil commercial banks up and down the country suspended payments and some forty eventually failed. A crisis of such magnitude had repercussions throughout the economy, hitting the small traders, artisans and domestic servants, the principal depositors with the savings banks. The government had already introduced a measure in 1824 to prevent the better-off from taking advantage of the relative security offered by the savings banks and the higher yields by reducing the annual ceiling on deposits from £100 to £50 in the first year and from £50 to £30 in subsequent years and imposed a limit of a total of £200 in any one account. This was still a princely sum for a savings bank depositor, representing five or six times the average annual wages of an artisan. Customers were required to sign an undertaking that they did not already have an account with another savings bank. At the height of the storm, the savings banks provided a safe haven from the battering that the commercial banks were taking. However, customers were forced to withdraw funds to meet difficulties caused by the crisis. By the end of 1826 there had been a net outflow of about £650,000, when interest payments are allowed for.

This was just the sort of emergency that the savings banks had been established to meet. Withdrawals might have been even greater if the government had not acted quickly to restore confidence by reforming banking law through the Bank Co-partnership Act in 1826. This allowed banks to be formed within a sixty-five-mile radius of London, with an unlimited number of partners who would collectively remain responsible for a bank's liabilities. Investors were reassured and, although the economy as a whole remained depressed over the next two years, savings banks deposits resumed their upward trajectory. Not surprisingly, the rate of growth was not as great as it had been earlier in the decade, but it was still impressive. Total deposits had climbed to over £15 million by 1828. The attraction of the savings banks in these years was undoubtedly the guaranteed rate of return and the security, together with the fact that deposits could be withdrawn on demand in contrast to registered friendly societies and the plethora of unregistered savings clubs – the principal means of saving for the working class. In some instances it was not as easy as it might have seemed to withdraw sums once deposited. At the Liverpool Provident Institution or Bank for Savings, all repayments were made by

Archdeacon Brooks, one of the senior trustees, who 'is reputed to have used the opportunity to make searching inquiries concerning the purpose of the withdrawal and to give sound moral advice'. There were pressures for change for the simple fact that it was costing the Treasury some £50,000 a year to subsidise the interest paid on the Savings Bank Fund. The principal critic of this loss of revenue was the radical MP for Aberdeen, Joseph Hume, well known to successive Chancellors of the Exchequer for his fastidious scrutiny of public expenditure. Legislation was introduced during 1828 by the new Chancellor of the Exchequer, Henry Goulburn, which cut the interest rates payable by the National Debt Office to savings banks

With growing surpluses, savings banks invested in premises
of their own. The West Somerset Savings Bank moved to this
building, in Taunton, formerly the Full Moon public house, in 1829.

from just over 4 per cent to 3.8 per cent. At the same time, the ceiling on annual deposits was reduced to a flat rate of £30, with a limit of £150 by any single depositor. Any sum over £150 was required to be returned to the depositor. The Act also required the rules of every savings bank to be approved by the barrister appointed by the Commissioners for the National Debt, John Tidd Pratt.

The immediate response to the Act was a sharp decline in deposits, which fell by over £1 million in total during 1829 as customers questioned the government's intentions, mirroring a general wavering in support for friendly societies. For more than a decade there had been growing concern about the conduct of many friendly societies, particularly the imperfections in the actuarial tables used to calculate premiums and benefits. An Act in 1819 had required that the rules of all new societies should be approved by two people with some actuarial knowledge, but this had proved less than adequate as it became apparent that satisfactory mortality tables for the 'working classes' did not exist. A Parliamentary Select Committee in 1825 revealed that in many localities there was growing hostility between friendly societies and savings banks. Although its terms of reference did not include savings banks, the Committee attempted to patch up the quarrel by declaring unequivocally 'for the particular purpose to which Friendly Societies are applicable. Savings Banks are entirely inefficient . . . Savings Banks should not supersede Friendly Societies, nor Friendly Societies, Savings Banks – the two are intended to help in achieving different ends.' The Committee's main concern was the financial management of societies, a theme examined in greater detail by another report in 1827. Following their findings, further legislation in 1829 attempted to improve financial management by requiring all societies to submit returns in 1835 'of the rate of sickness and mortality experienced'. Registered societies which failed to comply were to lose their legal protection in three years. According to contemporaries these Acts, smacking as they did of government interference, combined with frequent frauds and failures, caused a large number of societies up and down the country to dissolve and divide the box (the assets).

This crisis in confidence in the principal agents of self-help could not have come at a worse time. Expenditure on poor relief was fast moving back up to the levels of the immediate post-war years, re-awakening demands, at least in England and Wales, for a total reform of the Poor Law. The difficulties for the savings banks were compounded by bad harvests in 1829 and 1830, leading to widespread distress and causing total deposits to mark time for the following two years, 1830 and 1831. In an effort to boost public trust, John Tidd Pratt published his *History of Savings Banks in England, Wales and Ireland*, which catalogued the achievements of individual banks, piling up page by page the evidence for their vital role in the community. His statistical summary showed that there were 403,712 personal customers, less than 3 per cent of the population. However, his evidence suggested that the savings banks were beginning to fulfil the expectation that thrift could be practised by the less well-off even at a time when wages were drifting down, with over half the customers holding less than £20 in their accounts at an average balance of £7 4s 5½d. With weekly wages for labourers of between 8s and 16s, these were substantial savings even for artisans and miners who could expect to earn a little more. The average deposits recorded by Pratt for every county demonstrated that the appeal of the savings banks so far had been largely to the better-off. The lowest figure in England and Wales was Cardiff with 881 depositors and an average of £22. In London, which had almost 19,000 savers, the average investment was less than £25. In most counties the average was between £30 and £40, more than the total annual income of the majority of working men.

The agricultural distress in 1829 and 1830 coincided with further attempts at mechanisation on farms through the introduction of steam-powered threshing machines. Believing their position threatened, infuriated by seeing government interference in the conduct of their self-help organisations, and with their family budgets under pressure from rising prices, skilled farmworkers and other rural craftsmen took the law into their own hands. Throughout southern Britain there were a series of apparently spontaneous riots beginning in the autumn of 1830, characterised by attacks on the new machines and burning of ricks, inspired, it was rumoured, by the shadowy figure of Captain Swing. These disturbances came hard on the heels of a general election caused by the death of King George IV, in which the question of parliamentary reform had been hotly debated. Although the Tories did badly, they clung on to power. The overthrow of the French monarchy in July 1830 and the Belgian revolt later in the year increased anxiety at the possibility of political disturbances in Britain and made reform inevitable. The Tory Prime Minister, the reactionary Duke of Wellington, was forced from office to be replaced by the Whig, Lord Grey, at the head of an administration committed to a radical programme of reform. Immediately the new government set about abolishing sinecures, privileges and outmoded methods of doing business that had survived almost unaltered from medieval times. The centre-piece of their programme was to be the reform of Parliament by disenfranchising boroughs whose small population made representation laughable and redistributing seats to the new industrial towns. The franchise was extended to include a larger number of property-holders. Owing to the entrenched opposition of the members of the House of Lords, the Bill failed twice to reach the statute book. It was only after a general election and a wave of popular protest that the Reform Act was finally passed in June 1832.

Fundamental to reform was not only an attack on privilege but a commitment to the whole concept of individual self-determination. Nowhere was this more evident than in the proposals for the reform of the Poor Law advanced by Edwin Chadwick, formerly secretary to Jeremy Bentham, and Nassau Senior, an economist and disciple of Adam Smith, as members of a Royal Commission into its workings appointed in February 1832. The Committee sat for two years, but from the outset its conclusions were in broad outlines a foregone conclusion. Much of the assiduously collected evidence was partial, telling the Committee more or less what it wanted to hear. Witnesses testified to the deleterious effect of the Poor Law in stimulating saving. The Rector of Byfield in Northampton struck a common chord when he responded to the question 'Could a poor man save?' with the emphatic declaration 'With a family, it is scarcely possible he should lay anything out of his earnings, and if he could, he dare not let it be known, lest he should be refused employment under the present system of the Poor Law, though he is industrious and honest.' The final report published in 1834 recommended reforms that would effectively provide a powerful stimulus to self-help. The system of allowances on the Speenhamland model (see p.13) was to be swept away on the grounds that it caused rather than prevented poverty and idleness, encouraging men to abandon the 'less eligible' occupation of labour in favour of becoming paupers. In Chadwick's opinion, the position had to be reversed, making the pauper class 'less eligible' or less attractive by cancelling all outdoor relief and insisting that all paupers be accommodated in the workhouse. For the able-bodied the workhouse was to be a deterrent, to be avoided at all costs, where man and wife would be segregated and only subsistence rations would be provided. Although the report did not say as much, it was implied that dread of the workhouse would act as a powerful goad to savings both with friendly societies and savings banks. Encouragement to use the savings banks as a means of allowing for the vicissitudes of old age was provided in 1833 when it became possible to purchase through them government annuities of between £4 and £20. Most of the findings of the Royal Commission were incorporated later in 1834 in the Poor Law Amendment Act which severely restricted the scope of outdoor relief and abolished the law of settlement in England and Wales.

The new Poor Law was to be introduced progressively, beginning in the southern counties of England and Wales and moving gradually northwards. Although there were those who doubted the neatness of the theory which underpinned the reforms, at a time when the economy was recovering rapidly, there was little popular protest. In their second annual report the Commissioners had no doubt that the new system was more than matching its principal objective of converting 'paupers into independent labourers'. Due more perhaps to the upturn in the economy rather than the effects of the doctrinaire legislation, savings bank receipts advanced steadily. The improvement in deposits continued as real wages edged forward despite the scandal of the defalcation of the Hertfordshire Savings Bank in the summer of 1835, which sent shock-waves reverberating through the movement. The trustees of the bank, who included Lord Melbourne, the Prime Minister, had acted quickly to restore confidence by digging into their own pockets to make good half the loss resulting from fraud by the bank's agent at St Albans, a local clergyman who had embezzled the considerable sum of £24,000.

In Scotland, where the new Poor Law did not apply, the government, in 1835, extended the right of savings banks to invest all their funds with the Commissioners for the Reduction of the National Debt, qualifying for the title of National Security Savings Banks. The expectation that this permission would 'infuse new life and vigour into the Scottish Savings Bank system' was quickly borne out, with the formation, in April of the following year, of a National Security Savings Bank in Edinburgh where the existing Provident Bank was more or less moribund. James Cleghorn, the first actuary who was also much involved in the concurrent establishment of the Scottish Provident Life Assurance Society, immediately provided advice and assistance to a group of Glasgow businessmen keen to emulate Edinburgh's example. At the end of July the Savings Bank of Glasgow was established and within four months had attracted just over 2,000 customers and more than £19,000 in deposits.

Throughout Britain the government was keen to foster the expansion of other independent thrift organisations, which would not make any demands on the Treasury, in the same way that the savings banks and annuities did. Legal protection was given to building societies in 1836 through the Benefit Building Societies Act. The first society, designed to help members buy their own houses, had been formed in Kirkcudbright in south-west Scotland in 1816. Over the intervening twenty years, the number of societies had multiplied and they had come to be used as much as a convenient place for depositing savings as a means of purchasing property. Interestingly, the 1836 Act expressly forbade societies from investing their deposits with savings banks, unlike the friendly societies.

The boom in the economy faltered in 1835, a harbinger of a sharp downturn that persisted throughout the remaining years of the decade. As prices rose, wages fell and unemployment increased, the Poor Law Commissioners had the unenviable task of introducing the new regulations in northern counties. There were riots in several industrial towns in Yorkshire during 1837 and 1838. Antagonism towards the new Poor Law fuelled more general political protest after the Whigs' parliamentary majority was eroded in the election following the accession of Queen Victoria to the throne in 1837. Meetings were orchestrated up and down the country by prominent radicals to approve a People's Charter, with the chief objective of securing universal male suffrage. The first National Convention met in February 1839 to plan the campaign which was to include what amounted to a general strike and co-ordinated bank with-drawals in an effort to destabilise the fin-ancial system. As in the war years, the

A bill advertising forthcoming attractions at Edinburgh's Theatre Royal, 1839. Such entertainment was often condemned by the savings banks movement, both on moral grounds and because the theatres were believed to seduce working men into parting with money better put by for a rainy day.

authorities promptly prevented civil disorder by arresting Chartist leaders. However, unlike 1794, there was no attempt to repress societies that might act as seedbeds for revolution. On the contrary, the government gave official approval to membership of friendly societies, particularly the fast-growing affiliated Orders, as they were known, with lodges or branches throughout the country or in specific localities. The most successful were the Manchester Unity of Oddfellows and the Ancient Order of Foresters.

Both Whigs and Tories were shifting their focus away from savings banks with their close government involvement to the much freer and less restricted friendly societies. The advantage of belonging to a friendly society, as compared to a savings bank, was that it afforded immediate sustenance at times of ill-health and bereavement in the early years of membership well beyond total contributions. Nevertheless, the savings banks continued to attract customers and remained popular with leaders in local communities. The number of new foundations picked up in 1836, when nine new banks were set up in England and Wales, including the Tynemouth Savings Bank in Northumberland. This revival continued over the next three years with the formation of no less than forty-one new banks in the whole of mainland Britain at places as far apart as Plymouth and Inverness. Although deposits grew only sluggishly, reflecting the decline in disposable incomes, the number of depositors increased sharply, climbing from just under 550,000 in 1835 to almost 750,000 members in 1839. This increase in popularity at a time of economic difficulty was interpreted by managers as evidence that the savings banks were possibly reaching a little further down the social scale, providing a secure place for money needed to pay quarterly rents and for other major items of expenditure. It is more likely that the increase was due to a growth in the middle class as a result of the gathering momentum of industrial change even in rural areas. However, despite the growth in depositors, the savings banks still served only 5 per cent of the population, principally the aristocracy of the labour force and domestic servants. It was still believed that there were many amongst the remaining 95 per cent who could be persuaded to save by appeals from temperance campaigners, churchmen and other community leaders.

The recession reached the lowest level at the beginning of the 1840s and the economy began to recover very gradually from 1842. Wages remained depressed and did not return to the levels they had been in the mid-1830s for the rest of the decade. Nevertheless, the number of savings banks continued to grow. Hours of business and staffing varied widely. A few banks, such as Glasgow, now opened six days a week and employed full-time actuaries. The majority opened for less than ten hours a week and some just one day a month, and then only for two hours. The number of depositors exceeded one million in 1844 with total deposits of almost £30 million. Total deposits had increased rapidly in the previous two years as the pace of economic activity had quickened, fuelled by considerable investment in railway construction. The whole movement was encouraged by these results and the endorsement of the Royal Commission on the Scottish Poor Law, which concluded in its report published in 1844 that savings banks and friendly societies were 'two of the best preventives of pauperism'. The optimism of trustees was soon quenched by the introduction of a Bill in Parliament by the Chancellor of the Exchequer, Henry Goulburn, in response to long-standing criticism of the whole administration of the savings banks by none other than Joseph Hume, now MP for Montrose. The burden of Hume's criticism was that, since the interest paid on savings bank deposits was above consol rate, the scheme was too expensive to administer. His argument was couched in purely financial terms, with no reference to any of the social benefits of savings banks. Although he was adamant that he was not attacking the savings banks themselves, there were those who suspected that the better-off were taking advantage of the relatively high rates of interest available from the National Debt Commissioners. They would point to the annual reports of the savings banks themselves which showed their principal markets to be amongst domestic servants, artisans and mechanics, and clerks and warehousemen, the aristocracy of labour. There was evidence cited by John Bright, the radical MP for Durham, that some families of factory operatives in Lancashire were 'at present earning higher than the average of country surgeons, higher than the average of the clergy of all denominations, much higher than the average of the teachers of the rising generation and perhaps higher than the average of the middle classes of the United Kingdom generally'. Correspondence in *The Times* suggested that actuaries turned a blind eye to abuses of the regulations, notably opening accounts in different names and exceeding the limits on investments.

The Bill, introduced in the spring of 1844, sought to slash interest rates payable to depositors from about 3.45 per cent to about 2.66 per cent in line with the prevailing bank rate. In addition the annual limit on investment was to be cut to £20 and the limit on total deposits reduced to £120. These proposals evoked a storm of protest co-ordinated by the trustees of the St Martin's Place Savings Bank in London and its able comptroller and secretary, Edward Boodle. Up and down the country, trustees condemned the Chancellor's action. The Sheffield Savings Bank was typical in raising the spectre of panic withdrawals, with the attendant risk that investors would either 'keep the same in their possession unproductive, or invest it in plausible, but delusive, undertakings', or 'lured by the promise of a large rate of interest, will lend it to crafty and unprincipled persons and ultimately lose the whole', or 'unable to resist the temptation arising from the possession of an unusual amount of money, will spend it in useless extravagance or notorious dissipation, and thus destroy that character for prudence and sobriety which the institution of savings banks was intended to foster and encourage'. A mass meeting was held in London which appointed a 'monster deputation' to call on the Chancellor. The weight of criticism was so great that Goulburn was forced to make substantial amendments, lessening the reduction in interest rates and dropping his plan to curtail deposits any further. The Act, finally passed in August 1844, clearly spelled out that trustees were not liable for any losses should a bank default.

The campaign to modify the legislation was conducted against a background of mounting hostility in *The Times*, a long-standing enemy of the savings banks. The newspaper's antagonism derived from a firmly held objection to the 'prohibition of outdoor relief' by the Poor Law Commissioners and a conviction that people would not 'have it'. Friendly societies and savings banks were condemned as an integral part of a repressive system that had still not been totally implemented in the north of England. *The Times* tried to demonstrate the unfortunate effects of the unnecessary hoarding of money. The chosen examples were ill judged and overdrawn, unrepresentative of the vast majority of depositors, over 80 per cent of whom had less than £50 in their accounts. Its opinions were not shared by other newspapers, which believed that the savings banks exerted an 'unquestionable moral influence'. In their annual reports published at the end of the year, savings bank trustees attempted to make good the damage done by the new Act and onslaught by *The Times* by stressing the security of the investment. The Liverpool Provident Institution or Bank for Savings declared boldly: 'The money is invested in the public stock, for which the faith of the whole Country is pledged; the security thus obtained is of infinitely greater importance than any difference of Interest which is occasioned by the new Enactment.' Throughout the country, opposition and censure reinforced rather than reduced the determination of trustees to maintain the impetus of the movement. Inviting existing customers to encourage their friends to become depositors, Alexander Hector of the Edinburgh Savings Bank proclaimed: 'Let no one be deterred because they have but a small sum to begin with – small beginners are quite as welcome as large. They will gather by degrees faster than they will at present believe, and the very fact of gathering will justify their characters as well as their means.' Such appeals fell largely on deaf ears as the trustees of the Edinburgh Savings Bank might well have predicted. John Maitland, the actuary of the bank, noted in 1845 that despite the 'unusually large proportion of small accounts, and a still greater proportional number of small operatives' in the Edinburgh and Glasgow Savings Banks: 'It is notorious that, even in these cities, and during the periods of high wages, the labouring poor do not resort to the savings banks in the numbers they might do …' Two years later, when reviewing the savings bank movement, he reckoned that the savings 'of the industrious, labouring and operative classes, the domestic servants, and of course a vast number of persons; young and old in very poor circumstances' were unrepresented. He went on to suggest that there was no incentive for savings banks to pursue such custom vigorously because the legislation did not make adequate provision for expenses to cover a large number of trivial transactions. He believed that if this obstacle was removed 'five hundred or a thousand agencies, with tenfold that number of agents, aided by the printing press, could not then fail to produce a beneficial influence amongst the surrounding populations'. He condemned as evil the fact that 'at present, about one-third of the whole amount at the credit of private depositors in Savings Banks is in balances above £100 each'.

The economy slipped back into recession during 1845 and by the autumn interest available on government stock was higher than that paid by the savings banks. The rate of growth of members and deposits slowed sharply, confirming the impression that the more investment-conscious were using the savings banks. To make matters worse, the harvest failed in 1845 and 1846. In Ireland and the Highlands and islands of Scotland the potato crop was almost totally destroyed by blight, bringing conditions of near starvation to many areas. Food had to be imported that had to be paid for in bullion which, in turn, forced up interest rates, intensifying the economic crisis. In the spring of 1846, in response to the appalling conditions in Ireland, but after a campaign by free traders that had lasted a decade, the Corn Laws, introduced in 1815 to protect British agriculture, were repealed. This allowed grain to be imported into the United Kingdom whatever the price of home-grown cereals and heralded a change in policy towards free trade. Necessary as this reform was in the face of adversity, it did nothing to improve the state of the economy which was being made even more precarious by rash speculation in railway shares, often using money borrowed by those who could not afford it. By the autumn of 1847, interest rates reached an unprecedented 8 per cent.

In the circumstances it is surprising that savings bank deposits increased at all. As it was, they inched forward by a little more than the rate of interest in 1846 and 1847. In every part of the country trustees marvelled at this success at a time of profound agricultural hardship. The economy slumped in 1848 as Europe was torn by political disturbance and revolution. The spectre of revolution in Britain was briefly reawakened when the Chartists organised a popular petition for the establishment of a British republic. Signed by four million people, it was presented at a mass meeting in April at Kennington Common in London. When the police threatened to use force, the meeting dispersed peacefully and the danger of insurrection passed. It would have been difficult enough for savings banks to maintain deposits in this climate of economic and political uncertainty, but much-publicised frauds that came to light in Ireland at the same time as the Chartist disturbances on the mainland made the task impossible.

The St Peter's Parish Savings Bank in Cuffe Street, Dublin, had been known to

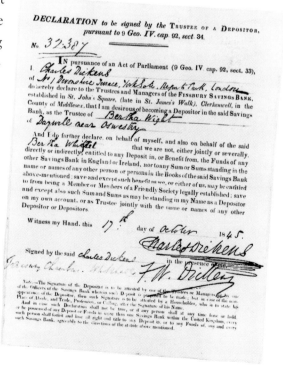

Charles Dickens believed deeply in the savings banks as a force for good, encouraging people to put a little by for a rainy day. In this declaration he has deposited money on behalf of Bertha White to tide her over such a period of adversity. Many of the small depositors were women.

be in difficulties by the Commissioners of the National Debt since 1826 when its actuary, the parish sexton, had been forced to resign. With advice from Pratt, the trustees had decided to keep the bank open, despite a large deficit due to the fraudulent activities of the previous management. This was an unwise decision and matters went from bad to worse. Rumours of imminent closure led to a serious run on the bank in 1845, precipitating its collapse three years later with debts of £56,000 due to more than 2,000 customers. Hard on the heels of this news came the fraudulent failure of two more Irish savings banks at Tralee and Killarney in County Kerry on the very depressed west coast. Confidence in the Irish savings banks was shattered. At Limerick Savings Bank in the adjoining county, the trustees took urgent action to stem the

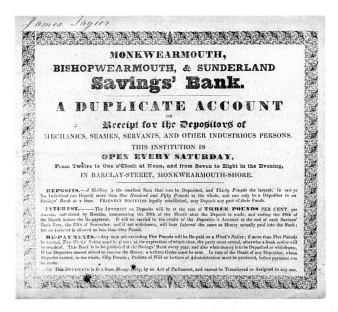

The cover of James Taylor's passbook for the Monkwearmouth, Bishopwearmouth & Sunderland Savings Bank, issued in 1847. Like most savings banks of the day, his opened for only a few hours each week.

panic by showing that there were sufficient assets to meet liabilities. At the same time, the Manchester Unity of Oddfellows was hit by scandal when the corresponding secretary, W. Ratcliffe, embezzled £4,000 and locked himself in the society's office, refusing to give up his records. His eventual acquittal on a technicality concerning the legal status of affiliated orders cast doubts on the reputation of thrift organisations on the mainland.

Whatever individual banks or societies might do to restore confidence, the damage was done. The suspicions voiced in *The Times* four years earlier, and repeated regularly ever since, appeared to be confirmed. Savings banks were condemned not only as advocating needless thrift, but as positively unsafe. A brief government inquiry did nothing to calm the fears formed by the press when it produced a report reckoned by Lord Bentinck, the Leader of the

Opposition, 'as remarkable for its brevity as for its vacuity – as brief as it is worthless'. Dismayed, the new Chancellor of the Exchequer, Sir Charles Wood, introduced a Bill requiring savings banks to appoint auditors, insisting that all depositors produce their passbooks for comparison with the ledger at least once a year and making every trustee personally liable for not more than £100 of any loss, in the expectation that these reforms would encourage better management and restore confidence. The reaction from the savings banks in mainland Britain, however, was swift and angry. In the face of determined opposition, the Chancellor was forced to restrict the operation of the Bill for the time being to Ireland. Even there, when it came into force at the beginning of the savings banks' financial year in November 1848, it was not entirely welcome.

Poster relating to the collapse of the Tralee Savings Bank in
Ireland, 1848.

The savings banks, suspicious of the Chancellor's intentions, expected a modified version of the Bill to be introduced in 1849, which would not only extend the new Irish regulations to the mainland, but also attempt again to reduce the ceiling on deposits. In anticipation that the limit would be set at £100, examples were paraded to demonstrate that large balances were not held by the well-to-do taking advantage of higher rates of interest than could be obtained elsewhere, but by genuine depositors. At Carlisle Savings Bank it was claimed that of the 134 investors with over £100 in their accounts, the majority were domestic servants who had been customers for between twenty and thirty years and would 'experience much difficulty in disposing of their money with safety, if compelled to withdraw their accounts'.

Amazed by the attitude of the savings banks in standing in the way of reform, *The Times* began a campaign in the spring of 1849 in support of an annual audit and insisting that the managers and trustees should be obliged to accept 'just sufficient liability to make them watchful against abuse and fraud, without making that liability so great as to deter gentlemen of small means from taking either office'. At the end of August, to head off the threatened legislation, the actuaries of the larger savings banks met in London to organise a petition to Parliament. Signed by over 79,000 depositors, it was presented in November and requested the Chancellor to leave matters as they were. *The Times* responded by publishing a series of letters from anxious depositors worried about the security of their savings. One letter purporting to come from a domestic servant with £100 in her account, expressed the fears of many depositors who had trusted savings banks 'entirely on account of the supposed security attending them; that alone has caused us to resist the tempting baits that are daily held out to us. Therefore I need not say, Sir, how great is our disappointment when we hear that we are quite at the mercy of any dishonest man who may be lucky enough to obtain the honorary situation of manager or auditor.' Such apprehensions were fuelled by the discovery of a huge fraud at Rochdale Savings Bank following the death of its actuary, George Haworth, the month before; a prominent local Quaker businessman with interests in wool, cotton and property, he had systematically embezzled almost £72,000 from the savings bank.

The extent of the Rochdale collapse added fuel to the agitation for reform. In late January 1850 – at a time when the boom in the economy was showing signs of running out of steam – *The Times* alleged that 'the public gained almost weekly fresh evidence of the rotten nature of these institutions on whose general soundness depends the well-being or ruin of many thousands of the industrious classes'. The editor went on to accuse actuaries of wilfully breaking the rules to attract large deposits from the better-off, particularly by allowing accounts to be opened in the names of fictitious customers and minors. Stung by these taunts, Prince Albert, the Prince Consort and President of the St Martin's Place Savings Bank, London, immediately asked the actuary to conduct a thorough investigation of the bank's accounts. This public questioning of the policy of the savings banks made the Chancellor of the Exchequer more determined than ever to reform the law. He introduced a new Bill at the end of April 1850 which proposed that trustees should be liable 'for wilful neglect and defaults'. A further clause gave the Commissioners of the National Debt powers to instruct Inspectors to investigate the accounts and affairs of any bank. It also included the predicted reduction in the ceiling on deposits to £100 and cut interest rates payable to savings banks to 3 per cent and to investors to 2.75 per cent. The final straw for the savings banks was a recommendation that the treasurers of every bank

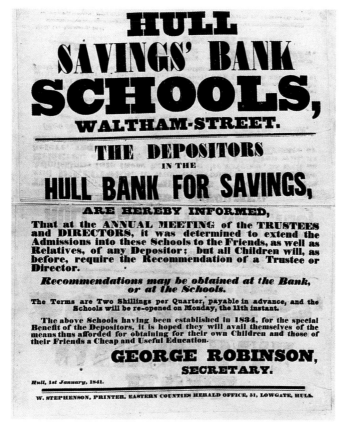

This special service for depositors at the Hull Savings Bank was introduced as an added incentive to save. The first and only savings bank school was closed in 1851 after the National Debt Office expressed doubts about the legality of the enterprise.

should be appointed by the government and receive salaries paid from the savings resulting from the reduction in the rate of interest.

The radical press greeted the Bill enthusiastically, but the savings banks were outraged. Trustees and actuaries noisily voiced their hostility to the Bill which challenged the principle of local management, fundamental to the success of the movement. Another meeting was held in London which unanimously condemned the measure and, when it became clear that many Members of Parliament also doubted its likely efficacy, it was withdrawn.

The Manchester Unity of Oddfellows and the affiliated Orders had already taken steps to secure legal safeguard. Following the acquittal of W. Ratcliffe on charges of fraud in 1848, they had pressed for a Select Committee hearing which recommended that affiliated societies should be brought within the scope of the law. A new Act was passed in 1850 for this purpose, which also required friendly societies to make annual returns of their funds to the Registrar and cut interest payable on deposits with the Commissioners of the National Debt to 3 per cent – the level proposed and rejected for savings banks. The Registrar was required to present a digest of the returns each year to Parliament. Having failed spectacularly to win the consent of the savings banks for a very similar measure, the Chancellor of the Exchequer, in consultation with Sir Alexander Spearman, the newly appointed Comptroller-General of the National Debt Office, issued a circular drawing attention to the provisions of the 1844 Act that depositors should produce their deposit book once a year for examination and suggesting that the opportunity should be taken for comparison with the ledgers. At the same time, Sir Alexander Spearman resolved to begin publishing a comprehensive annual financial return of all savings banks intended in great measure to allay public anxiety. There was no equivalent pressures for more general reforms of the banking system, largely because there had been no equivalent crisis in commercial banks.

In both 1849 and 1850 net deposits fell because of all the doubts shed on the integrity of the savings banks, despite the fact that real wages were higher than they had been for a century. The annual return for 1850 took more than a year for the National Debt Commissioners to compile and was not published until March 1852. It was the first comprehensive financial statement of the savings bank movement since John Tidd Pratt's *History of Savings Banks in England, Wales and Ireland* of twenty years before. Most savings banks now had at least two officers: a treasurer or an agent and an actuary or secretary. Treasurers were not normally paid, giving their services voluntarily, but actuaries received a salary. Levels of remuneration varied in the smaller banks from £55 a year in Abergavenny Savings Bank to £120 per annum at York Savings Bank. The few large banks had a hierarchy of staff. St Martin's Place Savings Bank, the largest savings bank in England, had sixteen staff under the day-to-day direction of Edward Boodle, the Comptroller and Secretary with a handsome salary of £700 a year. Beneath him were a chief cashier and accountant (paid £444 a year), two auditors (each paid £275 a year), three cashiers (each paid £279 a year), six clerks (each paid between £129 and £260 a year), two messengers (each paid between £57 and £99 a year), a constable (paid £168 a year), a superannuated officer (paid £50 a year) and two supernumeraries (paid £43 and £33 a year). In most banks the actuary was an important member of the local community, playing a part in a variety of other voluntary organisations.

The figures for the number of savings bank customers revealed wide disparities in penetration between different counties. The movement had been most successful in London, with almost 12 per cent of the population of Middlesex, some 223,000 people, holding accounts. This was followed by Devon with just under 9.5 per cent, then the East Riding of Yorkshire with a little more than 9.1 per cent, and Hereford with 8.2 per cent. Bottom of the league came Rutland with no savings banks, Westmorland with 2.3 per cent of the population, Durham with 2.36 per cent, and Cambridge with nearly 3 per cent. The average was between 5 and 6 per cent. There were also large variations in the average number of times depositors used the savings banks during a year; in Middlesex, for example, the 223,000 customers each made on average between one and two deposits, but only half withdrew money from the bank. In Cornwall just over half the customers made a deposit and less than half withdrew money. The figures for the number of withdrawals at more than twice the number of deposits suggested that the savings banks were by now firmly established as a means of short-term savings to meet projected expenditure such as rents and not for long-term thrift. This impression was confirmed by the turnover figures – the total amount of cash that passed through a bank's hands in any year – published in some savings banks' annual reports, but not included in the annual return. The volume of transactions presented trustees and actuaries with a considerable problem as they yielded almost no income to the banks. In the absence of the membership fees and fines imposed by friendly societies, the savings banks depended for their management expenses (overheads) on long-term deposits usually made by the bigger investor. It was for this reason that reductions in interest rates to or below the rates available on government stocks – consols – were so fiercely opposed.

Trustees and actuaries continued to believe passionately that the role of savings banks extended far beyond merely providing a watered-down commercial banking service for the better-off artisan and domestic servant. At a time when the government, influenced once again by Chadwick, was pre-occupied with improving the living conditions and health of the poorest sections of society, the movement played its part by enthusiastically experimenting with the establishment of penny banks to provide a haven for the savings of families with very little to save. Penny banks owed their

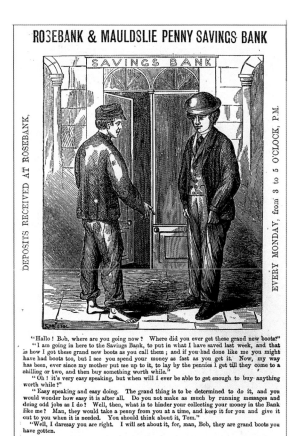

The Penny Banks adopted similar rhetoric to that of the savings banks to encourage thrift.

inspiration to J.M. Scott of Greenock on the lower Clyde in Scotland, who opened the first bank in 1847 to act as a nursery for the town's Provident Bank where investors would learn the virtues of thrift. As the name implied, penny banks were directed at those with only pennies to save, particularly schoolchildren and young people, preventing them wasting their money on luxuries. When a pound had been accumulated, an account was opened with the parent bank. The following year a similar bank was opened by the curate of Christ Church in the parish of St George's-in-the-East in London. Within a year, using Sunday School teachers and other volunteers, he had enrolled 15,000 depositors. Glasgow's first penny bank was inaugurated in 1850 in one of the poorest parts of the city, gaining 132 depositors on the first four Saturday evening openings. By 1851, penny banks had been established up and down the country in Sunday schools, schools, mechanics' institutes, and social clubs.

Despite the bruising experience of the scandals and criticisms of the late 1840s, the confidence of the movement was returning. Economic recovery, falling prices and growing prosperity gave trustees and actuaries a renewed sense of purpose. There was evidence for all to see that a significant and increasing proportion of the population had money to save. The most obvious testimony was the four million people who flocked to the spectacular Great Exhibition in the Crystal Palace in 1851 to witness not just Britain's engineering prowess, but also all the products for the home and the person from the country's mills and factories. The Exhibition epitomised the virtues that the savings banks had sought to promote, demonstrating the untold material rewards and moral improvement that could result from hard work and prudent living. Matching this more assured mood, total deposits with the savings banks recovered to above their 1846 level for the first time in 1852 and continued to grow faster than the rate of interest during the following year.

These were years of unparalleled affluence as British manufacturers reaped the benefits of free trade. The much-feared threat to home agriculture of cheap imports of grain following the abolition of the Corn Laws had failed to materialise and, on the contrary, farmers were enjoying high yields and good returns helped by industrially produced artificial fertilisers. At the Savings Bank of Glasgow, in the fastest-growing industrial city in the United Kingdom, deposits exceeded £500,000 in 1851. To mark this achievement, the trustees held a public meeting in the City Hall in February 1852 attended by over 3,000 people. In a celebration of saving, speaker after speaker extolled the merits of thrift, drawing a sharp contrast between the prodigal drink-sodden family and the temperate provident household. The Revd Dr Buchanan was typical when he quoted the example of one man: 'He is a boot closer to his trade and a crack workman. He could show you specimens of fancy stitching that might have been worthy of a place in the Great Exhibition. He can make 30 shillings a week with ease – and he has been in a position to do so for many years – and yet if disease or old age were to overtake him as he is, he would have no refuge but the workhouse, and would, when he died, have to be indebted to the poor's rates for his coffin.' He compared him with a man who had been introduced to the savings bank shortly after it opened and became a regular investor: 'And what has been the result? Two or three years ago a snug little business, in a country town, of a kind that suited him, was offered for sale. To purchase the stock and the goodwill together required a sum of about £500. Our prosperous merchant had by this time that sum at his credit . . .'. He concluded by declaring that the business had flourished and then carried a stock of £1,000. This story of 'canny' personal endeavour was true of the careers of a good number of the tradesmen and manufacturers who were, themselves, trustees of the bank.

In 1853 the Commissioners attempted to discover more about the social composition of the customer base of the savings banks. A questionnaire was sent to every savings bank inviting returns of the number of accounts by thirteen different classifications. Out of the 576 savings banks, 404 made a return, accounting for almost 80 per cent of all depositors. The largest group was 'tradesmen and their assistants, small farmers, clerks, mechanics and artisans not described as journeymen and their wives', with 235,333 accounts and deposits of about £6.4 million. These were followed by 'domestic servants, charwomen, nurses and laundresses', with 205,781 accounts and deposits of nearly £5.5 million. An analysis of depositors with the Savings Bank of Glasgow for the period 1836/59 by Professor Peter Payne in 1967, showed that 'in an average year, of every hundred new accounts, 28 were opened by mechanics (i.e. wrights, masons, smiths, joiners, ironworkers, etc), 13 by domestic servants, 11 by clerks and warehouse workers, 10 by minors (under 15 years old), 9 by labourers, carters and porters, 5 by shopkeepers and small trustees, 4 by female warehouse workers and sewers, and 4 by factory operatives.' From this analysis, Payne concluded that John Maitland, the actuary of the Edinburgh Savings Bank at the time, had been correct in his assumptions that the savings banks had persistently made little headway in attracting the industrial workforce. Charles Sikes, a manager of the Huddersfield Savings Bank, reported that the majority saved for 'wearing apparel, watches, books, or support during unemployment'.

Although during the 1850s the savings banks recovered much of the ground they had lost in the previous decade, this experience was shared by their principal competitors in the savings market. The affiliated orders of friendly societies, whose numbers had fallen sharply, stemmed the tide in the early 1850s. The Manchester Unity of Oddfellows, hard hit by fraud in 1845, marked time with 225,000 members, but the Ancient Order of Foresters had a record membership of nearly 90,000 in 1852. Benefit building societies were becoming increasingly popular, but no reliable figures for the United Kingdom as a whole survive for this period. Catering for the poorer sections of society, membership of burial societies, which simply provided insurance to cover the cost of funerals, also increased sharply. In what was becoming an increasingly complex, but still informal, market for savings, there was no sense of competition between the different types of provident organisations which, in many cases, shared common management. The advantage of the savings banks was that they offered ready access to money and, for all the scandals, a high degree of security. As in any period, but especially at a time when the range and variety of goods and attractions was expanding rapidly, all thrift organisations struggled, not simply to persuade people to save money they had, but also to stop them spending money they did not have. Everyone with access to money, from the richest to the poorest members of society, had new and exciting opportunities for spending in the great department stores being built in every part of the country, in gambling at race meetings, now easily and cheaply accessible with the coming of the railways, the new music halls, and, in the summer, at the seaside. Except for the well-to-do, who could borrow from commercial banks, credit was obtained chiefly from pawnbrokers by means of pledging clothes, jewellery, furniture, domestic utensils and even tools. Although despised by social commentators, the number of pawnbrokers had increased rapidly in the 1840s, meeting the urgent needs of many families in the exigencies of the depression.

The boom in the economy slowed in 1853. Real wages retreated and flattened out the following year at the levels they had been in the early 1840s. Savings banks' receipts were immediately affected, with total withdrawals in 1854 exceeding deposits for the first time for three years. More worryingly, turnover also declined for the first time since 1848. There were many explanations for this setback. Emigration from Scotland, Ireland and northern counties of England was blamed. The Savings Bank of the County & City of Perth reported that 'many of the best and steadiest operatives were drafted off to the Colonies and a large sum has left the coffers of the Bank in meeting the demands of these emigrants'. Others believed the cause to be the rising cost of living, especially of foodstuffs. In some places there was competition from other thrift organisations. The Leeds Skyrac & Morley Savings Bank was facing competition from the Leeds Industrial Co-operative Society founded in 1847 and the Leeds Permanent Benefit Building Society founded the following year. Some attributed the reversal in fortunes of the savings banks to the return of the uncertainty surrounding the movement caused by another attempt to reform the legislation by the new Chancellor of the Exchequer, William Ewart Gladstone. During the Parliamentary session 1853/4, he introduced three separate measures. The first two were, on the whole, uncontentious and became law, improving the method of buying government annuities through savings banks and restricting the freedom of the Commissioners of the National Debt to invest the proceeds of the Fund for the Banks for Savings. The third Bill, which proposed a reduction in interest rates payable to depositors from 3 per cent to 2.5 per cent and offered government guarantees for funds on certain conditions, encountered a storm of protest from trustees and managers. The savings banks disliked intensely the renewed suggestion that 'inspectors and receivers' should be appointed directly by the government and paid for out of the surplus in the Fund for the Banks for Savings. If individual savings banks failed to comply, the trustees would become personally liable for any loss of deposits.

In their annual reports published at the turn of the year, nearly every savings bank took the opportunity of drawing attention to the impracticality of the proposals. The trustees of the efficiently run Devon & Exeter Savings Bank, with deposits of almost £1 million, believed 'these alterations necessarily ensure the cessation of this Bank with all its numerous branches, as the proposed Government Receiver cannot be substituted for our numerous gratuitous and paid Receivers, and no Trustee or Manager will consent to the alternative of refusing the Government's offer by the personal responsibility of each of them for the total amount of Deposit'. Despite amendments to meet some of the criticisms, the Bill remained unacceptable to the savings banks and finally lapsed at the end of the session. Gladstone's warning that the Bill would be reintroduced was soon overtaken by the declaration of war on Russia in March 1854, followed by the despatch of troops to the Crimea in the autumn. As the troops were about to embark, Sir Henry Willoughby, a long-standing supporter of the savings banks and a trustee of the St Martin's Place Savings Bank in London, publicly accused the government of plundering the Savings Bank Fund to prosecute the war. Although it was true that the Fund had been used by the Chancellor to cover a temporary shortfall in public borrowing, the allegation that sums had been misappropriated was unfounded and quickly condemned in the press. As Willoughby should have known, such an accusation, however hotly denied by the government, could only serve to fuel depositors' anxieties.

The events of 1854 had a noticeable effect in England and Wales, with a further marked decline in deposits. Hardest hit was London and the south-east of England, with a loss of about £200,000 out of the £5 million deposited with the savings banks in Middlesex and about £30,000 out of the £500,000 with those in Sussex. By the end of the year, the outbreak of hostilities in the Crimea had forced the price of government stocks down to bargain basement levels with a consequent increase in yield, attracting many of the wealthier savings bank depositors in the south of England to switch their investment so as to obtain a higher yield. It is possible that such big investors, with first-hand knowledge of the London capital market, behaved differently from their counterparts in other areas of the country. The north of England and Scotland were largely insulated from the loss of confidence in the thrift movement and consequent temptation to invest directly in government funds. In Lancashire, where friendly societies were very well represented, the number of investors and total deposits rose. There was sustained growth in Scotland's smaller towns, where competition from the commercial banks which accepted interest-bearing deposit accounts, unlike their English counterparts, was more severe. In some cases there were specific local reasons for a decline in business, as in Hull where a prolonged lock-out by employers forced many families to draw on their savings. International tension eased in 1855 following the coming to power of Lord Palmerston as Prime Minister and the capture of Sebastopol after a long siege in September. There was, however, no general recovery in the economy and savings bank deposits continued to slide, influenced by rising food prices and the persistently low price of consols which, as a result, offered high rates of return.

Trustees marvelled that, in the circumstances, families were able to save at all. The superintending committee of the Brighton Savings Bank viewed a modest increase in deposits as 'satisfactory evidence that, though the prices of the necessaries and conveniences of life far exceed the average, the operative classes are still enabled, with industry and economy, to accumulate some savings'. Although withdrawals still exceeded deposits, the performance of the savings banks improved with the coming of peace in 1856. There were those who believed that, notwithstanding the recession, the savings banks could do much better if their management and organisation was improved. In December 1856, Charles Sikes of the Huddersfield Banking Co and a manager of the Huddersfield Savings Bank, published an open letter to the Chancellor of the Exchequer, now Sir George Lewis, in which he outlined various reforms. He also drew unfavourable comparisons between the rate of growth of the savings banks and the Post Office money order department, which he attributed entirely to the fact that post offices were open every day and savings banks 'generally are closed except for one or two days per week'. A firm believer in the utility of savings banks, he continued Florence Nightingale's recent declaration about the working class, 'Give them schools and lectures and they will come to them; give them books and games and amusements, and they will leave off drinking,' with 'Give them savings banks truly worthy of their confidence and easy of access, and yours may be the delight of beholding the savings banks presenting an annual balance sheet worthy of the *bank of the people.*' He could write with first-hand knowledge. His Huddersfield Preliminary Savings Bank, aimed at young people embarking on their first jobs, was an almost immediate success, attracting 359 depositors. He suspected that one reason people were deterred from using the savings banks was the fear that their employers would learn how much money they held in their accounts.

Dismissing some of Sikes's ideas as objectionable, there was a consensus amongst trustees that investors might well be encouraged to deposit more if interest rates were raised. Bank rate reached 7 per cent in November 1856, its highest level for a decade, and eased only fractionally in the opening months of the following year. In Scotland larger depositors sensibly transferred their savings to commercial banks and even in England, where such recourse was not possible, depositors sought other avenues of investment. In the late autumn, faith in the commercial banks was weakened by the collapse of the Liverpool Borough Bank in October, followed hard on the heels by the Glasgow-based Western Bank of Scotland in November. The Western Bank, just two years earlier, had taken over the business of the Paisley Savings Bank to prevent a haemorrhage of funds to the former actuary, who now represented the City of Glasgow Bank in the town. This was possible because the bank had chosen not to register under the 1835 Act. It was the public-spirited response of the other commercial banks in guaranteeing deposits that prevented the investors in the Paisley Savings Bank from losing all their money. Shortly after the collapse, the City of Glasgow Bank was forced temporarily to close its doors and other commercial banks in the west of Scotland were reported to be in difficulty. To stem the panic, the Bank of England immediately raised interest rates to an unprecedented 10 per cent, but this did nothing to encourage savings bank customers, who received interest at less than a third of bank rate, to maintain their accounts. At Glasgow there was a run on the savings bank which developed into a near riot because the Treasurer was also the manager of the collapsed Western Bank. At nearby Greenock demands for repayment from the Provident Bank (also not registered under the 1835 Act) were so large that three directors volunteered to help man the counters to relieve overworked officials. Liverpool Provident Institution or Bank for Savings was equally hard-pressed with the closure in November of over 2,000 accounts, some 10 per cent of the total. The crisis, coinciding as it did with the end of the savings banks' financial year, caused many actuaries to paint an exaggeratedly gloomy picture in their annual reports, provoked in part by a renewed proposal for legislative reform made earlier in the year by Sir George Lewis, Chancellor of the Exchequer.

The new Bill promised in 1854 had been introduced eventually in February 1856. This was much less contentious than the predecessor, offering total government indemnity to all banks that undertook to abide by its terms. No longer were paid receivers to be imposed on banks by the National Debt Commissioners, but instead simply be approved by them. This had been the more or less informal arrangement since the publication of the annual returns began in 1852 as these listed the names and designation of all bank officers throughout the United Kingdom with details of their salaries and the amount of security they had pledged for any loss resulting from their negligence or dishonesty. However, the legislation did propose that the Commissioners would be empowered to demand minimum qualifications for officers, to determine levels of salary and security, and to remove those who were considered unsatisfactory. The annual returns showed there were wide variations in the remuneration of actuaries reflecting their responsibilities and the hours of bank opening. In addition, the Commissioners were to appoint inspectors to supervise the movement and investigate complaints and cases of defalcation. To these reasonable reforms was added a recommendation that the ceiling on total deposits in any one account should be reduced from £200 to £100. In a letter to each savings bank, the Comptroller of the National Debt Office, Sir Alexander Spearman, explained that, to qualify for protection under the Act, all a bank was required to do was to demonstrate it was solvent and the accounts properly kept. This was to be achieved by the comparison of all customers' passbooks with the ledger under the surveillance of the inspectors. Since the discovery of the frauds at Rochdale in 1849, most of the larger banks had already adopted such an annual procedure as part of the audit.

The reception was mixed. The more far-sighted actuaries, such as William Meikle of Glasgow, were willing to endorse the measure on the one condition that the £200 limit on deposits was retained. The Liberal press welcomed it; the *Manchester Guardian* was delighted, believing that the numerous statutes currently in force suggested that the movement had 'its affairs in a muddle and rested on an insecure foundation'. The editor hoped that reform would attract savers and reduce the pernicious influence of the pawnshops. William Hatton, the actuary of the Brighton Savings Bank, tried to encourage a rational discussion of the suggested reforms by launching at the end of March the *Savings Bank Magazine*, an idea he had first experimented with more than ten years before. In the editorial of the first and only issue, he advocated the need for reform, but raised a number of practical objections to the details of the Act and cast doubts on not only the suggested ceiling on deposits but also the whole administration of the Savings Bank Fund by the National Debt Commissioners which he was not convinced provided the best yield. Donald Bain, describing himself as a 'Scottish Accountant', published two 'Notes' on the Bill which went further, picking holes in nearly every clause and raised the question of whether the movement could be more cheaply managed with better returns to investors if it was taken over by the commercial banks. He concluded that, without substantial improvement to the Bill, the Chancellor 'had better proceed no further'. Bain's views corresponded with those of the trustees and actuaries who distrusted the government's motives, particularly the permissive nature of the proposals which would allow banks that refused to register to operate outside the scope of the Act. Although the clause reducing the ceiling on deposits was abandoned, the opposition in Parliament had hardened and the Bill was lost. Disappointed at the harsh attacks on what he had believed to be useful and constructive proposals, Sir George Lewis agreed towards the end of August 1857 to the appointment of a Select Committee.

The Select Committee was not formally set up until February of the following year under the chairmanship of Sotheron Estcourt, MP for North Wiltshire. Its terms of reference were narrow: 'to inquire into the Acts relating to Savings Banks, and the Operations thereof'. The proceedings concentrated on accounts of the modes of operation of individual banks and consideration of the management of the Savings Bank Fund by the National Debt Commissioners. They were dominated by the evidence of John Tidd Pratt and Sir Alexander Spearman, with the latter at pains to point out that the use of the Savings Bank Fund to cover shortfalls in government expenditure was perfectly proper. The evidence from the savings banks was presented with one exception by representatives of the larger banks such as Edward Boodle of the St Martin's Place Savings Bank, London, James Shopland of the Devon & Exeter Savings Bank, J.H. Neild of the Manchester Savings Bank, William Meikle of the Savings Bank of Glasgow, and Charles Sikes of the Huddersfield Savings Bank. Sikes was deeply opposed to direct government interference in the affairs of the savings banks, believing that the management of the Savings Bank Fund should be removed from the direct control of the Commissioners and independent inspectors should be appointed to make spot checks on individual banks. He reckoned that, providing they paid the same rate of interest as the savings banks, commercial banks could be persuaded to take deposits from investors in the savings banks when they had reached their ceiling. W.N. Wortley of the Finsbury Savings Bank, on the other hand, was an enthusiastic supporter of the appointment of government inspectors and, although he considered a proportion of the Savings Bank Fund could be invested more profitably, he did not believe it should be removed from the supervision of the Commissioners. William Meikle proposed that the overheads allowed to a bank should take account of the number of depositors as well as the capital so as 'to hold out inducement to the banks to cultivate more than they have done small accounts, to attract to the banks the great masses of the labouring population, especially those who are verging on poverty'. The only savings bank witness who did not hail from a successful bank was Edward Taylor, the chairman of the committee which had investigated the Rochdale fraud. He came to be cross-examined about what could be done to prevent such abuses in the future, but refused to endorse the appointment of inspectors, preferring the creation of a Savings Bank Board with officers (in effect advisers) who would meet annually with boards of trustees.

In the face of such contradictory opinions, the Committee shied away from making any specific recommendations about the supervision of the individual banks and instead devoted its brief report to approving the establishment of a separate Savings Bank Board to manage the Savings Bank Fund. The Board was to operate the Fund entirely for the benefit of the savings banks with power to invest a third of its capital in other securities. It was to be authorised in general terms to specify how each bank was to keep its books and arrange its financial affairs, to certify banks and appoint officers 'for the proper audit and inspection of accounts'. The existing ceiling on accounts was to be maintained, but some measure of liability was to be restored to trustees. Most trustees welcomed the report and looked forward to the promised new legislation. The City correspondent of *The Times*, by contrast, concluded from the Committee's failure to address the central issue of public confidence that it were 'better the government abandons Savings Banks altogether – Government should not be mixed up in banking for any class'. The Archdeacon of Salop, John Allan, reacted angrily by forcibly restating the social purpose of the savings banks, 'We want to lead the poor, under God's blessing, to self-reliance and self-help . . . Many indulge largely in tobacco, without considering that for every ounce per week that is spent in thus weakening their energies, thirteen shillings in the year passes away in smoke. To be a depositor at a savings bank is to have the best certificate that I know of for sobriety and honesty.' By the time the report was published in July 1858, the Conservatives had come to power and Benjamin Disraeli was Chancellor of the Exchequer. He was implacably opposed to the idea of a separate Savings Bank Fund which would circumscribe the Treasury's room for manoeuvre in an emergency.

There was no time for trustees to regret the lack of action. The economy was improving and deposits had once again overtaken withdrawals in the teeth of growing competition from other thrift organisations. Since 1856 the Manchester Unity of Oddfellows had increased its membership from 250,000 to over 275,000 and the Ancient Order of Foresters from 114,000 to 135,000. Building societies were also reported to be doing well while collecting societies, such as the Royal Liver Society, Liverpool Victoria Legal Association and Scottish Legal Liver Burial & Loan Society, were gaining ground amongst the less well-off, the section of the community that the savings banks had been established to serve. Undeterred by their lack-lustre performance since 1853, trustees and actuaries such as Archdeacon Allan had not lost sight of their social responsibility to provide for the savings of the poorest sections of society through penny banks, which continued to be established eagerly in many parts of the country. By the end of 1859 the Savings Bank of Glasgow had no fewer than thirty-six penny banks with some 8,000 depositors. They operated in churches, schools, works, improvement societies,

An idealised image of contented old age,
and of a partnership of thrift and industry.

and from the homes of trustees. Their message to depositors was still the gospel of temperance and thrift. With faster, more powerful machinery, drunkenness was not just disagreeable but dangerous. Mr Nixon, the owner of a factory at Mountain Ash near Aberdare in Wales, told a party he hosted for his workforce: 'You ought to save a little money so that when you get old you may have a house over your head and something to fall back upon ... But I tell you this, I will not have a drunken man on the premises, for the drunken men are the pest of the neighbourhood, and I will have them weeded out.' With these concerns in mind, Colonel

Edward Akroyd in 1856 established a new savings bank, the West Riding of Yorkshire Provident Society & Penny Savings Bank, which was to conduct business through branches in every locality in the Riding. The success of this venture led to its extension to cover the whole county in 1859, renamed as the Yorkshire Penny Savings Bank. Unlike the Glasgow penny banks, the Yorkshire Penny Savings Bank was not connected to a savings bank, investing its funds instead with the Leeds Permanent Building Society.

Influential in the formation of the new bank was the redoubtable Charles Sikes of Huddersfield, whose pamphlet *Good Times or the Savings Bank and the Fireside* had been distributed to over 36,000 homes. Deeply committed to the concept of thrift as a means of economic and social advance for most families, he published in September 1859 another open letter to the Chancellor of the Exchequer, W.E. Gladstone, in Palmerston's second government. In it he went much further than before, condemning the savings bank movement for failing to achieve nationwide coverage and therefore not providing a bulwark against needless expenditure and the lure of the public house, the gambling table and the pawnshop. Developing his ideas, he advocated the creation not just of a Savings Bank Board as had been suggested by the Select Committee, but of a central savings bank to be conducted under the aegis of the Post Office's money order departments, selling £1 'Savings Bank Interest Notes' bearing interest of 2.5 per cent – in effect, national savings certificates. Pounds could be patiently accumulated in the penny banks independent of the savings bank. This scheme was redolent of proposals made over fifty years before by Jeremy Bentham's followers as a means of reducing the cost of the Poor Law. It had many attractions. It was relatively cheap to operate through an existing infrastructure of post offices open daily in every town and village of the United Kingdom, however remote. Gladstone, irritated by the resistance of the savings banks to change, immediately began to explore the practicality of the plan.

By the time Gladstone initiated these investigations, he was committed to introducing a new Bill in the coming year. Ignoring the findings of the Select Committee, he proposed in the Bill published in March that the Chancellor of the Exchequer should no longer have unfettered powers over the Savings Bank Fund and that a quarter of the Fund could be invested in higher-yielding securities. The members of the Committee were furious that their advice had not been taken. Sotheron Estcourt called for a much wider measure that would overhaul the whole legal framework in which savings banks operated: 'If the House passed this measure they would throw away a golden opportunity of placing these institutions on a better and more expansive footing.' Gladstone retaliated by attacking the Committee for its negligence in not addressing the problems of the internal management of the savings banks. The Committee members hit back by condemning the Bill out of hand and doing everything they could to delay its passage through the House by tabling amendments. Many of the attacks were preposterous, based on hearsay rather than fact. In July, when the Bill was in Committee, Mr Henley accused Gladstone of using the measure as a cover for reducing rates to depositors,

The Chester Savings Bank in Grosvenor Street. The building opened in 1852 and the bank's manager was provided with free accommodation on the premises. Gladstone, who passed by on his way to and from his home in Hawarden, probably had this bank in mind when he complained of the extravagance of erecting 'those beautiful buildings ... used for two or three hours a week for Savings Bank purposes and which formed very agreeable residences for those officers'.

implying that he had deliberately misled the House. Uncharacteristically, Gladstone lost his temper and struck out at the whole savings bank movement. He denounced the officers of the savings banks for wasting their overheads on unnecessarily opulent buildings which were open only a few hours a week, and formed very 'agreeable residences' for officers. This quite unwarranted onslaught sealed the fate of the Bill with the opponents of reform winning support of a House of Commons dominated by old men whose support for change had never been more than lukewarm. A simple measure to enlarge the National Debt Commissioners' power to invest in government stock similarly ran into difficulties in the House of Lords before passing into law at the end of the session in August. The protracted wrangling over the question of reform had done the savings banks movement little good. Supporters in the House of Commons, led by Sir Henry Willoughby, had presented an unfortunate image to the outside world of men more concerned to hurl brickbats at the Chancellor of the Exchequer for the government's supposed misappropriation of the Savings Bank Fund than to addressing the problems that troubled newspaper columnists and depositors.

The impression that the savings banks had lost their way in the 1850s was largely relative.

The returns for 1861 showed that although total deposits had risen by little more than the rate of interest, from £30 million to £41 million during the decade, the number of customers of the 645 individual banks had grown by almost 500,000, from 1,161,089 to 1,609,852. When compared with the population of the country, enumerated in the census of that year, performance in England varied from one county to another, but in all counties there were improvements. Trustees and actuaries could take comfort from figures which confirmed that they were matching Henry Duncan's expectations.

As trustees knew only too well, the achievement of the savings banks depended on the dedicated service of chairmen, actuaries and a growing army of clerks – many of whom had experience of working in commercial banks. By 1861 Devon & Exeter Savings Bank, with its countywide coverage of receiving offices that opened daily, employed thirty-three clerks who, in addition to their salary, were provided with a house. There had been a marked advance in the rewards of the actuaries of such larger banks. The actuary of the large Savings Bank of Glasgow was paid the princely salary of £600 a year compared to £350 ten years earlier. At Stamford in Lincolnshire and Staines in Middlesex, the Treasurer received no salary but was allowed to retain the 'floating balance' in hand at the end of the financial year – an average of over £500. Some actuaries and branch officials were paid a basic salary and commissions. At Beaumaris Savings Bank in Anglesey the four actuaries received a salary of £20 a year and a commission of 0.5 per cent on total deposits with their branch at the end of the financial year. At Chichester Savings Bank the actuary was allowed a commission of 9d for each new account that was opened. The actuary at the Glenlivet branch of the Inverness Savings Bank, William Skinner, had to provide a guarantee of £150 in return for a meagre salary of £4 a year. Apart from the work of receiving deposits and making repayments during opening hours, there were many other duties, 'the attention of the officers and clerks being much occupied with correspondence, attendance on trustees and managers at their meetings, half-yearly balances of accounts, preparation of returns to the Commissioners and to Parliament and various incidental matters ...'.

Over the forty-four years since the passing of George Rose's Act, the savings banks and their staff had played a vital role in the campaign to encourage providence and thrift. In a period which had seen the debate about the merits of thrift lose its national focus as expenditure on poor relief fell, the savings banks, like most other organisations for social progress, increasingly had come to rely on local initiatives and supporters in mobilising funds. Recognising the importance of the commitment of the trustees and managers of every bank, leaders of the movement had become very sensitive to any changes in the law which might cause them to withdraw. This had the unfortunate consequence of making the savings banks seem to be conservative institutions, a symbol of old reactionary Britain rather than the new free trade world constructed since 1846 and confirmed in Gladstone's great reforming budget of 1860 that swept away the last vestiges of import tariffs and duties.

# CHAPTER THREE

# APOSTLES

# OF

# SELF-HELP

## *1861–88*

In November 1859 John Murray pulled off a rare achievement in publishing; he brought out two bestsellers on the same day: *The Origin of Species* by Charles Darwin and *Self-Help* written by Samuel Smiles, an Edinburgh medical man turned railway manager. *Self-Help* was an apologia for the whole provident movement. A radical and ardent advocate of free trade, Samuel Smiles summarised and articulated a social theory shared by many of his contemporaries. Although he advanced the notion that in every apprentice's tool box, whatever the profession, was the key to the master's office, his argument was much less materialistic. In keeping with the attitudes of churchmen and social reformers such as Charles Kingsley, John Keble and Henry Newman, the objective of 'self-help' was as much moral improvement or individual fulfilment as financial reward. In Smiles's view, the struggle to live providently was an achievement in itself because man's natural state was prodigality. Combining the medieval notion that to work was to pray with Newton's ideas about the conservation of matter, he contended that, for all its tedium and repetition, labour was both honourable and pleasurable with results, even from the most humble tasks, that were never lost. It was this very sense of continuity that, according to Smiles, provided the motive for thrift as savings resulted in investment which in turn made for far more opportunities for work: 'The building of all the houses, the mills, the bridges, and the ships, and the accomplishment of all other great works which have rendered man civilised and happy, has been done by the savers, the thrifty; and those who have wasted their resources have always been their slaves.' Everyone had a moral duty to save: 'A penny is a very small matter, yet the comfort of thousands of families depends upon the proper spending and saving of pennies.'

Like many of the early apostles of thrift, there was something naïve about the repeated injunction to spend less than the family income. In Smiles's world there was no such thing as ill-luck or bad luck, just good and bad management. Poverty was projected as the true test of man's fortitude, sharpening wits and purifying spirits. Smiles's reasoning reflected his experience of lecturing in mechanics' institutes to those who, as skilled craftsmen, could expect to be employed for most of their lives and could, therefore, afford to save. He assumed incorrectly that even those at the very bottom of the social scale had only to put their domestic economy in order to avoid the terrors of debt and the pawnshop. He was no killjoy, however, freely admitting that people enjoyed the convivial drinking at friendly society meetings, which he believed helped to explain their growing popularity. Throughout, Smiles's philosophy was imbued with the perceptions of the free trader where the role of government was seen as a benevolent spectator of its hard-working, industrious and thrifty citizens: 'It is every day becoming more clearly understood, that the function of government is negative and restrictive, rather than positive and active, being resolvable principally into protection – protection of life, liberty and property. Laws, wisely administered, will secure men in the enjoyment of the fruits of their labour, whether of mind or body, at a comparatively small personal sacrifice; but no laws, however stringent, can make the idle industrious, the thriftless provident, or the drunken sober.' As far as encouraging providence was concerned, the role of the State, according to Smiles, was confined to ensuring that secure and reliable means of saving were available to every citizen, irrespective of social position, income, locality or age.

The fashion for direct government intervention in social affairs had waned during the 1850s after the far-reaching reforms of the previous two decades. There remained, however, a tacit assumption that the State, following Smiles's line of reasoning, had a duty to regulate society and institutions. Gladstone, as Chancellor of the Exchequer, had set the seal on the acceptance of free trade in his 1860 budget and had no doubt that the State should provide the infrastructure for individual self-development. Frustrated by the persistent resistance of the leaders of the savings bank movement to reforms that would at one and the same time increase government supervision and depositors' confidence, Gladstone turned his attention to the ideas of Charles Sikes for using the Post Office money order departments in local post offices to provide more readily accessible places for the deposit of savings.

Very shortly after the ideas canvassed by Sikes were published in their final form in 1859, the Post Office began to investigate the practicalities of its network of offices for collecting savings and making repayments on behalf of the National Debt Commissioners. Rowland Hill, the architect of the penny post and Secretary of the Post Office, was willing to countenance a scheme where the Post Office simply acted as the Commissioners' agents. Hill's brother, Frederic, who was head of the Post Office's Railway Department, concurred, arguing that money orders transmitted for the Commissioners should be charged at the full economic rate for fear of antagonising either existing savings banks or commercial banks. He also suggested that a lower limit of £1 should be placed on all transactions. Recognising that such a policy would effectively emasculate the proposed service, the less conservative and up-and-coming

W. E. Gladstone, an enthusiast for physical fitness, laying an axe to an old oak at Hawarden.

Post Office officials Frank Scudamore and John Tilley were willing to consider a far more ambitious plan put forward in November 1860 by George Chetwynd, bookkeeper of the Money Order Office. He advised that all the Postmaster had to do was accept deposits, enter the transaction in the investor's passbook and transmit the cash to a central savings bank in London along with the cash balances from the money order department. Withdrawals would be effected by means of warrants issued by the central savings bank. A charge of a penny on every transaction would ensure the service was profitable for the Post Office. Nothing could have been simpler and, as Sikes intended, the service would be able to attract relatively small deposits. Scudamore immediately seized the opportunity of extending the role of the Post

Office by suggesting that it should be responsible for administering the central savings bank, reducing costs and making for more effective management. The existing savings banks were thrown into a quandary. They could hardly object to any proposal which would extend the principle of thrift to communities that had no savings banks; on the other hand, they were deeply suspicious of the establishment of a national savings bank by the Post Office. The auditors of the Finsbury Bank for Savings echoed the opinion of other trustees when they told their investors in January 1861: 'The idea of facilitating the deposits of money in the Savings Banks through the Post Office agencies is most valuable, but that the creation of any new Institution for that purpose is quite unnecessary, because the extensive and well-proved machinery of the existing Savings Banks could be used with the greatest ease for the object proposed.'

Gladstone was deaf to such protests, seeing in the proposed Post Office Savings Bank a means of wresting the initiative away from the leaders of the savings bank movement who had so steadfastly opposed every measure of reform. In February 1861 he introduced a financial resolution to enable the Consolidated Fund to make good any deficiency arising in the Post Office money order department as a result of the operations of the Post Office Savings Bank, should one be established. The resolution was passed with little debate and three days later the Post Office Savings Bank Bill was introduced. Its terms were simple. Deposits of 1s or more could be accepted by money order departments designated as branches of the new bank. Identically with the savings banks, there was a limit on total deposits in any one year of £30 with a ceiling excluding interest of £150 on any account with a maximum balance of £200. Interest was set at 2.5 per cent, half a per cent below that paid to the savings banks. A clause allowed customers to move their investments to savings bank accounts and savings bank depositors to switch to the Post Office Savings Bank. Trustees of savings banks were also required, when a decision was taken to close a bank, to notify their customers of the facilities provided by the Post Office. In presenting the measure, Gladstone went out of his way to stress that he had no intention of fostering a competitor to the existing savings banks, but rather of providing a service for small investors in areas where there were no such institutions. It was impossible to challenge this objective as it was estimated at the time that there was a Post Office money order office open for seven hours every working day within three miles of nearly every home in the United Kingdom – something which could not be claimed for savings banks.

Throughout the debate in the House of Commons, Gladstone was conciliatory, allaying the fears of Members of Parliament such as Sotheron Estcourt, who had chaired the Committee on the savings banks three years before, that a deliberate assault on the existing system was intended. However often the supporters of the savings bank movement held up the spectre of the closure of existing banks in the face of this new competitor, Gladstone reassured Members that priority in forming branches of the Post Office Savings Bank would be given to places out of reach of existing banks. The Bill was piloted through the House of Lords by the Postmaster-General, Lord Stanley of Alderley, who was well briefed by his officials to meet any criticism.

Acknowledging defeat, Lord Monteagle, a staunch defender of the trustee savings banks, eloquently expressed his anxieties about the likely effects of a measure 'which seemed to him [was] meant to produce a breaking up of the existing savings banks and the substitution of the action of a salaried Government Department for what he might call a great public charity, directed by benevolent persons acting gratuitously in their own neighbourhood'.

Lord Monteagle's guess at the government's real intention was not far wide of the mark. Lord Stanley ensured that Frederic Hill should not be responsible for supervising the formation of the Post Office Savings Bank, as Rowland Hill had intended. Instead he placed it under the control of John Tilley, the progressive assistant secretary, who could be depended on to give Frank Scudamore, charged with the day-to-day management, his head. Despite the undertakings the Chancellor of the Exchequer had given to the House of Commons, Scudamore conceived of the Post Office Savings Bank as a vehicle for the 'gradual extinction' of the trustee savings banks. As soon as the Bill was on the statute book in May 1861, he and George Chetwynd energetically set about the practicalities of opening the first branches. They had the universal and enthusiastic support of social commentators such as Samuel Smiles and of the press. A contributor to Charles Dickens's periodical *All the Year Round* commented, 'If there's a philanthropist that's hard up for an object, I don't know that he could do better than go about distributing tracts setting forth the rules, regulations, and advantages of the Post Office Savings Banks.' After three months' brisk activity, 301 branches opened for business in September. By the end of the year the number had reached 1,700 and Scudamore let it be known that a branch would eventually 'be established at every Money Order Office in the United Kingdom'. From the outset he was determined that the service would be as widely known as possible. Taking Dickens's correspondent at his word, a simple pamphlet costing a penny was published giving forms and directions 'How to Deposit Money and How to Withdraw It'. Well aware of the potential appeal of the new bank to women, Scudamore selected as the publishers the Caledonia Press in Edinburgh which had only recently been established 'for promoting the employment of women in the art of printing'.

Scudamore followed up these formal instructions with two simple pamphlets, both published by Emily Faithfull & Co at the Victoria Press 'for the employment of women' in London. The first entitled 'Post Office Savings Banks – A few Plain Words concerning them' gave, as its title implied, straightforward advice to intending clients. The tone was even more helpful, dispelling doubts and answering questions, but at times as patronising as the rhetoric of the old savings banks, which the promoters of the Post Office Savings Bank had roundly condemned: 'You will not have to pay the postage of any letters which you may write, or receive from, the General Post Office in London with respect to your deposits, nor will any charge be made upon you for your numbered book, but if you lose it you will have to pay one shilling for a new book; you must therefore take great care of it, and you had better have a cover made for it, of linen or cloth or leather, to keep it clean and in proper condition.' Despite the provision in the Act for the transfer of funds from the Post Office Savings Bank to a trustee savings bank and vice versa, there was no mention of this facility. Throughout, the Post Office Savings Bank was presented as a national bank, providing a national service entirely confidentially. By the beginning of 1862, over 150,000 copies of this pamphlet had been distributed. The second pamphlet developed the ideal of saving echoing many of the ideas advanced by Henry Duncan and the early advocates of savings banks – the need to provide for sickness, old age, and death. Entitled 'Life Insurance by small payments – A few Plain Words concerning it', Scudamore showed how regular weekly deposits with the Post Office Savings Bank would allow most people to accumulate sufficient funds to meet an annual life insurance premium which could be transmitted to the insurance company by money order.

Although the careful reader of either of these tracts could have been in no doubt of Frank Scudamore's ambitions for the infant Post Office Savings Bank, most trustees and actuaries clung to Gladstone's commitment not to encourage competition. Early in 1862, a writer describing himself simply as 'An Old Actuary' wrote a widely circulated pamphlet dispassionately comparing 'the old system and new Post Office system', declaring at the outset, 'Let it be distinctly understood that the two institutions are not antagonistic. They ought to be regarded as friends, not rivals.' Except for a slight advantage for the trustee savings banks in interest rates and greater security, the 'Old Actuary' could find little to choose between the two institutions. He even went so far as to claim that 'a large amount of business may be done by [the Post Office Savings Bank] without any perceptive effect on the transactions of its neighbour, the old Savings Bank'. This view was widely shared by trustees and actuaries throughout the country who more often than not made similar reference in their annual reports. A few remained sceptical. The Revd Henry Renton of Kelso, a leading minister in the United Presbyterian Church, published a similar comparison where he praised the opening of branches of the Post Office Savings Bank in places without existing banks, but condemned as 'most strange' their opening in places where savings banks were already operating. Despite Scudamore's publicity campaign, he doubted if the Post Office Savings Bank could flourish in places where there had been no extensive promotion of the ideals of thrift by leading members of the community represented amongst the ranks of trustees and managers of the savings banks. Sensing that the Post Office would build on the foundations dutifully laid by trustees for almost half a century, he called on the government to come clean about its objectives. By the end of 1862 it was clear that the Post Office Savings Bank had got off to a good start with over 178,000 customers and total deposits of almost £1.7 million. This was a considerable achievement at a time when the economy had been pushed into recession by disruption caused by the outbreak of the American Civil War the year before. The early success of the Post Office Savings Bank was due almost certainly to its national coverage, the daily opening of all its offices and the fact that, unlike the trustee savings banks, money could be drawn in two days.

The savings banks blamed economic circumstances rather than the establishment of the

Post Office Savings Bank for a reversal in their fortunes. The chairman of the Paisley Savings Bank, providing for a large community in the west of Scotland dependent on the textile trades, commented on the decline in deposits towards the close of 1862: 'The extra wants of the winter season, combined, in many cases, with the lack of employment, have caused a number of depositors to fall back upon their saving.' Likewise, the trustees of Liverpool Savings Bank, based in the country's largest cotton port, attributed a rise in withdrawals to the 'general depression of trades and diminished employment, which has prevailed in this and surrounding

The staff of McLachlan & Brown's department store, Stirling, 1862.
The savings banks courted respectable working girls, encouraging them
to save for the day when they would marry and set up home.

districts'. The position of the savings banks was not helped by the discovery in January 1862 of a fraud of some £8,840, about a third of the total deposits, at Bilston Savings Bank in Staffordshire. The fraud had been perpetrated over several years by the vicar of Bilston, the Revd H.S. Fletcher, who had systematically and deliberately broken the rules laid down by the National Debt Commissioners by holding all the principal offices of the bank. *The Times* was quick to renew its criticism of the savings banks, condemning Fletcher as 'the meanest, the most cowardly, and the most cruel of swindlers', commending the Post Office Savings Bank as offering 'an escape from danger', and hoping that 'the day will speedily arrive when these fallible savings banks will all cease to exist'.

For the first time since the crisis year of 1848 the total number of savings bank depositors at the end of the year was lower than at the beginning. In November 1861 there had been a record 1,609,882 customers; a year later there were 51,663 fewer. Likewise, total deposits had also retreated in absolute terms, falling from a record of £41.5 million in 1861 to £40.5 million in 1862. As worrying was the closure of twenty-four of the 645 savings banks open in 1861, including those at Poulton-le-Fylde, Kirkby Stephen, Blackpool, Braintree and Finchley. No new savings banks were opened – something that had not occurred since 1815. The effect of the crisis was almost uniform throughout the country. Savings banks in rural counties as far apart as Cambridgeshire and Devon suffered as much as industrial and commercial centres. Although little mention was made of the Post Office Savings Bank in annual reports and at annual meetings, many of the larger savings banks had taken steps to mitigate the effect of competition by increasing their opening hours, improving confidentiality of accounts, altering their rules where necessary to make it possible for withdrawals of small sums to be made on demand, and paying interest on sums of less than whole pounds. These minor reforms were nevertheless significant as contemporary commentators had suggested that restricted opening hours and delays in making repayments had forced families to resort unnecessarily to money-lenders. In November 1861 the Savings Bank of Glasgow, anticipating the appeal of the Post Office Savings Bank to smaller savers, formed the Association of Penny Banks 'to sustain and extend the system of Penny Banks in and around Glasgow and to promote their efficiency and good management'.

Immediately after the passing of the Post Office Savings Bank Act, the leaders of the savings bank movement concluded that it would require more than local initiative to restore confidence and meet the challenge. A Savings Bank Extension Committee was formed in London with the support of Sotheron Estcourt and Sir Henry Willoughby 'to prepare a Bill to be laid before the Government prior to the next session of Parliament embodying the best practical suggestions from different savings banks for their improvement'. The Committee's deliberations were given added direction by the Bilston defalcation. The Bill as drafted made provision for tightening up the rules of the savings banks, for making trustees liable for any losses due to fraud or negligence, for introducing outside audits, and for insisting that all transactions should take place during opening hours. The savings banks objected on the grounds that the provisions were not sufficiently specific and that trustees would be liable for defalcations whatever the circumstances. The Extension Committee was hurriedly re-convened at the St Martin's Place Savings Bank, appointing a sub-committee to draw up more acceptable recommendations. These were circulated to all the savings banks for their approval; ninety-four out of the 600 banks troubled to reply. They endorsed the proposals and a new Bill, consolidating all the previous legislation, was drafted.

Designed to meet all the criticisms made over the previous fifteen years, the Bill passed easily through Parliament and came into force at the beginning of the savings banks' financial year on 21 November 1863. The chief provisions were that at least two persons must be present when deposits or withdrawals were made, that an independent auditor inspect the books twice a year, and that trustees and managers meet at least twice yearly, keeping minutes of their discussions. The trustees were liable for defalcations only if these rules were not observed, or if they did not hand over money they received personally, or if they did not obtain sureties from their officials. Customers were required to produce their passbooks at least twice a year to be compared with the ledger. Passbooks had to be checked against the ledger every time money was withdrawn and at the first deposit in each financial year. A book had to be available for public inspection in each bank containing an audited account of each customer's balance with the passbook number but not the name at the year end. The Act also made it possible for a depositor to transfer his account relatively easily from one savings bank to another. A clause in the 1828 Act which allowed savings banks to invest directly for individual customers in government stock was widened to include other securities, providing there was a balance of at least £50 in the customer's account invested with the National Debt Commissioners. To qualify as National Security Savings Banks all existing savings banks had to comply with these regulations and no new savings banks could be formed outside the terms of the Act. The use of the title 'savings bank' from now on was to be restricted to banks recognised under the Act. The passing of the Act was greeted with enthusiasm by trustees and managers throughout the United Kingdom heralding, in the words of the annual report of the Liverpool Savings Bank, 'a new era for savings banks'.

At first it seemed as if the Act had lived up to these expectations. The majority of savings banks chose to amend their rules to qualify for certification under the Act. During 1863, with trade beginning to improve after the setbacks of the previous year, the number of depositors lost fell to less than 1,350 and total deposits appeared to stabilise even though there was a decline in real terms. This modest success was only short-lived and for the next three years savings bank deposits declined steadily to £36.4 million by 1866, the number of customers dropped to just over 1.4 million, and the number of banks to 551. The decline was more or less uniform throughout England and Wales. The worst affected counties were those where banks closed, such as in Kent, which lost six banks and almost £350,000 in deposits, and in Warwickshire, with two closures and over £630,000 in deposits. A few counties bucked the trend, notably Northumberland where the number of depositors rose by 900 to 26,828 and total deposits grew by £55,000 to £954,000, and the West Riding of Yorkshire with a small rise in the number of depositors from 74,000 to 76,000 and no absolute fall in deposits despite the closure of four savings banks. In Wales, Carmarthen, Glamorgan and Pembroke recorded similar successes. In Scotland, where 4.8 per cent of the population had savings bank accounts in 1862 compared with 6.6 per cent in England and Wales, the savings banks fared better with a steady increase in the number of customers, a small advance in total deposits, and no closures. It was in Ireland that the savings banks suffered their most serious reverse. Ireland had the lowest percentage of customers per head of population of any part of the United Kingdom in 1862 with a little over 1 per cent, a consequence of the frauds detected in the late 1840s and the country's poor economic performance. By 1866 this percentage had fallen below 1 per cent and over a quarter of deposits had been withdrawn, falling to just over £1.5 million.

This disappointing performance took place against a background of an improving market for personal savings throughout the United Kingdom with real wages edging forward. Clear evidence of the popularity of the call for thrift made by Samuel Smiles and other commentators was the performance of the Post Office Savings Bank which had attracted almost 750,000 clients by 1866 and held total deposits of a little over £8 million, of which just 50,000 customers and £1.1 million had been transferred from closed savings banks. The appeal of the Post Office Savings Bank was to investors with little to save, with average deposits of nearly £1 compared to almost £26 with the savings banks. Small savers were traditionally an important target for the savings banks which were just as committed to preaching the gospel of self-help to the poorest sections of society as to the better-off families of craftsmen, small traders, and domestic servants, but friendly societies also courted the small saver, with conviviality and companionship to sweeten the price of saving. During the early 1860s the affiliated orders, such as the Manchester Unity of Oddfellows and the Ancient Order of Foresters, continued to gain ground rapidly, despite an attempt by the Post Office Savings Bank to win their business after the passing of the Government Annuities Act in 1864. This legislation was directed as much against new and determined commercial competitors for the investments of the smallest savers, the large national so-called collecting friendly societies and the industrial life assurance companies. The principal objectives of these organisations was to provide sufficient funds at death to cover the cost of the funeral and customary hospitality. Policies could be taken out on both adults and children, male and female alike. The largest collecting society was the Royal Liver Friendly Society and the biggest life company was the Prudential Insurance Company. Both collecting societies and life offices operated essentially for profit, paying generous commissions to their collectors responsible for drumming up custom by door-to-door visits. Subscriptions were usually a penny a week. Using aggressive sales patter drawing on the respectable rhetoric of thrift, the collecting societies and life companies won huge business in the 1860s. In 1863 alone, the Royal Liver Friendly Society wrote 135,000 new policies. Between 1860 and 1866 the Prudential Insurance Company increased its annual total of new policies from just over 33,000 to 163,423.

The savings banks confronted competition in the first half of the 1860s, not only at the bottom of their market, but also at the top. Although English commercial banks had done little deposit banking earlier in the century, most banks, by the 1850s, would pay interest on sums deposited for periods of three months or more – the longer the term, the higher the rate of interest. An added incentive to use commercial banks was the ability to settle accounts by cheque following the admission of the joint stock banks to the London Clearing House in

laying the foundation stone in the Savings Bank of Glasgow's new
head office, Glassford Street, 1865. The cost of the ground and
building was £13,683.

1854. Providing bank rate remained relatively low – 5 per cent or less – the availability of this
new means of investment posed little threat to the savings banks, paying 3 per cent interest.
Aside from 1857, bank rate did not rise above 5 per cent for more than a whole year until
November 1863. From then until January 1865 the rate did not fall below 6 per cent. Rates
eased in the spring and summer of 1865 but climbed inexorably from October to reach 10 per
cent in May 1866 when the United Kingdom was plunged into a financial crisis by the collapse
of London's biggest discount house, Overend Gurney & Co, with liabilities of over £1 million.
This long period of high interest rates made savings banks less attractive to larger investors.
Trustees regularly complained of the damaging effect of high interest rates on their business.
The managers of the Savings Bank of the County & City of Perth commented in 1863 that,
because of the prevailing high rates of interest, 'With the single exception of Glasgow, which,
dealing with a very large and wealthy field of labour, still shows progress at the Government
rate of 3 per cent, all the other leading institutions of the country in England, Scotland, and
Ireland, so far as their reports have come under the notice of the committee, indicate a large

withdrawal of funds beyond the sums deposited – seriously affecting the Banks of long-standing and large capital.' The Liverpool Savings Bank (which changed its name from Liverpool Provident Institution or Bank for Savings in 1863) attributed a 5 per cent decline in their deposits during 1865 partly to the 'very high rate of interest' which had widened 'the opportunities for investment to advantage'. The effect on large deposits with the savings banks was significant enough to be noticed but not dramatic. The Oxford Savings Bank, which closed its doors in 1865, was reported to have been losing larger accounts to the joint stock banks for some time.

Since 1850 the Perth and Dundee savings banks had sought to offset the effect of competition from the commercial banks through the creation of 'Chartered Bank Departments'. Taking advantage of the clause in the 1828 Act that allowed savings banks to invest depositors' money other than with the National Debt Office, these departments were to be used for transferring funds to commercial banks when rates were high. By 1865 over 90 per cent of the Savings Bank of the County & City of Perth funds were deposited with two Scottish commercial banks. Other savings banks, concerned about the danger of placing funds with commercial banks at times of economic crisis, lobbied the National Debt Commissioners to allow depositors to invest in higher-yielding government stock. The Commissioners rejected this appeal and advised the savings banks to invest in local funds such as those raised to meet the cost of large public works.

Before savings banks could experiment in deploying funds in this way, the country was overwhelmed in May 1866 by the Overend Gurney crisis. Confidence in the whole banking system was rudely jolted and there were wild rumours that the Bank of England's bullion reserves were insufficient to meet bank calls. Many commercial banks and savings banks called urgently for gold specie from the Bank to meet withdrawal repayments. In the aftermath of the catastrophe some English commercial banks were forced to suspend payments and some collapsed. Even before disaster struck, the savings banks had experienced exceptional withdrawals by depositors. Directly the news broke, in the words of the actuary of Finsbury Savings Bank, 'the excitement which arose took away all discrimination and judgement – every Bank of Deposit was doubted – until the doubt almost extended to the value of Bank Notes and Coin was largely required by those who valued their money by its weight in the hand'. Financial markets began to return to something like normal during the summer months despite the persistence of problems in some parts of the country, such as the Black Country where the Birmingham Banking Company collapsed in July. As conditions eased, bank rates drifted down to 3.5 per cent by the end of the year. With the threat of competition from the commercial banks waning, the more determined savings banks were quick to remind their customers that the collapse of commercial banks could not undermine the value of their deposits held by the government, which could be relied on to make repayments in cash on demand. They also took the opportunity, somewhat gratuitously, to tell customers 'there are no risks allowed – no lending of money in discounts, loans or mortgages – and no speculations of any kind'. Such brave talk was, perhaps, designed to counter the damaging effects of the well-publicised defalcation the year before at the Canterbury Savings Bank which had forced its closure and the transfer of some £150,000 in deposits to the Post Office Savings Bank. In the wake of this fresh crisis, ten more savings banks shut during 1866 with the loss of nearly £212,000 in deposits, of which £127,000 was transferred to the Post Office Savings Bank. The largest closure was at Greenwich which had 2,711 customers and total deposits of £68,874.

The attraction of government security for savings bank deposits, combined with very low rates of return available on government securities and from commercial banks in 1867 and 1868, allowed the savings banks to stage a modest recovery. Although the number of depositors continued to fall, mostly at the bottom end of the market, total deposits held steady at between £36 and £37 million. This was a creditable performance as the trustees of no fewer than a further thirty-eight savings banks had decided to close their doors, with the loss of almost £1 million of which £537,785 was transferred to the Post Office Savings Bank. Most of the savings banks that closed, like the majority of all savings banks, had total deposits of less than £30,000. There were only two relatively large closures – Chichester Savings Bank, with deposits of over £107,000, and Portsmouth with deposits of £146,000. By now it had become customary, when the decision had been taken to shut a savings bank, for the trustees to call for assistance from the Post Office Savings Bank, which, without charge, posted circulars to all depositors and sent staff to help wind up the accounts. During the period of the closure, a temporary Post

The Preston Savings Bank, Fishergate, and its banking hall. Built in 1872, it was one of many fine mid-Victorian buildings erected by the savings banks.

Office Savings Bank was opened in the savings bank so that customers could open accounts on the spot and transfer their deposits. The Post Office officials were prepared to go some way to protect clients' confidence. Wives, who did not wish their husbands to know they held accounts for either themselves or their children, could arrange for all correspondence to be sent to a Post Office Savings Bank branch rather than to their home address.

Persistent low interest rates from 1869 to 1872 took the pressure off the savings banks. The pace of closures slowed and those that did shut their doors were small. Although total deposits resumed their upward trend after four years of decline, the advance barely kept pace with the annual rate of interest. The Post Office Savings Bank, with its national coverage, by comparison performed far better, with deposits climbing by almost £6 million to £19.3 million by 1872 and a 30 per cent increase in the number of customers to 1.44 million. For the first time, the Post Office Savings Bank had more customers than the savings banks, due in great measure to its national coverage and longer opening hours. Most savings banks still opened for only a few hours each week. Howden Savings Bank in the East Riding of Yorkshire opened for just one hour each Saturday and on the day after the Martinmas feeing day, when farm servants were hired for the year.

Despite the success of the Post Office Savings Bank, this was a period when saving for spending took precedence over saving for old age or times of illness and unemployment. The growth in membership of friendly societies and life assurance companies appears to have slowed. These four years were ones of rapidly advancing prosperity, particularly in urban areas. Food prices were falling with the arrival of cheap imports first of all from northern Europe and later North America. The advent of ready-to-wear clothes, made with the help of the newly invented sewing machines, slashed prices enlarging the market for fashionwear. By 1870 there was little that could not be mass-produced. In every town and city there were magnificent new stores to entice the unwary shopper. This was a period of booming house construction with the building of well-appointed villas and spacious terraces for the better-off and rows of comfortable terrace houses for the families of artisans, clerks and labourers. New homes, which were mostly rented, had to be decorated and furnished.

Even Samuel Smiles, the apostle of self-help, did not believe that thrift should be practised at the expense of domestic comfort, including the occasional indulgence. In his second bestseller *Thrift* (1879) he advised: 'Why not have some elegance in even the home? We must of course have cleanliness, which is the special elegance of the poor. But why not have pleasant and delightful things to look upon? ... Why not hang up a picture in the room?' Of course, he remained firmly committed to the belief that all such expenditure should be incurred prudently and never undertaken on credit: 'People do not know what trouble they are brewing for themselves when they run into debt ... It hangs round a man's neck until he is relieved of it. It presses like a nightmare upon him.' He condemned as heinous, unscrupulous small loan societies that had driven many a working-class family into penury. Like *Self-Help*, *Thrift* was crammed with examples of the powerful effect of saving and its handmaid, the temperate use of alcohol.

In the more materialistic world of the early 1870s, those involved in the savings bank movement appreciated that they had a moral duty to spread the gospel of thrift to prevent debt and drunkenness. Consumption of beer, wines and spirits was again on the increase, causing concern to employers at a time when more and more machinery was being used in the

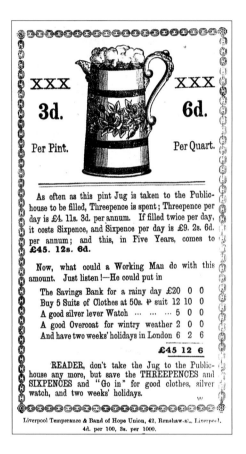

A flyer produced by the Liverpool Temperance & Band of Hope
Union attacking the demon drink and extolling the virtues of savings.

workplace. The savings banks combined with temperance organisations to publish tracts extolling the virtues of saving and prudence in domestic economy. These were widely distributed in an effort to warn of the dangers of overspending and to extend knowledge of the facilities of the savings banks. Some were simple notices, like that produced by the Liverpool Temperance & Band of Hope Union (available at 3s per thousand copies) which displayed a frothing jug of beer and explained what a working man could expect to gain by a year's abstinence. Others took the form of simple homilies or moral tales. Typical was *Plain Facts for Plain People* in which a savings bank actuary discussed Pawn Offices, Thrift, and Penny Banks.

The tone was overtly moralistic: 'There is no doubt whatever but that the pawnbroker thrives to a large extent upon the humiliation of his fellow creatures and the attractive warehouse, with the significant three balls, are just so many places where, in most cases, persons find a ready means of procuring money to satisfy the cravings of a depraved appetite.' The stories were more beguiling, either cautionary tales of improvidence, such as 'The Rainy Day', or anecdotes of the triumph of thrift, like 'Bob Sim's Resolve'.

My Lady: *I'm afraid I must give up the pineapple, Mr Green.*
*8 shillings is really too much.*
Successful collier: *Just put 'un up for me ther mester. 'Ere's arf a sovereign,*
*an' look 'ere yer mek keep the change if you only tell us 'ow to cook un.*

*Punch* lampooned the working man of the 1870s, as a dullard whose
greater earning power gave him ideas above his station. The savings
banks made every effort to ensure that at least a portion of his
new-found wealth was saved.

Many trustees appreciated that propaganda to win the custom of the poorer sections of society had to be matched by equal effort to retain and enlarge the saving opportunities of the better-off, on whom the savings banks depended to earn their operating margins. However, it was these customers who were most likely to be tempted to spend their money on the new luxuries that were readily available. For those with good incomes, these extended beyond clothes and household furnishing to include the increasingly popular music halls and, in the summer months, seaside excursions. The only inducement that the savings banks could hold out was to offer higher rates of interest by taking advantage of the clause in the 1863 Act that allowed them to invest customers' deposits other than with the National Debt Commissioners. The crisis of 1866 had, if anything, made trustees and actuaries more cautious than before about opening investment accounts with commercial banks when bank rate was higher than that paid by the Commissioners. During the autumn of 1870, William Meikle, the influential actuary of the Savings Bank of Glasgow, proposed that the service to larger customers should be extended by allowing those whose accounts had reached their limit, to invest directly in government stock which the bank would buy in £50 lots. This scheme was rejected by the Comptroller of the National Debt who repeated his advice to invest in 'safe local securities' which were now readily available in the larger towns and cities.

As a result of the passing of the Sanitary Act in 1866, local authorities throughout the United Kingdom had powers to raise loans on the security of the rates to pay for a variety of improvements, from the provision of water supplies, sewage treatment, housing refurbishment, to the construction of hospitals and schools. Such investments appealed to the Glasgow trustees; they were safe, and guaranteed by the rates. Typically, local authorities paid 1 or 1.5 per cent more than the Commissioners. Moreover, they provided a means whereby depositors could contribute directly to the well-being of the local community. William Meikle lost no time in preparing a plan and an Investment Department was opened in January 1871. Access to the department was restricted to customers whose accounts had been continuously open for five years and reached the limit of £200. Like the commercial banks, which paid interest on deposit accounts, customers were required to give three months' notice of withdrawals. Despite these tight regulations, the new department was immediately popular, attracting deposits of nearly £50,000 in the first eleven months. Meikle was delighted, telling the annual meeting: 'The accommodation thus afforded has been much appreciated by many of the Bank's earliest and most exemplary depositors, who have thereby been enabled to resume the deposit of small savings in their former accounts.' By the end of the following year, when the

The Savings Bank of Glasgow, which pioneered the Special Investment Department.

balance had more than doubled, Glasgow's example had been copied by the Leeds, Skyrac & Morley Savings Bank with less circumscribed rules allowing deposits to be made by customers with £100 in their accounts which had been open for only two years. The Manchester & Salford Savings Bank and the Preston Savings Bank followed suit in 1874.

Just as Glasgow was deciding to experiment with this radical innovation to maintain the support of its larger customers, John Tidd Pratt, the Barrister to the Savings Bank movement since 1828 and Barrister and Registrar to Friendly Societies since 1829, died at the age of seventy-three. A small dynamic man with firm opinions, he had for more than forty years been a self-styled 'minister of self-help to the whole of the industrious classes'. He had worked tirelessly, not only to promote the ideal of thrift in all its shapes and forms, but also to improve the financial management and policy of savings banks and friendly societies. As barrister to both movements, he was not afraid to criticise rules that fell short of the standards set by the legislation and those in positions of responsibility who failed to discharge their duties either correctly or honestly. In an age impressed by statistics, he had patiently collected figures to demonstrate the growth and impact of savings banks and friendly societies. He had published several books and pamphlets giving practical advice. His death triggered a crisis in the relationship between the government and 'self-help' organisations. Although the spirit of the times increasingly favoured growing government involvement in society, Gladstone, Prime Minister since 1868, and his cabinet questioned the future role of the Registrar. Influenced by the Chancellor of the Exchequer, Robert Lowe, who believed that the government should not interfere in economic affairs, a Bill was introduced to abolish the position of Registrar, offering friendly societies the option of adopting limited liability status. The whole thrift and provident movement was outraged that the gains of half a century should be so capriciously swept away.

Bowing to the strength of feeling, the government appointed a Royal Commission on Friendly and Benefit Building Societies, under the chairmanship of Sir Stafford Northcote, a leading Conservative, and as secretary, J.M. Ludlow, a Christian Socialist whose nomination as Registrar had been rejected by the Chancellor of the Exchequer. As an interim measure, the talented W.H. Stephenson, Assistant Solicitor to the Treasury, took over as Registrar of Friendly Societies and Barrister to the Savings Banks and the Post Office Savings Bank. The Commissioners applied themselves diligently, inquiring into every aspect of friendly societies and publishing no fewer than five bulky reports over the next four years. Although they had considerable difficulty in obtaining accurate information about the membership and assets of societies, they calculated that there were over 1.8 million members of registered societies and an estimated 4 million belonging to all societies. The total assets of all the societies were reckoned to be over £11 million, well short of the £42 million deposits held by the savings banks and the £23 million by the Post Office Savings Bank. However, no one questioned that the affiliated orders and collecting societies had gained ground rapidly in the last decade. The final report was published in 1874. Far from recommending that the post of Registrar should be scrapped, the Commissioners, taking over from where Tidd Pratt had left off, proposed that the office should be strengthened by the appointment of deputy registrars and trained actuaries to assist the Registrar in supervising the work of the societies, particularly in ensuring that contributions were sufficient to match the expected benefit. Following the example of the 1863 Savings Bank Act, the Commissioners insisted that there should be an annual independent audit of accounts and a valuation of assets every five years. Nearly all the Commission's proposals were incorporated in the Building Societies Act of 1874 and Friendly Societies Act of 1875. J.M. Ludlow was appointed the first Chief Registrar under the Act. The following year, under separate legislation, the post of Barrister to the Savings Banks and the Post Office Savings Bank was abolished and the duties transferred to the Registrar of Friendly Societies, who, as a result, became responsible for certifying the rules of savings banks and adjudicating in disputes between banks and their depositors.

With the principle of government supervision of the whole thrift movement reaffirmed, the savings banks breathed a sigh of relief, even though they cannot have welcomed the appointment of Ludlow, a known critic of the savings banks and supporter of the Post Office Savings Bank. While the government was deliberating about the future of Pratt's offices, as Barrister to the Savings Banks and Barrister and Registrar of Friendly Societies, the savings banks had been quick to see the opportunity of the Education Act of 1870 which established School Boards in England and Wales bringing schools under State control. Two years before the Act, the Savings Bank of Glasgow, which had helped to pioneer penny banks, had published a list of the 874 penny banks operating in the United Kingdom, declaring confidently:

> The general result aimed at, however, is less the accumulation of money than the training of the young to habits of forethought and independence; habits which will influence them beneficially throughout their lives ... Government should attach the Penny Bank to every school receiving aid throughout the country, and should enjoin the teachers of these schools to instil into their pupils the lessons of industry and providence.

William Meikle, the bank's actuary, published a booklet, *Penny Banks: Their Formation and Management*, with specimens of the books and forms in use. By 1870 the Savings Bank of Glasgow already had a few banks based in schools open outside teaching hours. The education system was not reformed in Scotland until 1872 when the Savings Bank of Glasgow launched an intense campaign to persuade the newly elected School Boards to inaugurate penny banks. Articles were published in the local press advertising the success of school banks in the Belgian city of Ghent in persuading 10,000 of the city's 16,000 children at school to save. In the meantime the Liverpool Savings Bank had followed Glasgow's lead by establishing a Penny Bank Association in 1870 and sought the sanction of the School Board to open school banks. The negotiations in both Liverpool and Glasgow were protracted and it was not until April 1874 that the first school banks were opened by the Glasgow Highland Society Schools. Within a week 600 children had enrolled, depositing almost £37. Although the teacher was responsible for collecting the cash, the pupils took it in turns to fill in the depositors' books and the school cash book.

The following year the Liverpool Savings Bank held a public meeting by invitation of the School Board which was addressed by the Revd T.E. Crollan, chaplain of the County Asylum at Haywards Heath in Sussex. Explaining his efforts to establish penny banks in Sussex and Wiltshire, he condemned the state of British society 'as pretty well saturated with extravagance, and the result was a good deal of waste, squalor and misery, full unions, crowded gaols and gin

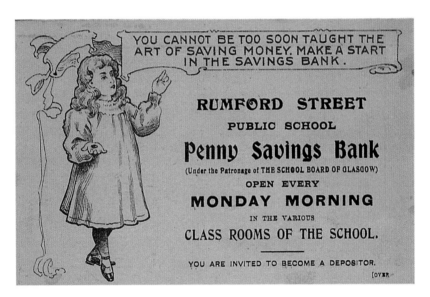

The Penny Banks produced attractive advertising material
designed to appeal to schoolchildren.

palaces. If they could advocate the people to be thrifty then instead of waste, squalor, and misery, there would be economy, decency and comfort, instead of poverty, drink, and vice, there would be general sobriety, prosperity and honesty.' He held up a vision of a Utopian future if only children were inculcated with habits of thrift while at school. The School Board did not require much persuasion and accepted the idea in principle. However, the Liverpool Savings Bank had more difficulty in convincing school managers and teachers who believed penny banks 'involved expense and time and trouble'. By 1880 penny banks had been opened in thirty-one schools in Liverpool, less than 30 per cent of all the city's State schools. Other large banks took similar initiatives, including, in 1874, the Devon & Exeter Savings Bank in a part of the country where there were no existing penny banks and in 1876 the Sheffield Savings Bank, which already operated a dozen or so penny banks.

The prosperity which characterised the early 1870s and drew the anger of the Revd Crollan continued until the end of the decade. New house construction boomed with roughly a 25 per cent increase in the number of homes. Real wages also rose sharply, partly because the cost of clothing and food drifted persistently lower. To cater for the newly affluent middle class, town and city centres became shoppers' paradises. More and more families were enjoying holidays at the seaside. Although paid holidays were not common for labourers and craftsmen, the growing army of clerks that maintained the fabric of Victorian society could expect a week or a fortnight's paid leave a year. Bank holidays were made official in 1871, leading to similar holidays being taken in shops, offices and factories. In 1879 almost a million passengers arrived at Blackpool station to enjoy some time in the fashionable north-west resort. On the Clyde, the Thames and the Severn, river steamers had become popular for summer excursions. From round the coast there were reports that holiday-making was extending well down the social scale.

During the decade the Post Office Savings Bank maintained its onward momentum with a doubling in the number of account holders from 1 million in 1870 to over 2 million by 1880 and in total deposits from £15 million to £32 million. The Post Office was helped by the Married Women's Property Act of 1870 which declared that deposits made by a woman in a savings bank were her own property. On expeditions away from home an account with the Post Office Savings Bank was more flexible than one with a savings bank as money could be drawn at any branch office, providing the necessary withdrawal forms were dispatched well in advance. The savings banks could not match the Post Office's achievement with growth in deposits falling well behind the rate of interest and the number of clients rising by only little more than 120,000. By 1880 the Post Office Savings Bank was taking almost twice as much a year in deposits as the savings banks, some £1.15 million.

The success of the Post Office Savings Bank, at a time when the population of the United Kingdom was growing at about 10 per cent every ten years, had made serious inroads into the representation of the savings banks in nearly every area of Britain. The only real overall gain achieved by the savings bank movement between 1861 and 1881 was in Scotland, where the percentage of depositors almost doubled from 4.6 per cent to nearly 9 per cent due largely to the efforts of William Meikle, the actuary of the Savings Bank of Glasgow. In 1861 the bank had won the custom of 10 per cent of the city's population; by 1881 it had achieved an outstanding 23 per cent by the skilful use of penny banks and branch banks, making it the bank with the largest number of depositors in the United Kingdom. Despite the poor showing of savings banks in England as a whole, there were a few savings banks in urban settings similar to Glasgow that recorded equivalent gains. In Lancashire, where the percentage of depositors remained more or less stable at 6 per cent, the Liverpool Savings Bank more than doubled its total deposits from £863,000 in 1861 to £1.83 million in 1881 and its customers from under 30,000 to almost 70,000.

For all its brilliant ascendancy, the Post Office Savings Bank had failed to eclipse the savings banks as Frank Scudamore had so confidently anticipated in 1863. Lewin Hill, who had succeeded Scudamore as Controller of the Post Office Savings Bank, reckoned in 1876 that 'at the present rate of closing it would take about seventy-four years to close them all'. Concerned that investment departments would be opened by most of the larger banks in the foreseeable future, he proposed to Sir Stafford Northcote, the Chancellor of the Exchequer in Disraeli's Conservative administration, that legislation should be introduced to close all the savings banks and transfer their assets to the Post Office Savings Bank. The Treasury was less than enthusiastic about this 'heroic remedy', but agreed that the pace of closures should, if possible, be quickened. The Post Office volunteered to feed the Chancellor with defamatory material about the savings banks on the strict understanding that it 'should not appear as the accuser of the old Savings Banks'. In the short term the attention of the Treasury and the financial institutions was directed away from the savings banks to the commercial banks by the spectacular collapse of the City of Glasgow Bank in the autumn of 1878, with losses of over £5 million resulting from the fraudulent activities of the board of directors. In addition to its commercial business, the Bank also ran a so-called 'Savings Bank Department' opened with the deliberate intention of competing with the fast-expanding Savings Bank of Glasgow. Confidence in the whole banking system was badly shaken, contributing to the end of the speculative boom that had lasted for almost the whole decade. The Governor of the Bank of England, Horsley Palmer, took emergency action lifting interest rates to 6 per cent, the highest for four years, intensifying the anxiety of the Post Office Savings Bank about the prospects of competition from savings bank investment departments. The financial community, in an effort to limit the damage, lobbied the Chancellor to improve banking accountability and supervision in the Companies Act of 1879. Although the catastrophe exacerbated the distress in Glasgow and the west of Scotland pushing bankruptcies up to record levels, the Savings Bank of Glasgow weathered the crisis without a serious run on its funds. Withdrawals were, however, greater than deposits as families hit by the recession drew on their savings to tide them through. The trustees believed that this experience could serve only to reinforce commitment to thrift.

The economic setback of 1878, which coincided with a very poor summer, heralded a serious crisis for rural Britain, which had enjoyed thirty years of unparalleled prosperity characterised by 'high farming' with the liberal application of the newly developed artificial fertilisers. Foreign producers, who had unfettered access to the British market since the repeal of the Corn Laws in 1846, had lacked an efficient cheap transport system to make the most of this privilege. Technical advances in the design and construction of ships and locomotives during the 1870s, combined with the building of many thousands of miles of railroads, particularly in North and South America, reduced freight rates. As a result grain prices in Britain tumbled and many farmers were faced with ruin, especially those on the heavy clay lands of East Anglia and on marginal lands in the Highlands and Ireland. The agricultural depression, which persisted without respite into the 1880s, spelt hardship for many families dependent on farm work.

Although cheap imports of food created problems for the agricultural community, they benefited Britain's now large urban population, and the cost of living fell sharply in the last five years of the 1870s. At the same time wages in towns and cities began to climb once again after the setback in 1878. By the middle years of the 1880s, families whose members were in regular employment enjoyed a higher standard of living than ever before. Housebuilding, which was seriously disrupted by the financial trauma in 1878, resumed in the early 1880s at the same pace as before. In this environment of rural poverty and urban prosperity, the performance of the savings banks was again dwarfed by that of the Post Office Savings Bank. Despite the popularity of special investment departments opened by the larger savings banks, with total holdings climbing from £2 million in 1880 to over £4 million, the total deposits still failed to keep pace with the annual rates of interest, reaching £52 million in 1887. However, the number of transactions (deposits and withdrawals) and the cost of administering individual savings bank accounts climbed by 12 per cent between 1879 and 1885, reaching a total of just over £2 million. The Post Office Savings Bank continued to attract funds rapidly and overtook the savings banks in 1887 with total deposits of nearly £54 million in the names of almost 4 million depositors. The building societies also did well. Nevertheless, only thirty-seven small savings banks shut their doors between 1880 and 1886.

Charles Dickens's popular character from *David Copperfield* exhorts
Glaswegians to save; and the Savings Bank of Glasgow's 'mission
statement' of the 1880s.

The credit for this repeated success of the Post Office Savings Bank was due largely to Henry Fawcett, the blind Member of Parliament, whom Gladstone appointed Postmaster-General after the Liberal landslide victory in the 1880 general election. Within weeks of taking office, Fawcett was urgently addressing demands for a reduction in the minimum deposit of a shilling. This proposal was dismissed on the grounds of the prohibitive cost of processing small transactions. However, on the advice of George Chetwynd, who had drawn up the bank's original regulations in 1861, Fawcett introduced, in September 1880, a scheme of penny savings, using postage stamps. It was tested experimentally in six English counties, two Scottish and one Irish, and was in such demand that at the end of the year the scheme was extended to the whole country. At the same time, Fawcett sought to head off the challenge of the savings banks' special investment departments through legislation, which allowed customers of both the Post Office Savings Bank and the savings banks with more than £10 in their accounts to buy government stock – consols, annuities and local loans stock. This new facility proved popular with larger depositors in the Post Office Savings Bank, who transferred £127,000 in six weeks. To the dismay of the savings banks, the legislation also reduced the interest received from the National Debt Commissioners from 3.25 per cent (where it had been fixed in 1844) to 3 per cent. This alteration was done to bring the rate paid to depositors by the savings banks into line with the Post Office Savings Bank – 2.5 per cent. Only the larger better-managed savings banks could afford to pay 2.75 per cent. Taking a leaf out of the book of the more progressive savings banks with their well-developed publicity material, Fawcett pressed the Post Office Savings Bank's advantage through an extensive campaign of promotion using the postal services. Advertisements were distributed from door to door, in many instances along with a pamphlet by Fawcett himself, *The Post Office and Aids to Thrift*, which was received enthusiastically.

The larger savings banks were well placed to fight off this challenge. Even paying the 2.75 per cent allowed by the Commissioners, they offered competitive rates of return at a time when bank rates had retreated to between 2.5 and 3 per cent. The savings banks also counter-attacked by mounting their own promotional campaigns. For example, in 1880 the Hull Savings Bank, following the lead of others, introduced an annual essay competition on the subject 'Advantages to be derived from the habits of thrift' for 'Working Men's prizes' of £5, £3 and £2. Savings banks, which had not responded to pressures to extend their opening hours in the 1860s, did so now. Others improved facilities for customers by enlarging their banking halls and adding to branch networks. Opening hours of the smaller banks were extended, but rarely to more than ten hours a week. All these improvements required additional staff, including the recruitment of the first women clericals and 'receivers of deposits'. Although the commercial banks could not match the returns offered by the savings banks except for very short periods when rates were high, they sought to compete for bigger accounts by offering more flexible facilities – ready access to cash and settlement by cheques. They were also concerned to prevent the savings banks or the Post Office Savings Bank from persuading the Chancellor to raise the upper limit on deposits for fear that it would rob them of many of their smaller commercial clients.

Just as the savings banks seemed to be stemming the tide of the fresh onslaught from the Post Office, disaster struck when it became known in April 1886 that J.E. Williams, the actuary of the Cardiff Savings Bank who had recently died, had embezzled £30,000 – some 15 per cent of its deposits – over a period of twenty years. Most of the funds that had been embezzled had been deposited with him 'irregularly' out of hours, contrary to the law. Some of these deposits had been made by trustees and managers themselves, who must have been well aware of the irregularities but probably not of the fraud. The Committee of Management of the Cardiff Savings Bank, attempting with good reason to avoid any personal liability for the loss, handled the subsequent investigation ineptly refusing to make any repayments to account. Depositors, angry at the terms of a proposed settlement of 17s 6d in the £1 for all depositors, including those who had made irregular payments, appealed to the Registrar of Friendly Societies who ordered that all the regular depositors should be paid in full. The Cardiff trustees foolishly refused to comply, drawing down on the whole savings bank movement the wrath of the press and those MPs and government officials who supported the Post Office Savings Bank. The potentially damaging consequences of the Cardiff fraud were self-evident.

All too conscious of the effectiveness of the central Post Office Savings Bank inspired by a man as forceful as Henry Fawcett, the larger savings banks lost no time in identifying the need for concerted action in the face of potential disaster. Although savings banks had been in the habit of acting together at similar times of tension, there was no formal mechanism for regular meetings. In May 1886 the Committee of Management of the Manchester & Salford Savings Bank, following a discussion of the Cardiff fraud, resolved that 'an association of Trustee Banks should be formed'. In making this plea they were following a well-trodden path. The building societies had formed an association in 1869 in a similar crisis. At first the proposal met with little support from trustees. It was a bad time to make such an appeal; the whole country was gripped by the debate about the Irish Home Rule Bill introduced by Gladstone in April in the wake of his victory at the general election two months before. Passions on either side were intense, dividing families throughout the country. The Liberal Party split and the measure was defeated. The government collapsed in August and was defeated in the ensuing general election. Throughout the turmoil the managers of the Manchester & Salford Savings Bank had never lost their commitment to the formation of an Association and, once the political situation had settled, they made a fresh approach. Trustees, reflecting on their personal positions, warmed to the idea and by the end of November the proposal had the support of forty-two of the larger banks out of the 400 or so banks. The first meeting took place in Manchester in February 1887 attended by representatives of twenty-six savings banks, when the rules were adopted, and it was agreed that the object would be 'to watch over and protect the interests of savings bank depositors, and to provide the means of affording the help of advice and co-operation in matters of a general character in which savings banks or their depositors may be interested'. Led by the elder statesman of the Trustee Savings Banks, William Meikle, actuary of the Savings Bank of Glasgow, the members of the new Association took immediate action to challenge critics of the savings bank movement in the wake of the Cardiff fraud.

Ten days before the gathering at Manchester, George Howell, MP for North-East Bethnal Green, had raised the question in the House of Commons of the extent of the deficit at Cardiff and the use by the savings banks of the words 'Government security'. The Conservative government's response was to emphasise the security of the Post Office Savings Bank and to promise some tightening of the legislation. Meikle's reaction was to propose that the Association should at once open negotiations with the Chancellor of the Exchequer, G.J. Goschen, and the National Debt Commissioners to find out on what terms the government would provide an indemnity for the savings banks. This practical advice was rejected by the members of the Association, who believed the most prudent course of action would be to circulate all the savings banks, reminding them of their statutory responsibilities. It took six months to draft a suitable pamphlet, *Remarks on the Management of Savings Banks*, and to gather together a mailing list. The whole savings bank movement was to pay dearly for this vacillation and delay. In the meantime, harried by a volley of questions from George Howell, the government had agreed to push a Bill quickly through Parliament, enabling the Treasury to apply to the High Court for the appointment of a Commissioner to examine the circumstances in which a bank was wound up. Directly the Bill became law in September 1887, a Commissioner was appointed to investigate the Cardiff fraud.

At the same time in the spring of 1887, under another proposal, measures relating to 'the purchase of small government annuities and to assuring payment after death', the Treasury attempted to lift the ceiling on annual deposits with the Post Office Savings Bank and to reduce the minimum amount that could be invested in government stock. The Trustee Savings Bank Association protested vigorously. A large deputation of trustees from all over the country called on the Chancellor in June to register the movement's disapproval. The commercial banks, concerned that the State-controlled Post Office might start to poach their business, added their voice to the opposition. This was orchestrated in the House of Commons by three Members of Parliament – Lord Claud Hamilton, Edward Whitley and J.W. Maclure – who together succeeded in having the clause relating to the alteration in the ceiling on annual deposits with the Post Office Saving Bank dropped, and the other clauses in the Act extended to the savings banks. Delighted at the outcome at a time when trustees were beginning to lose their nerve, the Council of the Association warmly thanked the three Members of Parliament for their support.

Well aware that the savings bank movement was not out of the woods and that some changes in the law were inevitable, William Meikle of the Savings Bank of Glasgow, and his brother, Christopher Meikle, the actuary of the Edinburgh Savings Bank, spent the winter months drafting a paper on 'Suggestions for the Reform of Savings Banks'. This was presented to the meeting of the Council of the Association in February, which endorsed several of the proposals. These were that the security provided by officials should be increased; that the weekly returns of the savings banks to the Commissioners should be signed by two officials; that trustees should appoint a chartered accountant as auditor; and that every year as large a number of passbooks as possible should be compared with the ledger. These proposals were to be printed and circulated to all member banks. Within three weeks, the attention of the savings banks was diverted by the Chancellor of the Exchequer's decision to take advantage of the prevailing low rates of interest to convert the whole of the National Debt of £600 million from 3 per cent to 2.75 per cent at the end of the fiscal year 1888–89, with a further reduction to 2.5 per cent in fifteen years' time. This gigantic operation was approved by Parliament in March and carried through almost without a hitch. The consequence of this achievement for the savings banks was a reduction in May of the interest paid by the National Debt Commissioners to 2.75 per cent with a maximum rate of 2.5 per cent paid to depositors bringing it directly into line with that paid by the Post Office Savings Bank.

No sooner had the rate been cut than the Commissioner investigating the Cardiff fraud, E. Lyulph Stanley, submitted a scathing report highly critical of the savings banks. He accused the trustees and managers of negligence, if not fraud, and suggested in so many words that the savings banks should be amalgamated with the Post Office Savings Bank. In June George Howell introduced a resolution in the House of Commons to remove all reference in savings banks literature to government indemnity or security. The drift of his speech was less contentious, demanding reform rather than abolition. Sir Albert Rollit, MP for North Islington and a trustee of two savings banks that were members of the Association, found little to quarrel with in responding on behalf of the movement. Rather than tabling the proposals of the Meikle brothers, he opted for the compromise of a government inquiry. The Chancellor of the Exchequer concurred and in June he announced the appointment of a Select Committee on Trustee Savings Banks under the chairmanship of the Rt Hon G.J. Shaw Lefevre. These events were too much for some managers and trustees. Eighteen banks closed, with total balances of £1.1 million of which £890,000 was transferred to the Post Office Savings Bank. The banks that closed included Bristol, with deposits of £577,477; Farringdon Street in London with £60,297; and Hereford with £191,872 – all members of the Association. In these circumstances the savings banks did well to lose only £550,000 in deposits during the year.

The appointment of the Select Committee marked a victory for the savings banks in the twenty-seven-year-long struggle with the Post Office Savings Bank. There was now no question that Scudamore's plan drawn up in 1863 for the total eclipse of the savings banks by a long campaign of attrition would ever again be taken seriously. Since then attitudes to saving had changed; no longer was 'self-help' simply a matter of providing for times of illness, unemployment and old age, but as an important way of providing without recourse to borrowing for the comfort of the home and new pleasures and pastimes. This transformation was partly a reflection of increasing prosperity combined with cheaper and more widely available mass-produced goods, and partly an outcome of the restatement of the individual's relation with the State by political theorists, such as the Oxford philosopher T.H. Green, who argued that personal freedom could be achieved only by a degree of State direction and control. He and his followers again began to question whether it was morally right for the poor to be encouraged to save when they appeared to have barely enough income to cover the basic necessities of life. These were very different attitudes from the repressive authoritarian outlook of the reformers of the 1830s or Samuel Smiles's conviction that hardships and struggle allowed an individual to escape from a natural state of prodigality into one of self-determination. By casting doubt on the principles of 'self-help', the new school of social thinkers were challenging the whole ethos of thrift, but they lacked sufficient empirical evidence about family budgets and expenditure to prove their case. With thrift beginning to move away from immediate political debate, government could allow the trustee savings banks to exist side by side with the Post Office Savings Bank as two complementary, but not necessarily competing, services in the community, just as Gladstone had promised so disingenuously in 1862.

Thrift Strangling Poverty:
a common theme in Victorian
savings bank rhetoric, here
represented in a sculpture
by A. McFarlane Shannan
in 1908.

# CHAPTER FOUR

# SAVINGS BANKS

## ON THE

## DEFENSIVE

## *1888–1914*

Threading The Select Committee on Trustee Savings
Banks was appointed at a time when the mood of the country was confident and buoyant in
the wake of Queen Victoria's Golden Jubilee celebrations the year before. For the first time
since the death of her husband, Prince Albert, in 1861, the Queen had appeared regularly in
public in Britain's major cities and towns with huge celebrations in London attended by
reigning monarchs from all over Europe. The carnival atmosphere, coinciding with rising
wholesale prices, made for the business optimism that allowed for the conversion of the
National Debt from 3 per cent to 2.75 per cent to proceed smoothly. In keeping with the
times, the tenor of Lord Salisbury's Conservative government was benign toleration.

In his speech promising the establishment of the Select Committee, the Chancellor of the
Exchequer, G.J. Goschen, had made it clear that he was not contemplating an attack on the
savings banks, simply reform which would restore confidence after the uncertainty following
the Cardiff fraud. He was quick to point out that in comparison to the total savings bank
deposits, the number and size of frauds was trivial – no greater than those in the commercial
world. He endorsed the savings banks in glowing terms: 'It is only the disasters with which the
House of Commons and the public are acquainted; we see little of the considerable service and
magnificent working of many of the larger institutions which have done so much credit to the
country.' The terms of reference of the Committee were to inquire into and report on the
administration of Trustee Savings Banks, the powers, duties, and liabilities of the trustees,
managers and officers, the relations of the banks to the Commissioners for the Reduction of
the National Debt, the Registrar of Friendly Societies, and other offices or departments of the
government, and 'the alleged assumption by certain Trustee Savings Banks of designations
calculated to mislead depositors'. The Committee comprised sixteen members in addition to

the Rt Hon G.J. Shaw Lefevre, including George Howell, the most outspoken critic of the savings banks, and Edward Whitley, their champion.

Work began immediately and just eleven days after its appointment the Select Committee met in June to interview the first witness, John Ludlow, the Registrar of Friendly Societies and a known opponent of the savings banks. Living up to his reputation, his evidence was highly critical: 'If the security of the depositors is the only object to be considered, then I think that the whole business of the Trustee Savings Banks should be handed over as soon as possible to the Post Office Savings Bank which would give entire security to the depositors.' However, he was prepared to admit that if this was not the government's intention, the law must be amended to improve the position of depositors, preferably by giving them a say in the direction of the individual savings banks. His own choice was to bring the savings banks directly under friendly society legislation, failing which he suggested that depositors should have the right to elect a third of the managers (responsible for the day-to-day administration) and to confirm the election of new trustees (responsible for the overall supervision). He wanted the powers of the Registrar of Friendly Societies to intervene in disputes strengthened and he denounced the trustees at Cardiff, who had deliberately invested larger sums than the rules allowed. When pressed, he conceded that it was possible for frauds to be perpetrated in branches of the Post Office Savings Bank and that in some respects the savings banks enjoyed an advantage, principally because 'the trustees and managers are people of a superior station to the ordinary postmaster'. His chief objection was that unpaid managers had no real incentive to devote their time and effort and he proposed that in future they should be paid.

The force of Ludlow's evidence was mitigated by that of his assistant, Edward Bradbrook, who followed him as a witness. He was totally opposed to the merger of the savings banks with the Post Office Savings Bank and was adamant that losses through fraud were trivial when compared with total transactions since 1817 of over £1,000 million. The only area of the law with room for improvement, in his opinion, was that relating to the liability of trustees. Sir Charles Rivers Wilson – the Secretary to the Commissioners for the Reduction of the National Debt – who was called next, had no particular axe to grind, giving his lukewarm support to the idea of turning savings banks into limited liability concerns with no consideration as to how they were to earn sufficient returns to pay dividends to their investors.

After this disappointing start for the savings banks, E. Lyulph Stanley, the Commissioner who had investigated the Cardiff fraud, came forward with some constructive proposals based on his findings, and observations on the organisation of savings banks more generally. He contrasted the high quality of the management of the larger savings banks, such as Glasgow and Liverpool, with smaller banks, whose functions he believed could be much better and more safely performed by the Post Office Savings Bank. He had no doubt that frauds like that at Cardiff could easily be prevented by ensuring that the rules were observed and by rigorous audit. The assurances about the conduct of the larger savings banks were confirmed by the evidence of the first witness to speak on behalf of the movement, Thomas Newton, the secretary of the Liverpool Savings Bank and one of the honorary secretaries of the newly established Trustee Savings Banks Association. He described in detail the regulations introduced by the trustees and managers to safeguard against any possibility of fraud. Managers met monthly to discuss the bank's affairs and were in daily attendance to countersign returns and cheques. Newton was able to show that in a savings bank as large as Liverpool, with nearly 85,000 customers and almost £2.5 million in deposits, the cost of each of the 357,310 transactions a year was about half that of the Post Office Savings Bank. He believed passionately that in most large cities people preferred the savings banks to the Post Office: 'It is the natural appearance of it; it is a bank, it is not a shop ... it is their bank.' He had no quarrel with the Post Office Savings Bank. Arguing that 'there seems to be business for both of us,' he showed that there was a two-way traffic in deposits between the two banks which, in the case of the Liverpool, favoured the savings banks. Most of his evidence followed the line agreed by the Association, with the exception of his condemnation of special investment departments and suggestions that these should be closed and the proceeds invested in government stock. Although such an arrangement would have been easy to administer, it was argued that it would deny local authorities access to funds raised in their area, urgently needed for a variety of improvements.

The Select Committee adjourned at the end of the session in November and was not reappointed until March 1889. The members of the Trustee Savings Banks Association were furious at Newton's remarks about special investments. At their next meeting in February, he resigned as one of the three honorary secretaries, despite attempts by William Meikle and the Leeds actuary, Mr Heppner, to persuade him to stay on. Meikle was anxious that there should be no break in ranks at this critical moment with the outcome of the Select Committee as yet undecided. He was still to give evidence and was determined to present a programme of reform, an extension of the ideas sketched out the year before. These he summarised under four headings: (1) increased security from officers; (2) efficient audit; (3) increased limit of deposit of £50 a year and £300 in total; and (4) investments under section 16 in local bonds under proper limits. Efficient audit was to be supervised by a Board of Inspection to report each year on the probity of savings banks. To avoid a repetition of Newton's resignation, Meikle was at pains to ensure that he had the full approval of the Council of the Association before he was called as a witness in May. He also suggested that the Association should pre-empt the findings of the Committee by having a private member's Bill introduced into the House of Commons as soon as possible.

The Select Committee had resumed the task of hearing evidence in April 1889 and completed their work by mid-May. The key witness was undoubtedly Meikle, whose testimony was authoritative and statesmanlike. With a Scotsman's suspicion of central government, he was concerned that the members of the proposed Board of Inspection 'of persons experienced in the management of savings banks' should not be nominated directly by the Treasury. He stated that the Savings Bank of Glasgow had sounded out the opinion of the larger savings banks and confirmed that they were willing to contribute towards the cost of the inspectorate out of their management expenses. Correcting the impression given by Newton, he stoutly defended special investment departments. He went on to explain that the savings banks needed this facility to meet the demands of larger depositors whose interest they served just as much as the mass of customers with only a few pounds in their accounts. The only part of his evidence that lacked force was in response to questions about smaller banks where he was obviously on unfamiliar territory.

This shortcoming was more than compensated for by the Revd Alexander Shaw Page, the vicar of Selsley near Stroud in Gloucestershire and the manager of the Cairncross Provident Bank for Savings. Although this bank, like many other smaller banks, was 'just holding its own' and not growing, the Revd Shaw Page was adamant that it had a vital part to play in encouraging thrift in the neighbourhood: 'the people are used to it, and country people are very conservative . . . There they know the actuary and managers; they find in them friends and advisers as to money affairs.' He welcomed the idea of annual inspection, 'making, as we say in regard to our schools, visits with notice and visits without notice'.

Within a fortnight of the Committee's last hearing, the savings bank movement was stunned by the discovery of another fraud at Macclesfield Savings Bank in Cheshire where a junior clerk had embezzled £4,000 'by tampering with the passbooks, receiving money from deposi-tors without corresponding entries in the ledgers, paying in money from depositors without passbooks and by falsifying the liabilities of the bank at the end of each year, in order to cover the amount he appropriated'. The news could not have come at a worse time. A Commissioner was immediately appointed to investigate the matter. He had an interim report in the hands of the Select Committee by the end of July 1889, accusing the trustees and actuaries of gross negligence and carelessness in allowing so easily detectable a fraud to be perpetrated.

It took the Select Committee two months to agree the final report which was published in August. It was a very short document of only five pages. Following the note struck by the Chancellor when the Select Committee was appointed, the Report fully supported the savings banks: 'It appears, therefore, that there is room for both Trustee and Post Office savings banks, and your Committee, while thinking it preferable that many more of the smaller trustee banks may be merged in the Post Office, would regret the general disappearance of such banks.' Nevertheless, its findings were vague and couched in general terms, calling for improved audits to be supervised by independent boards of audit and making mild comment on the risks involved in special investment departments. The proposed government inspection was rejected on the not altogether convincing grounds that it might entail government guarantee of deposits with savings banks, 'making them practically a branch of the public services as much as the Post Office Bank'. The only specific recommendation was that every savings bank passbook should make it clear that the government was not liable for any deposit. There was no reference to Meikle's suggestions for increased security for officers or the raising of the limits on deposits. The Macclesfield fraud simply confirmed the Select Committee's view that audit should be strengthened.

In anticipation of the publication of the Report, Meikle had been hard at work drafting a Bill based on the proposals presented in his evidence. Although the Council of the Trustee Savings Banks Association was happy to scrutinise the draft clause by clause at their meeting in June, they lacked the confidence either to seek the wider approval of their membership or to submit the Bill to the Committee. Meikle, refusing to take no for an answer, pressed for a further discussion a fortnight later. When he was again rebuffed, he accused the Council of throwing away 'a golden opportunity'. Even when the Report was published, the Association still vacillated, leaving Sir Albert Rollit, MP for North Islington, to take the initiative. He invited the Chancellor of the Exchequer, Goschen, to inspect the Hull Savings Bank, of which he was a trustee, to witness at first hand how a well-managed savings bank operated. Prompted by Rollit, the Chancellor wrote to the Association in October, inviting suggestions for legislative reform. At once Meikle's supporters – the Edinburgh, Glasgow, Hull, Preston and Lincoln savings banks – demanded a meeting in October. Those in attendance were deeply divided, but this time Meikle was able to summon enough support not only to defeat a motion that it was 'not expedient for this Association to take steps in promoting legislation'; but also to secure the appointment of a committee to initiate dialogue with the government. After protracted negotiations, Rollit introduced in February 1890 a private member's Bill, embodying most of Meikle's ideas. No sooner had it been tabled than the government announced that it would frame its own measures.

The Bill, published in late April, confirmed all Meikle's worst forebodings of the short-comings of the government's intentions. It was proposed that all passbooks in future should bear a statement that the government was in no way liable for savings bank funds and, if this was not enough, the clause in the 1863 Act that allowed the operation of special investment departments was to be repealed. An Inspection Committee was to be established, but the Chancellor called for advice on its constitution and terms of reference. The Association was powerless to respond constructively. Broken by the disagreement it was left representing only a rump of seven savings banks: Bloomsbury, Devonport, Leeds, Manchester, Preston, Sheffield and Warrington. The other larger savings banks, such as Hull, St Martin's Place in London, Glasgow and Edinburgh, rather than risk further argument and delay by the Association, opted for an immediate and decisive campaign under the leadership of Sir Albert Rollit. In the belief that the legislation as framed 'really meant the extermination of the Trustee Savings Bank system', a meeting representing as many savings banks as possible was arranged at St Martin's Place Bank in June. Over seventy MPs attended and went on to present the savings banks' case to the Chancellor.

So impressed was Goschen by the size and importance of the delegation that he agreed to

Sir Albert K. Rollit (1842–1922) MP, LLD, DCL, from a portrait by Sir
Hubert von Herkomer. Rollit was a trustee of both the Hull and
Finsbury savings banks, and became the movement's staunchest ally in
the House of Commons.

make substantial amendments to the Bill, including abandoning the abolition of special investment departments and raising the limit on deposits. To save time, the Chancellor proposed that all the amendments be dealt with in Committee, bringing a storm of protest about his ears. Under relentless pressure from backbenchers, the Bill was abandoned in early August. A new Bill incorporating all the changes was introduced by the government in February 1891. Although it raised passions in Parliament over points of detail, there was not the same determined opposition as the year before. The main points of contention were the degree of government control over the Inspection Committee; the embargo on the opening of further special investment departments; the prohibition on investment in mortgages on land and in property itself which could be interpreted to include loans secured on the rates; and the smallness of the increase in the limit on deposit first set in 1828 from £150 to £200. Apart from a few modifications, the Bill became law in July.

The most significant reform was the creation of the Inspection Committee to be nominated by a committee named in the Act: E. Lyulph Stanley; three MPs: Lord Francis Hervey, Sir Albert Rollit, John Ellis; T.C. Wright, chairman of the Association and of the Bloomsbury Savings Bank; John Ure, Lord Dean of Guild of Glasgow and a trustee of the Savings Bank of Glasgow; and Henry Court, the recently retired Assistant Comptroller of the National Debt Office. They set to work at once, holding their first meeting four days after the Act was placed on the statute book, when it was decided that the Inspection Committee should consist of seven members, three of whom were to represent the savings banks themselves. The remaining four were to be nominated by the Governor of the Bank of England, the Council of the Institute of Chartered Accountants in England and Wales, the Council of the Incorporated Law Society, and the Chief Registrar of Friendly Societies. The Inspection Committee had wide powers to investigate every aspect of savings bank affairs and to discipline savings banks that failed to observe the statutory regulations in the most extreme cases by forcing closure.

The Inspection Committee, as finally constituted, comprised Sir Albert Rollit, John Ure and Thomas Newman (a trustee of the Bloomsbury Savings Bank) representing the savings banks; Horace Bowen, Chief Accountant of the Bank of England; Thomas Walston, President of the Council of the Institute of Chartered Accountants; William Walters, President of the Law Society, and John Ludlow, who had just stood down as Chief Registrar of Friendly Societies. The Committee then set about grouping the savings banks into districts and appointing local inspectors who were to investigate at least a third of the savings banks in their area each year. They included amongst their ranks a number of distinguished accountants, such as W. B. Peat in Middlesbrough, and F. Whinney in north London. Under the chairmanship of Sir Albert Rollit, the Inspection Committee saw themselves as upholders of the savings bank movement, protected by legislation that had steadily been improved since the first Act of 1817. Their first report to Parliament, published at the end of January 1893, was as much a review of the history and development of the savings banks as of the Committee's work during the year, with statistics and appendices for every ten years from 1859 and a digest of all the legislation relating to the banks.

The Report itself made sorry reading. The Committee regretted 'to find that in many instances the statutory requirements relative to the conduct and management of Savings Banks have been neglected, either through ignorance of the law or through general laxity in management. It has been found that some Banks even ignore their own rules.' Out of the 178 savings banks inspected, there were 167 where irregularities had been discovered and reported by the local inspectors, principally the failure to include a copy of the rules in the passbook. The inspectors were astonished to find that 105 savings bank officers were over the age of sixty-five with twenty-eight over seventy-five. The Committee at once opened negotiations with the National Debt Office with a view to establishing a superannuation fund for officers. Despite their disappointment, the Committee adopted a cautious approach, carefully explaining the regulations in a circular to all the savings banks in November 1892 in the hope that they would put their house in order without compulsion. They were to be sadly disappointed. The results of the second year's inspection were no better than the first. The Committee was forced to take tough action, closing Folkingham Savings Bank in Lincolnshire for flagrantly ignoring the regulations and forcing St Clement Dane's Savings Bank in London to comply. More worry-ingly, a serious fraud of £14,000 was discovered at Sudbury Savings Bank in Suffolk, which was compulsorily wound up. The Inspection Committee issued a stern warning at the end of their Report, particularly to the smaller banks, that the movement must put its house in order. The savings banks were not alone in being criticised for poor management. The building societies, whose affairs had been reformed by the 1874 Act, were condemned for making speculative advances that threatened their viability. In September 1892 the Liberator Building Society, the brainchild of Jabez Balfour, collapsed along with his London & General Bank and associated companies. The total loss to depositors was a staggering £8 million. The directors were subsequently sent to prison for fraud.

The lowering of the rate of interest in line with the Post Office Savings Bank in 1888, combined with the lack of leadership from the Association during and after the inquiry and the close scrutiny of the Inspection Committee and the difficulties of the Liberator Building Society, proved too much for the managers and trustees of many banks. Between 1889 and 1893, 115 savings banks closed their doors, with the withdrawal of £4 million in deposits and the direct transfer of over £2 million to the Post Office Savings Bank. The majority of the savings banks that closed were very small; a few were relatively large, such as Bath with total deposits of almost £330,000.

The trustees and actuaries of the largest savings banks, which had operated special investment departments before the 1891 Act, were so disturbed by the apparent threat to their future that they sought to revive the Association. The initiative was taken by the Leeds and Preston savings banks in calling an open meeting of the Association in May 1892, to discuss a draft Bill to allow funds in the nineteen existing special investment departments legally to be invested in debenture stock, mortgages and local authority loans. The first meeting was a flop, with representatives of only five of the savings banks operating special investment departments present, and the noticeable absence of any representatives from Edinburgh and Glasgow. Nevertheless, it agreed to obtain Counsel's opinion on the interpretation of the Act and to promote the draft Bill in the current session of Parliament. Nothing came directly out of this plan; but in November 1892 the Association secured a meeting with Sir Albert Rollit, and the Meikle brothers and their supporters were persuaded to withdraw their boycott. As a result, the Edinburgh, Glasgow, Hull and Derby savings banks were represented at the meeting. Although the Meikle brothers would have liked to have had a general discussion with Rollit, they were over-ruled in favour of restricting the agenda to the deployment of special investment department deposits and the proposed legislation. Contrary to their Counsel's opinion, Rollit told the members of the Association they were no longer able to invest special investment funds in local authority loans and these had to be called in and replaced by securities other than those secured on property. His advice was that it would be difficult to introduce another savings bank Bill so soon, but he did offer helpful suggestions. Discussions dragged on for months.

In the meantime, the newly elected Liberal government introduced a Bill to enlarge customers' investment opportunities by lifting the ceiling on annual deposits from £30 to £100; raising the limit on the purchase of government stock from £100 to £200 a year, and the total from £300 to £500. The large commercial banks, which had developed out of a series of recent mergers, objected strongly to the big increase in annual ordinary account deposits at a time when they themselves were attempting to build their deposit business by borrowing ideas from thrift organisations. After a heated debate the ceiling was raised to £50. Despite assurances from the Chancellor of the Exchequer, the Association failed to secure the inclusion of a clause widening the investments available to special investment departments. Disappointed once more with the apparent failure of the Association to act decisively, the Meikle brothers opened negotiations for separate legislation for Scotland to reinstate special investment departments. Although their approach was similarly rebuffed, the Scottish savings banks once again ceased to support the Association. Sir Albert Rollit himself tried to put matters right by introducing Bills supported by the Inspection Committee in 1894 and 1895; but these, along with another Bill put forward by Lord Macnaghten in 1895, failed to win government blessing. While being unwilling to accommodate the larger savings bank investors, the government reached an understanding with the building societies in 1895, allowing them to pay interest free of income tax in exchange for a composite tax payment from the societies themselves.

While the larger savings banks were engaged in these fruitless discussions, the pace of closures had continued. A further twenty-two, mostly small, banks ceased to operate during 1894 and 1895 with the withdrawal of some £880,000 in deposits, of which about £500,000 was transferred to the Post Office. In the majority of cases the trustees gave as their reason competition from other thrift organisations and the retirement or death of one of the bank's officers. Although the rate of closure slowed in 1896 to seven, the whole movement was saddened to learn that amongst this number was the St Martin's Place Savings Bank, which had, even as recently as 1890, provided a much-needed focus for the movement as a whole. The trustees had decided to give up the now unequal struggle with the Post Office Savings Bank in London and recommended that customers should transfer their funds. Almost 90 per cent of the bank's deposits of £857,949 were thus switched to Post Office Savings Bank accounts.

Despite this continuing haemorrhage of funds, the savings banks as a whole markedly improved their fortunes during the 1890s. Real wages in the larger towns and cities maintained their upward surge, reaching an all-time high by the beginning of 1897, reflecting a sharp decline in food prices. Families with members in continuous employment had never been so well-off, with more money to save and spend. Total deposits which had drifted steadily down from 1888, reaching a low of £48 million in 1892, began to recover in 1894 following the changes in the limits on individual accounts the year before. This revival was maintained over the next two years with deposits advancing, even in 1896 when the St Martin's Place Savings Bank closed. Revival was accompanied by an increase in turnover in the ordinary departments which, from 1888 to 1894, was about £10 million a year. From 1894 it began to rise, reaching £12 million in 1896. Much of this success was due to the continuing advance of the larger savings banks notwithstanding the restrictions on special investment departments. Total deposits with the Liverpool and Manchester savings banks climbed from £3 million each to almost £4 million and with the Savings Bank of Glasgow from almost £5 million to more than £7 million. Although the downturn in the rural economy persisted, some smaller savings banks in agricultural districts recorded similar achievements to the delight of the Inspection Committee.

National statistics were not kept of the social backgrounds of the new depositors responsible for this upsurge in deposits. They were compiled for some individual banks. At the Aberdeen Savings Bank the largest group of new depositors were students and scholars, followed by unmarried women, probably mostly domestic servants. Collectively the majority of new depositors, as had always been the case, were artisans and craftsmen, but there was a significant growth in deposits by agricultural labourers; for labourers' families, saving demanded considerable sacrifices as wage levels were so low. An analysis of customer base of the Sheffield Savings Bank at this time by Roger Lloyd-Jones and M.J. Lewis has shown that 'the number of depositors associated with the basic industries of Sheffield, the light and heavy steel trades, was actually declining, while numbers in the service and tertiary sectors were increasing'. Their investigation confirms the experience at Aberdeen of a growth in savings by and for children. The reasons that there were so many accounts held by those in service was that employers often refused to pay all their wages in cash, preferring to place a good proportion in savings bank

Agricultural labourers were valued customers of savings banks serving
rural areas. These workers were photographed in East Lothian, 1912.

accounts. The actuary of Derby Savings Bank recalled in the 1920s: 'If the servant had no
account then the farmer would stand over him while he opened one.'

The better fortunes of the savings banks in the 1890s were dwarfed by the gains of the
whole thrift movement. Registered friendly societies saw their membership swell to reach 4.8
million by 1897, with total funds of £30.5 million. The number of paid-up policies with
industrial life assurance companies soared from less than 10 million in 1890 to over 17 million
by 1897. The friendly collecting societies experienced an equivalent advance in membership
and funds. Most notable of all was the meteoric progress of the Post Office Savings Bank,
helped in part by the closure of so many savings banks. The number of clients leapt from 4.8
million in 1890 to 7.2 million in 1897 and total funds from £67 million to £115 million. Apart
from the rising tide of prosperity, the popularity of these types of investments reflected the low
rates of return available on cash deposited with the commercial banks. From 1892 to 1897,
except for the occasional month or two, bank rate remained between 2 and 3.5 per cent.
However, the commercial banks were reluctant to see their market rates fall below the 2.5 per
cent return paid by the savings banks and the Post Office Savings Bank for fear of losing funds
to these competitors.

When bank rate held at 2 per cent in 1895, the commercial banks were quick to complain
about the higher rate of interest available to the savings banks. There was strong pressure on

the Conservative government of Lord Salisbury, returned in 1895, to cut the rate paid to the savings banks and the Post Office Savings Bank, particularly as government stock was trading well above par, bringing down the yield to below 2.5 per cent. *The Times* joined the attack, declaring that the better-off should not be entitled to higher rates of return than those available generally in the money market. The answer, the newspaper believed, was to lower the annual limit and the ceiling on deposits. In his first budget speech in the spring of 1896, the new Chancellor of the Exchequer, Sir Michael Hicks Beach, observing that the number of customers depositing the maximum of £50 a year was growing rapidly, speculated that there should be different scales of return for small and large depositors. Sir Albert Rollit jumped to the savings banks' defence and, to the annoyance of the commercial banks, nothing was done. The Chancellor promised, however, the rate would be lowered when interest on government stock was again cut under Goschen's 1889 scheme in 1903 (see p.96). The debate about the rate raged in the banking press throughout 1897.

The tireless work of the Inspection Committee in putting the savings banks' house in order served only to fuel the argument. By the end of 1896, Rollit and his colleagues were sufficiently confident that they had turned the corner to reduce the inspecting staff and submit a much-abbreviated report to Parliament. They took comfort from the fact that most of the banks found to have inadequate management in 1892 had shut their doors and that there was every indication only a few more closures would follow. Despite the confidence of the Inspection Committee, the larger banks with special investment departments remained uneasy about future prospects, particularly as they were still under notice to redeem investments no longer permitted by legislation.

Frustrated by the failure to secure any amendments to the 1891 Act, William Meikle explored the possibility of the Savings Bank of Glasgow establishing an investment trust registered under the Companies Act to take over securities held by the special investment department. After taking legal advice and informing the Inspection Committee, the bank established the Savings Investment Trust Ltd in April 1896. Bound only by the regulations of the Trustee Investment Act of 1889, the Trust could place deposits in local authority loans secured on the rates. This bold initiative by the country's largest savings bank stimulated considerable interest both from customers and other banks. Although the Trust was instantly popular, Glasgow had no immediate imitators, although an abortive attempt was made by the Hull Savings Bank to set up an associate banking company for the same purposes. The other three Scottish banks with special investment departments – Edinburgh, Dundee, and Perth – were spared the need of resorting to such an expediency by the passing of the Trusts (Scotland) Act of 1898, which allowed savings banks north of the border to invest 'in loans on bonds, debentures, or mortgages secured on any rate or tax levied under the authority of any Act of Parliament by any local authority in Scotland authorised to borrow money on such security'. The Trustee Savings Banks Association, which continued only to represent the larger English savings banks, was irritated by this separate legislation and immediately attempted to have the provision extended to England and Wales.

During the closing decade of the century, the whole thrift movement had more fundamental worries about its aims and objects than just being able to capture the deposits of the better-off. Socially concerned men and women began to investigate the problems of poverty in greater detail. Their findings revealed that beneath the growing prosperity of many families, about a third of the population lived on or below the poverty line. Early socialists took practical steps to help improve conditions in the worst areas of Britain's largest cities and towns by working for a variety of voluntary welfare organisations, particularly University settlements with origins in Toynbee Hall in London. Shocked by the grinding hardship experienced by many poor families, this new generation of social reformers became convinced that there was no moral imperative to encourage the very poor to save even pennies when they lacked the resources to maintain everyday life. This view was confirmed by the penetrating inquiry into the conditions of the London poor conducted by Charles Booth, a wealthy Liverpool shipowner, between 1889 and 1903. By scrupulous analysis of family budgets, he showed that the poor simply did not have the wherewithal to put anything aside to provide for times of sickness or for old age. Social commentators drew the conclusion that it was for the government to provide a more humane alternative to the workhouse for the old, the sick and the unemployed. This approach to the problem of poverty called into question the *raison d'être* of the savings movement fuelling the doubts of trustees and managers as they decided to comply with the regulations demanded by the Inspection Committee or give up.

During 1897 the trustees of the Leeds Skyrac & Morley Savings Bank, with deposits of well over £1 million and 29,000 customers, considered carefully whether their bank was 'fulfilling its object, viz., the assistance of the thrifty, and whether its place would be adequately filled if they discontinued'. A scrutiny of the accounts showed that more than two-thirds of deposits were of sums less than a pound and that the balance in three-quarters of accounts was under £20. On the basis of these figures they averred that for all the doubts of social commentators, the savings banks still performed a useful service which could not easily be supplied by the commercial banks even with their new-found enthusiasm for private client business. The Inspection Committee, praising the Leeds trustees' decision to keep going, drew attention to the average balances of other large banks such as Glasgow, where three-quarters of the 197,000 clients had average deposits of £11 6s 3d. Although such figures did not address the moral question of whether the poor should be persuaded to save, the Inspection Committee reminded the government that the savings banks were 'worthy ... of full encouragement by the State, whose best interests they serve and none should be closed without the clearest possible proof of inefficiency or inability to continue'.

The immediate threat of further reduction in savings bank interest rates passed in 1898 as bank rate edged higher, driven up by a gradual rise in prices and in the autumn of 1899 by government borrowing to meet the cost of the Boer War in South Africa. However, Sir Michael Hicks Beach was well aware that the problem had to be addressed before rates on government stock were reduced in 1903. If the interest payable to the savings banks remained at their present level of 2.75 per cent, the deficit in the Savings Bank Fund (see p.33) would accrue rapidly. As a first step he announced in his budget of 1899 that the fund of £2.8 million held by the Treasury to redeem the existing deficit established in 1887 would be converted into terminable annuities yielding 2.5 per cent from 1903. The management of this fund was a bone of contention with the savings banks which believed that any surplus accruing in the fund due to the rise in value of the government stock in which it was invested should be attributed to the Savings Bank Fund and not confiscated by the Exchequer. The Trustee Savings Banks Association protested loudly at what they interpreted as a prelude to a reduction in the interest paid to depositors. Encouraged by the Association, Francis Channings, MP for East Northamptonshire, urged the appointment of a Select Committee to investigate the investment of the Savings Bank Fund. Although the Chancellor of the Exchequer was not anxious for yet a further inquiry, he was undecided how to proceed. Almost immediately Sir Albert Rollit and his colleagues on the Inspection Committee seized the initiative by framing their own Bill to correct the shortcomings of the existing legislation identified in their reports. These included cancelling the requirement to obtain security for officers, permission for banks to use the surplus in their management accounts without restriction, the establishment of a superannuation fund for bank staff, wider powers to invest special investment funds, and the establishment of a mechanism for the amalgamation of banks. When the Bill was published in mid-July the Trustee Savings Banks Association summoned a special meeting which resolved to write to every savings bank encouraging them to lobby their MP to support the measure. The Bill was introduced too late in the session to pass, but was reintroduced early in the 1900 session. Before the second reading took place, the Chancellor asked Rollit to withdraw it so that the government could bring forward its own measure.

The government's Bill was introduced on 16 May, embodying most of the Inspection Committee's reforms with the exception of the reinstatement of the special investment departments for new customers, but also proposing that the rate of interest paid by the Post Office and the savings banks should be set each year by the Treasury at a minimum of one month's notice. To meet the criticism from the savings banks, the whole of the deficiency fund was to be transferred to the Savings Bank Fund to cover deficiencies or depreciation rather than being credited to the Exchequer. The Association protested vigorously at the threatened cut in interest rates and again lent its support to the appointment of a Select Committee. An open meeting was held at the Westminster Palace Hotel in June, attended by representatives of thirty-four banks, including for the first time for six years the Edinburgh and Glasgow Savings Banks. The meeting received a message from Sir Albert Rollit that he had finally persuaded the Chancellor of the Exchequer to appoint a Select Committee. Despite this promise the government took no immediate action largely because the price of government stock plunged during the winter of 1900 and into 1901, effectively pushing rates above 2.5 per cent, making it impractical for the Chancellor of the Exchequer to cut the rate payable to the savings banks. Disappointed that the Select Committee had still not been set up by February 1902, the Association sought the help of Sir Albert Rollit to put pressure on the Chancellor. A general meeting in March even went so far as to draw up a list of MPs considered suitable to serve and urged the Chancellor to take action on the proposals put forward by Rollit and the Inspection Committee almost three years earlier. The Chancellor of the Exchequer at last responded appointing a Select Committee under his own chairmanship in March 'to inquire into the general condition of both Savings Bank Funds in respect of their capital and income accounts and the authorised investments thereof, with special reference to the loss of income which will be incurred by the reduction of the rate of interest on consols in 1903'. Only three of the members of the Select Committee, including Sir Albert himself, were drawn from the list nominated by the Association. Some of the members were openly hostile, notably Sir Frederick Dixon-Hartland, a director of Midland Bank since its acquisition in 1891 of his private family bank, Lacy, Hartland, Woodbridge & Co, which specialised in the London cattle trade.

The Select Committee began its sittings in April and had completed its work by early July. The principal official witnesses were George Hervey, the Comptroller of the National Debt; Sir George Murray, the Secretary of the Post Office; H.A. Daniell, the Government Broker; and Sir Edward Hamilton, the Assistant Secretary of the Treasury. Their evidence focused on the management of the funds of the two savings banks by the National Debt Commissioners, particularly the possibility of enlarging the scope of investments and the likely outcome of the reduction in interest on government stock. The options for treating the deficiencies in the funds were probed extensively. Although fascinating, much of their evidence was technical, addressing the mechanism of the market for government securities rather than the operation of the savings banks themselves. The first witness to speak for the savings banks was Leonard Tatham, chairman of the Manchester & Salford Savings Bank and of the Trustee Savings Banks Association. His evidence repeated much of what had been said by the savings banks' witnesses at the previous inquiry thirteen years before. He stated explicitly that large savings banks such as that at Manchester depended for their operating costs on the income generated from accounts with large stable balances, and was certain that these accounts would be badly affected by a cut in interest rate. Fed questions by the Chancellor, he outlined the reforms the Association considered desirable, especially the reinstatement of the special investment departments, which any bank with deposits of more than £200,000 should have authority to open. James Fairbairn, secretary of the Norfolk & Norwich Savings Bank, made a radical suggestion that the Savings Bank Fund should be managed by the savings banks themselves or the Inspection Committee. He also wanted powers to sell life assurance on the model of the government annuities that could be purchased through the Post Office.

The Scottish savings banks, none of which had been included in the Association's Parliamentary Committee to attend meetings of the Committee, were represented by the actuary of the Aberdeen Savings Bank, Thomas Jaffrey, and W.B. Malcolm, one of the two accountants of the Savings Bank of Glasgow. They were adamant that deposits with savings banks in Scotland by customers with large accounts were sensitive to interest rates and could be easily lost to joint stock banks when bank rate was high. Jaffrey quoted the example of the winter at the turn of the century when commercial banks in Scotland for some four months paid between 4 and 4.5 per cent on deposit accounts compared with the meagre 2.5 per cent available from the savings banks. During these months the Aberdeen Savings Bank experienced the withdrawal of £73,000, some 6.5 per cent of its deposits. He attributed the fact that the loss had not been greater to the fact that for the majority of customers, who held small deposits, movements in rates, however large, were of no significance. Malcolm stated that during the same months, the Savings Bank of Glasgow had made exceptionally large repayments as customers took advantage of the high rates available on Glasgow Corporation stock. Both Jaffrey and Malcolm were concerned that if the rate paid by the savings banks fell below 2.5 per cent, the outflow of funds in a similar crisis might be much more severe. For the same reasons they were against the Chancellor having power to vary rates annually, preferring a fixed rate. The case for the reforms wanted by the savings banks and the Inspection Committee was ably and eloquently reinforced by Sir Albert Rollit, who himself gave evidence. With the exception of the formation of a superannuation fund, these reforms were largely accepted after a tussle by the Select Committee. However, the Select Committee was not persuaded that a reduction in the rate of interest would badly damage the thrift movement, nor did they see any compelling reason for altering the management and range of investments of the two savings bank funds. They recommended a cut of 0.5 per cent in the rate paid to customers with the Post Office Savings Bank and the savings banks. Shortly after the Committee's findings were published in July 1902, Lord Salisbury resigned as Prime Minister and Sir Michael Hicks Beach stood down as Chancellor, being replaced by Charles Ritchie. As a result no immediate action was taken.

While this debate about further reforms and reducing interest rates was rumbling on, the climate for saving was changing. Total deposits continued to rise between 1896 and 1899, reaching more than £58 million, helped by the slowing to a tiny trickle of closures. Encouragingly, the number of customers climbed by over 100,000 – some 7 per cent. These were boom times for British manufacturing industry, when those in full employment enjoyed the last four years of Victorian prosperity, with an unparalleled growth in opportunities for spending. More new homes were built than at any time for the last fifty years and more people, at least in England, began to buy their own homes by taking out mortgages with building societies. As in the 1880s, shopkeepers in every town and city vied with one another to win custom for furnishings, furniture and fashions, which more and more people could afford. Holiday resorts around the coast experienced an enormous influx of visitors, encouraging the construction of

Leisure activities flourished in the 1890s:
this poster advertises the attractions of Blackpool,
about 1893; and (BELOW) a picnic party of customers
outside a public house in Hulme, 1897, shows that
despite the propaganda of the savings banks and
temperance movements, the public house remained
at the heart of working-class social life.
(RIGHT) Cycling also became very popular during
the late nineteenth century. The bicycle offered
women a cheap and 'respectable' means
of taking exercise.

greater numbers of boarding houses and well-appointed hotels. By the end of the century Blackpool could claim 3 million visitors a year and on the other side of the country Great Yarmouth had some 800,000 visitors, with more than half staying for several days. On holiday and at home there were new and exciting means of entertainment catering for an ever-widening market: music halls, ballrooms, winter gardens, and opulent pavilions. Music halls, with their garish interiors and their variety shows, were the craze throughout the year. Sport, particularly

'Penny Dreadfuls', with their lurid covers and subject matter, tempted
the working man to part with hard-earned cash which might
otherwise have been invested in the savings bank.

football, cricket and boxing, were fast becoming popular entertainment, attracting huge crowds. Race meetings, once the preserve of the very rich, were also drawing record attendances where ordinary people might catch a glimpse of the great and the good. More people were taking part in sport, stimulated by social reformers who had come to appreciate the moral and physical virtues of exercise.

This craze for enjoyment in the late 1890s did not lack critics who objected to the over-indulgence, particularly by those who could barely afford it. They inveighed against the drinking associated with popular entertainment in music halls and condemned the increase in gambling surrounding sport and race meetings. There was a lack of balance in such blanket condemnation, when expenditure on alcoholic drink had reached an estimated £190 million by 1899 – over 8 per cent of a family's budget, while gambling was believed to account for just under £5 million and entertainment less than £20 million. Nevertheless, as far as could be judged, spending was not at the expense of saving. Again it was not only the savings banks which experienced significant gains. The Post Office Savings Bank repeated its success, with deposits advancing from a total of £115 million in 1897 to £135 million at the end of the century. Notwithstanding the doubts cast on the ethos of saving by some progressive commentators, the story was much the same across the whole thrift movement.

Queen Victoria died in January 1901 and was succeeded by her eldest son who became King Edward VII. His accession to the throne heralded a marked change in attitudes away from the stuffy atmosphere of the Victorian world towards a much freer climate in keeping with popular aspirations. It also coincided with a downturn in Britain's economic fortunes due in part to a reduction in public expenditure as the campaign against the Boers in South Africa began to wind down. Taken by surprise, some well-known businesses, like Earle's shipyard and engineering works in Hull, collapsed or were taken over. Unemployment rose and the outlook seemed bleak. The recession halted recovery in savings bank deposits in the first four years of the new century. Although withdrawals exceeded deposits from 1900, turnover did not decline, but continued to rise. In 1905, for the first time, over £13 million was paid in to the savings banks and over £14 million withdrawn, suggesting that, recession or no recession, customers were increasingly using their accounts for short-term deposits to meet expected items of expenditure, such as rent and rates. The number of depositors edged forward. In response to their changing expectations and use of accounts, opening hours were again extended, requiring more staff. The number of women working in the savings banks was growing fast. Gravesend Savings Bank and Gainsborough Savings Bank, for example, had female actuaries. Even the male-dominated Scottish savings banks, with the notable exception of Glasgow, had begun to recruit women – Aberdeen Savings Bank had a female clerk, Forfar Savings Bank a female assistant receiver and Fettercairn Savings Bank a female assistant actuary.

With the recession biting, the Post Office Savings Bank, which had outstripped the savings banks for so long, also began to feel the pinch as depositors found it more difficult to save and large account holders switched to more lucrative investments. Net total deposits with the Post Office Savings Bank slowed in 1900 and became a net outflow in 1903. Contributing to this setback was developing competition from the commercial banks, such as the Nottingham Joint Stock Bank, which began opening savings departments. In the closing decade of the century many small provincial commercial banks had been acquired by large London-based banks. The small banks simply became part of a fast-expanding branch network to cater for the financial needs of a growing middle class. Only in Scotland was there reluctance to open savings departments by the commercial banks, which preferred to leave this side of the business in the capable hands of the savings banks. In addition, local authorities throughout the country began to accept deposits of not less than £10 secured against the rates and yielding 3 per cent interest.

Commercial banks and local authorities on the whole sought only to win the custom of the larger savings bank depositors. They were not interested in the smaller accounts that made up the bulk of the business of both the savings banks and the Post Office Savings Bank. There were other indications that the small saver was experiencing difficulty. Growth in membership of the affiliated orders began to sag. The only element of the thrift movement left relatively unaffected was the steady growth of paid-up policies and premium income of the industrial assurance companies and friendly collecting societies.

Many observers blamed falling savings, not on the economic circumstances, but on extravagant expenditure on entertainment and amusement. In December 1903 the Lord Provost of Glasgow reported that for the first time for many years deposits with the Savings Bank of Glasgow had failed to keep ahead of the interest received from the National Debt Commissioners, which he blamed on extravagant expenditure on 'luxury' and 'amusement'. After blaming the threatened reduction in interest rates, he was of the opinion: 'A reason was also to be found in the fact that for a long period of years the working classes had been accustomed to unexampled, almost unparalleled prosperity, and in that prosperity, continuing year after year, they were apt to forget the rainy day which comes to every individual; and in increased luxury, and perhaps in an undue amount devoted to mere amusement, they were in danger of sapping the best qualities of their manhood.'

The dawn of the more liberal Edwardian age and the twentieth century had had a powerful effect on taste and fashions. The sombre styles of Victoria's later years gave way rapidly to brighter clothes and functional furnishings. The music halls became more risqué and even more popular. There was a gaiety about society which belied the problems of the economy even in the hard-pressed manufacturing cities in the north of England and Scotland. There were many in the savings banks who still firmly believed that for most families thrift was an essential virtue, safeguarding health and happiness. The very poor may have been an exception to this rule, but neither the savings banks nor the Post Office had ever really attracted many deposits from those far down the social scale. In an effort to bolster business, advertising was intensified, and those savings banks which still did not open daily began to do so. However, trustees and actuaries were well aware that until the question of future interest rates was settled and legislation reformed in line with the findings of the Select Committee, it would be difficult to drive home this message. The Chancellor of the Exchequer, Charles Ritchie, had increased the anxiety by promising legislation late in 1902 and again in 1903. It was only when Sir Albert Rollit pressed him in the House of Commons in mid-August 1903 that he admitted that no Bill would be introduced that year. In January 1904, with interest rates stubbornly refusing to fall below 3 per cent, his successor as Chancellor of the Exchequer, Austen Chamberlain, announced that there would be no cut in the rates paid to either the savings banks or the Post Office Savings Bank in the foreseeable future.

With this contentious matter out of the way, Sir Albert Rollit took the initiative and introduced a Bill in February incorporating all the improvements he had proposed as long ago as 1900, particularly legalising special investment departments and the amalgamation of savings banks. Provision was made for the superannuation of officials and compulsory retirement at the age of seventy-five, an issue that had concerned the Inspection Committee since its formation. For the first time, savings banks were allowed to cover the expenses of the annual audit of penny banks. Chamberlain happily supported the measure, himself introducing Treasury amendments to bring the Post Office Savings Bank within its scope. Sir Albert supervised the Bill's progress through the House of Commons without a division at any stage of the proceedings, and it became law in August. The Trustee Savings Banks Association, delighted by this turn of events, circulated a copy of the Bill to every savings bank a month after it was published, with the suggestion that MPs should be lobbied to support it. Its terms finally healed the breech in the Association's ranks, with the Scottish savings banks resuming active participation. Rollit and the Inspection Committee, leaving nothing to chance, wrote to each bank spelling out the reforms affected by the Act and prepared draft rules for the establishment of special investment departments by savings banks with more than £200,000 in their ordinary departments. Their concern was groundless; within a year fifteen banks had successfully applied to open special investment departments and a further sixteen were engaged in negotiations. To head off the challenge from local authorities and commercial banks, Edinburgh, Glasgow, Huddersfield and Leeds savings banks had raised interest rates in their special investment departments. Despite this flurry of activity, the outcome for the year was disappointing with the manufacturing industry in the north and farming still deeply depressed.

Within weeks of the end of the savings bank financial year on 20 November 1905, the Conservative government that had been in power for ten years collapsed, and was replaced by a Liberal administration with Sir Henry Campbell-Bannerman as Prime Minister. No one expected the Liberals to retain power for long, but in a snap general election in January 1906 they won a landslide victory. Although social policy had not been high on the agenda during the campaign, many of the new MPs who supported the government, particularly those from the Labour Party, believed strongly in State intervention to solve problems of poverty, old age and ill-health. One of the final acts of the Conservative government in 1905 had been to appoint a Royal Commission on the Poor Laws and Relief of Distress, the first general inquiry since 1834. A writer in the *Ladies' Field* summed up contemporary Liberal opinion: 'There is nothing ennobling in being poor in England today ... Of all the influences poverty is today the most deadening, affecting not only the body, but the mind and the soul, stunting and depressing them, crushing out ideals, reducing the possibilities of life to a mere question of making both ends meet.' Such attitudes were not universally shared. There were those who still adhered to Samuel Smiles's contention that poverty enriched human experience and were happy to support the notion of less eligibility fundamental to the 1834 Act. A press reporter in the Savings Bank of Glasgow's head office in 1905 observed a shabbily dressed widow making a deposit: 'She can only go on working and fighting till the end with what spirit she can. There is heroism in the conflict, too, all the greater perhaps because it is unremarked by any, and least of all by the poor woman herself.'

Much of the evidence to the Commission confirmed the findings of social investigators such as Charles Booth that, despite a growth of thrift organisations in the last half-century, a large part of the population 'have not the ambition or the ability to establish out of their wages a fund to which they may turn in times of stress, and thus in 1896–1905 we still have a million adult paupers – a larger number than in the period 1871–9'. The Committee was not so naïve to lay the blame solely at the door of improvidence. By examining the statistics, they identified more fundamental explanations, particularly an ageing population as life expectancy became greater, and the emergence of structural unemployment as old industries and crafts declined. It was estimated that the agricultural depression had resulted in the loss of a million acres of farmland since 1894 and a 20 per cent reduction in the workforce. Other industries were identified as being either in retreat or subject to rapid cyclical movements. Consequently, many people, particularly the unskilled, could expect long periods of unemployment. Part of the problem derived from the casual nature of much employment for a specific contract. A large class of unemployables was identified, extending beyond the mentally ill and the alcoholics to include the physically unfit, those who had lost their jobs through changing work practices, and those thought to be too old to work. The Committee concluded that since 1834 'forces have come into operation affecting employment, its regularity, its cessation and expansion, which are quite beyond local control', and called for measures 'more elastic and varied than the simple method which, eighty years ago, was sufficient to cope with able-bodied pauperism in agricultural districts'. There was no talk of thrift as providing a way out of the poverty trap.

By now, well aware that the savings banks did not exist as a bulwark against expenditure on poor rates, the more far-seeing trustees and managers took care to modify their rhetoric without reducing the force of the call to save. Selfishness was to be avoided. Extravagance and unnecessary expenditure, particularly on alcohol and gambling, were identified as the principal threats to a family's financial security, sentiments with which the supporters of the Liberal government would have agreed whole-heartedly and which were corroborated by much of the testimony to the Royal Commission on the Poor Laws. 'A great weight of evidence indicates drink as the most potent and universal factor in bringing about pauperism.' Some witnesses also indicted gambling as a serious and developing cause, but 'gambling, though it wastes the resources of its victims, does not lead to such physical and moral degradation as drink'. The joint actuary of the Savings Bank of Glasgow, Robert Crawford, who had succeeded William Meikle in 1903, explicitly pointed the finger at gambling in his evidence presented in May 1903: 'too many signs are visible that money is spent in ways that are inconsistent with the practice of a reasonable economy. There appears to me to be too large a proportion of the earnings of the people thoughtlessly spent in sport and amusement, and that large sums are misspent in betting by many members of the community.' He went so far as to calculate the following year that there were over 8 million attendances each year at theatres and music halls in Glasgow, whose population was less than 750,000, with a total expenditure of nearly £322,000.

This continuing concern with the apparently growing improvident habits of many families was stimulated by the persistently poor performance of the savings banks even after the question of interest rates and the legality of special investment departments had been settled. The gap between withdrawals and deposits widened sharply in 1907 to over £2 million on a turnover

The TSB Association and friends at Eaton Hall,
near Chester, 1908.

of £15.2 million. Total deposits slipped back and failed to grow faster than the rate of interest in 1908. However, there was no overall decline in the number of depositors. It was scarcely any comfort that the Post Office Savings Bank was still faring little better. There was another contributory factor to the decline in savings. Despite the economic difficulties, the number of new houses built between 1901 and 1907 remained at a high level, causing larger savers to withdraw deposits to buy new furniture. The savings bank movement, however, did not lose confidence in the need to continue to provide an alternative to the Post Office Savings Bank and the commercial banks. Between 1905 and 1909 four new savings banks were opened in Scotland at Hamilton, Bathgate, Kilmarnock and Ayr. In both England and Scotland the

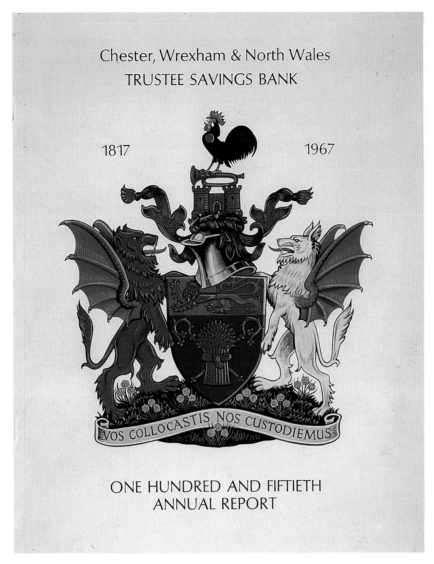

The armorial bearings of the Chester, Wrexham & North Wales TSB,
created by a series of amalgamations beginning in 1906.

larger banks sought to increase their representation by opening new branches, particularly in developing suburban residential areas.

During 1906 the Wrexham Savings Bank was prevented from closing, on the resignation of the actuary, by amalgamation with the Chester Savings Bank, the first amalgamation to be approved under the terms of Sir Albert Rollit's Act. Other banks soon followed this example. In 1909 the West Somerset Savings Bank amalgamated with the Wells Savings Bank, and the Guildford Savings Bank with the Horsham Savings Bank. In the face of adversity, the Trustee Savings Banks Association, now speaking with the authority of the whole movement, was ready to reply to any criticism, turning on the Inspection Committee for censuring certain unnamed banks in their annual reports of 1907 and 1908 for taking general expenses direct from the till without obtaining the specific approval of committees of management. A deputation met Sir Albert Rollit, still the chairman of the Inspection Committee, securing a promise that such allegations would not be made again. To demonstrate good faith, he let the Association representatives have a sight of the draft of the next year's report, which was couched in more positive terms: 'improvements have been effected in matters of administration, and ... much has been done by the Trustees and Managers to meet our views upon various details of management.'

Although there were now clear signs that the worst of the long depression was over, the savings banks were too preoccupied with the Liberal government's unfolding social welfare programme to take much encouragement from the Inspection Committee's endorsement. Early in 1908, Herbert Asquith succeeded Sir Henry Campbell-Bannerman as Prime Minister and appointed the radical Welsh MP David Lloyd George as the Chancellor of the Exchequer. Lloyd George believed passionately that fiscal policy should be used to redistribute wealth from the better-off to the poorest members of society. His first 'war budget', as he dubbed it – introduced in the spring of 1909 – was intended to raise the funds needed 'to wage implacable warfare against poverty and squalidness', tackling the problems identified in the Royal Commission on the Poor Laws. Duty on alcoholic drinks, tobacco and petrol were raised sharply and income tax and death duties set at record levels. The House of Lords rejected the budget and plunged the country into a constitutional crisis. Trustees and managers, in common with the majority of business people, were hostile to the government's plans, suspecting that as social policy became more ambitious it would be small investors who would be forced to shoulder the bulk of the tax burden. Nevertheless, the Liberals won another resounding victory in the general election in January 1910. Undeterred, the Edinburgh Savings Bank planned a national and international gathering at Edinburgh in June to celebrate the centenary of the founding of Henry Duncan's first savings bank at Ruthwell.

The occasion could not have been staged at a more unfortunate time. In late March the elected representatives in the House of Commons took steps to circumscribe the power of the House of Lords to reject Bills which they had introduced. The controversial budget was passed, but the constitutional question remained unresolved. Before any action could be taken, King Edward VII died and was succeeded by his second son, King George V. A constitutional conference was hurriedly summoned, preventing several of the more distinguished guests, including the Archbishop of Canterbury and the Earl of Rosebery, the former Prime Minister, from attending the savings bank celebrations. In a gloomy letter regretting his inability to be present, Rosebery cast a shadow over the proceedings: 'Grinding taxation, and a total disregard for economy in public affairs, offer nothing but discouragement for thrift. Moreover, everything points to further burdens, and nothing to any spirit of saving or retrenchment. In private life, too, luxury and the passion for pleasure disdain thrift ... For thrift is character, the basis of sound national as well as of individual character.' Although such opinions were not uncommon, Sir Albert Rollit was quick to point out that it was possible to view the Liberal government's social policy as a natural outcome of the arguments advanced by Duncan and the founding fathers of the movement. He believed that the payment of old age pensions to those over the age of seventy, far from threatening the savings banks, complemented their activities. The question of State benefits was to dominate British politics and the thrift movement for the next two years.

The constitutional conference collapsed and a further general election was called in November. The Liberals won again but could form a government only with the support of the

The banking hall at Preston Savings Bank's head office in Church Street, 1911; 37,588 people – one third of the borough's population – held accounts with the bank.

Labour Party and the Irish Nationalists. Lloyd George pressed ahead with his welfare programme, which had been modified after complaints from thrift organisations and the greater than anticipated cost of old age pensions, to include a contributory element. The National Insurance Bill was introduced in May 1911, providing contributory schemes for health insurance and the payment of unemployment benefit by those engaged in certain cyclical industries: building, construction, shipbuilding, mechanical engineering, ironfounding, vehicle construction and sawmilling. The National Insurance was to be controlled by the State, but was to be administered by approved organisations, insurance companies, friendly societies and even trade unions. These were authorised to deposit funds with approved bankers, including the Post Office Savings Bank, but not the trustee savings banks. The Bill was published too late to be considered by the Association's annual meeting in May, but immediately aroused a storm of protest from trustees and actuaries. Some attacked the measure as encouraging improvidence. Others, following Sir Albert Rollit's argument, saw it as an opportunity to encourage thrift. All were dismayed that there was no reference to the savings banks. W.A. Barclay, the actuary of the Savings Bank of the County & City of Perth, who had no quarrel with the principle of

A typical savings bank depositor:
Miss Nellie McGill, domestic servant,
at Gullane in 1911.

national insurance, hurriedly prepared a memorandum for consideration by the Association's council in mid-June, in which he called on the Association urgently to seek amendments which would bring the savings banks within the scope of the Bill. He believed this to be vital as he was certain that one outcome of the measure would be that 'a new and very general desire will arise among men to augment the State allowance, which is theirs in certain emergencies, by some extra effort of their own, for they will have the State's assurance that sickness and unemployment, the grim spectres which have hitherto confronted the working man, will not rob them of a penny of their savings'. Once again the Association's council vacillated, only agreeing to refer the matter to its Parliamentary Sub-Committee. As a result the trustee savings banks were omitted from the Act which received the Royal Assent in December.

Although concern remained amongst some trustees that Liberal social policy in the long run would undermine the cause of thrift, prospects for the savings banks had begun to improve in 1910 as the economy recovered. In 1910 total deposits advanced above the rate of interest for the first time since the end of the century, due entirely to a growth in deposits in re-established special investment departments by the larger savers in the bigger banks. In the ordinary department, where all other deposits were held, withdrawals remained persistently above deposits although the gap had narrowed to about £1.2 million on a turnover of just under £15 million. There was scarcely any increase in the number of depositors whose social

After the National Insurance Act in 1911, the voluntary movement
believed that it still had a role to play in moral reform as these before-
and-after photographs show.

composition, as far as can be judged, remained much as before. There was still a large representation of domestic servants encouraged or compelled to invest by their employers, who were advised in popular housekeeping manuals that 'a good servant can save much of her earnings, if she is so disposed'.

An investigation, *How the Labourer Lives: A Study of the Rural Labourer Problem*, by Seebohm Rowntree and May Kendall completed in 1911 concluded:

> On going through the whole of the weekly balance sheets and extracting every item of expenditure upon luxuries, the exceeding slenderness of these outgoings is revealed. We have defined it as including everything apart from food, household sundries, rent, clothing, medicine, and insurances, and we find that the amount spent in this way per week only averages about 6d per family, or $\frac{3}{4}$d per person. If out of this we allow the labourer $3\frac{1}{2}$d for a weekly ounce of

tobacco (a few of us would grudge him what he often seems to look upon as one solace), there is 2½d left to supply the household with newspapers, stamps, books, railway fares – indeed with any kind of luxury or recreation which costs money.

These findings were corroborated for urban Britain by the findings of Maud Pember Reeves's study of working-class life published under the title *Round about a Pound a Week* (1913): 'Experience, however, went to prove that married men in full work who keep their job on such a wage do not and cannot drink. The 1s 6d or 2s which they keep for themselves has to pay for their own clothes, perhaps fares to and from work, smoking and drinking. It does not allow much margin for drunkenness.' The only instance of thrift she could identify was burial insurance, not because families could afford it, but because 'these respectable, hard-working, independent people . . . like to squander money on funerals.' She believed that burial insurance was largely fraudulent and that the poor would have been far better to have invested a penny a week in the Post Office Savings Bank.

From 1911 to 1914 British industry and commerce enjoyed a substantial boom. Wages returned to the levels they had reached in the 1890s and total deposits with the savings banks climbed, exceeding £72 million by 1914. Growth continued to come entirely from the special investment departments, deposits in which rose from £9.7 million in 1909 to over £15.5 million in 1914. In ordinary departments, turnover maintained its upward trend, exceeding £16 million in 1913, but withdrawals were still in advance of deposits with the gap widening once more. This confirmed the impression that for families in continuous employment, savings bank ordinary accounts were being used for current expenditure as much as for long-term saving. Again, the Post Office Savings Bank enjoyed a more marked revival in its fortunes, with an upturn in deposits and a significant advance in the numbers of customers. There was much evidence to suggest Barclay had been right, with the industrial assurance companies and friendly societies now writing a large volume of business and attracting more and more members in the wake of the National Insurance Act. It was also clear that the Liberal government believed that thrift, especially if it encouraged temperate behaviour throughout society, was as much the handmaid of its new social order as it had been of the new Poor Law.

The government went out of its way to give official blessing to school penny banks. In February 1911 Sir John Struthers, Secretary to the Scottish Education Department, wrote to every School Board in Scotland recommending the establishment of penny banks. Taking the hint, the Association at once issued a circular to all the savings banks in the United Kingdom 'pointing out the importance of approaching the respective local Education Committees with a view to Penny Banks being established'. The response was encouraging. Nine savings banks opened school penny banks during the year. By the close of 1912 there were no fewer than 562 penny banks with 138,543 depositors in Liverpool, Manchester and Salford. The Charity Organisation Society (COS), which had been formed in 1869 to rationalise philanthropic endeavour and become a staunch defender of 'self-help', took up the cause, proposing to the

Board of Education in 1913 that 'something in the nature of a National System of Penny Banks' should be established, issuing simple rules for their conduct. The COS wanted thrift to be included as part of the Board's syllabus of work for elementary schools. The Parliamentary Secretary to the Board of Education, Charles Trevelyan, told a deputation from the COS and the savings banks that it was not policy 'to make the establishment of Penny Banks or any other subject compulsory, but that being in agreement with the views expressed by the speakers as to the great value of training children in the habit of thrift, the Board were willing to encourage the development of Penny Banks in the schools in every way short of compulsion.' This reassuring news came hard on the heels of final recognition of the trustee savings banks as approved banks by the National Health Commissioners under the National Insurance Act of 1911.

By 1914 the savings bank movement had good cause to be pleased with its achievements since the appointment of the Select Committee twenty-six years before. The savings banks now operated within a well-defined and almost watertight legal framework. They were policed by an Inspection Committee which, under the able and sympathetic chairmanship of Sir Albert Rollit, had greatly improved standards of management and raised public confidence. The frauds and defalcations that had bedevilled the savings banks were a thing of the past. Such problems as were now revealed by the Inspection Committee were minor irregularities that could easily be put right. Rollit himself had been the architect of new legislation which restored the special investment departments and allowed amalgamations, making it possible for the savings banks to compete for larger customers with the commercial banks and continue to preach the gospel of thrift to the less well off. After the disagreements at the beginning of the century, the Association now represented the whole movement and could speak to governments with a cohesive voice. It was largely thanks to the Association that the movement had found a way of coming to terms with the Liberal government's social programme.

# CHAPTER FIVE

# WELFARE

# OF THE

# WHOLE NATION

## *1914−31*

After the murder, on 28 June 1914, of Archduke Franz Ferdinand, the heir to the Austrian throne, the international money markets were thrown into confusion. By the end of July the London bill market, which kept the financial wheels of Britain's international trade turning, was on the verge of collapse, casting doubts on the future of a number of banking houses. When Austria-Hungary declared war on Serbia on 28 July, panic seized the financial institutions. Alarmed by the speed of events and worried about the safety of their deposits, customers flocked to the clearing banks and the savings banks seeking to withdraw their savings in gold specie. The Bank of England, concerned that in a moment of crisis a run could precipitate the total breakdown of the financial system, ordered that payment should be made in £5 notes and not gold. Anyone who wanted to withdraw a sum smaller than £5 was to be refused. This was a serious mistake, as many people wished to take out only sufficient funds for the forthcoming August bank holiday weekend. Huge queues formed in Threadneedle Street outside the Bank of England of people seeking to convert their notes into gold. In an effort to persuade investors to leave their deposits where they were, the Bank of England doubled interest rates from 4 to 8 per cent.

When Germany declared war on Russia on Saturday 1 August, interest rates were lifted to 10 per cent, which had been reached only once in the nineteenth century at the time of the collapse of the Overend Gurney bank in 1860. All financial institutions were to remain closed after the Monday bank holiday for the remainder of the week while the United Kingdom waited for events to unfold. On the bank holiday, the Treasury granted a moratorium on bill payments to provide relief for the hard-pressed merchant banks and discount houses and in so doing froze a proportion of the assets of the clearing banks. The savings banks were expressly excluded from the moratorium. On the evening of 4 August, Britain declared war on Germany.

The government announced that when the banks reopened on Friday, repayments could be made in Bank of England £1 and 10s notes. The National Debt Office urgently made arrangements for the savings banks to have sufficient notes to meet any foreseeable run, waiving the rule that not more than £10,000 could be withdrawn from a bank in any one day. The Chancellor of the Exchequer, announcing that interest rates would be pulled back to 6 per cent on Friday, appealed to savers not to hoard specie or notes.

As was to be expected, withdrawals from the savings banks were far higher than normal on the Friday and the Saturday, but there was no panic. Up and down the country tellers had been instructed to reassure nervous customers, advising them not to take out more money than they needed for their immediate use. Over the next fortnight there was confusion and anxiety in every home. With Britain's international trade completely dislocated, firms were forced to lay off staff. Consumers, worried about the outcome of the war, stayed away from all except grocery shops. Young men flocked to join the colours. By the end of September, three-quarters of a million had joined up. The government, anxious to prevent a total collapse of the domestic

Depositors queue at the counter of the Liverpool Savings Bank head
office in Bold Street, about 1914.

economy, called a meeting of London storekeepers, asking them not to dismiss staff and to attempt to restore customer confidence with the slogan 'Business as usual'.

By the end of August the savings banks were reporting that deposits and withdrawals were returning to normal. There were still serious problems for those larger banks that operated special investment departments. With bank rate still well above the 3 per cent available from most special investment departments, larger investors could find more profitable outlets for their money. Deposits rapidly fell away and withdrawals accelerated. Because of the dislocation, the savings banks could not rely on the normal mechanisms for covering such shortfalls, the sale of stock exchange securities, calling in of local authority loans, and borrowing temporarily from local branches of commercial banks. In the third week of August the Sheffield Savings Bank approached the National Debt Commissioners inquiring if the special arrangements made for the clearing banks, whereby they were allowed to borrow up to 20 per cent of their balances from the Treasury, could be extended to the savings banks. No response was forthcoming before the local authorities sought the permission of the Local Government Board to declare a moratorium on the repayment of loans on the grounds that deficiencies were expected to arise because ratepayers would be unable to meet rate demands. The Comptroller was sympathetic to the savings banks' position but was unwilling to offer specific help. However, he wrote to all savings banks with special investment departments on 5 September, telling them to write to report any difficulty in meeting withdrawals.

When nothing further was heard for three weeks, the Trustee Savings Banks Association called an emergency session on 29 September. The meeting adjourned to allow two members to call on the Comptroller. Again he refused to provide government assistance because no bank had reported being in difficulties. He did suggest that, as emergency relief had been made available to the local authorities, there was nothing to prevent the savings banks calling in their loans. Dismayed, Robert Thomson, a member of the Association's Council, suggested that the Association should lobby the Chancellor of the Exchequer, Lloyd George, to take over all special investment departments for the duration of hostilities. This radical proposal was rejected and instead the meeting cast about for other ways that savings banks could avoid insolvency. A committee, appointed to review the options, could see no alternative but for savings banks to invest a part of the funds held in their special investment department in government securities. By this time such an outcome was financially practical. With the government borrowing heavily to fund the cost of the war, interest rates had remained high at between 4 and 5 per cent. When the first emergency war loan of some £350 million was issued later in the month, the rate was set at 4 per cent, providing bonds were held to maturity allowing savings banks a comfortable margin for paying the higher interest available in special investment departments. Before the National Debt Commissioners could reach agreement with the Treasury, the imposition of controls on new capital issues on 18 January made it difficult for local authorities to raise loans, effectively robbing the savings banks of their home for special investments.

Shortly afterwards the Commissioners, acting with the Inspection Committee, devised a scheme for the savings banks to purchase Treasury Bills for the duration of hostilities. For legal and technical reasons these were to be held on behalf of individual savings banks by the Bank of England. The Inspection Committee took the opportunity to remind savings banks that they disapproved of investments in 'securities of fluctuating values ... it is difficult to reconcile the promotion of thrift with speculative investments'. Nevertheless, several of the larger savings

Soldiers of the 10th Battalion of the Highland Light Infantry bid
farewell to wives and sweethearts, Glasgow 1914.

banks were forced to borrow heavily from the clearing banks during 1915 to avoid selling such investments at prices considerably below their book value.

The muddled Treasury thinking about the position of the special investment departments was part and parcel of more widespread confusion about the civil conduct of the war. Before the outbreak of hostilities there had been virtually no consideration of how a prolonged campaign might be supported or financed, largely because it was assumed that a European war would be over quickly. When it became apparent that the conflict would be long and intense, demanding a constant supply of men and materiel, the government stepped up recruitment and issued contracts for the mass-production of munitions and equipment. Unemployment was soon a thing of the past as young men joined the services and were replaced by old men and women working for the first time. In factories engaged in war work, jobs were plentiful. The savings banks themselves were not immune. Several banks lost up to half their staff and were able to maintain services only by recruiting those 'disqualified by sex, by age, or otherwise, from military service'. Even then they were forced to rely heavily on the voluntary efforts of trustees and managers who were themselves equally hard-pressed in their own occupations. Sir Albert Rollit appealed in vain to the War Office to make actuaries of savings banks a reserve occupation, with the issue of official badges indicating that staff were engaged 'on service essential to the successful prosecution of the War, although in a civil and not a military capacity'.

With no government policy to control inflation, prices advanced sharply. Nevertheless, many households found themselves much better off than before; for, as a result of improved employment, prospects, wage rates and family income grew more rapidly than prices. Neither the savings banks nor the Post Office Savings Bank reaped any benefit from this renewed affluence. Deposits in both the ordinary and special investment departments of the savings banks which had fallen in the opening months of the war, failed to be replenished at an equivalent rate when withdrawals began to stabilise in November. One of the reasons was that poorer families used their new-found prosperity to buy goods that had been beyond their purchasing powers before the war. These were not necessarily luxuries, but better food – more fruit and vegetables, and eggs – and new clothes. For those who had been in the habit of saving before the war, failure to resume deposits was undoubtedly due to the attractive rate of return and inducements available on the first war loan. Although the loan had been directed towards institutions and larger investors, the annual return of 3.5 per cent was insufficient. Anxious not to see the government left in the lurch, the Bank of England offered to pay the full issue value of the loan to any investor at 1 per cent below bank rate at any time in the next three years. Many small investors, spotting the advantage of this offer, combined with an interest rate of 3.5 per cent, subscribed – guaranteeing the loan's success. The savings banks protested that they might have attracted some of these funds if the limits on deposits had been waived for the duration of the hostilities. This would have the advantage of adding directly to the Chancellor's war chest at a lower rate of interest. In the spring of 1915 John Mallaband, actuary of the Sheffield Savings Bank and a member of Council of the Trustee Savings Banks Association, wrote to the Chancellor of the Exchequer pointing out 'that the present limits of deposits fixed twenty-two years ago are out of all proportion to the present wages of working men'. He suggested that lifting the limits would be one of the best ways of raising money for the war, as, in his opinion, most savers preferred the security of 2.5 per cent deposits to investing in 3.5 per cent stock. There was no response.

In May Lloyd George was appointed Minister of Munitions with oversight of all war production and was replaced as Chancellor by Reginald McKenna. The Trustee Savings Banks Association immediately took up the petition for a removal of the limits along with the prohibition on holding accounts in both the savings banks and the Post Office Savings Bank. Like his predecessor McKenna turned a deaf ear and pressed ahead with the issue of a second war loan of £600 million bearing interest at 4.5 per cent, available in multiples of £100. Flying in the face of the arguments of Mallaband, this loan was to be directed specifically at the private investor, particularly women. Highly emotive advertising called on people at home to support the men at the front with their money. The publicity campaign, with its appeal to patriots, persuaded many of the larger savings bank depositors that it was their duty to subscribe. Hard-pressed staff had to work long hours to process the volume of applications. By the time the loan was fully subscribed on 10 July, £4.2 million had been invested by savings banks through their government stock departments and £15.9 million by the Post Office Savings Bank. In addition there had been heavy withdrawals for direct investment in the loan. While the issue was progressing, there was a clear indication that the government now recognised the important contribution the thrift movement could make in a prolonged and expensive campaign. At the start of July the Board of Education wrote to all Local Education Authorities in England and Wales, encouraging the establishment of penny banks in schools to mobilise funds for the war effort and advising them that both the savings banks and the Post Office Savings Bank could be called on for advice and assistance. The savings banks responded enthusiastically, supplying the requisite books and stationery free of cost and providing guidance on the management of school penny banks and their place in the curriculum. There was also government support for wider initiatives to develop State Collecting Savings Banks in more populous districts by savings banks and other organisations involved in the thrift movement. McKenna, however, was convinced that savings in whatever form could not meet the mounting cost of the war. In his first budget he raised direct taxation and enlarged the tax net by lowering the threshold to £30. The taxation of manual wage earners was introduced through a quarterly assessment. However, as the majority of the population still did not pay any tax, he did not lose sight of the importance of thrift, unlike some sceptics who with the editor of *Drapers Record* believed that: 'If trade is to be maintained at a satisfactory level, if unemployment is to be prevented, money must circulate. To store food excessively is recognised as harmful to the community; to store money with abnormal care is almost as bad.'

Disregarding such advice, McKenna proposed in November the issue of £1 War Loan Bonds at 5 per cent to be redeemed in three years. As the savings banks were quick to point out, no interest was to be paid for the first six months. The Chancellor, unsure as to how best to launch the stock, appointed early in December 1915 a committee on War Loans for the Small Investors chaired by Edwin Montagu, the Chancellor of the Duchy of Lancaster. The committee included Lord Cunliffe, the Governor of the Bank of England, John Bradbury, joint permanent secretary to the Treasury, Stanley Baldwin, and several other MPs. The savings banks were represented by Alexander Cargill, the actuary of the Edinburgh Savings Bank. The committee was instructed to report as rapidly as possible. The Trustee Savings Banks Association met once again in emergency session two days before Christmas, setting out a number of options for increasing deposits, the removal of limits on accounts; higher interest rates; extending penny banks, particularly in schools; house-to-house collections, using the model of the insurance companies; popularising investment in war loans through all types of saving institutions; and establishing saving societies in factories and churches. Within days the Montagu Committee had presented an interim report recommending the removal of the ceiling on deposits with savings banks and the issue of exchequer bonds in denominations of £5 and more which would be made available through the Post Office Savings Bank. McKenna accepted these early conclusions and put them into effect on New Year's Eve. The speed of his action was a response to growing evidence of a High Street boom as families spent rather than saved their higher wartime incomes. Encouraged by the Chancellor's decision, the Trustee Savings Banks Association immediately refined its proposals into a 'Scheme for Raising Money for War Purposes and the Best Method of Ensuring its Success amongst the Working Classes'. This was forwarded to the Montagu Committee along with a request that savings banks should also be brought within the scope of the new War Loan. On 6 January the Comptroller-General of the National Debt Commissioners replied to the secretary of the Association expressing anxiety about the likely effect of the £1 War Loan on the savings banks 'as should it result in a large withdrawal of deposits it may have serious effects on the margin available for management expenses'. In the meantime the savings banks acted immediately to inform their customers that the limits on deposits had been removed.

The final report of the Montagu Committee was published on 26 January 1916, with four further recommendations: the organisation of voluntary savings associations in every part of the country; the issue to such associations of Treasury Bills (National Savings Certificates) in smaller denominations than £1,000; the introduction of an instalment scheme for buying £1 War Savings Deposits through the Post Office Savings Bank; and the appointment of committees to co-ordinate propaganda campaigns and devise model schemes. The Committee gave pride of place to the need to assure small savers that investments would not fall in value and that they could be withdrawn on demand. They emphasised the necessity of savings to reduce 'consumption by all classes' as the government's chosen weapon against the inflationary pressures in the economy caused by high expenditure on war materiel. Despite their conclusions, the Committee doubted if this strategy would work. Like many commentators since the eighteenth century, the members were not convinced that the poorest sections of society had money to save even with higher wartime wages and enlarged employment opportunities for women, boys, and elderly men. They would have preferred the government to have paid for much of the cost of the war by pushing income tax even higher. The savings banks were incensed that the Committee had specifically rejected raising their interest rates to 5 per cent in line with the new War Loans on the expedient grounds that it would impose a heavy charge upon the taxpayer. They were also annoyed that, unlike the Post Office Savings Bank, the savings banks were to receive no extra expenses for sales of war bonds which were in heavy demand – placing intolerable strain on their already slender management resources.

McKenna, ignoring the Montagu Committee's misgivings about the thrust of his policy, appointed two national committees in February 1916: the National Organising Committee for War Savings and the Central Advisory Committee for War Savers. The responsibility of the National Organising Committee was to oversee the establishment of the voluntary War Savings Associations, and that of the Central Advisory Committee to provide an independent panel of experts to mediate between the Treasury and the Associations. Neither committee contained any representatives from the savings banks. The first action of the committees was to attack the continuing consumer boom by a massive propaganda campaign urging self-denial and denouncing extravagance. At the beginning of March a public meeting was held in the Guildhall in London, addressed by the Chancellor of the Exchequer and Lord Kitchener, Minister of War, to launch a campaign to establish local committees in every part of the country. The response was encouraging, with men and women from all walks of life offering to help. By April it had become apparent that the work of the two committees could not readily be separated and they were amalgamated to form the National War Savings Committee. When the committee reported at the end of the first year in March 1917, 800 War Savings Committees had been established and 26,500 separate War Savings Associations in schools, churches, the armed services, commercial offices and factories. They were kept abreast of events by the National Committee through the columns of its official bulletin, the appropriately named *Silver Bullet*. By the end of December 1916 they could claim to have been responsible for raising almost £42 million through the sale of War Savings Certificates (originally War Savings Deposits). Although trustees and actuaries in many parts of the country had agreed to serve on local War Savings Committees and played an active role in the management of Associations, this first report omitted to make reference to the savings banks.

Throughout 1916 the savings banks had been irritated by the government's attitude, particularly by the refusal to bring interest rates into line with those available on government securities and even on building society deposits. However, despite the concern that savers would switch their investments into the higher-yielding War Loan, deposits in the ordinary and special investment departments as well as government stock department increased during 1916. The Inspection Committee was delighted with this achievement in a year when the consumer boom had continued unchecked, believing that it reflected 'the increased earning capacity of the working classes, the growth of habits of saving among them and unabated confidence in the Savings Banks'. The heavier workload of the staff in most savings banks, caused by the departure of men to join the forces, and the transfer of deposits into War Savings Certificates, led the Inspection Committee to call for greater efficiency through amalgamation. During the year the York Savings Bank took the savings banks at Retford and Worksop under its wing and the London Savings Bank was formed through the amalgamation of the four

The Lambeth Savings Bank, 1915. The following year, it amalgamated
with the London Savings Bank.

existing banks in the capital. Encouraged, the Inspection Committee suggested that all the
savings banks in each county should be brought together 'where this unit of local government
provides a convenient basis of organisation'.

This suggestion was almost certainly designed to meet any possible threat from the formation
of local authority savings banks as part of the war savings campaign. In April 1916 the Lord
Mayor of Birmingham, Neville Chamberlain, had put forward a plan, backed by the council,
to establish a municipal savings bank in the absence of a savings bank in the city since 1864.
Conceived as integral to the war savings campaign, deposits were to come largely from voluntary
deductions from individuals' income at source (a progenitor of Save As You Earn schemes) and
were to be invested with the government at 3.5 per cent. The Treasury raised no objections
and a Bill was introduced into Parliament to allow any local authority with a population of
more than 50,000 to set up a municipal bank. The clearing banks objected vehemently and the
measure was defeated, but Chamberlain was not to be thwarted. After an intense campaign and
detailed discussions with the National War Savings Committee, he secured the passing of the
much more limited Municipal Savings Bank (War Loan Investment) Act in August. This
restricted the formation of banks to municipal boroughs with a population of over 250,000.

Deposits could be received from employees only through employers and there was a limit of £200 on each account; 80 per cent of deposits was to be invested in Treasury bills or advances through the National Debt Commissioners; all banks formed under the Act were to be wound up three months after the end of hostilities. By the end of September, Chamberlain had launched the Birmingham Municipal Savings Bank, with the enthusiastic J.P. Hilton as its first manager. It got off to a slow start, attracting just £18,000 in deposits before the end of the year.

Any expectation that the success of the savings banks in 1916 could be repeated in the coming year was dashed when Andrew Bonar Law, who had succeeded McKenna as Chancellor of the Exchequer at the close of the year, launched the third War Loan on 11 January. This was divided into two parts: the first bearing 5 per cent interest was subject to tax, and the second tax free yielded 4 per cent. The Treasury at once called on the whole financial community to collaborate in an enormous publicity drive. For the first time, the savings banks were formally

The increasing role of women in industry, and their greater earning power,
made them natural targets for appeals such as this one, from 1918.

The centenary dinner – no expense spared –
at the Cork Savings Bank in 1917.

invited to assist in raising a staggering £9 billion by 16 February. Throughout the country savings bank staff worked far into the night and at weekends to process applications from depositors either to buy stock or convert existing holdings into the new loan. Altogether savings bank customers subscribed over £9.5 million directly through stock departments. Although part of this sum was withdrawn from accounts, a large proportion represented new investments which would probably otherwise have found its way into special investment departments. The savings banks again renewed their demand for financial help in dealing with the volume of business, but to no avail. However, the National Debt Office wrote to all the savings banks informing them that their staff were engaged in work of national importance and could, therefore, be exempted by Military Tribunals from military service. By the end of the year total deposits in both the ordinary and special investment departments had fallen back, but by less than the new investments in government stock. The fact that savings bank deposits had held up delighted the movement, which celebrated the centenary of the passing of George Rose's Act in 1817 at a reception at the Mansion House in London at the end of October.

With the German unrestricted U-boat campaign threatening the United Kingdom's vital supplies of food and materials, the government appealed not just for households to save money but also to show restraint in the consumption of food and of anything else that could conceivably be used to help prosecute the war. The National War Savings Committee, the principal vehicle for the economy campaign, met with an enthusiastic response to calls to stamp out waste. To

Tank Week in York, February 1918, when £1.5 million was invested
in war savings by the city's inhabitants.

the alarm of the Inspection Committee some savings bank clerks were over-zealous in their search for old papers, even passing for salvage ledgers that were no more than twenty years old. During 1918 the Treasury raised no further War Loans, relying instead on the sale of National War Bonds, which were heavily promoted by the National War Savings Committee and local associations. This, combined with a slackening in interest rates, attracted funds into the savings banks from men and women enjoying unprecedentedly high wages driven up by wartime inflation. Deposits with ordinary departments soared by a record £8.5 million, some 16 per cent, to reach nearly £61 million. The Post Office Savings Bank experienced an equivalent gain. Even the National War Savings Committee conceded that the advance of almost £89 million in deposits from the savings banks and the Post Office Savings Bank made a substantial contribution from the small investor to the war effort. With income tax at record levels, this was a notable achievement, suggesting that the Montagu Committee had been wrong in doubting the willingness of the poorer sections of society to save something out of their increased wartime income. Reluctantly, in February 1918, the Treasury, through the National Debt Commissioners, decided to provide some compensation to the savings banks for the costs involved in issuing War Loan and other emergency stock.

This welcome decision could do nothing to prevent further loss of staff as even more men were recruited for the spring offensive which, it was hoped, would terminate the war. At the end of May the Association expressed its grave concern in an open letter to the National Debt

Commissioners 'at the serious position in which the Banks stand owing to the heavy and continuing depletion of their staff for military service and the lack of any form of Government protection'. Although savings bank actuaries were specifically excluded from military service, there were complaints from different parts of the country that they were frequently called before Military Tribunals to be cross-questioned, amounting at times to harassment.

By the spring of 1918 the government was beginning to look beyond the war to the peace; towards the reconstruction of the whole economy. Keen to maintain confidence in the savings bank movement as a useful tool of economic management, the Treasury took action to resolve the problems encountered by special investment departments at the beginning of hostilities.

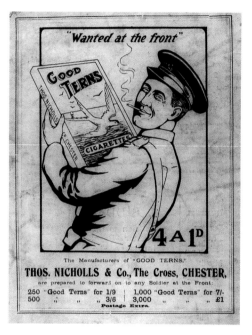

Hundreds of thousands of servicemen were introduced to the habit of cigarette smoking during the war, receiving free supplies from well-wishing civilians. Smoking was deplored by savings bank officials as harmful to health and wealth.

After protracted negotiations with the banks operating special investment departments, legislation was passed in April 1918. This brought all special investment departments directly under the control of the National Debt Commissioners, from whom permission had to be obtained before making or realising an investment. To prevent the liquidity problems that affected savings banks with special investment departments in the opening months of hostilities, it was no longer possible for savings banks to invest in securities that matured in more than one year, unless there was a clause allowing them to be called in at six months' notice. This provision was acceptable to local authorities and public utilities – the principal place of investment of most special investment department deposits. All investments had to be valued in balance sheets

To the annoyance of the savings banks, servicemen were encouraged
to cash in their savings certificates issued on demobilisation at the
Post Office. Staff there were not always willing or able to transfer
money to trustee savings bank accounts.

at current prices rather than their book value. A guarantee fund to meet any deficit was also established from the reserves of all banks with special investment departments along with those of banks that had closed. By securing the position of the special investment departments, the Act ensured that the savings banks would be able to continue to attract and retain deposits from their larger customers, particularly at times when interest rates were high.

Three days after the Armistice was signed on 11 November 1918, the Association convened a special meeting to consider the future of savings banks in peacetime. Spencer Portal, the architect and chairman of the amalgamated London Savings Bank, criticised the banks for their failure in the past to co-operate with one another. His views were supported by W.C. Jackson,

'When the boys come home, we are not going to keep you on any longer, girls.' After the war, many women lost their jobs in Britain's factories and workshops to make way for returning servicemen.

one of his deputy chairmen, who advocated area committees, not dissimilar to the county savings banks suggested in the midst of the war by the Inspection Committee. This idea was readily accepted and at the end of January five regional committees were formed. George Anderson, the honorary secretary, wrote to all savings banks explaining the Association's firm conviction that 'the experience of the War Years, and the great campaign of economy and thrift which has made such a striking appeal to the loyalty and prudence of all classes, will greatly increase the extent and value of Savings Bank work in future years.' The secretaries of the new committees numbered some of the most far-sighted actuaries with a clear vision of how the movement might develop, including W. Louis Lawton of the York County Savings Bank, W.A. Barclay of the County & City of Perth Savings Bank and R.A. Drean of the Belfast Savings Bank. The new structure was no sooner in place than the savings banks learned that the War Savings Committee was to become a permanent National Savings Committee. At the end of May it was used as a vehicle for launching a 4 per cent Victory Loan of over £750 million. The savings banks were infuriated when the Post Office Savings Bank pleaded lack of staff as an excuse for failing to transfer to the savings banks war gratuities paid to demobilised servicemen who were their customers. As a result 3.5 million new Post Office Savings Bank accounts were opened with £56 million at their credit.

In planning their future role, the secretaries of the new regional committees were well aware that changing attitudes to thrift were just one of the consequences of the profound effect of the war on the fabric of British society. By the Armistice nearly three-quarters of a million men, mostly in their late teens or early twenties, had been killed. There were few families in which someone had not died or been left disabled. Nevertheless, those who survived the front or who had toiled long hours in munitions factories expected material rewards for victory: better housing, a higher standard of living, secure employment, and improved State social provisions. Lloyd George, the Prime Minister, predicted, in a speech delivered thirteen days after the Armistice, that the task was now 'to make a fit country for heroes to live in'. Such expectations in the immediate aftermath of war were not easily fulfilled. Men returning from the front naturally counted on returning to their old jobs, many of which had been taken over by women, men too old to fight and boys. Most of these were laid off in the immediate aftermath of the war. Tensions in British society in this difficult period of re-adjustment were evident in race riots over coloured immigrants and industrial disputes. Local authorities were persuaded that they had an important part to play in improving living conditions by constructing new homes. Such a policy required large-scale finance which some authorities believed could be raised by establishing savings banks.

In June 1919 Birmingham City Council sought Parliamentary sanction for the conversion of their wartime municipal bank into a permanent bank for this purpose. Since its foundation in 1916, the bank had been outstandingly successful. Riding on the back of the war savings campaign, the bank had attracted over £600,000 in deposits and had made repayments of £295,000. Under the terms of the Birmingham Corporation Act (1919) the council was allowed to continue to operate a savings bank, using deposits for its own purposes or investing them in securities approved by the Treasury. The Birmingham Municipal Bank was authorised to inaugurate a housing department to make advances to depositors for house purchase. There was concern that other local authorities, keen to raise funds for building homes under the recently introduced Housing & Town Planning Act, would seek similar legislation. Already Glasgow Corporation had approached the Savings Bank of Glasgow, proposing that they should collaborate in asking permission for the bank to be converted into a Municipal Savings Bank. The Savings Bank of Glasgow reacted sharply, telling the Corporation that as part of the savings bank network it was impossible to take such unilateral action. There was no response until the spring of 1920 after a speech by the Prime Minister, Lloyd George, at a national conference on housing finance in which he encouraged the formation of municipal banks. Before meeting members of the Corporation, James Munro, the Glasgow actuary, sounded out the Association whose members were in no doubt that nothing should be done to disturb the relationship between the savings bank and the State. No other local authorities were prepared to draft a Bill, but three Scottish burghs – Kirkintilloch, Irvine and Clydebank – registered savings banks under the Companies Act.

Despite all the obstacles, the confidence of savings bank customers was maintained and deposits soared. Total investments with ordinary departments jumped in three years by a further £14 million to reach £75 million in 1921 and in special investment departments from under £15 million to over £19 million. This striking accomplishment did not blind the eyes of the

Staff at their stations in the York Savings Bank, about 1920.

more perceptive actuaries to the necessity of continuing to press for the rationalisation of the savings bank structure. A meeting was held in Derby in May 1919 at which W. Louis Lawton strongly recommended amalgamation: 'The past year provided more valuable experience of the great advantages to the smaller savings banks of amalgamations, with, as a rule, the nearest Savings Bank having a Special Investment Department.' In full agreement, the Inspection Committee wrote in May to all the savings banks extolling the benefits of amalgamation and offering advice and support in any negotiations. Some savings banks did not require encouragement. The following day the Southampton and Guildford Savings Banks joined the London Savings Bank. Others were prompted into action by the Inspection Committee's letter. Towards the end of the savings bank year in November 1919, the small savings bank at Stanhope in Co. Durham amalgamated on the death of its actuary with the large Newcastle Savings

Bank. During 1920 the Newcastle Savings Bank also acquired the Middleton-in-Teesdale Savings Bank. At the same time the Brighton Savings Bank, which had merged with the London Savings Bank in 1917, seceded and joined the Midhurst Savings Bank. A large amalgamation was completed in May 1921 when the savings banks at Boston, Horncastle, Louth, Sleaford and Spalding in Lincolnshire joined to form the Boston & District Savings Bank. With these examples, no small savings bank now needed to close its doors when it became difficult to find men willing to serve as trustees or actuaries.

Although no one questioned the advantages of mergers, there were problems, particularly for the staff. Some jobs became redundant and there was competition for senior posts in the new banks. Until the end of the First World War, the staff of the savings banks, and joint stock banks for that matter, had no formal organisation to represent them in meetings with employers. Before the outbreak of war, it had been possible for anyone who worked in the savings banks to discover what employees of other banks earned as the salaries of every single member of staff down to messengers and junior clerks had been published since 1859 in the annual Return of Trustee Savings Banks to Parliament. Salaries of full-time senior officers in the larger banks were roughly comparable and competitive. The junior staff, like those in the joint stock banks, were not well paid, earning between £50 and £250 a year. In the immediate aftermath of the war, staff were unsettled, not only by the threat of mergers but more generally by the return of servicemen to resume their peacetime duties and the departure of some of those recruited during the war. For those who had been away some of the work was unfamiliar as the banks now dealt in a great deal more government stock than before the war. Worryingly for those committed to a career in the savings bank or the commercial banks, salaries had been seriously eroded by wartime inflation. During 1919 staff of the joint stock banks formed the Bank Officers' Guild and the Scottish Bankers' Association to negotiate salaries and conditions of service at a time when there was much talk of amalgamation in the commercial sector. Savings bank staff were invited to join. By the midsummer of 1920 clerks in most of the larger savings banks had joined one or other of the organisations. Although both the joint stock banks and the savings banks agreed that wages should be raised, they were reluctant to recognise the new unions. Adopting the attitude that they were not on the same footing as commercial banks, the savings banks refused to participate in discussions. When talks in Scotland appeared deadlocked in June 1920, a strike ballot was taken which came to nothing. However, it did have the effect of hardening the resolve of the Trustee Savings Banks Association to seek higher management expenses from the National Debt Commissioners and also to introduce uniform superannuation and life insurance schemes.

A one-eighth of a per cent rise in interest for management purposes was sanctioned by the Savings Bank Act of May 1920, which allowed the salaries of junior clerks to be raised immediately. Under its terms, all limits on deposits in all savings bank departments were removed until six months after the 'official' end of the war – an arbitrary date to be selected by

The Savings Bank of the County & City of Perth published an
attractive colour brochure after the First World War, describing the
luxuries the saver might one day afford.

the Chancellor of the Exchequer. In addition the Act made the National War Savings and Scottish War Savings Committees permanent, changing their titles to the National Savings and Scottish Savings Committees. In anticipation of this decision the National Committee was overhauled to include six representatives elected by the National Savings Assembly which, in turn, was composed of representatives elected by the local savings committees. The Post Office Savings Bank, the Trustee Savings Banks and the National Union of Teachers, because of their members' vital role in managing penny banks, were also offered seats on the committee. George Anderson, actuary of the Preston Savings Bank and a member of the Council of the Association, became the savings banks' first representative.

The conversion of the wartime savings campaign to peacetime purposes was just an element in the Treasury's policy of cooling down the economy. While the measure was making its way through Parliament, the Chancellor of the Exchequer had intervened directly to discourage expenditure and encourage saving by raising the Treasury Bill Rate and consequently bank rate to 7 per cent. Such a tough stance was urgently needed to push up prices so as to dampen consumer demand, which despite the continued high levels of savings was booming as goods came back into the shops after the wartime austerity. Rates on National Savings Certificates remained unaltered at 5 per cent to the annoyance of some savings banks which would have liked the government to bring the rate payable on ordinary deposits more or less into line. The Council of the Association were reluctant to press the matter on the spurious grounds that £54 million out of the £75 million total ordinary department deposits had been lodged before the war when interest rates had been generally lower: 'It would appear, therefore, that any advance of interest given at present would be largely at the expense of the general taxpayer.' With sales of National Savings Certificates of nearly £45 million in 1920 many savings banks refused to be fobbed off in this fashion and in February 1922 forced a resolution on the Association regarding the 'National Savings movement as at present conducted as being inimical to the interests of the savings banks.' At the beginning of the following month the Chancellor of the Exchequer officially declared that the war had ended. Under the terms of the 1920 Act, a limit of £500 a year was imposed on deposits in ordinary departments, but no overall ceiling. However, total deposits in special investment departments were pegged at £500.

The response of the larger savings banks with special investment departments to competition from National Savings Certificates was to take advantage of the high prevailing interest rates to lift the rate paid to depositors during 1920. The economic boom that had followed the war came to an abrupt end in the autumn. Throughout Britain men and women engaged in manufacturing industry were laid off in large numbers, straining the national insurance scheme to the limits. Orders for everything from Atlantic liners to clothes were cancelled or postponed. The situation in the countryside was equally grim with the government unable to honour a wartime commitment to compensate farmers if prices fell below certain stipulated levels, which they began to do as cheap imports from the United States and Australia resumed. As in the late nineteenth century falling food and commodity prices left families with members in employment better off. Real wages remained well above their pre-war levels. Even for those out of work there was now social provision available from the State to cushion them from the worst. Fulfilling the government's deflationary policy, those who could afford to, chose to save rather than spend. Consequently the recession had almost no perceptible effect on thrift organisations, whose appeal remained principally to skilled workers, to those employed in clerical jobs and to domestic servants. A real decline in total ordinary department deposits of the savings banks from about £75 million to £73 million in 1921 was partly compensated for by a marked advance in takings in special investment departments from £16 to £19 million. The number of depositors, which had climbed to a record 2.25 million the year before, fell back by 30,000. The Post Office Savings Bank, without the benefit of a special investment department and with a far greater number of small savers, was less fortunate. Deposits declined and the number of account holders fell by more than 2 million – over 16 per cent.

With savings bank customers having over £30 million invested in government stock at the end of the year, the Association was bitterly disappointed not to be represented on a departmental committee appointed by the Chancellor of the Exchequer in November 1922 to investigate the sale of savings certificates and the relations between the National Savings Committee, the Scottish Savings Committee, the Post Office, the Post Office Savings Bank and the Trustee Savings Banks. The Association, however, was invited to give evidence. Sir Thomas Jaffrey, the actuary of the Aberdeen Savings Bank, and Walter Cobbett, chairman of the Manchester & Salford Savings Bank, were nominated to appear before the Committee. They argued that the whole national savings scheme had been misconceived, drawing funds from the better-off, because of the competitive interest rates and exemption from income tax rather than winning the support of small savers. Jaffrey claimed that out of the 575 million National Savings Certificates sold, only 50 million or so had been bought by small investors. He explained to the Committee that there had never been any competition between the Trustee Savings Banks and the Post Office Savings Bank. They both suggested that the national savings campaign would have been far more effective if the effort had been channelled through the savings banks and the Post Office Savings Bank and on this basis called for the abolition of the National Savings Committee. The only flaw in their testimony was Cobbett's assertion that even with the higher rates available on savings certificates, deposits in savings banks' ordinary and special investment departments had 'continued to increase in a very satisfactory manner'.

The Committee was not convinced by Jaffrey's assertions. After careful scrutiny of the sale of certificates, they were able to show that well over half had been bought in units of less than £25, and £132 million in £1 certificates. This discovery called the whole of the Association's evidence into question, leading the Committee to conclude that neither Jaffrey nor Cobbett had much knowledge of the work of the Savings Associations. The Committee went on to conclude that far from being abolished, the National Savings Committee should be strengthened, developing its publicity machinery further to promote thrift, particularly through the establishment of school penny banks in association with the Post Office Savings Bank. Since branches of the Trustee Savings Banks were local and concentrated in urban areas in the north of England and Scotland, the Committee could identify no role for the Association at a national level. Picking up Cobbett's observation that deposits with the savings banks remained buoyant, they were certain there was no competition from savings certificates. However, greater co-operation between Local Savings Committees and branches of the Trustee Savings Banks was recommended in order to promote thrift by whatever means.

Even before the report was published, the savings banks had sensed trouble ahead when it had been rumoured early in March that a £500 limit on total investments in both the ordinary and special investment departments was about to be imposed. There was relief when James Munro and Sir Thomas Jaffrey wrung a concession from the National Debt Office that the limit would apply only to ordinary departments. The Association's publicity committee, appointed twelve months before, hurriedly set about shaping the movement's national identity by adopting a 'universal emblem' that would be used by all Trustee Savings Banks on all their

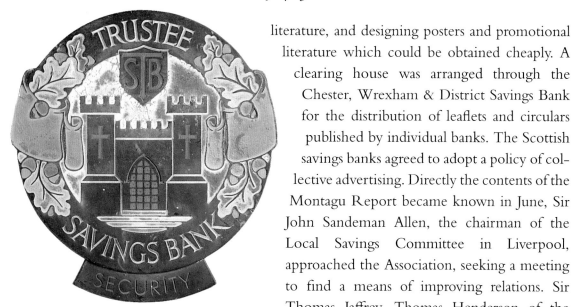

The Keep motif designed by the Association's publicity committee for use throughout the movement; and (BELOW RIGHT) the famous key symbol and slogan of the Birmingham Municipal Bank.

literature, and designing posters and promotional literature which could be obtained cheaply. A clearing house was arranged through the Chester, Wrexham & District Savings Bank for the distribution of leaflets and circulars published by individual banks. The Scottish savings banks agreed to adopt a policy of collective advertising. Directly the contents of the Montagu Report became known in June, Sir John Sandeman Allen, the chairman of the Local Savings Committee in Liverpool, approached the Association, seeking a meeting to find a means of improving relations. Sir Thomas Jaffrey, Thomas Henderson of the Savings Bank of Glasgow, and four officials of the Association were nominated to open negotiations. Despite some disagreement about the role of the penny banks, these progressed well.

Any hope of reaching an agreement was quashed in late September when Jaffrey attacked savings certificates in an interview with the *Aberdeen Journal*, repeating much of what he had said in his evidence. The National Savings Committee was deeply offended and Jaffrey's apology that he had no intention of causing offence seemed less than genuine. After an exchange of hard words on either side, negotiations came to a halt not entirely to the regret of some savings banks, which were annoyed by the attempts of Local Savings Committees to substitute savings associations for penny banks in schools. Attempts were made to get them restarted, including a meeting between Sir William Schooling, a vice-chairman of the National Savings Committee, and Jaffrey. Despite every encouragement, Jaffrey refused to concede that his opinion of the merits of the National Savings Certificates was erroneous.

By this time the attention of the savings bank movement had switched towards another potential threat to their future livelihood – the opening of additional municipal banks on the Birmingham model. The concept of municipal banks as a means of raising funds for local development, particularly housing, had been gaining ground since the end of the war, especially amongst the ranks of the more radical members of the fast-expanding Labour Party. Even on the left there were those who counselled caution, pointing out that depositors would expect repayment on demand, which would prove difficult at times of economic crisis if capital was locked in property

and other fixed assets. It was for this reason that in mid-May 1922, Glasgow Corporation had thrown out a motion from the Labour group to establish a municipal bank in the city. Both Bristol and Swansea tried unsuccessfully to obtain Parliamentary authority for banks. During 1923 Labour MPs introduced a Bill similar to the emergency wartime legislation which would allow any town with more than 150,000 inhabitants to open a bank. The proposal was rejected. Despite pressure from some Members, when Labour briefly came to power the following year, the Bill was not re-introduced. During 1924 another Scottish local authority, the burgh of Motherwell and Wishaw, set up a bank under the Companies Act. Unsettled by these developments, the Association half-heartedly toyed with the idea of mustering support to re-establish the Bristol Savings Bank and to open others in southern England where the movement had been under-represented since the closures in the 1890s.

The savings banks were able to debate the issue from a position of growing strength. Although the economy made only a faltering recovery between 1923 and 1924, deposits with the savings banks advanced faster than the rate of interest. The biggest gains were in the ordinary departments, with special investment and stock departments marking time. The number of customers also edged forward. Turnover fell back from its record level of over £39 million in 1920 to about £34 million, still well above the pre-war levels, suggesting that more and more customers were using the savings banks as safe places of deposit for their incomes, which could be withdrawn at any time to meet their daily needs. Throughout the country trustees and actuaries were surprised and delighted with this achievement. Everywhere the banks were at pains to point to the scale of lending to local authorities, meeting the challenge of municipal banking head-on. John Watson told the customers of the Hull Savings Bank that depositing with a special investment department gave 'everyone an opportunity of having a stake in the country'. He believed the banks 'to be a great bulwark against anarchy'. The movement was heartened by the active encouragement of Philip Snowden, the Labour Chancellor of the Exchequer who was deeply committed to financial orthodoxy. In June 1924 he wrote to the banks, trusting that 'in the future, the Banks may have a still greater measure of usefulness in helping to build up the character of the people, and in fostering that spirit of self-help and independence, which will make for the welfare of the whole nation'.

Other thrift organisations also benefited from the buoyancy of the market for personal savings. The Post Office Savings Bank barely recorded any gains, but sales of life insurance policies reached new heights. The most striking advance was in deposits with building societies, which climbed from nearly £71 million in 1921 to more than £127 million by 1925. Membership increased from 789,000 to 1,129,000, reflecting tax exemption, competitive rates of interest, often above that available on special investment departments, and the growing ambition amongst better-off families to own their own homes. National Savings Certificates continued to attract customers, with net investments of £57 million in 1922, followed by £12 million a year in 1923 and 1924. The appeal of building societies and National Savings

Certificates seems to have been mostly to middle-class depositors whose income had grown significantly during and since the war and who were keen to earn as much from their investments as possible. Their popularity amongst larger investors was almost certainly at the expense of the savings banks' special investment departments.

The Conservatives came to power after the collapse of the Labour government in November 1924 and in the following April appointed another committee to investigate national savings, this time to consider what should happen when the first issue of War Savings Certificates expired the following year. Thomas Henderson, the actuary of the Savings Bank of Glasgow, gave evidence on behalf of the Association. Following the line of argument of Sir Thomas Jaffrey when he appeared before the previous inquiry two years before, he attacked proposals for a further issue of savings certificates. Using figures drawn from the Savings Bank of Glasgow he attempted to demonstrate that the higher rates of interest available on savings certificates had dented investments. The Committee were deaf to his petition for savings certificates to be converted on redemption to deposits with the National Debt Office at the same rate of interest as that paid on deposits in the Post Office Savings Bank or savings bank ordinary departments. Instead the members recommended in an interim report that savings certificates should be extended to 1932 at the existing rate of interest. In a final report in February 1926 the national savings scheme was endorsed, with a proposal that War Savings Certificates should be converted into savings bonds, yielding 4.5 per cent rather than the current 5 per cent, in line with current market rates. The government, anxious to restrain inflationary pressures in the economy, accepted these findings.

While the Committee had been sitting, a fragile economic recovery had been nipped in the bud by the persistent problems besetting international trade, driving up unemployment and forcing depositors with both the savings banks and Post Office Savings Bank to draw on their investments. In 1925, for the first time since the beginning of the war, withdrawals from the savings banks exceeded deposits reducing income for management expenses. Turnover, nevertheless, remained buoyant at about £40 million, adding to the problems of the savings banks. Trustees were concerned to get across the message that there was still an important role for the savings banks in times of economic crises.

The Bishop of Manchester told the annual meeting of the Manchester & Salford Savings Bank: 'Everybody should realise the welfare of each person was bound up with the general welfare in such a way that it was not possible, even if he should desire it, to promote his own interests at the expense of the general good, and nothing contributed to that end more than institutions like this bank.' The Bishop was making an oblique reference to the recent introduction of contributory widows' pensions and old age pensions for those over sixty-five which appeared to remove one of the pillars in the rhetoric of the savings movement. The benefit, however, was small and thrift organisations had no difficulty in declaring with the Bishop that they still had a role to play. They could point at the persistently high level of

The first Wembley FA Cup Final, 1923, when 200,000 spectators
gained entry to the stadium. There was a massive increase in
attendances at football matches after the First World War.

unemployment; the lack of comprehensive State health insurance for the whole family; and, despite the recession and heavy taxation, at the continuing high level of demand for alcoholic drinks which still accounted for between 8 and 9 per cent of the expenditure of families living above the subsistence level. There had also been a noticeable increase in smoking and gambling since the war reflecting the higher real wages. The proportion of family incomes devoted to essential expenditure on food and rents was falling fast. Rising living standards, coupled with better social provision, convinced some actuaries that appeals to save had to find a new vocabulary. Thomas Henderson published a pamphlet in 1926 advocating the introduction of 'Save to Travel' schemes in partnership with railway companies, in which he argued:

> To many thoughtful minds in the savings bank movement it has been apparent for some time that, if savings banks are to maintain their hold upon the community, they must adapt their methods to the changing needs of the day, they must realise that the old conception of their function which was limited very largely to making provision for a rainy day, must give place to a wider conception of their usefulness in order to enable them to render a still more effective service to the community and meet, more adequately, present-day requirements.

S.C.W.S. Ltd.                                        Drawing-room Furniture

Prices can be obtained at any Co-operative Store, or from the S-C-W-S Limited

Fashionable furnishings for the home were much in demand in the
mid-1920s. Following upon a sharp increase in house-building and a
fall in prices, more and more people were able to buy their own homes.

The need for new services was most striking at the top end of the savings spectrum, where larger deposits were under pressure, not just as a result of the recession but also because of a revival in new house-building. There had been almost no house-building between 1917 and 1919 and then a sharp upturn with a marked fall in price. During 1924 over 130,000 new houses were completed. The following year the total reached an all-time high of 174,000 and was set to climb even higher in 1926 and 1927. Much of this new housing was constructed by local authorities financed by loans, but a substantial proportion was private. With a rapid decline in the numbers of children in families to two or three, the new homes of the 1920s were smaller than their Victorian predecessors, fitted in many instances with labour-saving gas stoves and electric lighting. More and more people could afford to buy their own homes, particularly in the Midlands and the south of England where real incomes were rising rapidly. Many of the new home owners were established savings bank customers who had been accustomed to using their accounts prudently to accumulate reserves to meet their rents. The managers of the Coventry Savings Bank were struck by the number of depositors who withdrew savings in 1925 to buy houses: 'The purchase of a house is an excellent use to make of savings, and the most satisfactory and economical way of doing so is to save the money to pay for it.' The majority of such savings were held in special investment departments, which as a result experienced a large rise in turnover. Once savings had been withdrawn for this purpose and mortgages taken out with building societies, there was little likelihood of the depositors being retained by the savings banks.

Although withdrawals in ordinary departments continued to run ahead of deposits during 1926 and 1927, the movement did not falter in the endeavour to win additional customers by intensifying publicity campaigns. This was co-ordinated by the Association's newly appointed Development Committee. In the meantime, services to customers continued to be improved by extensions to the branch network and upgrading of existing branches, but principally by further amalgamations which, as before, allowed more and more customers access to special investment departments. Largely for this reason, during 1926 no fewer than fourteen banks amalgamated with seven larger banks already operating special investment departments – Aberdeen, Newcastle upon Tyne, Finsbury & City of London, Derby, Devonport, Oswestry, and Somerset Savings Banks. In some areas the development of the branch network was

During the 1920s, an ever-increasing range of electrical appliances came within the means of the ordinary householder. (RIGHT) The Army & Navy Stores published this price list at the same time, but the number of British domestic servants, who were among the most faithful savings bank customers, was declining rapidly.

designed to fill gaps created by past closures; otherwise the majority of new branches were established in new housing areas. In Scotland in 1927, the Savings Bank of Glasgow built a branch at Anniesland to the west of the city where a huge corporation housing scheme was under construction. In England the Newcastle upon Tyne Savings Bank took similar action in inaugurating a branch at Percy Mains to the east of the city where there was equivalent housing development. In an effort to remain competitive with the clearing banks, which were becoming more and more interested in private client deposit-taking, savings banks' opening hours were once again lengthened; in some of the larger banks to a full hour beyond the closing time of clearing bank branches at 3 p.m. in the afternoon.

Neither the clearing banks nor the savings banks, however, could match the rate of growth of the building societies as enthusiasm for home-ownership swept middle-class Britain. The societies won customers and promoted mortgage services by bold and aggressive advertising that left the rest of the thrift movement at a disadvantage. Usually still paying higher interest than either clearing banks or savings banks, total building society deposits overtook total savings bank deposits in 1926 and had reached £213 million by 1928. The savings banks called in vain for an increase in the interest rates paid on ordinary department deposits by the National Debt Commissioners. The London Savings Bank protested in March 1927 at the unsatisfactory level of current rates, when 'in the market other stocks carrying this guarantee earn an interest of over 4 per cent'. This reference to savings certificates was not entirely apposite, as the National Savings Committee was also experiencing difficulty in attracting funds. Pending a response from the Treasury, the savings banks tried to play the building societies at their own game by following Coventry's example of extolling investment in special investment departments for house purchase.

Despite the runaway success of the building societies in the mid-1920s, they were not the main cause of concern for the savings bank movement, partly because, for the majority of savers, home-ownership in the foreseeable future was an impossibility. The greatest worry for the larger banks was renewed interest amongst members of the Labour Party in the potential of municipal banks for funding ambitious schemes for local authority housing. The Labour Party had no great love for the savings banks, which had been repeatedly held up since the war as bastions against Bolshevism or State socialism on the grounds that people with savings, especially if they were invested with the State, were unlikely to become involved in political agitation. Ian MacIntyre, a Scottish Conservative MP, voiced opinions typical of trustees throughout the United Kingdom when, at the annual meeting of the Edinburgh Savings Bank in 1926, he likened the 126,000 depositors to 'an army marshalled against revolution'. Even without such polemics, the Labour Party was considering fundamental reform of the banking system when it next came to power. Early in 1924, within months of losing office, Philip Snowden was toying with the idea of setting up Labour Banks on the American model, to collect savings from members and invest them directly in the manufacturing industry. In March the Independent Labour Party's Financial Inquiry Commission proposed the formation of municipal banks, 'with a view to the financing of municipal developments and local trading', and at the same time the extension of credit facilities through both the Post Office Savings Bank and the savings banks. Believing that such a proposal was inimical to their principal objectives of encouraging thrift, the Post Office Savings Bank and the savings banks were openly hostile. In February 1926 the Labour MP for Mile End, John Scurr, introduced the Municipal Banks Bill allowing any municipal authority to form a bank on the Birmingham lines. Although the Bill failed, a number of local authorities, including Liverpool, Nottingham, Bristol and Grimsby, expressed interest in taking the idea a stage further. Following Snowden's suggestions, the Labour Party in County Durham favoured the foundation of a Labour Bank which would not only finance house-building, but also take over derelict industrial sites for re-development. When the Birmingham Municipal Bank, which also provided mortgages, reported another healthy year in June, discussion intensified. Even quite small boroughs, such as Hornsey in north London, explored the possibility. Every attempt to include powers to form a municipal bank in a local authority Bill was vetoed by Treasury officials to the annoyance of the Labour Party. So high did excitement run that in September Winston Churchill, the Chancellor of the Exchequer, intervened and appointed a committee to investigate the matter, chaired by Lord Bradbury.

Believing that 'the deadening hand of tradition and usage must not be allowed to hinder our acceptance of new ideas and methods', the Development Committee of the Trustee Savings Banks Association had already been actively investigating ways of countering the challenge of municipal banks and responding to the needs of the many newly affluent depositors. Immediately after its formation, W.A. Barclay was asked to prepare a Memorandum on the Development

The Birmingham Municipal Bank exploited every opportunity
to publicise its services.

of the Trustee Savings Bank System with the advice of Thomas Henderson and Noël Griffith of the London Savings Bank. This was to be used as a basis for consultation and discussion. In it Barclay demanded an annual review of interest rates and an immediate increase to bring rates available into line with the 4 per cent currently paid on Treasury Bills. He wanted all banks, irrespective of their total deposits, to be allowed to open special investment departments, mobilising capital for investment in local utilities. He hoped that this reform, together with powers to use bank surplus funds to support local authorities, would meet all the arguments advanced for the formation of municipal banks. In addition he made two radical suggestions: the introduction of cheques by the savings banks and mortgage finance for house purchase by customers. The Memorandum was widely circulated, along with observations from members of the Development Committee and a questionnaire. The initial response was encouraging and the Committee's proposals were endorsed in June 1926 at the Association's annual meeting. To prevent confrontation with the Birmingham Municipal Bank, the Association came to an informal understanding with the manager, J.P. Hilton, for the exchange of information and opinions. The Development Committee urgently sought to improve the movement's coverage by publishing a map showing the 115 towns of over 30,000 inhabitants where there were no savings banks. Most of them were in the south of England where new industries were flourishing, despite the recession in the traditional manufacturing centres in the north, Wales and Scotland. In response, the pace of branch opening intensified, but no new savings banks were established. During 1927 in replying to the demand for higher rates of interest, the National Debt Commissioners raised the maximum rate payable on special investment departments to 4 per cent.

In the meantime, the Committee on Municipal Savings Banks had been collecting evidence. The savings banks had been represented by Cobbett and Henderson, both of whom, not surprisingly, were outspoken in their condemnation of municipal banking. This did nothing to prevent further investigation of the potential of municipal banking by a number of towns and cities in 1927, particularly Bristol, Glasgow and Swansea. Early in 1927 Glasgow Corporation agreed in principle to form a municipal bank in the belief that as a result 'a greater portion of the savings of the citizens should be made available for municipal purposes than at present is the case'. Throughout the year there was a lively public debate with the advocates of municipal banking showing a disturbing disregard of sound banking and believing naïvely that if there was a crisis of liquidity the government would come to the rescue. In November the editor of *Lloyds Bank Monthly* attempted to quash the enthusiasm:

> What then would happen if there was a sudden demand by the depositors for the return of their money? The bank would have to call in its loans to the corporation, and the corporation would have no means of repaying them except by borrowing elsewhere, which might not always be easy. It is one thing to entrust your money to a bank run by the Birmingham Corporation. It would be quite another thing to keep a deposit account with the local

authorities of, say, West Ham, or other areas, the financial affairs of which … had to be taken out of local control because of their extravagance and mismanagement.

For this reason the Treasury continued to veto any Parliamentary proposal to sanction individual municipal banks.

The report of the Committee was published in January 1928, finding against any further extension of municipal banking, at least in the foreseeable future. The Committee was concerned that the establishment of a municipal bank would almost certainly be at the expense of the branches of the savings banks which would have a damaging effect on government finance. This would make it difficult for the Treasury to convert the £900 million war debt that matured in the next ten years to lower rates of interest, vital if rates generally were to be brought down to stimulate economic activity. They were also worried that access to municipal bank funds would encourage councils to overspend with attendant risks to customers' deposits. On the whole, the Committee favoured improving the services offered by both the Post Office Savings Bank and the savings banks. With their strong local affiliations, the savings banks were identified as an ideal vehicle for raising funds through special investment departments to meet local needs. It was recommended that there should be far greater co-operation, nationally and locally, between the savings banks and the national savings campaign, and that the path should be smoothed for the opening of new savings banks in places without them. Delighted by this outcome, Thomas Henderson wrote a short pamphlet for the Association, *Trustee Savings Banks: The Case for Disinterested Service*. He believed that the success of the savings banks was because they 'set themselves to cultivate the personal touch with their depositors which in the course of the years has been the means of endearing them to the affections of the customers they serve'. The quality of personal service was undoubtedly the hallmark of the savings movement.

Not everyone welcomed the findings of the Bradbury Report. Many members of the Labour Party suspected the Committee of class prejudice anxious to perpetuate outdated paternalistic institutions. Contrasting the high rate of return of 5 per cent from war loan with the niggardly 2.5 per cent paid on savings bank ordinary department accounts, Tom Johnston, the Labour MP for Dundee, condemned the report out of hand as the product of 'banking leeches already growing steadily in commercial business circles'. Encouraged by such emotive criticism, councils where the Labour Party was strongly represented continued to press the issue. By the end of March, the establishment of municipal banks had become official Labour Party policy, supported by the leader Ramsay MacDonald. With this assurance, many Labour-controlled local authorities shelved their plans until the political climate was more propitious.

The government responded to the findings of the Bradbury Committee by giving notice that legislation would be introduced in the near future to put the findings relating to savings banks into effect. By now the process of consultation resulting from the Association Development Committee's circular and questionnaire was complete. Five key reforms had been identified: (1) increase in the ceiling on special investment departments; (2) extension of period of investment for special investment department funds; (3) the use of the reserve fund from closed savings banks for the opening of new banks; (4) increase in the rate of interest in the ordinary department; and (5) power to take over uncertified savings banks (of which only a handful remained) guaranteeing any losses.

The National Debt Commissioners agreed to implement the first three proposals, but were unable to endorse the last two in view of the precarious state of government finances as a result of the recession. Apart from these general concerns, the savings bank movement as a whole

Staff working on the ledgers at Ashton-under-Lyne, 1927. Working
conditions for junior staff changed little after the war.

remained worried by the continuing lack of a superannuation fund for savings bank staff, demanding that this should be incorporated in any legislation. The new Act passed uneventfully, reaching the statute book in June and coming into force at the beginning of the savings bank year in November. It followed the tenor of the Association's advice, making it impossible for trustees to close a bank without the permission of the Association and the Inspection Committee, and allowing customers to operate more than one account and also to hold accounts in savings banks and the Post Office Savings Bank. Permission was also granted for the National Debt Commissioners to make advances from the surplus fund on the recommendation of the Inspection Committee and the Association towards the cost of opening new savings banks.

More significantly, individual banks, at the discretion of the Association and Inspection Committee, were also allowed to extend their services to include any business which was 'of a nature ancillary to the purpose of the bank and calculated to encourage thrift'. In anticipation of receiving these legal powers, the Association had already registered itself as a limited liability company with the permission of the Treasury. The Permanent Secretary commented wryly, 'I do not see anything in the long-winded articles to which we need object.' On incorporation, the Association appointed a statutory executive committee, took steps to establish a London office with a permanent secretary, and began publishing a *Gazette* to provide members with news of the movement. One of the first successes the executive committee was able to report was an understanding with the National and Scottish Savings Committees for joint savings schemes in schools and for the affiliation wherever possible of penny banks with savings banks in preference to the Post Office Savings Bank.

While the debate about municipal banking and the future role of the trustee savings banks had been raging, the economy had been showing signs of modest recovery, particularly in the more prosperous south of England. There was a general mood of confident optimism. Unemployment had fallen back during 1927. The Conservative government had also taken steps to mitigate the horror of being without work for long periods of time, through transitional payments introduced in the Unemployment Insurance Act. The improvement was short-lived and unemployment began to rise again, stabilising at 11 per cent of the insured workforce in 1928 and 1929. The national figures disguised wide regional disparities with high levels of unemployment in Scotland, the north of England and in rural areas, reflecting the serious difficulties of the older manufacturing industries and agriculture, and low levels in the south of England where much of the new industry was located. However, those who remained in employment even in depressed areas, still found themselves better off than before. Wages were reduced, but prices were falling more rapidly, allowing for even greater discretionary expenditure on luxuries – the cinema, drink, gambling and holidays.

Total deposits with the savings banks, which had declined in real terms between 1925 and 1926, began to recover, reaching a total of £124 million by the end of 1929. Unlike the early 1920s, this growth was entirely attributable to savings by the better-off. In the ordinary departments, withdrawals remained above deposits; the former reached £43 million in 1929 with deposits of just over £39 million. Of the gap between withdrawals and deposits, over £2 million was accounted for by the Scottish savings banks, where unemployment was severe and where special investment departments were well established. Out of the £2 million, over half was transferred to special investment departments, bringing the average balance in special investment accounts north of the border to over £237. In England and Wales total deposits with special investment departments climbed from £17.3 million in 1926 to £27.9 million by 1929, with an average balance of £219. This improvement was achieved largely through the opening of new special investment accounts by ordinary account holders with the required minimum balance. The number of depositors with special investment accounts rose from 120,000 in 1926 to 677,000 in 1929. Encouragingly for the savings banks the number of depositors in ordinary departments also continued to grow, reaching almost 2.5 million by 1929. As before the gains of the savings banks were as nothing compared to the continuing advance of building society share capital which jumped from £147 million in 1926 to over

A 1930 campaign to promote 'purpose saving' in Glasgow.

£250 million by 1929 as even more people sought to buy their own homes. Not all thrift organisations experienced this growth in their net receipts. The Post Office Savings Bank deposits drifted downwards and the number of depositors, which had been about 10.5 million in 1924 declined to less than 9.8 million in 1929 as smaller savers withdrew their cash and closed their accounts to meet the vicissitudes of the recession. Similarly the National Savings Campaign slipped into the doldrums with repayments above new subscriptions.

The success of the savings banks in maintaining their business during the late 1920s, in the face of economic recession and strong competition from the building societies, was not achieved

Customers of the future? Birmingham Street urchins at a Birmingham
Municipal Bank branch opening ceremony.

without a struggle. To meet the challenge of the bold advertising of the building societies, the
Association geared up its publicity, encouraging individual banks to canvass for new custom
door-to-door, particularly when new branches were opened; the striking results of such
campaigns were well publicised, reminiscent of the stories recounted by the pioneers of the
movement. The Inspection Committee noted the case of a couple who had been persuaded to
deposit their life savings, some £1,300, kept in £1 notes and gold under a flagstone in their
kitchen. All the larger savings banks opened more branches, targeting towns with no savings
banks and middle-class housing areas where they competed directly with the clearing banks.
During 1927, Stockport Savings Bank opened a branch at Reddish and York Savings Bank, a
branch at Acomb – both towns with no savings bank representation. A total of eighteen
branches were established in 1929. Efforts continued to be made to inculcate habits of thrift in
young people through penny banks, the heavy promotion of home safes (piggy banks) and the
introduction of thrift stamps and cards. As an experiment the Union Bank of Devonport &
the County of Cornwall introduced a cheque system for depositors, but the Association's

Development Committee was unable to win support for a widening of the scheme. In an effort finally to silence advocates of municipal banking, Edinburgh Savings Bank, under the permission granted in the 1929 Act, began providing a rate collection service for the city.

At the general election in June 1929, the Labour Party returned to power with the support of the Liberals. There were immediate calls from up and down the country by left-wing councillors for legislation to allow municipal banking. Cardiff and Derby were both reported to be seeking individual powers to establish banks. Following the findings of the Bradbury Committee, the Liberals were hostile to such proposals. The banking community once more raised questions of liquidity. They found a ready supporter in Philip Snowden, again Chancellor of the Exchequer, who was grappling with a rapidly deteriorating outlook for government finance. After the collapse of the speculative boom on Wall Street in October 1929, which quickly turned depression into slump, there was no further question of general legislation. However, some Labour supporters in large local authorities still believed that municipal banks could provide a simple solution to their financial needs. These had been increased by the 1929 Local Government Act, which had transferred the administration of the Poor Law to local authorities with instructions to form Poor Law Assistance Committees for the relief of the able-bodied – no longer to be known by the demeaning name of 'paupers'.

As unemployment began to rise inexorably during 1930 to almost 20 per cent – some 2.5 million – of the insured workforce (see p.123), the financial problems of both local and national government grew steadily worse. In several local authorities, notably Bristol, Cardiff, Derby, and Glasgow, there was a fierce dispute about municipal banking. Even where councils approved the idea in principle, there was no prospect of securing the necessary Parliamentary approval as the Chancellor and the Treasury remained firmly opposed to any such schemes, not least because of the threat they posed to deposits with the savings banks and branches of the Post Office Savings Bank – vital to the funding of the National Debt at a time when conversion of the War Debt to a lower rate of interest was again being explored. By the end of 1930, the only concern of the Chancellor was how to continue paying unemployment benefit at the levels set in 1928 without risking a currency crisis. In February the Labour government agreed to the appointment of the May Committee to find ways of making economies in public expenditure. In the meantime, Snowden pressed ahead with secret plans to convert the War Debt by the end of the year. These were interrupted when the May Committee reported in July recommending a variety of cuts, including a 10 per cent reduction in the dole. The Cabinet split, precipitating a political and monetary crisis. To restore confidence, Ramsay MacDonald, the Prime Minister, and Snowden were persuaded to remain in office and form a national government with the objective of leading the country out of the slump. Although interest rates were raised to 6.5 per cent to protect sterling, the government was committed to a long-term policy of cheap money which would stimulate investment and employment.

The effect of the crisis took trustees and other champions of thrift by surprise. Although deposits and the number of accounts in the ordinary departments of the savings banks fell slightly, the number of depositors with special investment accounts rose by 30 per cent between 1929 and 1931, and total deposits from £45 million to £65 million. The gains were distributed fairly evenly across the country, even in the north of England and Scotland, where the effects of the slump were most severe. These increases in investments, reflecting the continuing advance in real wages, were experienced by other thrift organisations. The National Savings Committee, whose relations with the savings bank movement had become much more harmonious following the findings of the Bradbury Committee, experienced a £3 million fall in investment in National Savings Certificates during 1930, followed by an advance of over £12 million in 1931. The growth in the share capital of the building societies was dramatic, rising by almost £100 million during 1930 and 1931, with a corresponding advance in membership. Likewise, membership of friendly societies, which offered a variety of benefits similar to those available from the State, increased with total funds reaching a record £63.5 million in 1931. It was evident that the bulk of these savings came from the better-off. The Post Office Savings Bank, which experienced a modest recovery in its fortunes in 1929 and 1930, suffered a further reverse in 1931. The premium income of the life assurance companies, which had peaked at nearly £70 million in 1929, retreated, with a record £30 million in surrendered policies. Observers found a ready explanation for the growth in personal savings of the middle class in the lack of confidence of investors in the stock market and in the words of the chairman of the Aberdeen Savings Bank – 'prudent people restricted their expenditure and increased their savings'. Savings bank actuaries detected a large influx of 'hot money' into special investment departments from so-called 'undesirables' who, they believed, would withdraw their funds as soon as market conditions improved. One commentator has described this sudden flow of deposits as 'a rush – almost a frantic rush – among investors for security above all considerations'. What it certainly was not was a sudden alteration in habits by the less well-off. Estimates suggest that there was little change in patterns of expenditure; spending on leisure, recreation, drinking and smoking in the 1920s remained surprisingly stable, despite the recession.

By 1931, in the seventeen years since the outbreak of war, the thrift movement had been transformed first of all by the National Savings Campaign to help meet the heavy cost of prosecuting the war and subsequently by the circumstances of the post-war years. The recession, accompanied by better benefits for the unemployed and the old, had made it both more difficult and less necessary for those less well-off to save. For the better-off, the emerging middle class and skilled artisans, there was a new purpose in savings – the purchase of a home, along with furniture and fittings. They could also afford to save more. Incomes had risen dramatically during the war and, for those who kept their jobs, the gains were not entirely eroded during the recession. Consequently, deposits with special investment departments accelerated at the expense of the ordinary departments. Although the savings banks lost to the building societies in the race for the savings of would-be home-owners, their function was also changing.

Increasingly, ordinary departments and even special investment departments were being used as retail banks where money could be lodged for short periods to meet daily expenditure. As a result, turnover had increased far more rapidly than total deposits.

Well aware of these changes in their market and function, the savings banks, through a revitalised Association, had defended themselves against the ambitions of the National Savings Committee, winning official representation both nationally and locally. They and other circumstances had defeated the advocates of municipal banking, enhancing their role as important conduits of funds for local and central government. In the new post-war environment for savings, individual savings banks had made every effort to secure the custom of home-owners and the tenants of the new council houses by opening branches and by amalgamations, allowing more and more customers access to special investment departments.

With the encouragement of the Association, the first new savings banks to be established in England and Wales since the foundation of the Post Office Savings Bank were opened in Bournemouth and Portsmouth in 1931, towns which had benefited from the prosperity in the South and the boom in home-ownership since the war. The Association had supported the initiatives of all the individual banks by co-ordinating publicity and promotional literature. The passing of the 1929 Act had finally set a seal on the position of the savings banks within the complex market for personal banking and thrift, allowing the introduction of services that matched clients' requirements.

# CHAPTER SIX

# THE

# TRINITY OF

# THRIFT

## *1932–50*

Lhe formation of the National government in 1931 and the subsequent general election, which left the Labour Party with only forty-nine seats in the House of Commons, marked a turning point in British social and economic policy. The National government was faced with two apparently competing priorities: the maintenance of international confidence in sterling, while, at the same time, ensuring that the unemployed and their families were protected as far as possible from the rigours of the recession. Although sterling left the gold standard in September and the exchange rate was allowed to float against other currencies, economic orthodoxy demanded that public expenditure should be seen to be held in check to prevent the value of sterling falling too far and also to allow all-important interest rates to be reduced. As a result, the 10 per cent cut in unemployment benefit proposed by the May Committee in 1930 that had helped precipitate the political crisis was imposed. In future benefit was to be limited to twenty-six weeks. Thereafter, transitional benefits – renamed transitional payments – were to be made available on a strictly means-tested basis by local Public Assistance Committees. The means test was comprehensive, including all sources of income, interest payments and the paltry earnings of children to provide themselves with pocket-money. This was a complete reversal of the policy of the 1920s which had been firmly opposed to the means testing of national insurance benefits. Its introduction was bitterly resented by applicants – the long-term unemployed – and heavily criticised by thrift organisations on the grounds that it militated heavily against their objectives of encouraging savings to meet such vicissitudes.

The economist John Maynard Keynes and his disciples argued that this strategy was misconceived, believing the cuts in government expenditure to be unnecessary, if not positively harmful, at a time of deep recession. They were convinced that there would be little risk of further depreciation in the exchange rate if the government budgeted for a deficit to tide the economy over short-term difficulties. Additional government spending would have a multiplier effect on trade and industry, hastening the recovery. Keynes and his followers took the thinking of the socialists at the turn of the century a stage further by declaring there was not only no moral imperative to save, but in fact for those who could afford it, a moral imperative to spend to reinforce this multiplier effect. Such radical policy alternatives did not find favour with the government, the Treasury, the Bank of England and the financial institutions and were firmly

A typical window display of the 1930s.

rejected. Sir Josiah Stamp, speaking as a member of the Economic Advisory Council in a broadcast to the nation in 1931 on national savings, declared emphatically, 'that free spending in excess of the normal surplus would bring to a standstill the accumulation of capital without which no expansion of industry is possible'.

With this fast about-turn in government policy in relation to the means test, the savings banks lost no time in registering their protest. Individual banks reported there was concern amongst depositors that details of their accounts would be disclosed to the Public Assistance Committees, despite assurances to the contrary. By March 1932 the Association, in joint committee with the National and Scottish Savings Committees, had concluded from the evidence so far collected from the savings banks and branches of the Post Office Savings Bank

that the means test 'must have a far-reaching effect upon the future of institutions concerned in teaching thrift'. One Scottish savings bank maintained that a local Labour MP had told his constituents 'to close their accounts and have a good time'. Under intense pressure from the Association and the National Savings Committee for clarification, the government announced in December 1932 that savings up to a limit of £50 would not be means tested. The thrift organisations hurriedly informed their members and depositors of this important concession.

The measures taken by the National government to ensure financial probity had begun to take effect by the spring of 1932. In keeping with the government's cheap money policy, bank rate was reduced progressively to 3.5 per cent by the middle of March and, after steps had been taken to prevent speculation against sterling, to 2 per cent on 30 June. On that summer evening, Neville Chamberlain, now the Chancellor of the Exchequer, told an astonished House of Commons that the outstanding £2,000 million of War Debt would be converted from a yield of 5 per cent to 3.5 per cent. The Chancellor appealed to the patriotism of investors to convert rather than take the cash alternative. In effect he was inviting them to accept a sharp reduction in income in the national interest of reviving and restructuring the economy. As part of the package the rate of return on National Savings Certificates was correspondingly reduced. During July, when the conversion would take place, new issues by public authorities and private sector companies were to be prohibited. Within days it became clear that investors were prepared to respond magnificently to the Chancellor's call. By the closing date at the beginning of August, although the number of savings bank depositors with government stock accounts had fallen slightly, total holdings had increased. Over £68 million of the National Savings Certificates were converted and an astonishing £1,920 million out of the total £2,000 million of War Debt. Savings bank staff had to work night and day to process all the necessary documentation, earning the gratitude of the Treasury and the National Debt Office. Part of the explanation for the success of the conversion was the lack of other investment opportunities yielding a more competitive rate except for the savings banks' special investment departments and building societies. In current conditions, the stock market was too risky except for the most seasoned campaigners.

The conversion may have put the economy on the long road to recovery; it spelled immediate difficulties for thrift organisations paying interest above bank rate and that available on National Savings Certificates. With the stock market still depressed, the better-off personal investors poured money into the building societies and the special investment departments of the savings banks. Total deposits with the special investment departments rose by a further £9 million in 1932. Building society share capital soared by £40 million to over £380 million because they could offer more competitive rates of interest since mortgage rates were not

Neville Chamberlain, a piece of paper in his hand, at the opening of
the Birmingham Municipal Bank head office in Broad Street, 1934.

controlled by either the government or the Bank of England. Building society managers and savings bank actuaries were thrown into confusion as they endeavoured to find an outlet for the flow of funds which showed no sign of subsiding.

From July 1932, the building societies began progressively to reduce interest rates and more importantly to limit investments, particularly by new members. As early as September 1931, the executive committee of the Trustee Savings Banks Association had appointed a committee to review the placing of loans by banks operating special investment departments. The Committee reported in April 1932, by which time many savings banks were having difficulty in securing a home for the funds in their special investment departments at a reasonable rate of return. The Committee's findings came down strongly against competition between banks for municipal loans and cast doubt on the wisdom of using the plethora of agents, who made a living from placing loans at the most advantageous rate. After discounting a proposal to restrict the number of agents as invidious, the Committee explored the practicality of the Association establishing its own Central Agency, but this was rejected on further consideration. They preferred that banks should deal directly with local authorities which were to be circulated with details of the conditions on which savings bank loans could be made available.

By the close of 1932, special investment department interest rates had been reduced to between 3 and 3.5 per cent, from 0.5 to 1 per cent less than the yields available on building society share accounts. Nevertheless, funds continued to flood in, partly because larger investors were prevented by newly imposed restrictions from unlimited access to building society accounts. In the spring of 1933 the savings banks were obliged to follow suit, reducing the annual amount that could be placed in a special investment account from £200 to £100. The problems for those banks which operated special investment departments were compounded as local authorities, seeking to take advantage of cheap money, tried to slash interest rates every time a loan was renewed at the six-monthly intervals required by the legislation. The savings banks called for wider powers of investment, but the National Debt Office chose instead to impose in November 1933 a ceiling on interest rates of 2.25 per cent on new deposits, with 3 per cent available on application for deposits made before this date. This was still a full 1 per cent below building society rates. Of equal concern in this very fluid market for savings was the liquidity of special investment departments if there should be a sudden withdrawal of funds. A survey by Thomas Henderson, the actuary of the Savings Bank of Glasgow, revealed the alarming fact that some banks had less than 5 per cent of their special investment funds in readily realisable securities and would be forced to rely, possibly illegally, on bank borrowing in a crisis – a fact that curiously had escaped the attention of the Inspection Committee. This problem was rectified by the Trustee Savings Bank (Special Investment) Act of 1934 passed in response to a sharp reduction in local authority borrowing which allowed up to 30 per cent of balances to be invested in government securities and a further 10 per cent in municipal stocks which could be realised quickly in the event of a crisis. By 1933 the pressure was beginning to ease as the stock market began to pull out of the slump and investors' confidence returned.

Throughout 1932 and 1933 the savings banks were at pains to counter any suggestion from Keynes and his supporters that the nation was saving when it should have been spending. Chairing the annual meeting of the Association in 1933, Sir Spencer Portal of the London Savings Bank, who had been knighted two years before for his services to the movement, cautioned:

> It would be unwise to assume from these increased deposits that there is too much saving by individuals today. It is only some seven or eight years since the Colwyn Committee [on National Debt and Taxation] . . . came to the conclusion that we were not saving enough as a nation. I find it difficult to believe that there has been such a marked increase in individual thrift or such a complete change in the country's economic position since then that we are now saving too much.

By way of justification, the Association reported that special investment departments were now investing funds with 862 different local authorities and utilities who were using them 'for promoting employment'. Seventeen new branches were opened during 1932 to improve services to customers. Convinced that savings banks still had an important role to play both in providing funds for central and local government and in promoting thrift, the Association's Development Committee forged ahead with plans to enlarge their representation in England, where many savings banks had closed in the aftermath of the formation of the Post Office Savings Bank.

Encouraged by the enthusiasm which greeted the establishment of the banks at Bournemouth and Portsmouth, the Development Committee sought to bring together groups of potential trustees in other cities and towns. In July 1933 the Oxford Savings Bank was inaugurated, supported by a 'very representative body' comprising 'the Mayor, several City councillors, a clergyman, several well-known tradesmen, members of the University teaching staff and a Labour JP (the local secretary of the National Union of Railwaymen)'. This was followed in October by the opening of the Wolverhampton Savings Bank which had taken over two years and a voluminous correspondence with Godfrey James, the Association's newly appointed Development Officer, to bring to fruition. Within a week of opening, the new bank took nearly £4,000 in deposits and opened seventy-two accounts – an auspicious start to what the Development Committee hoped would result in the re-establishment of savings banks in Staffordshire. By the end of the year there were sufficient volunteers to act as trustees for a savings bank to be opened early in 1934 at Walsall, six miles away from Wolverhampton, at Luton in Bedfordshire and at Northampton.

Just as the savings banks seemed poised on the verge of a new era of regeneration, the threat of municipal banking once more clouded the horizon. The savings banks had hoped that the question had been finally answered by the findings of the Bradbury Committee in 1929, but, as a precaution, had gone to some lengths to ensure that prominent local members of the Labour Party were represented amongst the trustees of the new banks to guard against any suggestion that savings banks did not really represent the interests and aspirations of working-class depositors. Serious discussion of municipal banks as an alternative to savings banks had resumed in the left-wing press in the spring of 1932. The influential Scottish ILP newspaper *Forward!* carried an article on 27 February supporting a municipal bank for Edinburgh which, it was claimed, was prevented by 'the determination of the Moderates to protect the vested interest of the financiers'. It was argued, as it had been in the past, that a municipal bank would give the council access to much cheaper funds than the current loans from savings banks. The opening of the Kilsyth Municipal Bank (registered under the Companies Act) the following month by Tom Johnston, who had resigned as MP for Dundee in 1931, added fuel to the argument. Johnston, a long-standing advocate of municipal banking, was delighted to be able to point a finger at the Tory Chancellor of the Exchequer, Neville Chamberlain, the instigator of the Birmingham Municipal Bank, and declare that this was no longer a party issue. However, it was not until October that a committee of Glasgow Corporation, which was now Labour controlled, recommended the establishment of a municipal bank. The decision to proceed was not taken until April 1934. In a highly charged statement, Bailie Hector McNeill claimed that the new bank would 'save thousands', as 'Managing its own bank, Glasgow can lend to Glasgow when Glasgow most needs the loan.' No sooner was the bank, registered under the Companies Act, about to start trading in October than a ratepayer, John Kellock, secured an interim interdict against the Corporation, preventing the use of the City Chambers as a registered

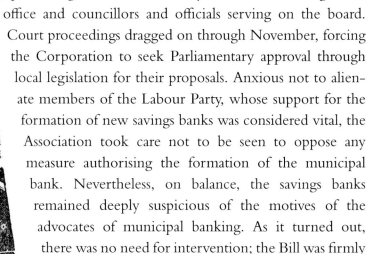

office and councillors and officials serving on the board. Court proceedings dragged on through November, forcing the Corporation to seek Parliamentary approval through local legislation for their proposals. Anxious not to alienate members of the Labour Party, whose support for the formation of new savings banks was considered vital, the Association took care not to be seen to oppose any measure authorising the formation of the municipal bank. Nevertheless, on balance, the savings banks remained deeply suspicious of the motives of the advocates of municipal banking. As it turned out, there was no need for intervention; the Bill was firmly

A cartoon illustrating the defeat at the hands of
Duff Cooper of the Glasgow Corporation Bill
to establish a municipal bank in 1934.

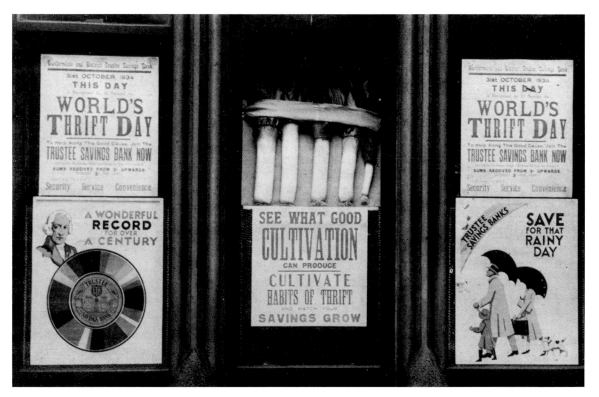

Window display at the Dunfermline Savings Bank
on World Thrift Day, 1934.

rejected by a Conservative-dominated House of Commons. In the wake of this defeat, Stoke-on-Trent and Sunderland abandoned similar Bills. The spectre of municipal banking was exorcised for the foreseeable future.

In the meantime, the Joint Committee between the Association and the National and Scottish Savings Committees had been extended to include the Post Office Savings Bank. The three savings organisations were keen to build on the concordat on school penny banks which was working well. A challenge from the Yorkshire Penny Bank was fought off in the spring of 1933, resulting in a non-aggression pact. The savings banks were persuaded by Louis Lawton, the actuary of the York Savings Bank, to replace local thrift stamp schemes with a national thrift stamp common to the Post Office Savings Bank and the National Savings Campaign. Stamps would allow purchasers the option of investing in either a savings bank, the Post Office Savings Bank, or National Savings Certificates. They would be distributed through existing outlets and National Savings Clubs, formed for the purpose and staffed by volunteers, mostly women, whose duties would include explaining the scheme and making weekly door-to-door collections. The new scheme was launched in September, evoking a good response from investors at the lower end of the savings market. By the autumn of 1935, 665 National Savings Clubs had been formed, of which 147 were registered with the savings banks. In addition,

30,000 of the 37,000 National Savings schemes were now being managed and promoted jointly between the National and Scottish Savings Committees, the savings banks, and the Post Office Savings Bank. The success of the national savings movement in the early 1930s almost certainly reflected a marked redistribution of incomes through taxation in the inter-war years. At the same time there was, with increasing reliance on contraception, a continuing sharp decline in

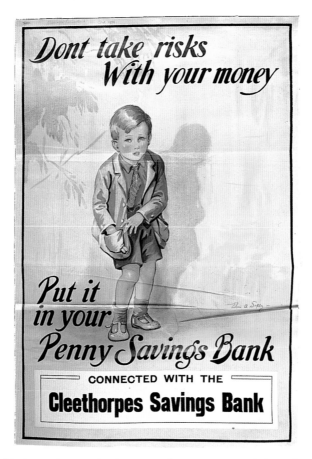

This Penny Savings Bank poster of 1936 anticipated the style of
advertisement adopted by the National Savings Committee during
the Second World War.

family size at the lower end of the social scale allowing more to be saved. The average size of families fell from 4.1 in 1921 to 3.7 in 1931 and the trend was continuing downwards.

One unpredicted consequence of the cheap money policy introduced in 1932 was a boom in new house construction. There was pent-up demand for home-ownership, particularly in the south of England, evinced by the huge advances in the share capital of building societies since 1918. New house building had retreated from its peak of 254,000 in 1927 to a low of 200,000 in 1930, but had never fallen back to pre-war levels due largely to the maintenance of local authority programmes. Recovery came quickly in 1933, with an all-time record of 365,000 new houses in 1936. The growth in construction came almost entirely from the private sector at a time when local authority finances were under pressure from the high cost of financing benefits for the long-term unemployed. The average cost of a new semi-detached house with a bathroom and garage was £450, with mortgages at interest rates of 5 per cent readily available

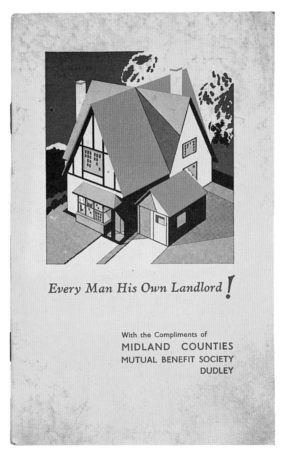

This Mutual Benefit Society would lend two-thirds
of the value of a property to those seeking to
become home owners in 1937.

from building societies flush with funds. With salaries of white-collar workers of between £225 and £368 and of skilled artisans of between £175 and £288, home ownership for the first time was in range of that section of the population that had traditionally been savings bank depositors. With the dramatic increase in income tax in the second 1936 budget (see p.180), there were also powerful tax advantages for a middle-class family to have a mortgage. Between 1930 and 1936, the percentage of all mortgages advanced to weekly wage earners as opposed to those drawing salaries climbed from 34.8 per cent to 50.5 per cent. It has been estimated that in this period 90 per cent of the increase of £198 million in mortgages can be attributed to working-class families. Mortgage advances by building societies climbed from £82 million in 1932 to over £130 million in 1935 with the number of investors fast approaching 2 million and share capital £447 million. Expenditure on furniture and household goods also accelerated in a period when prices generally were falling and wages and salaries recovering to their wartime levels. The biggest increase was in sales of recently developed electrical appliances, notably

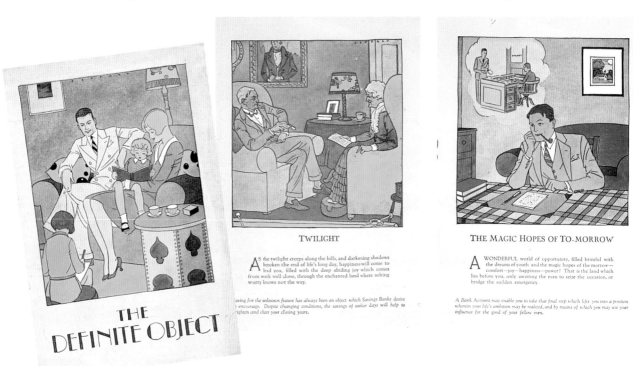

'The Definite Object' of this savings bank booklet was to woo
depositors from the building societies, with illustrations of what could
be achieved through saving at a savings bank.

vacuum cleaners, fires, radios and gramophones. Rising personal investment in houses and household goods after 1933, combined with the restrictions on annual deposits, helped staunch the flow of funds into special investment departments. The advance in total deposits slowed to little more than the annual rate of interest in 1935, despite a continuing sharp advance in real wages.

The slowing of activity in the special investment departments was accompanied by a revival of ordinary departments after a decade of stagnation. As employment prospects began to recover, the smaller depositors gradually began to return, pushing the total back over the 2 million mark in 1933 and to over 2.1 million by 1935. By 1935 they had more to save. Income tax was reduced in the budget and personal allowances increased to take many savings bank depositors out of the tax net. Deposits advanced to above £107 million in 1935 as customers, denied access to building society and special investment department accounts through the newly introduced restrictions, took advantage of the higher returns available in the savings banks; 2.5 per cent as compared to the very low yields paid on deposit accounts with the clearing banks. Indicative of a shift away from the clearing banks was a steady advance in ordinary department turnover. Deposits increased from just over £42 million in 1932 to almost £52 million in 1935, while withdrawals moved up from a little under £42 million to a new

THE FUTURE HOME

WHAT is this house in the heart of the world? It is Home that we shall build of dreams made real. It will be filled with love, with beauty, with laughter, with happiness. There, romping children will run to meet you, and with the joy of living in their faces, make complete the life which lies before you.

*But this "Home" can only be built by forethought and thrift. Your money in the Savings Bank will work and build for you. Make your decision to open an account to-day.*

EDUCATION

WHAT of these bright, young children when Time comes to take you down the valley of night! Have you given them that golden key which, as youth unfolds to manhood and womanhood, will open for them the doorway into a happy world of opportunity?

*The sacrifice entailed by saving and thought for your young people's future will be borne cheerfully, but it will be lightened by the cultivation of the Savings Bank habit. Begin your connection with the Savings Bank now. Do not wait until to-morrow.*

TRAVEL

SAVE TO TRAVEL is a familiar slogan on the windows of the Savings Bank. A leading Journal wrote regarding it: "He was a genius who invented this slogan, for the small visitor suddenly sees, beyond the shiny counters and the grills of the local Savings Bank, the picturesque chateaux of France, the roads of the North, the blue waters of the Mediterranean, all his particular castles in Spain, and knows the weary art of thrift is but a crossing to lands prodigal of delight."

*But money for travel must be saved in advance; it must be saved ere one embarks upon his journey. A weekly visit to the Savings Bank will make holiday a red letter event in your life.*

high of £45.6 million in 1934. This was a concern to the clearing banks which found themselves losing in the race for depositors. Although the upward thrust of turnover presented administrative problems for the bank staff, there were no complaints with the rise in deposits more than covering the cost. By 1935 the average deposit in ordinary departments was £50. Northern Ireland, where there were less than 100,000 customers, still headed the national league with an average of £83, followed by Scotland, where building societies played a less significant role, with £56, and then England and Wales with £44. The Post Office Savings Bank, paying the same interest as the savings banks, was equally popular. The seemingly relentless decline in the number of depositors was reversed in 1933. As with the savings banks some, but not all, of the ground lost in the slump was recovered by 1935. Prospects looked good, recruitment being bolstered by heavy promotion of branches of the National Savings

Club through advertisements in the press, exhibitions, window displays, films and the *Post Office Bulletin*. Total deposits reached £390 million in 1935 with deposits of £116 million and withdrawals of a little under £90 million.

Advancing turnover in both the Post Office Savings Bank and the savings banks was testimony to rising expenditure across the social scale, over and above that on the home. The savings banks were no longer hostile to spending for its own sake, providing it was undertaken wisely and sensibly. There was, however, a marked change in personal spending patterns in the

James R. Fiddes, who was appointed a CBE
in 1943 and created a Knight Bachelor in 1948
for his distinguished service with the TSBs.

aftermath of the slump. Sales of beer, often a good barometer of spending, slumped to less than 20 million bulk barrels in 1932, and did not recover to even their 1929 level before 1938. Total sales of all alcoholic drinks remained below their 1930 level, itself depressed, until 1938. Instead, expenditure was switching to other sources of entertainment, particularly the cinema following the advent of talking pictures, football matches, travel, and betting, particularly on dog racing and football pools, made legal in 1927. There was also evidence of more socially desirable spending, particularly on health care.

Upturn in savings bank business stimulated further expansion of the network and services. Opening hours were again extended in many banks and more save-to-travel schemes started in conjunction with the railway companies. The Association was concerned that there was no coherent approach to the introduction of new services and the possible initiatives sketched out by W.A. Barclay almost ten years before were in danger of being overlooked as the fortunes of the savings banks improved. J.R. Fiddes, the honorary secretary and actuary of the Savings Bank of Glasgow, chaired a committee to investigate the matter. In presenting their findings to the annual meeting in 1935, the committee warned that because one savings bank did not wish a new service, 'that bank should not stand in the way of it being made available to others'. They endorsed Barclay's proposal for a cheque system 'of a limited character', possibly in conjunction with the Post Office Savings Bank. This was immediately challenged by Major B.L. Fletcher of Liverpool who 'thought that the making of new depositors, particularly amongst the poorer section of the population, was of more importance than the conferring of further benefits on existing depositors. As things turned out, the Post Office was not enthusiastic, fearing it would be inconsistent with the payment of interest on ordinary accounts. By the following year, in addition to cheque services, the committee had considered the introduction of travellers' cheques, standing orders for periodic payments, advances for house purchases, and powers to act as executors and trustees.

J.R. Fiddes was disappointed that disagreement between the individual savings banks had again prevented progress, especially as the National and Scottish Savings Committees and the Post Office Savings Bank had launched 'new schemes for effective service'. He wondered if the cumbersome central control of the movement through the National Debt Office and the Inspection Committee was now more of a hindrance than a help. At least he wanted a proper development organisation within the Association and higher standard of training for savings bank staff. The reaction was mixed. Some committee members believed that the individual savings banks were already doing all they could for depositors by

Like savings bank accounts, football pools were promoted to attract the ordinary working man.

'collecting rates etc.' Others wanted to go further, bringing all the banks together under central control. Sensing from the mood of the meeting that radical change was impossible, Fiddes was able only to persuade the Council to explore some of the less controversial ideas, particularly staff training, and appoint a sub-committee to consider the practicalities of savings banks entering the buoyant life assurance market. The savings banks were not alone in disagreeing about the way forward. Despite the growth in their business, the National Association of Building Societies, which represented only a third of societies, was riven with internal dissent about the question of competition. In 1936 the Association was dissolved and the Building Societies Association immediately formed by those members subscribing to a code of ethics. Those societies, who refused to subscribe, set up a rival organisation – the National Federation of Building Societies. However strained the debate within the Trustee Savings Banks Association, there had never been such a public division of opinion.

By this time the climate for public finance had changed decisively. Since December 1933, when Hitler had taken totalitarian powers in Germany, the international situation had become increasingly tense. Germany was rearming, with the obvious intention of re-establishing hegemony in central Europe. The National government was thrown into a quandary. To meet force with force would, necessarily, require greater public expenditure which, in turn, might jeopardise the cheap money policy and recovery by driving up both interest rates and taxation. It was not until the Defence White Paper of March 1935 that the decision was taken to rearm, but little was done in practice until after the general election in October when the National government was returned, now with the Conservative Stanley Baldwin as Prime Minister. At first the additional defence expenditure was to be met entirely from revenue by raising taxation without recourse to borrowing. Standard rate tax was raised to 4s 9d in the pound and the reduced rate for those with incomes of less than £500 a year to 1s 7d. To sweeten the pill, allowances for married couples were raised from £170 to £180, and from £50 to £60 for each child.

Fundamental to this strategy was a continuing commitment to national saving through the combined efforts of the Trinity of Thrift – the Trustee Savings Banks, the Post Office Savings Bank, and the National, Scottish, Welsh and Irish Savings Committees. Taking advantage of the new medium of the wireless, Sir Spencer Portal, as President of the Association, broadcast to the nation on behalf of the campaign: 'You will not miss the little sums paid into your savings banks, but the big sum that will come out when you need it will surprise you. And you will have the satisfaction as well of knowing that your money, while you do not use it, is helping your country and your fellow countrymen.' Nevertheless, the Treasury was quickly forced to resort to borrowing to fund rearmament, but was determined that as far as practical the cost of borrowing would not rise. Under the Defence Loans Act of March 1937, £100 million 2.5 per cent National Defence Bonds were issued the following month. Despite the deepening crisis in international affairs, the public was unenthusiastic possibly because of the mounting burden of taxation. Sales of national savings certificates also declined. To attract private depositors, the government was forced to raise interest to the more competitive level of 3.5 per cent on an additional £81 million bonds launched in June 1938.

Higher rates of taxation did little to dent personal savings with institutions between 1936 to 1939. In savings banks, deposits with ordinary departments continued their onward progress, rising from £120 million to £152 million. There was a steady advance in new customers with an additional 230,000 new investors by 1939. Many of these were recruited through a further

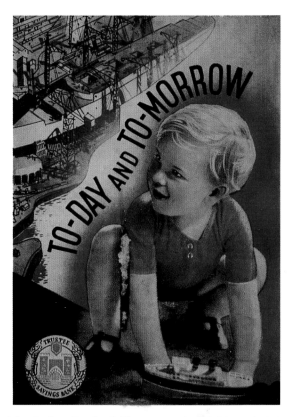

The Savings Bank of Glasgow produced this optimistic
advertisement in 1937.

extension of the branch network and new banks. Two more banks were opened – at Stoke-on-Trent in 1936 and Cardiff in 1937. In an effort to achieve efficiency and improved service, there were more amalgamations, including Newcastle upon Tyne and Morpeth Savings Banks in 1936, Glasgow and Kilmarnock in 1937, and Reading and Henley Savings Banks in 1938. With the rate of interest equivalent to that available in ordinary departments and now subject to official restrictions on annual deposits imposed by the National Debt Office in April 1936, deposits with special investment departments maintained their sluggish performances.

Keeping a careful watch on the building societies and the life companies whose popularity showed no sign of waning, the Association pressed on with the detailed investigation of various means of enhancing the range of services available to savings bank customers. E.C.C. Evans, the actuary of the Manchester & Salford Savings Bank, was an enthusiastic advocate of the savings banks entering the life assurance market, particularly after the existing life companies had been heavily criticised in 1936 for their sales-pressure tactics by a House of Commons Select Committee. Encouraged by the example in the USA of the Massachusetts Savings Bank, which successfully operated an insurance scheme, Evans calculated that the savings banks would have far lower overheads than insurance companies and, on the basis of the Massachusetts scheme, could anticipate a much higher degree of customer loyalty. At the same time, the Executive Committee reviewed the operation of ordinary and special investment departments; hire purchase, which was proving an increasingly popular method of buying consumer goods; and staff training. There was general agreement that the regulations concerning the investment of funds in special investment departments should be relaxed to allow unsecured loans to be made to local authorities. Many savings banks were worried that unless more was done to assist local authority finances, there was a danger that a future Labour government might revive proposals for the formation of municipal banks. Walter Cobbett, chairman of the Manchester & Salford Savings Bank, was convinced that the best defence against this danger was powers for banks with large surpluses in their administrative accounts to be allowed to make grants available for the formation of more new banks. Predicting Labour policy, others believed that the savings banks would simply be nationalised and amalgamated with the Post Office Savings Bank into a single national bank. In any event, a draft Bill was prepared, incorporating many of these suggestions and discussed with the National Debt Commissioners.

The Treasury and the National and Scottish Savings Committees, from a different perspective, were also concerned with the whole concept of saving for spending, aroused by a proposal from a book on the subject by Professor Levy and Sir Arnold Wilson, a Conservative MP. They were appalled at the authors' apparent dislike of 'all spending, for its own sake'. Max Nicholson, general secretary of the National Savings Committee, summed up the new approach to saving:

> Jam tomorrow and never jam today seems to me equally unsound in the moral as in the economic sphere, even admitting that we are our poor brethren's keepers. The real issue is, given the right amount of saving from the saver's point of view, what monetary or economic measures are necessary to ensure sufficient aggregate spending to keep activity and employment going – or to get them going, as the case may be.

Improvement in the control of hire purchase by the 1938 Hire Purchase Act persuaded some actuaries, again inspired by Evans, that it was now prudent for savings banks to provide this service. Recognising that hire purchase, by its very nature, was incompatible with the principle of 'wise saving for wise spending', its advocates presented their case carefully. They argued that there was no moral objection to the purchase of 'houses or other necessities of life by instalments' and, providing strict regulation was observed, there was no danger of undermining the essential purpose of encouraging thrift. Any suggestion that the savings bank movement should become involved in hire purchase was bitterly opposed by a large number of trustees, who believed it to be morally indefensible. The Revd Beaumont James, the vicar of a working-class parish in London, spoke for them all in denouncing even:

> house purchase ... as one of the most pernicious forms of hire purchase. Often those who went into a house to be purchased under some such plan came from a social class which had no experience of possession before; they were ignorant of all that they were committing themselves to, and sooner or later found themselves in difficulties. They never obtained any substantial ownership, and often lost all they had paid – whereas in council houses, obtainable at a moderate rent, they were able to live within their income, to bring up children and make a contribution to the social life of the centre in which they lived.

There could have been no clearer statement of the differences in outlook and perception which divided the movement between those anxious for improved services to maintain the loyalty of larger depositors, and those who held a rigid interpretation of thrift and providence, entirely appropriate and relevant in certain contexts.

There was still ample evidence that, despite growth in real wages, the working population at the bottom of the social scale still lacked the wherewithal to save and therefore could not afford to take on liabilities such as mortgages and hire purchase. Nevertheless, poor families continued to invest in burial insurance policies to the fury of social commentators like Seebohm Rowntree, who conducted a survey of the town of York in 1941. He found that poor families were spending between 5 and 21 per cent of their income on insurance: 'that they should pay so large a proportion of their inadequate income for "death insurance" is a serious matter. They were going short of food and fostering their death in order to ensure a decent burial.' At the other end of the social scale, Rowntree found much to support Evans's views; since his first survey at the end of the nineteenth century, he could report a big advance in house ownership amongst those families where the 'chief wage earner' took home less than £250 a year, with over 10 per cent of his sample owning their own homes. He was confident enough to believe that Britain was 'already within measureable distance of abolishing poverty ...'.

There was no disagreement amongst the savings banks about the urgent need to improve the quality and training of staff. Minimum entrance qualifications were recommended in February 1937, when the formation was mooted of a Savings Banks Institute to act as an examining body, modelled on the well-established Institute of Bankers in London and the Building Society Institute established in 1934. It was envisaged that the Institute, in addition, would serve the needs of the Birmingham Municipal Bank, and the Post Office Savings Bank. The idea evoked an enthusiastic response, but a final decision was delayed until the outcome of negotiations with the Scottish Institute of Bankers for membership by savings bank staff was known. When the Scottish Institute refused late in 1938 to follow the lead of the English

Institute in agreeing to admit savings bank members, the Association had no alternative but to explore the proposal further.

All discussion of future plans and developments was brought to an abrupt halt by the rapid deterioration in relations with Nazi Germany during 1938, culminating in the Munich crisis during the autumn, when war seemed imminent. At the time, the government believed that hostilities would be dominated by heavy indiscriminate bombing of cities and towns, resulting in huge loss of life and property. Businesses were encouraged to maintain duplicate sets of records away from obvious targets, such as large industrial conurbations. Of equal concern was the possible effect of the threat of war on customer confidence. In the weeks before the outbreak of the First World War, the international financial markets had been paralysed and banks had experienced abnormal withdrawals. Since then measures had been taken to ensure

The story of Scottykin and Mopsy and their sixpences, produced for
the 1938 Scottish Empire Exhibition.

stability in international markets, reducing the danger of steep rises in interest rates to hold the exchange at times of crisis. Nevertheless, savings banks made arrangements to be able to call on sufficient liquidity should there be heavy demand. The immediate danger of war passed, but every department of government was soon preoccupied in planning for war and no progress could be made with the suggested Savings Bank Bill.

Of greatest concern to the Treasury was the rising cost of the defence programme and a possible downturn in the economy. Personal savings assumed an increasingly important role in the preparations for financing the war. The National and Scottish Savings Committees worked tirelessly with the Savings Banks and the Post Office Savings Bank to promote National Savings Groups. Throughout Britain there were heavily publicised 'National Savings Weeks'. By June 1939 there were over 45,000 National Savings Groups, of which 85 per cent were run jointly with the Post Office and trustee savings banks. With tension mounting and the outbreak of war more and more likely, the emergency procedures drawn up the previous year were elaborated. The Association set about devising a national scheme to deal with an anticipated surge in withdrawals in the event of forced evacuation following the first heavy German bombing raids that were expected to devastate Britain's cities. The government had prepared plans for the compulsory evacuation of people in the worst affected areas and it was believed others would wish to move voluntarily – 'The first thing they would need would be money.' J.R. Fiddes, consulting with actuaries of other large savings banks, concluded that, given many staff would have been called up and arrangements be in hand to ensure the safety of buildings, it might be difficult to cope with the rush immediately, and such conditions might easily give rise to panic. A simple plan was devised whereby any savings bank depositor would be able to obtain £3 in cash on production of a warrant at any Post Office or clearing bank. Under severe pressure from the government to have a workable plan in place by the end of July, there followed tense negotiations with both the Bankers' Clearing House and the Post Office, neither of which was prepared to co-operate without the support of the other. Eventually, the Association undertook, with the consent of the National Debt Office, to open temporary banks in parts of the country where there were no banks, to which people were evacuated in the event of such an emergency.

The Association had taken advantage of the respite in international tension in the spring of 1939 to develop proposals for an Institute. During April help and advice was solicited from the Association of Building Societies, the Institute of Municipal Treasurers and Accountants, the Chartered Insurance Institute and the Chartered Institute of Secretaries. At a meeting in early May the objectives of a Savings Banks Institute were discussed. Membership was to be available to all savings bank staff whose 'education, efficiency, progress and general development' were to be the Institute's responsibility. The Institute was to have its own professional examinations. There was also a suggestion that it should have certain pastoral functions, like some other similar institutes – caring for those who had fallen on hard times and supporting widows and orphans. Until there was sufficient subscription income, the Institute was to be financed initially out of a levy of 1s on every £10,000 of deposits. The urgent preparations for war made it impossible to implement the proposal, at least for the time being. By the summer many of the men, who could have been the first members of the new institute, had left their desks to join their territorial army units in anticipation of imminent hostilities.

War was declared on 3 September and as it turned out, at least in the opening phase of the conflict, predictions of heavy bombing appeared to be wholly exaggerated. Taking advantage of this unexpected lull, the chairman of the Association, Sir George Rainy, sought an immediate meeting on 8 September with the Treasury. His purpose was to ensure that the savings banks played their full part in funding the war in a way which had been denied them in the previous conflict. Responding to an invitation to let the Treasury know their views, the savings banks compiled a memorandum at very short notice against a background of rapid loss of staff of military age to join the forces. The outcome was an invitation for representatives of the savings banks to attend a meeting at the Treasury on 26 October when plans for a new issue of National

Savings Certificates and another security for small investors were explained. Delighted to be taken 'much more frankly into confidence . . . than had been customary in the past', the savings bank representatives insisted that the savings banks should be given their due place in the war savings campaign. There was disappointment that no joint propaganda was envisaged and that the National Debt Commissioners were unwilling to remove the ceiling on deposits in special investment departments imposed in April 1936. The Treasury, for its part, had no desire to see any growth in special investment departments with funds that could be invested at the discretion of the individual banks. Almost immediately investment opportunities for special investment departments were dramatically curtailed by restrictions on local authority borrowing powers to ensure there would be no competition for war funds. Similar restrictions were applied to private enterprise.

With the broad agreement of all the financial institutions, the War Savings Campaign was made public on 22 November 1939. In making the announcement, Sir John Simon, the Chancellor of the Exchequer, made it clear that there were three ways the personal saver could contribute to the war effort: through the purchase of 3 per cent seven-year Defence Bonds, with a 1 per cent bonus on maturity; through National Savings Certificates yielding 3.5 per cent if held for ten years and, as in the past, exempt from income tax; and through deposits with either the Post Office Savings Bank or the trustee savings banks. Arrangements could be

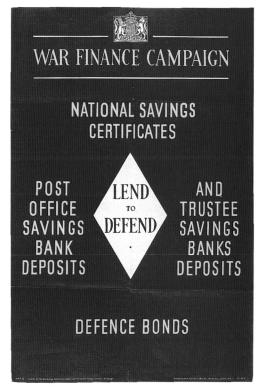

Four ways to Lend to Defend, 1940.

made by employers for the tax-free purchase of National Savings Certificates by direct transfer from their employees' wages. Despite this declaration, press advertising and posters about the campaign published over the next few days referred only to the issue of the two new government securities. To the alarm of actuaries, customers began transferring their deposits into National Savings Certificates and Defence Bonds. Sensitive to the importance of maintaining good relations with the savings banks, the Chief Commissioner of the National Savings Committee, E.C.H. Jones, acted quickly and decisively to put matters right, by explaining that reference to the savings banks had been omitted on the advice of leading publicity agents who believed it would confuse the public. He reassured the savings bank movement that, once the message about the new securities had been got across, the emphasis would be placed on popularising National Savings Groups. On his advice, the Association voiced their complaints directly to the Treasury, the architects of the campaign, but did agree to use the publicity material of the National and Scottish Savings Committees for the duration of the war, providing it was adjusted in the way the Chief Commissioner had described.

Although the Treasury and the National and Scottish Savings Committees took immediate steps to ensure that War Savings advertising carried reference to the savings banks, the members of the Association remained on their guard for any failures to comply with the Chief Commissioner's undertaking. In mid-January 1940 they insisted that a film on war savings must be remade to give prominence to savings banks; censured Sir Robert Kindersley, the President of the Campaign, for deleting reference to savings banks in the agreed text of a broadcast speech; and demanded full representation at all public meetings. They had good grounds for complaint. With as yet no clear public signal from the Treasury, customers were still transferring appreciable sums into National Savings Certificates and Defence Bonds, over £2.75 million in the last few weeks of 1939. Nevertheless, the savings banks were willing to comply with an instruction issued by the National Debt Commissioners on 19 December 1939 that all new money deposited in special investment departments would be invested in the new government securities. The sensitivity of the savings banks to omissions in publicity continued to the frustration of Treasury officials, who increasingly believed that trustees and actuaries had little understanding of the difficulties of formulating fiscal policy in wartime.

There were economists led by J.M. Keynes, who believed that the voluntary nature of the War Savings Campaign was inherently flawed:

> No amount of saving by the rich nor any amount of taxes levied upon the rich will suffice to reduce the spending of the poor out of their enhanced incomes. It is not reasonable that the lower income groups will suddenly develop habits of saving which will render reliance on voluntary saving a satisfactory anti-inflation policy. Peacetime quiescence in the injustices of economic inequality cannot be perpetuated in wartime by mere appeals to the patriotism of the poor. A family which had not been able to afford roast beef before the war is not likely to refrain voluntarily from indulging a little during the war when its income has risen ...

At the turn of the year Keynes called for a compulsory Government Savings Deposit Scheme deducted from income at source; in other words, deferred pay. Such a policy would have left the savings banks with no new business and might even have threatened existing deposits. His argument was given greater credence by the failure of the Treasury's first large issue of War Loan to the financial institutions and large savers on 12 March. Disappointed, the government renewed its call to smaller savers, having already reassured trade union leaders that war savings would not be used to hold down wages. Deeply concerned that a compulsory savings programme might be taken seriously, the savings banks made even greater efforts to attract savings for the war effort, particularly through the formation of new group schemes, especially in the workplace with the co-operation of the trade unions, and war weapons weeks modelled on those mounted during the previous conflict. Deposits poured in, with takings averaging £5 million a week until the middle of May. Following the German blitzkrieg on France and the evacuation of the British Expeditionary Force from Dunkirk later that month, the nation responded by giving all it could to help defend the country against what seemed imminent invasion. For the week ending 18 June deposits with the savings banks reached a striking £20 million. The possibilities of invasion came even nearer at the end of the month when German troops invaded the Channel Islands. Before the occupation, the books of the Jersey and Guernsey Savings Banks had been sent to the London Savings Bank, which carried on their business until liberation. On 12 July all banks were circulated with instructions as to what to do in the event of an invasion. These included the purchase of 'a sack or bag for the speedy removal of currency etc.', the removal of all keys from the premises, and the advice that on the approach of the enemy, currency – notes and coins – must be destroyed before a creditable witness to prevent accusations of frauds.

The flood of new savings at this time of crisis was not entirely an outcome of appeals to save, but also of the increasing disincentives to spend. The War Savings Campaign was balanced by a commitment from the government to hold down inflation of living costs by controlling prices and by rationing. Despite instructions to every trade association not to raise prices during the emergency, the cost of living had climbed by about 10 per cent by the New Year with wages lagging well behind. Rationing was introduced in January 1940; everyone was issued with ration books entitling them to specific amounts of all the more important foodstuffs. Spending on non-essential goods, including clothes, was to be held in check by both the imposition of purchase tax in the spring budget and by sharp reductions in the goods supplied to the home market. To the dismay of shopkeepers, the government tried to dissuade customers from buying even the merchandise that remained on the market by calls for greater savings for the war effort. At the end of July the new coalition government, with Winston Churchill as Prime Minister, set the standard rate of purchase tax on all goods except food at 33.3 per cent, with an additional 16.3 per cent on luxuries. The result of this indirect approach to compulsory saving in the face of imminent invasion and nightly bombing was a transformation of attitudes.

The evacuation of children from cities and towns to the countryside gave rural Britain, for the first time, direct knowledge of the hardship of life in industrial areas worst affected by the depression. High taxation of the better-off, combined with shared experiences in air-raid shelters and of shortages of goods and food rationing, made the socially divisive policy of the means test less and less acceptable. The Labour Party, as a member of the coalition, was determined to address changing expectations with a radical programme of reform. Already the previous Chamberlain government had extended the means test in March 1940 when supplementary benefits were introduced under the Old Age & Widows' Pensions Act to help offset the effect of inflation since the beginning of hostilities. Trade unions and thrift organisations protested that the £50 savings exemptions were no longer adequate. Under pressure, and anxious to do nothing to disturb the War Savings Campaign when the war was intensifying, the Chamberlain government promised to amend the Determination of Needs Act 1935 as soon as practicable, and immediately raised the limit on new money lent for war savings to £375. The legislation was delayed by the formation of the coalition government in July and the appointment of the trade union leader, Ernest Bevin, as Minister of Labour. Consequently, when the measure was introduced later in the year, it went much further than the Chamberlain government had envisaged, mitigating the worst features of the means test by abolishing the rigorous personal inquiry into an individual's resources. Contemporary reports suggest that raising the limit so generously had the desired effect, encouraging those who had hoarded cash at home for fear of the means test to invest in war savings; this was particularly noticeable in cities and towns bombed nightly.

The political consensus achieved immediately by the coalition government, necessary to prosecute a total war, contrasted starkly with renewed protests from the savings banks that they were continuing to be overlooked in the campaign for war savings. At the postponed annual meeting of the Association in mid-September 1940, there were complaints that the Post Office Savings Bank was still repeatedly referred to in advertisements and broadcasts while scarcely any mention was made of the savings banks. When the savings bank year ended in November, fences had been more or less mended by the efforts at a local level of the National and Scottish Savings Committees. This new sense of common purpose was reinforced by the punitive blitz of Coventry on 14 November 1940 which destroyed 60,000 out of 75,000 buildings in the city, including the head office of the Coventry Savings Bank. Responding to this appalling testimony to the effects of modern aerial warfare, annual reports from savings banks up and down the country endorsed war savings with such slogans as 'Save to Defend', and the wordy 'Make the Country's Economic Position IMPREGNABLE – RETRENCH WISELY, MOBILISE YOUR SAVINGS FOR THE COUNTRY'S SERVICE by depositing them in the SAVINGS BANK – Victory depends on it'. Chairmen in their speeches and messages to shareholders stressed the close and amicable relations with local savings committees. All reported the formation of new savings groups in 'workshops, offices, organisations, etc.' By the end of the year these efforts had contributed to a further marked growth in ordinary departments. Special investment department holdings rose by little more than the rate of interest, but new investments in government stock (Defence Bonds) through the banks totalled almost £5 million. The number of depositors rose by over 200,000. The Post Office Savings Bank recorded even greater percentage gains. Deposits climbed and a million new customers were recruited to bring the total to nearly 13 million.

The New Year of 1941 brought no cheer for the British people. The tentacles of the German military machine spread to ensnare most of Europe and reached into North Africa by midsummer, threatening Russia in the north and Egypt in the south. The nightly bombing of Britain's cities and towns intensified. A raid on London on 10 May left devastated a third of the streets in the docklands and killed almost 1,500 people. One unexpected consequence of the raids was a sudden advance in deposits, as people looked for a secure home for the cash savings they had hidden away in their homes. After the raid on Clydebank, the home of John Brown's shipyard, on 13 March 1941, over £500,000 was deposited with the Savings Bank of Glasgow made up mostly in £1 notes. The bombing took its toll of savings banks. The principal office of the London Savings Bank in Southampton was destroyed and one of the branches of the Hull Savings Bank. Remarkably, despite the heavy raids in Plymouth, the head office in the city centre escaped almost unscathed – 'an oasis in a centre of desolation'. Throughout the country bank staff prided themselves on maintaining the service in the face of appalling odds. The air raids and consequent evacuation tested the regulations for emergency withdrawals devised on the eve of war.

The need for funds to fight the war was more urgent than ever. Weekly savings news programmes began to be broadcast in February 1941 immediately after the six o'clock evening news when many families could be expected to be listening. Savings films were shown as trailers in cinemas up and down the country, and millions of leaflets and posters were distributed. Between March 1940 and March 1941, total sales of National Savings Certificates exceeded a startling £170 million. There were those, however, who were convinced that more could be achieved, pointing an accusing finger at the high level of spending in the weeks before Christmas, which put inflationary pressures on the money supply. The censure was even greater for official encouragement for people to take summer holidays. There was good sense in this decision, giving men, women and children bruised by the blitz time for refreshment and relaxation. Holidays, however, cost money. Individuals and families naturally drew on their savings to pay for what might be their last opportunity for enjoyment together for a long time. Some trustees and actuaries found this decision difficult to comprehend, inconsistent with the campaign for war savings, and called for the government to request that holidays should be taken near home to avoid unnecessary cost. The zealous voicing of such opinions reinforced the unfortunate impression that the savings banks were out of step with the political consensus

The National Savings Committee's message in 1941 was clear.

THE SIGNAL IS SAVE

vital for the successful prosecution of the war. Nevertheless, relations between the savings banks, the Post Office Savings Bank and the National and Scottish Savings Committees continued to improve, becoming more amicable and co-operative.

The closing months of 1941 were ones of setbacks and disappointments for Britain as the Japanese, following Hitler's example in Europe, established their military hegemony in the Far East. The unprovoked attack on 7 December on the American Pacific fleet in Pearl Harbor brought the United States into the war, holding out the promise of eventual victory to the Allies. There was no doubt that it would be a long and expensive campaign. Nevertheless, it was not anticipated that the cost would increase by much more than £1 billion over the £5 billion set aside in 1941, although even that figure was far in excess of pre-war predictions. When government expenditure stabilised during 1942, the Treasury, keen to ensure that it was

Humour, as well as appeals to patriotism, was used in promoting war savings. Posters such as this one from 1942, provided welcome light relief for Britons on the Home Front.

met in roughly equal proportions from revenue and borrowings, urged the National and Scottish Savings Committees to maintain the levels of personal saving achieved in 1941. This was easier said than done. Most personal accumulations of cash had been gathered in and the bulk of future savings would have to come from incomes. Despite higher taxation and the increased cost of living, real family incomes were rising as more and more men and women found employment. Spurred on by the National Savings Committee, the savings banks and the Post Office Savings Bank began a fresh drive to capture a bigger proportion of family incomes from existing depositors and to win new custom. They were helped by further restrictions of spending; rationing of food was tightened and rationing extended to clothes and furniture as the U-boat campaign made supplies harder and harder to obtain. To meet the challenge, the government had launched an urgent building programme for corvettes, destroyers and merchant ships. The National and Scottish Savings Committees sponsored 'Warship Weeks' the length and breadth of the country, in collaboration with savings banks and the Post Office Savings Bank to reinforce local initiatives. This appeal was made against a background not just of the rapidly intensifying Battle of the Atlantic, but also of the continued nightly bombing of Britain's cities and towns.

In solemn mood the savings banks, their staffs more than halved by conscription, devoted much energy to carry the war savings message into the workplace, with the aim of enlarging the direct transfer scheme (see pp.186–7). Savings banks were opened in large factories. In July the Oxford Savings Bank inaugurated a branch at the Pressed Steel Company's plant at Cowley, declaring: 'Many employees prefer an account in the Trustee Savings Bank to other forms of National Savings as they appreciate the opportunity to save in privacy, the friendly help and service which the Bank gives and the facilities for speedy withdrawals when necessary.' When the war in North Africa entered a critical phase later in the year, the National Savings Committee inaugurated a nationwide 'Tanks for Attack Campaign'. In Sheffield the vigorous promotion resulted in a 25 per cent increase in all forms of small savings for the year. The Warship Week at Aberdeen yielded an astounding £3 million and the Tanks for Attack Campaign, £500,000. Altogether, ordinary department investments in the United Kingdom climbed by about £50 million and the number of customers reached over 3 million. The advance in the Post Office Savings Bank was even more startling, with an additional £180 million, taking deposits over £1 billion for the first time.

By the end of 1942, there was at last tangible proof that Hitler's military might was not invincible. General Montgomery's crushing defeat of Rommel's German and Italian army at El Alamein in October marked a turning point in the war in the West. In the East the Russians had brought the German advance to a standstill at Stalingrad and in the Far East, on Guadalcanal, the Americans were stemming the tide of Japanese conquests. Matching the more optimistic mood, the chairmen of savings banks lost no opportunity when reporting the largest increase in the movement's history in stressing the importance of collaboration with the Post Office

Hull Savings Bank's East Branch,
destroyed in an air raid, July 1941.

Savings Bank and local Savings Committees in maintaining the level of war savings. They were fulsome in their praise of staff who had struggled to maintain services to the customers. Many offices were damaged by bombing; some seriously. In May the head office of the Devon & Exeter Savings Bank was completely destroyed, killing seven fire-watchers, including the bank's chief cashier, W.H.W. Beazley; within days, a new temporary office had been opened. Throughout the country savings banks reported that as more men and women were called up, there was insufficient staff to cope with the volume of business. In many savings banks, the only member of staff left with any pre-war experience was the actuary; the rest were mostly young women recruited since the outbreak of war. Apart from being forced to close early during the winter months because of lighting restrictions, many were obliged to shut at lunch-time – a period of peak business – owing to lack of staff. Tentative discussions were held with the joint stock banks with a view to sharing services; but there was agreement that as they catered for different sections of society nothing would be gained. With the movement operating an almost skeleton staff, the Association wrung a promise from the government in the autumn to exempt women from call-up and defer indefinitely the conscription of senior staff of serviceable age.

At the very moment the war began to move in the Allies' favour, the government published a report, *Social Insurance and Allied Services,* by Sir William Beveridge, commissioned the previous year. Beveridge went beyond his original brief and addressed every aspect of social policy,

Pirelli–General Cable workers line up at their 'branch' of the
Southampton Trustee Savings Bank.

calling for the final annihilation of the five giants of Want, Disease, Ignorance, Squalor and Idleness. Building on the evidence collected by social commentators such as Rowntree, he proposed an ambitious social insurance guaranteeing benefits covering sickness; medical treatment; pensions for widows, orphans and old people; maternity; industrial reform; and the cost of funerals. The means test was to be abolished, along with the last vestiges of the Poor Law. In reaching his conclusions, Beveridge assumed that the government would pursue economic policies that would ensure more or less continuous full employment. The report, with its emphases on equity and consensus, struck a popular chord and quickly sold out. Some representatives of the savings movement were sceptical that the proposed benefits would make it almost impossible to persuade people to save. Others wondered if it would add so much to industry's costs that British manufactured goods would be priced out of overseas markets, fuelling the unemployment it was designed to cure. Sensing the tenor of the nation, more progressive trustees and actuaries intervened to support the report, advancing the same argument that had been used when national insurance had first been introduced thirty years before. Dr Guy Worman, Bishop of Manchester, president of the Manchester & Salford Savings Bank told the bank's annual meeting:

> I suppose the real purpose of this bank is to rid people of necessity and to give them a sense of
> security. Now we are told by some people that that sense of security and all the virtues
> connected with it are likely to be taken away and nullified by such a report as that of Sir William

Beveridge. I have seen it suggested more than once that the Beveridge Report is going to make us thriftless and careless. I do not for a moment believe it. During the last fifty years we have moved one stage up by degrees ... I believe a measure of security will tend to make us more careful. Some sort of provision is made in the Beveridge Report, I understand, for the 'rainy days' of life. If some provision is made, I believe people will try to add to that provision.

Necessary as such statements were in keeping the savings banks in tune with public opinion, the debate about the Beveridge Report remained largely academic. Churchill, preoccupied with the prosecution of the campaign, sought to quieten discussion for fear of raising hopes that could not be fulfilled.

Whatever their expectations, no one was in any doubt that in the immediate future there would be further privations and suffering until Hitler was finally defeated. Local Savings Committees renewed their call for a sustained effort with slogans like the Belfast Savings Bank's 'SAVE FOR VICTORY AND YOURSELF' or 'Convert your SAVINGS into MUNITIONS by taking them to CHORLEY TRUSTEE SAVINGS BANK', or the Nottingham Savings Bank's 'Patriotic Pounds', or the Stoke-on-Trent Savings Bank's more prosaic 'Play YOUR part in the War Finance Campaign by depositing your savings regularly at the bank'. Apart from local promotions, the principal drive for the deposits of smaller savers was to be through an extension of what had

become known as the Savings in Works scheme. Savings bank staff were well aware that the scheme could be successful only with the full co-operation of both management and employees. Securing the support of management, well represented in the ranks of trustees, was straightforward; employees were more difficult. In each works, every effort was made to gain the confidence of the shop stewards and to assure would-be depositors that transactions would be treated in complete confidence. To prevent there being any chance of an employer finding out the details of any account, the bank encouraged customers to hold two accounts: one with the branch in the works and another with a normal branch. Throughout the spring and summer of 1943, meetings were held in factories and offices. Local initiative was supported by another national promotion, this time with the slogan 'WINGS FOR VICTORY – SPEED THE WINGS BY SAVING', designed to be a sort of poetic justice for Hitler's claim that he would use aircraft to terrorise the world. The results from an increasingly co-ordinated campaign were better than even the most optimistic predictions. Net sales of National Savings Certificates climbed from £206 million to over £250 million. Turnover at the Post Office Savings Bank was, for the first time, more than £425 million, with total deposits reaching £1.24 billion. The turnover in the savings banks was £154 million and total deposits surpassed £0.5 billion (£500 million). Rising turnover did not always produce a net gain in deposits. In mining areas, where there

had been a reluctance to use savings banks before the war, the novelty led many new customers to use their accounts as current accounts. The Savings in Works scheme was an instant success as savings were shown along with income tax and national insurance as a deduction on the pay slip. Instead of leaving their savings in their accounts, many new customers simply withdrew their balances to spend on beer unbeknown to their wives!

During 1943 the war had turned steadily to the Allies' advantage. The Germans were driven from North Africa and in September Italy was invaded. On the eastern front the Russians had gone on to the offensive and in the Far East the Japanese, in a series of bloody confrontations, were forced to yield

Poster launching the 'Wings for Victory' campaign; and (OPPOSITE) Wings for Victory Week at the Birmingham Municipal Bank, 1943.

territory. Stimulated by the recent success of the War Savings Campaign, and with more funds urgently needed to open the second front on the mainland of Europe, an even more ambitious promotion was launched for the months of March to June 1944 during the build-up to D-Day and after the Normandy landings. Using the caption 'Salute the Soldier', an exceptional series of posters was designed for the National Savings Committee. As the details of the year's savings drive were being put together, the Treasury and the National Debt Commissioners began to look forward to the coming of peace. Starting out from the premise that a high level of personal savings would be needed to help meet the cost of post-war reconstruction, a questionnaire was sent to all savings banks to sound out their views about continuing the War Savings Campaign on much the same lines in peacetime. Suspecting a premeditated attack by government on their independent local role, the savings banks were less than enthusiastic. They were particularly infuriated by the suggestion that all new money deposited in special investment departments should continue to be invested in government securities rather than with individual local authorities. There was considerable apprehension at the use by the Commissioners of the phrase 'full partnership'. Many actuaries were keen to know whether, when the so-called partnership was eventually

Saluting the Soldier, 1944; and (OPPOSITE) Salute the Soldier Week, Birmingham Municipal Bank, June 1944.

dissolved, the savings banks would receive a share of the national savings they had helped to create. It soon became clear that the room for manoeuvre of savings banks operating special investment departments would be very restricted as the Treasury intended to put a tight rein on local government expenditure for fear that funds would be diverted away from central government. Wrong-footed, the Trustee Savings Banks Association, speaking for its members, grudgingly accepted that the restrictions would have to remain in force at least for the time being.

Consideration of the post-war funding of local and national government was of central importance to the policy decision being put forward on the basis of the Beveridge Report. In February 1944, a white paper was published, proposing the creation of a National Health Service. This was followed by further white papers, *Full Employment in a Free Society* in May and *Social Insurance* in September. It did not take long for the more far-sighted trustees and actuaries to appreciate the implications of these policies for the traditional rhetoric of the savings movement. Sir George Rainy told the annual meeting of the TSB Association that the members 'would have to face the problems and see how far the functions of Trustee Savings Banks might be modified now that public provision was to be made for many of the needs to

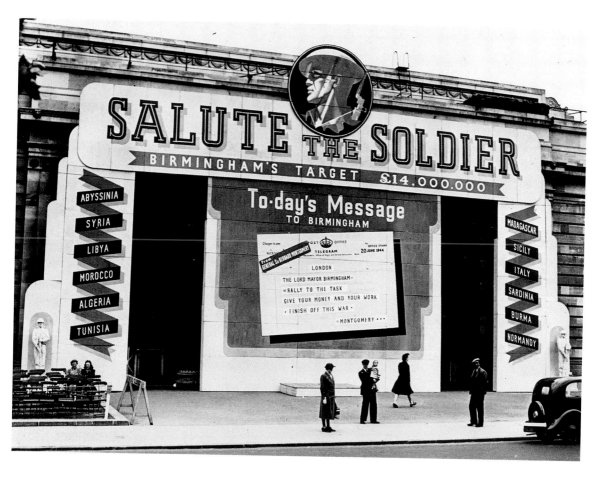

provide for which saving had been advocated in the past'. In the short term, as long as the movement accepted the importance of maintaining the level of national savings in the coming peace there was no obstacle to promoting the ideal of thrift. Sir Kenneth Stewart, deputy chairman of the Association and chairman of the Manchester & Salford Savings Bank, explained his strategy for the peace:

> The real crisis will come in the three to five years after the war. Our fighting services will feel entitled to some relaxation, but, to my mind, the hope of a prosperous and worthy future for this country will be very largely in the hands of the workers in the National Savings Movement. If they continue to work for savings and continue to bring before the public the absolute necessity for providing the Government with money for all the vast schemes of building and social betterment in this country and all over the world, we can look for a grand future for our fighting services who have borne the heat and burden of this fearful war. If the National Savings workers and, in consequence, the country relaxes in its efforts, I fear we shall face a repetition of the disasters that followed the last war.'

Disappointing as such an outlook was to those who hoped that the cessation of hostilities would bring an opportunity for the introduction of services so widely debated before the war, Sir Kenneth believed that the Association should take positive action to improve staff training and co-ordinate 'development' which, for the time being, would be through further branch extension. The concept of a Savings Banks Institute was revived during 1944 and a committee appointed by the Association to work out the details.

Concern for the future was tempered by the achievement of the Allies in securing the Normandy bridgehead and carrying their offensive across France towards the German border. Against this background, the 'Salute the Soldier' campaign had been an outstanding success. With victory predicted early in 1945, the next campaign was planned as a 'Thanksgiving', driving home the message to keep saving to win the peace. When victory finally came in Europe in May and in the Far East in August, the profile of personal saving and expenditure had been profoundly altered since the outbreak of war. Rationing, coupled with purchase tax and increased savings, had slashed consumer expenditure from an estimated 87 per cent of national income in 1938 to 57 per cent in 1944. Savings had reached a remarkable 15 per cent of after-tax incomes when at times in the pre-war years it had been negligible. As a result, by 1945 small savings were almost double what they had been in 1938. National savings, including deposits with the Post Office Savings Bank and the savings banks, accounted for the bulk of the increase, £3,909 million out of a total of some £4,725 million. Within the field of National Savings, the sale of government stock (Defence Bonds) by the Post Office Savings Bank, recorded the largest percentage increase, up 450 per cent on the pre-war total, followed by sales of National Savings Certificates up 362 per cent. Deposits with the Post Office Savings Bank were in third place with a rise of 349 per cent and the savings banks were in last place with 250 per cent. There was an equivalent gain in the number of customers, introducing more people to the concept of banking than ever before. The number of Post Office Savings Bank account holders doubled to over 22 million, while savings bank depositors advanced by a third to over 3.6 million. This uneven experience was attributed to the strong appeal of Defence Bonds to those who had previously invested in the stock market, and to the promotion of National Savings, associated more closely with the Post Office Savings Bank than the savings banks. Thrift organisations outside the War Savings Campaign fared less well. With the cessation of house building during the emergency, deposits with the building societies failed to keep pace, rising by little more than the rate of interest. By 1945 the building societies' share of total small savings had fallen from 17.5 per cent to 9 per cent. More puzzling was the lack-lustre performance of the life assurance and provident societies whose share fell from 34 per cent to

The NSC was eager to ensure that civilians
continued to save once the war was over.

25 per cent – due possibly to an unwillingness in the uncertainties of war for people to commit themselves to long-term savings. Although the clearing banks experienced a huge advance in deposits, much of this was the consequence of the introduction of Treasury Deposit Receipts in 1940 rather than any expansion of private client business.

At the end of the war it was estimated that there were few families in which at least one member did not have some form of savings account, but there was some debate as to how far the twin effects of restrictions on expenditure and encouragement to save had really altered attitudes to thrift at the lower end of the social scale. Two wartime surveys into personal savings suggested that the bulk of deposits were still held by the better-off. The first conducted in Leeds during 1942 suggested that 44 per cent of families had no National Savings. The second, based on a national survey two years later, was more optimistic, concluding that only 13 per cent of families had no savings at all, but of the rest, 39 per cent had no more than £50 of savings. The savings banks were quick to cast doubt on these findings, pointing out that 30 per cent of those questioned had refused 'to give full information on these very personal money matters'. Nevertheless, it was estimated that the number of large savers had risen sharply during the war, principally because of the lack of opportunities for spending. To the alarm of the Treasury, there was agreement that, when goods returned to the shops, the new savers would simply withdraw their deposits and close their accounts.

The 1945 'Thanksgiving' campaign, designed to prevent a sudden outflow of cash when the government was strapped for funds, was delayed by the general election in April, which resulted in a landslide Labour victory. The new government, led by Clement Attlee, was committed not just to the implementation of the Beveridge Report but also to a costly programme of nationalisation of essential services and basic industries. Almost immediately the country was plunged into a fresh crisis when in August the United States abruptly cancelled the wartime lend-lease and denied the United Kingdom any long-term aid to cover her dollar indebtedness. The government's financial plight reinforced the role of national savings in the eyes of the Chancellor of the Exchequer, Hugh Dalton. The Treasury acted quickly to force down short-term interest rates to below 2 per cent and to control local authority borrowing through the Public Works Loan Board and prescribed permissible periods of borrowing under the Local Authority Loans Act. This action effectively forced the savings banks to invest new deposits in special investment departments in government stock, obliging them to bring their rates down from 2.75 per cent to 2.5 per cent. The Treasury was anxious that large investors looking for a home for their cash should not take advantage of the higher rates available from the savings banks. At the end of the year, for the first time since the First World War and to the irritation of the Association, a limit, albeit generous, of £2,000 was placed on aggregate deposits by one person with the savings banks and the Post Office Savings Bank.

Although the National Savings Campaign was to continue, the savings banks were determined to re-affirm their separate identity. The Savings Banks Institute was successfully inaugurated in 1945 financed by a subscription of £25 each from the eleven largest savings banks and the Birmingham Municipal Bank. Its principal aim was staff training. A syllabus for the first examinations was issued, causing panic amongst the staff of the Birmingham Municipal Bank who could not obtain copies of the *Master of Ballantrae* and *David Copperfield*, required reading for one of the papers. University graduates, bank managers, and other academically qualified employees were entitled to membership without examination, but the need for a professional examining body to set standards was now greater than ever. During the war savings banks, finding it almost impossible to recruit staff, had freely admitted there had been a decline

An NSC poster from 1946 encourages saving for peacetime pleasures.

in the educational standards of new recruits. The larger banks had already taken the initiative by mounting training schemes for three categories of staff: 17–27-year-old new entrants; 24–30-year-old intermediate; and over 30-year-old management staff. The first examinations of the Institute were held in May 1946 when eight out of twelve candidates were successful. At first the Institute was administered by the staff of the Association. On New Year's Day 1949 it moved to its own premises near Clerkenwell Green in the former head office of the Finsbury & City of London Savings Bank which had amalgamated with the London Savings Bank in 1942 to form the London Trustee Savings Bank. On that day the Institute's first full-time secretary,

Keep *A GOOD BALANCE* in the
**POST OFFICE SAVINGS BANK**
or a **TRUSTEE SAVINGS BANK**

The first of the 'Keep a Good Balance' series, 1946.

J.F.D. (Freddie) Miller, recruited from the Reading Trustee Savings Bank, took office. The Institute's own *Journal* was launched in September 1948. Fundamental to the Institute's examinations was a thorough knowledge of the law relating to savings banks. From 1905 these were summarised in *The Law of Savings Bank* by John Y. Watt. In 1949 Charles L. Lawton, the joint actuary of York County Savings Bank and the son of W. Louis Lawton, published *A Guide to the Law of Trustee Savings Bank*, which quickly became the definitive authority on the subject.

At the same time as the Institute was established in 1945 a scheme for making inter-bank transactions was introduced, which allowed customers to make withdrawals from any savings bank. The Association's publicity was overhauled with a new distinctive series of posters. Some of these had a historical theme, a direct reference to the centenary celebrations to commemorate Henry Duncan's death. Delegates came from throughout the world to a service of commemoration held in Ruthwell Church on 12 May 1946. The centrepiece of the Association's post-war promotion was to be the publication of *A History of Savings Banks* by Oliver Horne, previously its secretary and now actuary of the Aberdeen Savings Bank. Sadly, exhausted by war work, he died at the age of fifty-one in December 1946 and publication was delayed until the close of the following year. Horne's history and Lawton's guide soon became the bibles of all aspiring junior savings bank staff.

At the same time, the Association revived the Bill drafted seven years before to allow for the introduction of a common superannuation scheme for all staff and for the bigger banks with large surpluses in their administration accounts to provide funds for the extension of the branch network. There was broad agreement that there was an urgent need for a branch at least in every town of over 10,000 inhabitants if a national service was to be achieved. It was estimated that this target required 122 new branches to be opened in the Association's north-west area; 130 in the north-east; and 212 in the south, excluding Wales, London, Bristol and Birmingham. Sir Kenneth Stewart, who had succeeded as chairman of the Association on the death of Sir George Rainy in January 1946, continued to sound out ideas. He was adamant that development, supported by mutual aid, should be planned and co-ordinated by the Association. With the introduction of social security, family allowances and the inauguration of the National Health Service in 1948, there were demands that the movement should focus on educating young people on the prudent use of money as a foundation for good citizenship. The possibility of the savings banks entering the mortgage market was re-examined, but rejected.

Maintaining the level of savings in the peace proved every bit as difficult as the Treasury had forecast. During 1946 the rate of personal savings remained relatively high at just over 10 per cent of after-tax incomes. However, the following year it collapsed to less than 4.5 per cent, dwindling to under 3 per cent in 1950. The effect on National Savings was catastrophic, sliding, as people withdrew their investments, from 7 per cent to −0.07 per cent of after-tax incomes in 1950. The trustee savings banks fared a little better with a decline from 0.95 per cent to 0.52 per cent of after-tax incomes. In the circumstances the savings banks could take some comfort in a rise in their share of the market for savings from just under 6 per cent to 8.25 per cent. Despite this relative fall in the level of personal savings, turnover in the savings banks continued to rise, touching almost £300 million in 1950. The decline in personal savings was due primarily to a rapid advance in spending on food as rationing was relaxed, explained by a sharp rise in the number of consumers as men were demobilised from the army. There was also a marked increase in recreational spending after the deprivation of wartime: during 1946 one-third of the population went to the cinema at least once a week and 13 per cent twice a week; football matches drew record crowds.

With total deposits continuing to climb, trustees had little immediate cause for concern, particularly as from 1946 the Post Office was doing much worse due largely to the readjustment of personal expenditure to peacetime. R.D.A. de la Mare, the vice-chairman of the Oxford Trustee Savings Bank, told his depositors in 1947: 'The increases recorded in the Report have been made at a time when small savings generally have been far below the figures of recent years and are convincing evidence that the Trustee Savings Bank is now recognised as the most convenient medium for small savings.' Lt-Colonel G. Christie-Miller, chairman of the Stockport & District Trustee Savings Bank, concurred: 'The steady and continued progress of the Bank proves Trustee Savings Bank facilities fill a particular requirement in the life of the community.' There were doubters, not least the chairman of the Association, Sir Kenneth Stewart, who publicly questioned whether inflation was steadily undermining the whole ethos of thrift. He supported his misgivings by comparing prices in 1939 with those in 1947. Even when purchase tax, introduced during the war, was discounted, he was able to demonstrate that prices were substantially higher. A refrigerator bought for £50 in 1939 cost £105 in 1947, including £33 purchase tax; a vacuum cleaner, £6 in 1939, £15 in 1947 with £3 purchase tax; home decoration £10 in 1939, £45 in 1947 with no purchase tax, and a popular second-hand car £80 in 1939, £300–£350 in 1947, with no purchase tax. Although he believed there was only one conclusion to be drawn from these figures as long as inflation persisted – namely that there was no purpose in saving – he was still able to plead for savings by falling back on the 'national interest.' Against a background of a crisis in the economy, he wrote: 'The over-riding consideration is that our national requirements make it almost wicked for anyone to spend money or demand goods and services that can be done without.'

By the time Stewart's article was published, Hugh Dalton had already acted in his emergency autumn budget to reduce demand by raising taxation, principally excise and purchase tax, in the hope that, as during the war, higher prices would stimulate savings. He believed that once inflation had been squeezed out of the system, with full employment real wages would increase. Keynes, despite his encouragement to spend in the depths of the slump in 1931/2, had argued that in these circumstances savings as a proportion of after-tax income would rise. In this expectation, the Association had pressed ahead with plans for post-war development, particularly securing the new legislation vital if the network was to become truly national. The Treasury, anxious not to upset the savings banks at a critical time, agreed to sponsor the Bill

The NSC's 1946 appeal to savers, to defer expenditure on luxury items for a little longer, was not entirely successful.

The executive committee of the TSB Association,
sailing on the River Clyde in 1948.

and to secure the agreement of the Ministry of Labour and Ministry of Works to give priority
to the release of the necessary labour and materials for the construction of new savings bank
buildings. The 1947 Act created the Mutual Assistance Scheme which allowed banks with cash
surpluses of over £10,000 in their administration accounts to make interest-free loans to less-
well-placed banks for opening new branches and for the construction of new buildings. Loans
could also be used to cover losses incurred while custom was being won. The scheme was to
be administered by the Association and run for five years from 1948 in the first instance. The
Act also established a superannuation fund for male staff. To discourage large investors, a limit
was imposed on deposits in special investment accounts of £500 in total and £250 per annum.
The ceiling on aggregate deposits remained unchanged at £2,000.

By the time the Act reached the statute book, Hugh Dalton had been replaced as Chancellor
by Sir Stafford Cripps, committed to a policy of severe restraint in government expenditure.
One of his targets was to trim the rate of interest paid to savings banks to prevent the bigger
savings banks accumulating large surpluses at the government's expense. On 9 and 10 December
1947, the National Debt Office held a conference with representatives of the Association at
which the contents of a further 'so-called' non-contentious Bill were outlined. The Comptroller, G.H.S. Pinsent, proposed that surpluses should not exceed a certain proportion, in the

order of 1.5 per cent of a bank's total assets. Any surplus over and above this amount would be paid into a Mutual Assistance Account controlled by the National Debt Commissioners, bearing no interest, to be used to make loans for developing the network of banks. In other words, the National Debt Commissioners would take direct control of the mutual assistance scheme. The Association was deeply concerned. The proposed cut in interest rates would have two unfortunate consequences: smaller banks would either have to cut the rates paid to depositors or incur losses, and the larger banks would have less to lend for development. The savings banks, anxious not to let their rates fall below those of the Post Office Savings Bank, protested vigorously. The Glasgow, Belfast and Liverpool savings banks, which had large surpluses, agreed that in order to maintain a uniform rate any bank that suffered a loss as a result of the proposed cut in interest rates would have a statutory right to claim compensation from the Mutual Assistance Fund. Applications for grants and loans would continue to be made to the Association, which would evaluate them before passing them to the National Debt Commissioners for authorisation. Their proposals were incorporated in the Act which was passed in 1949. Under its terms, all savings banks that wished to participate in the Mutual Assistance Scheme, which was to run for five years in the first instance, were required to pass resolutions of acceptance. When this Act came into operation, over £250,000 had been advanced under the original scheme. The Act also cut interest rate payable to savings banks on ordinary department deposits from 2.875 per cent to 2.8 per cent.

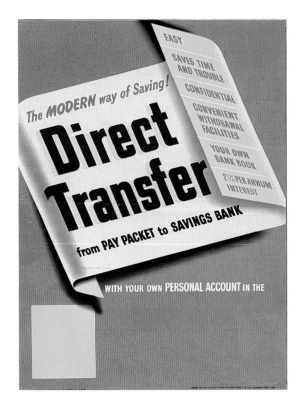

An advertisement for the
Direct Transfer Scheme, 1949.

The Association was delighted by the new Act. The new Mutual Assistance Fund was more broadly based than its predecessor and the cut in interest rates was much less than had been feared. With savings perceived as a powerful weapon against inflation, government spokesmen had gone out of their way to praise the work of the savings banks during the passage of the Bill through Parliament. It took several months for the Association to work out the details of the operation of the scheme. Savings banks were divided into three classes: A banks that contributed to the Fund; B banks that neither contributed nor benefited from the Fund;

and C banks that benefited from the Fund. No grants were to be made from the Fund until the loans made available by the Association under the 1929 and the 1947 Acts had been repaid.

In pursuing the policy of extending the network in the south of England, the Association was encouraged by figures which showed that deposits south of the border were growing faster than those in Scotland. It was estimated that in 1948 in Scotland, 33 per cent of the population had savings bank accounts, with deposits which had grown from £105 million in 1939 to nearly £255 million – an advance of 141 per cent. In England only 10 per cent of the population had accounts, with deposits which had climbed from £171 million in 1939 to £640 million – an advance of 273 per cent. As 1950 progressed, it became evident that, despite an eroding market for small savings, the total deposits with the savings banks would exceed £1,000 million for the first time. Celebrations were planned to be held in the Guildhall, City of London, on 20 November. In reporting this achievement *The Times*, so long the scourge of the savings banks in the nineteenth century, compared their development with the Post Office Savings Bank since the war:

> The comparatively greater progress made by the Trustee Savings Bank is persistent, and it seems to support with a new emphasis the claims which the Trustee Savings Bank usually make for the social virtue of their own savings medium. They can offer neither better interest rates nor better security than the Post Office. But they specialise in the banking function, and there seems to be solid grounds for their claim that they can and do show a more sympathetic concern for the personal needs of the customer.

This admission by *The Times* represented a triumph for the savings banks after eighteen years of constant struggle to maintain their separate identity within the National Savings Campaign. Since the advent of 'cheap money', the government had circumscribed the savings banks with regulations that had denied them the opportunity to expand special investment departments with marginally higher rates of interest. From the outbreak of war they had become simply a cog in the wheel of a national savings machine, vital to the financing of the war. In the welter of wartime activity with custom and turnover soaring, the ambitious plans for adding new services so hotly debated in the inter-war years had been all but forgotten. As peace drew near these had been revived by the Association which increasingly viewed the savings banks as a national homogeneous movement that required national coverage to achieve its objective. Distancing itself from the War Savings Campaign, the Association laid the foundations for expansion, particularly in the south of England where they were very under-represented.

In securing reform in the legislation from a Labour government, the experience of working with trade unionists in the works savings schemes helped greatly to change the image of the savings banks from vaguely paternalistic organisations to people's banks. Despite this achievement, the outlook remained obscure. The high levels of personal savings achieved during the war had not been sustained in peacetime and it remained to be seen if increased wages would indeed lead to higher savings.

# CHAPTER SEVEN

# COMPETING IN

# THE COMMERCIAL

# WORLD

## *1950−71*

The opening of the new decade of the 1950s was heralded as a watershed by the people of Britain, who hankered for a prosperous future with secure employment for all after the previous decade's hardship and sacrifice. The austerity programme introduced three years before by Sir Stafford Cripps was beginning to yield results, following the devaluation of sterling and further cuts in public expenditure in 1949 in response to a balance of payments crisis. After the narrow Labour victory in the general election in February 1950, recovery came quickly. Exports boomed, the balance of payments returned to the black, and trade and industry flourished. Wartime controls, including rationing, began to be swept away by the zealous young President of the Board of Trade, Harold Wilson. The new optimistic outlook was to be reinforced by a national celebration in 1951: the Festival of Britain, designed, like the Great Exhibition a hundred years before, to provide a show-case for all things British – art, architecture and artefacts. The tone would combine the pomp and circumstance of patriotism with a progressive vision of a future characterised by innovation and experiment.

This more confident, almost jaunty, mood was out of keeping with calls for personal sacrifice and self-denial in which the thrift movement was still firmly rooted. Failing to catch the change in the nation's temper, most TSB chairmen and actuaries continued to couch their appeal for savings in the language of the Depression and the Second World War. A.W. Heneage-Vivian, the President of the South-West Wales Savings Bank, wrote to customers in 1950: 'The Trustees would again stress the need for caution in spending, as a check to inflationary tendencies, as by so doing depositors will help materially in the recovery of the economy of

The NSC ensured that advertisements for the TSB conformed with
the optimistic mood of 1950.

Open a 'holiday' account in the

# TRUSTEE SAVINGS BANK

ASK FOR DETAILS OF THE T.S.B. TRAVEL CREDIT SCHEME

the country and at the same time provide themselves with financial security against the future.' Those officials, such as H. Martin Scantlin of the Lambeth Savings Bank, a branch of the London Savings Bank, who wanted 'new services to entice joint stock bank customers' were condemned as heretics, denying the role of savings banks as thrift organisations: 'It is the inculcation of that virtue which is our primary function.' Even the special £1,000 million TSB savings stamp looked dated, more reminiscent of a Victorian Sunday School than of a forward-looking movement.

The TSBs could be forgiven for this misjudgement. The outbreak of the Korean War in

Despite greater efforts to produce national advertising in-house, the
TSBs continued to rely heavily on NSC material during the 1950s.

June 1950 forced the Labour government to rearm, committing a sizeable budget to a three-year programme. This was to be paid for by stiff tax increases announced in the April 1951 budget, which included the taxation of interest received on savings accounts. At the end of the coming fiscal year in April 1952, a return had to be made by all savings organisations of accounts bearing interest of £15 or more. In the case of savings banks these returns would be made for those with £600 or more in their accounts – more than the annual average income of most families. The introduction of National Health charges split the Cabinet, leading to the resignation of Aneurin Bevan and Harold Wilson. Despite the official return to restraint, most people would not tolerate the privations of wartime to finance a campaign so far from Europe.

The Festival of Britain, opened at the height of the crisis, won an instant appeal, drawing huge crowds and spawning many local festivals up and down the country. The striking architecture and design style set a distinctive fashion that was to change the decade. Still unable to sense that the Festival accurately mirrored popular aspirations, the TSBs on the whole remained wedded to their outmoded rhetoric. Colonel M.K. Mathews, the chairman of the London Savings Bank, reporting on the 1951 result, reiterated the call to 'ameliorate inflationary pressures by deferring consumption and depositing money thus saved in this Bank'. Although there were undoubtedly inflationary pressures at work in the economy, far-sighted actuaries continued to be aware that to attract custom, the emphasis in advertising and promotion had to change towards what was termed 'purpose' saving 'for the eventual purchase of a home, some business or at least a definite object'.

An *ad hoc* committee on promotion, set up by the Association in the spring of 1950, recommended the immediate formation of a Thrift Promotion Department 'in view of the forthcoming celebrations in connection with the £1,000,000,000 [deposits with the TSBs] and the Festival of Britain'. The new department's terms of reference were most ambitious:

> It would operate centrally and on a national level. It would take advertising space in the national daily papers and the main weekly and monthly journals and provincial dailies. It would hold regular conferences, and correct from the inside some of the many misleading ideas that were prevalent about the place of TSBs. It would initiate ideas for posters, pamphlets and broadsheets.
>
> It would be an organisation operating for the sole function of TSBs.

There was widespread support for this initiative amongst younger staff and trustees, who demanded that the remit of the *ad hoc* committee be widened to consider new business developments such as the introduction of small loans in direct competition with the clearing banks. Tom Broad of the Border Counties Savings Bank told a meeting of the Scottish Area that was calling for an overhaul of the Executive Committee, to 'make it smaller, more representative of larger and smaller banks, and more effective in designing a strategy for the future'. His proposal addressed head-on the chief obstacle to internal change: the structure of the Association which allowed all eighty-five TSBs, irrespective of size and status, equivalent membership and gave the right to every chairman and actuary to participate in all general meetings. An opportunity to realise at least some of the Association's objectives was provided in October 1950 when Lord Mackintosh, chairman of the National Savings Committee, offered to provide matching funds and design expertise for a TSB promotion campaign. On the understanding that there would be no interference with individual savings banks' promotions by individual TSBs, a joint committee was established.

The following month the International Thrift Institute (which the Association had helped to found in 1910) held a conference in Stockholm to consider publicity. The three British delegates were struck by the quality and scope of the promotional activities of the Swedish Savings Banks Association, coming back with the impression that the use of publicity in Britain was inadequate. On returning home one of the delegates, Archie Hunter, the actuary of the Wigan Savings Bank, persuaded the Association's publicity committee to consider the question of producing publicity material that would be used nationally. The members of the National Savings Committee, believing this was their territory, were displeased and tried to thwart the initiative. Hunter, appointed chairman of the publicity committee, was not easily dissuaded. Despite misgivings from some TSBs, particularly those in Scotland, that central control would

Series of three NSC posters, 1952.

inhibit local initiatives, by the autumn of 1951 he had wrung a commitment from the Association to establish a publicity department to build directly on the work of the joint committee. A year later the advertising agents, Sells Ltd, were appointed as publicity agents. The account was handled by the managing director, Gordon Miller, who believed that 'most people save nowadays for something specific which they wish to enjoy in the future. It may be a television set, or it may be getting married, or buying a house. This type of saving is relatively short-term and it is among short-term savers that I believe TSBs are likely to find their most fruitful ground in opening new accounts.' His first poster campaign followed this line of attack, personalising saving for spending with no reference to either the national interest or the misfortunes of life. With the blessing of the Association, he and his partners had to persuade the individual banks to allow them to handle their advertising. Within a year they had won contracts from forty banks for their services.

In this more confident mood of 1951, the London Savings Bank completed a new head office on the corner of Cannon Street and Queen Victoria Street. A savings bank was also opened in May in Bristol, where the original bank had closed in 1888. The new bank was formed with financial support from the Liverpool and Manchester savings banks and took over three of the branches of the Somerset & Wilts Trustee Savings Bank in Bristol.

While the Association had been taking its time to bring the image of the savings banks up to date, the political and economic environment continued to change. The Labour government had run out of steam in October 1951 and been defeated at the polls. The incoming Conservative administration had developed an alternative strategy for managing the economy – a combination of cuts in government expenditure, accompanied by tax reductions, and the use of interest rates and other measures to control credit, to stimulate savings, and thus to restrain demand. On taking office, the Chancellor of the Exchequer, R.A. Butler, at once imposed sweeping cuts on imports and raised bank rate from 2 to 2.5 per cent, presaging the end of cheap money. With signs that the success of the savings banks in winning deposits in a declining market since the Second World War was beginning to wane, the Association pressed the new government hard for a relaxation in the tight Treasury control of special investment departments and for an increase in ordinary departments interest rates. In his first budget in March 1952, Butler pushed bank rate up to 4 per cent, its highest level for twenty years. So as to encourage saving, the ceiling on deposits with ordinary departments was lifted from £2,000 to £3,000. One consequence of this about-turn in monetary policy was a sharp fall in the value of government stocks, bringing the yield into line with current market rates. Small savers, who had responded so patriotically to the wartime propaganda to buy War Loan, saw the value of their holdings plummet. Unable to sell their investments except at a substantial loss, they had no alternative but to hold on to their stock in the hope that they would recover their value. Many families felt deeply betrayed, losing in many cases most of their life savings.

By the autumn there was plenty of evidence that higher interest rates had succeeded in taking the heat

Poster relays the message to those who did not hear the budget speech, March 1952.

out of the economy. Bank advances were falling and, as a result, the government could afford to relax its control of the capital market. The requirement that local authorities had to borrow exclusively from the Public Works Loan Board was lifted, although capital projects had to be authorised by the Treasury. With local authorities once again back in the market for loans, the larger TSBs were able to resuscitate their special investment departments (still with government-imposed limits of £500 per account), modestly raising interest rates on new investments to attract the larger saver. The TSBs, believing the Treasury regularly treated them as the Cinderellas of the thrift movement, pressed for further concessions. Early in 1953 the Treasury, no longer concerned to capture all savings to fund government expenditure, gave notice that the wartime scheme which required the greater part of funds deposited with special investment departments to be held in Treasury Deposits would be abolished by May of the following year. The Treasury, 'recognising the increased scope that the special investment departments gave to the savings banks', raised the ceiling of £500 on total deposits in special investment departments to £1,000. This alteration was welcomed enthusiastically by actuaries of savings banks whose

Local advertising could be very effective. During the early 1950s, the
Devon & Exeter Savings Bank introduced Jack Thrift and Joe Drift
to illustrate the advantages of regular saving.

ordinary departments were in retreat, as a result of the low return and a general collapse of small savings.

By the end of 1952 savings with the TSBs as a proportion of small savers' average personal expenditure had fallen substantially from 0.53 per cent in 1950 to 0.11 per cent. This reflected the continuing decline in small savings which fell from just under 3 per cent of personal expenditure to a little over 2 per cent. However, within this dwindling market, deposits with TSBs as a percentage of all small savings held their own at 8.25 per cent. There was a variety of explanations for the continuing overall downward trend in personal savings: persistent inflation, particularly in the cost of foodstuffs; expenditure deferred because of wartime restrictions; and the coming into force of the requirement in the 1951 budget that a return had to be made to the Inland Revenue of the names and addresses of depositors who received interest of £15 or more. According to Alderman Harvey, chairman of the North Staffordshire & District Trustee Savings Bank, the failure of deposits to recover after the large withdrawals before Pottery holidays in July, could be attributed to the interaction of all these factors – 'It seems evident that not only has the margin available for saving been reduced, but also that the cost of household requirements has tended to cause increased withdrawals. In addition, the recent increases in the yield on Government and Corporation Securities has caused transfers from deposits.'

A survey of savings patterns in 1952 conducted by the Oxford Institute of Statistics, but not published until 1955, showed that the greatest decline in deposits with the Post Office Savings Bank and the TSBs, and in holdings of National Savings Certificates and Defence Bonds, was amongst the better-off, those earning more than £1,000 a year and most likely to be affected by the new tax regulations. The survey could detect any real increase in savings only amongst those under the age of twenty-four. Most disturbing for the TSBs and the Post Office Savings Bank was the discovery that there was little or no saving in any form amongst those whose incomes were less than £600 a year – the majority of the population which the thrift movement had always professed to serve. With turnover rising relentlessly to over £400 million by 1952/3 as more and more customers simply used their TSB accounts as a secure short-term home for their cash, it was vital that larger savers should be persuaded to halt their withdrawals. Without their deposits the TSBs would have diminishing income to cover the cost of managing the steadily advancing number of transactions or to contribute to the Mutual Assistance Scheme. Already the scheme was having an effect, with the balance of business moving away from the north of England and Scotland towards the south, where the bulk of the 100 offices opened between 1950 and 1952 were created.

An extra incentive for accumulating savings had been provided in February 1952 when hire-purchase controls were introduced as part of the Conservative government's policy to take the heat out of the economy. These stipulated minimum down payments of 33.5 per cent on cars and radio and electrical goods, and 12.5 per cent on furniture and floor coverings, and a maximum repayment period of eighteen months. Taking these regulations together with the promotional strategy of Sells Ltd, many actuaries drove home the message of saving for spending. The Oxford Trustee Savings Bank was typical in telling depositors:

> In many cases saving through the Bank is for short periods only, but the Committee believe that this type of savings, for example, to meet commitments for household expenditure, or for holidays or Christmas, is a form of Thrift no less valuable than the old established conception of saving as being the accumulation of small sums over a long period of years, often with no particular end in view. Experience has shown that the short-term saver, having learnt the values of his short-term saving, becomes a long-term saver.

The first posters designed by Sells reinforced this message, which by 1953 had almost totally eclipsed the concept of saving in the national interest, left over from the Second World War. This approach, combined with higher interest rates, lifted deposits in special investment departments.

Despite the rise in the volume of business, TSBs throughout the country had continued to experience considerable difficulty in recruiting staff of the right calibre, partly because of the government's full employment policies and partly because of the impact of the introduction of National Service in 1948. Methods of recruitment varied from bank to bank, but there was agreement that there were three possible pools of additional labour: women, university graduates and men returning from National Service. Women, whom the male-dominated TSBs believed had aptitude for routine work, were discounted because their average office life was only ten years before they left to have children. University graduates were treated with suspicion, as they were by the commercial banks; they were thought not to be as easily trained as a clerk who had entered the bank at the age of sixteen. After some discussion at Savings Banks Institute meetings, the TSBs decided to focus attention on school-leavers (mostly males), weeding out the less efficient before they became eligible for National Service at the age of eighteen. Having made this choice, the role of the Institute was of paramount importance in maintaining standards. Training was delivered by external agencies through correspondence courses and evening classes at local technical colleges. In an effort to increase awareness of the problems and perspectives of different banks and to encourage greater uniformity of practice, the Institute staged its first vocational school at Worcester College, Oxford, in January 1952.

To the delight of trustees and actuaries in the continuing stagnant market for personal saving total annual deposits with the TSBs climbed from £122 million in 1952 to over £292 million in 1954, with only a marginal decline in ordinary department deposits. Renewed confidence was reflected in the heightened profile of some TSBs, with redesigned annual reports, carrying advertising. The back page of the report of the Ashton-under-Lyne & District Trustee Savings Bank showed a photograph of a smiling baby in its bath with the caption: *Portrait of a growing investor – in happiness.* As in other years since the Second World War the Post Office Savings Bank continued to lose ground, suggesting that the small saver was

The TSB Association at Alnwick Castle, 1952.

continuing to be squeezed, a view once again corroborated by further surveys by the Oxford Institute of Statistics which confirmed previous findings that it was the better-off who did most of the saving. Nevertheless, the TSBs had persisted in endeavours to gain the custom of smaller savers, largely through the extension of 'direct savings' in the workplace, community savings groups and school banks, operated jointly with the National Savings Committees. Although these schemes were expensive to operate, they contributed substantially to the recruitment of 1 million new depositors between 1952 and 1954 and a rapid advance in turnover. Many of these new recruits were undoubtedly won from the Post Office, which offered a poor service through a network of rundown sub-offices. To meet mounting overheads the TSBs pleaded with the Treasury and the National Debt Commissioners to increase the rate of interest paid to the banks.

Since the cost of the rising volume of transactions bore most heavily on the newer banks in the south of England, the Treasury would consider lifting rates only on condition of the renewal of the Mutual Assistance Scheme which expired after its initial five years in 1953. Internal discussions about the shape of a new scheme started in 1951 and formal talks were initiated in the spring of 1952 by Lord Mackintosh, chairman of the National Savings Committee, at the instigation of R.A. Butler, the Chancellor of the Exchequer, who was concerned

at the collapse of personal savings since the Second World War. In addressing the question posed by Lord Mackintosh as to how National Savings could be improved, the Association had responded by requesting that a proportion of deposits in ordinary departments should be tax-free and that a development grant equivalent to 0.5 per cent of ordinary department deposits should be made available annually. The grant was intended to make good a shortfall in the funding of the Mutual Assistance Scheme, in consequence of the interest rate cut in 1949. In the last five years management expenses had risen dramatically from £1.4 million to £2.8 million, while income had risen from only £2.7 million to £3.1 million, leaving almost nothing over for re-development. Advance in turnover at whatever the administrative cost was a direct consequence of the objectives of the National Savings campaigns. In this knowledge, the TSBs made it clear that in the approaching fiscal year the Mutual Assistance Scheme would be able only to strengthen the balance sheets of existing banks rather than to fund branch extensions. Notwithstanding the concessions available to the building societies, the Treasury rejected tax-free investments in ordinary departments out of hand, but was sympathetic to a development grant. As it was not legally possible for such a grant to be paid to the Association, it was proposed that the additional interest would be paid to the individual TSBs, providing undertakings had been made that the whole sum would be made over to the Mutual Assistance Scheme. Not all the TSBs were enthusiastic. Some were openly hostile on the grounds that they had no responsibility to bail out other TSBs. Deeply worried by the weakness of the balance sheets of many smaller TSBs, the Association pressed ahead with the negotiations.

Sir Kenneth Stewart, still the chairman of the Association, played a crucial role in holding the TSBs together as the details of the new arrangements were negotiated during the autumn and winter of 1952. At the turn of the year, he fell ill. Deprived of his leadership and vision, the Association's Executive Committee tried to disconnect the rise in interest rates from the future of the Mutual Assistance Scheme. The request, put bluntly, met with an ultimatum that firmly linked a rise in rates to a re-negotiated scheme. The executive committee, thrown into confusion, was uncertain how to proceed. Some of the larger TSBs, notably Glasgow – the principal contributor to the original scheme – doubted if their trustees would be persuaded to renew the Mutual Assistance Scheme in such circumstances. In the event the Glasgow trustees, in the words of their own minutes, 'to their eternal credit agreed that Mutual Assistance was the price of their freedom and were ready to pay'. Sir Kenneth was back at his post by the end of March 1953 and discussions once again became more purposeful, to the relief of the Treasury. A draft of the terms of the new scheme was settled in early April. Unlike its predecessor, it was to be an income scheme, not based on grants from the surplus funds of the larger TSBs but calculated on a sliding scale at fixed percentages of surpluses. The Treasury was anxious to

Sir Kenneth Stewart, Bt, GBE,
Chairman of the TSB Association, 1946–66.

support the plan, but assumed that the Chancellor of the Exchequer would provide no help if any part of the additional interest was not deployed for development. Unfortunately, four TSBs – Ashton-under-Lyne, Blackburn, Chorley and Sunderland – failed to sign the renunciation making over the additional interest to the Mutual Assistance Scheme. J.C. Campbell, the chairman of the Savings Bank of Glasgow, was dismayed that these banks should be willing recklessly to throw away £200,000 badly needed to support the newer small TSBs which were on the verge of insolvency, when his bank had contributed so much to their development. The four banks were challenged to give an undertaking at the annual meeting of the Association in May. They remained firmly opposed on the grounds 'that the matter had been badly handled and it was time a stand was taken against the methods employed'. Sir Kenneth, there and then, authorised the notification of the National Debt Office by telephone that the proposal had collapsed. The Treasury was willing to be sympathetic and agreed to make a once-and-for-all grant of £200,000 available pending a solution to the impasse. Sir James Fiddes, honorary secretary of the Association, disappointed by the parochialism of many trustees, called for unity that would bring the banks together in a 'common bond'.

Only too conscious of the increasingly precarious state of the balance sheets of many of the smaller TSBs, Sir Kenneth was determined to secure agreement for the Mutual Assistance Scheme during the breathing space offered by the Treasury. The haggling continued throughout the summer, with the individual banks flexing their muscles, hedging the negotiating committee about with petty restrictions and tiresome requests. The Treasury found it hard to understand what the difficulty was. By October 1953, Sir Kenneth, Sir James and Charles Lawton, chief actuary of the York Savings Bank, had amended the scheme to meet most of the objections. Briefly, the scheme allowed individual TSBs the right to refuse to participate in any venture proposed by the committee; ensured that the priority of the fund should be to keep all banks solvent making available additional grants as required; continued the endowment grants (providing there were sufficient resources) for opening new branches; and allowed the committee to assemble funds for building projects either through inter-bank loans, drawing on the Closed Bank Fund, or borrowing directly from the National Debt Office. The draft was circulated to every TSB with two questions: Was it acceptable if interest rates were raised to 2.75 per cent; and was it acceptable if the increase was lower? They made clear their impression that the Treasury would impose different rates on the savings banks if the scheme was not accepted. The response was an overwhelming 'yes' for the first question and an almost blanket 'no' for the second. The Treasury, after pressing the Association to come to a conclusion, dragged its feet. At the end of October it was agreed that interest rates would be lifted to 2.75 per cent as a temporary arrangement, but the draft of the scheme was rejected by the Treasury on the grounds that it failed to distribute the surpluses of the larger TSBs equitably. The Treasury remained adamant that unless there was unanimous support for the Mutual Assistance Scheme, differential interest rates would be imposed whether the TSBs liked it or not. The

Association was in a quandary; if it stood out against differential rates the implication would appear to be that it supported the Treasury line in opposition to some of its members. When a handful of TSBs still steadfastly refused to accept the scheme, the Association was forced reluctantly to consent to the Treasury taking powers to impose differential rates on the culprits in exchange for a rate of 2.75 per cent with no fixed duration for the rest of the banks. As finally agreed, the new scheme, in the words of Sir Kenneth Stewart 'was not intended primarily for the establishment of new offices, but was a scheme of redistribution of resources and further expansion would only be possible if that could be achieved without asking the Treasury for more money'. It also incorporated inducements for TSBs to improve their efficiency by reducing their management expenses. The Association had been considering, in a desultory fashion, means of reducing management expenses for some time through the Administration and Extension of Services Sub-Committee. The incentives to improve efficiency gave purpose and direction to the committee's investigations, particularly the use of the mechanisation of ledger posting that had been adopted by the Birmingham Municipal Bank.

As soon as the new Mutual Scheme was accepted, the Treasury and the National Debt Office began drafting new legislation, taking into account proposals for amendments from the Association. These included the raising of the percentage of the surplus on the special investment fund that could be used for the purchase of property, the removal of the ceiling on the interest rate that the Treasury could pay on ordinary department deposits withou refer-ence to Parliament and possibly smallsecured advances to established customers. To offset some of the tax advantages enjoyed by buil-ding Societies, it was proposed that the first £15 of Interest earned on savings bank deposits in the ordinary department

A poster announces the new tax concession.

should be tax-free. This would represent an important concession to large savers – those with more than £600 to invest – who were being deterred from deposit with the savings banks by the Inland Revenue rule that interest payments of more than £15 had to be notified and therefore taxed. Individual TSBs, however, had been reluctant to support the introduction of small secured loans of not more than £100 on the grounds that they contravened the objectives of the movement. As a preliminary step a non-controversial consolidating Act was passed in November 1954. Further legislation was disrupted by the general election in May 1955, which gave Anthony Eden – now leader of the Conservative Party – an easy victory, and by the Suez crisis that followed. Parliamentary time to incorporate the major changes could not be found until the autumn of 1957. The Bill, published in October, crucially lifted the ceiling on the interest paid to depositors on ordinary accounts to 3.25 per cent and extended the range of investments that were available to special investment departments and incorporated many of the minor charges requested by the Association. Directly the Act was placed on the statute book, the National Debt Office raised the rate paid to the TSBs from 2.87 per cent to 3.04 per cent.

While these protracted negotiations had been dragging on, the government had become even more concerned about the decline in savings, particularly after the removal of hire-purchase controls in July 1954. A new National Savings drive was launched in October by the Duke of Edinburgh with the aim of attracting 'Two Million New Savers' by the end of March in the following year. The message of the campaign was 'Save to spend' – short-term savings rather than long-term thrift. It was again chaired by Lord Mackintosh and supported by both the Chancellor of the Exchequer, R.A. Butler, and the shadow Chancellor, Hugh Gaitskell. Targets were set for each region and every large town. The TSBs were to play a prominent role in winning new custom, supported by a poster campaign and press advertising. Within two months over half a million new savers had been enlisted, many in group saving schemes. When the campaign ended, the total fell just short of the target, which was achieved a month later. A jubilant Lord Mackintosh declared: 'The campaign has proved a great stimulus to the whole Movement and has undoubtedly been a contributory factor to the great improvement in National Savings figures during the last six months.' Despite this brave assertion, the campaign had failed to staunch the outflow of funds completely. Repayments from the various components that made up the National Savings remained in advance of the receipts, but the difference was reduced from £170 million in 1953/4 to less than £10 million. On the plus side, sales of National Savings Certificates were £50 million ahead of repayments and sales of the current issue of defence bonds yielding 5.75 per cent (if held to maturity in seven years), almost £25 million in front. The TSBs sustained a loss of deposits in ordinary departments, but this was more than compensated for by a growth in special investments bearing between 2.5 per cent and 3 per cent interest. Everywhere the actuaries and trustees paid tribute to the National Savings Committee's role in this achievement. An analysis of the new deposits by Sir Kenneth confirmed the impression that, thanks to the Mutual Assistance Scheme and the Development

Committee, new savings were much more evenly distributed across the country. It was also evident that the TSBs attracted fewer but larger depositors than the rest of the National Savings due, it was believed, to the fact that they offered 'facilities . . . attractive to people of moderate incomes who want something more than the Post Office can offer but do not wish to incur the expense of a current account at a joint stock bank'.

The Post Office Savings Bank fared less well, but not as badly as the year before, with repayments £59 million above receipts. Apart from its down-market image, the Post Office Savings Bank was also hampered by having to deliver its service through staff with a variety of other duties, by limits on withdrawals and the periodic return of pass-books to London headquarters for certification. One of the principal impediments to new saving was the record levels of new house building in both the public and private sectors as families used all their available resources to buy and furnish their new houses. A revival in demand for home-ownership attracted savings into the building societies from those whose incomes were subject to persistently high rates of tax. Building society share capital which had advanced little since the end of the Second World War climbed quickly in 1954 and 1955. As in the 1930s housing boom, deposits with TSBs were withdrawn to pay for furnishing outright or by hire-purchase. Although the TSBs no longer disapproved of saving for spending, the majority of trustees condemned hire-purchase as a menace.

The closing stages of the National Savings campaign coincided with considerable speculation against sterling as the economy showed signs of over-heating. The government was forced to take urgent action, principally by restricting credit through higher interest rates of 4.5 per cent and re-introducing hire-purchase controls. These policies had the desired effect of reducing inflation, partly by stimulating thrift. In January 1956, Harold Macmillan succeeded R.A. Butler as Chancellor of the Exchequer. Committed to maintaining his predecessor's policies, bank rate was raised again in February and hire-purchase controls tightened. Although National Savings Certificates and defence bonds had continued to attract funds, the TSBs had begun to lose depositors as investors sought more lucrative returns. In his 'Savings and Savers' Budget' he bowed to pressure from the TSB Association and at last allowed the first £15 of interest earned on ordinary accounts to be free of tax. This was an important concession, making for most depositors investment with a TSB ordinary department as competitive as with a building society. The successful National Savings New Savers campaign was to be extended with additional publicity. New issues of defence bonds and National Savings Certificates were announced, both yielding 4.5 per cent with generous terminal tax-free bonuses, more than outweighing for larger investors the tax concessions on savings bank accounts. The Queen, speaking in May at the fortieth anniversary celebrations for National Savings in London's Guildhall, told her audience: 'My husband and I, my children, and my sister, play a part in this: we are all members of the savings group in the Royal Household.' In an effort to stimulate savings further following a budget announcement, premium savings bonds with tax-free prizes selected by ERNIE the computer, were introduced in November. The TSBs were to act as selling agents, but it soon became clear that depositors, lured by the large prizes, were simply transferring funds from existing accounts. This irritated the TSBs intensely, as the commission paid on sales of premium bonds, National Savings Certificates and defence bonds did not cover their costs. By March 1957 the budget savings package had made a notable impact, the total purchases of National Savings Certificates had soared to £335 million and defence bonds to

A letter from ERNIE: the dream of every premium bond holder; and
the TSBs advertise their accounts for children.

£131 million. Repayments, however, were also up as investors sought to take advantage of the higher rates. The TSBs, by offering heavily advertised competitive rates of interest in special investment departments, were able to prevent depositors switching to the new National Savings securities.

No sooner had premium bonds gone on sale than Britain was plunged into an international crisis as a result of Nasser's take-over of the Suez Canal. Early in November, French and British troops made an inopportune landing in Egypt in an attempt to overthrow his government. After intense international pressure, Anthony Eden was forced to accept a humiliating withdrawal and stepped down as Prime Minister in January 1957, to be succeeded by Harold Macmillan.

Although the pound came under pressure, interest rates were not raised until later that year. While these momentous events were unfolding, the Association renegotiated the Mutual Assistance Scheme, simplifying its operations and restricting its objectives to strengthening balance sheets, making good deficits, and repaying loans negotiated under the previous scheme. With costs rising as turnover continued to climb inexorably, several TSBs had slipped into deficit. The Treasury agreed under the terms of another Savings Bank Act to make good the deficit for the whole movement for 1957 with an *ex gratia* payment not exceeding £300,000 (£225,000 was paid) and to raise the rate of interest paid on ordinary departments to the savings banks participating in the scheme, to £3.12 per cent.

By 1958 turnover in the TSBs had almost doubled in six years, largely as a consequence of the growing number of depositors, who either were members of works savings schemes or who chose to have their salaries paid directly into their accounts. The Association investigated these 'salary credit' accounts, as they were termed, and concluded 'that this type of business was costly to the Banks by reason of the abnormally heavy proportion of withdrawals and, in addition, administrative difficulties were experienced as the impact of salary credits usually coincided with peak periods of counter activity'. This caused queues and delays at counters as staff wrote new balances in customers' passbooks and copied them into the ledgers in the same way as they would have done 150 years before. A few banks had installed adding machines to help speed up the work. Manchester Savings Bank was the most progressive with machines in every branch, but, curiously, no typewriters! A handful, including the Guernsey Savings Bank, had introduced mechanised systems of posting passbooks, ledger cards and record sheets following the example of the Birmingham Municipal Bank. At the end of 1955 the Association's Administration and Extension of Services Sub-Committee had appointed, on the initiative of

# THE GAMBOLS . . .
## by Barry Appleby

George and Kay Gambol discuss the benefits and drawbacks of savings
accounts, 1958.

the Southern Area, an Ad Hoc Committee to Investigate Mechanisation to solve the problem of delays at the counter. Under the chairmanship of A.E. Walker of Aberdeen Savings Bank, the Committee had begun examining systems already in use and reviewing existing manual procedures. It was obvious from the outset that one of the chief obstacles to mechanisation was the lack of any standard manual practice and procedures in the various banks. The Committee was deeply divided with some members keen to press ahead in response to urgent demands for ways of speeding up counter service and others concerned that mechanisation might undermine the savings banks' 'long tradition of courteous personal services'. In setting up the Committee, the Association was almost certainly influenced by the decision of the Committee of London Clearing Banks to form a special electronics sub-committee at the same time. Concerned at the mounting administrative costs, several TSBs, without reference to the Ad Hoc Committee, began to explore the possibility of using the newly available small Ferranti Pegasus computer, the next generation of Burroughs adding machines and NCR equipment for repetitive tasks and calculations, particularly the payment of the increasingly popular standing orders. The London Savings Bank decided to install a centralised data processing unit, which held out the possibility of marked gains in productivity.

There were those, such as F. R. Whitehead, actuary of the Derby Savings Bank, who questioned the assumption implicit in moves to increase efficiency that the TSBs were seeking total market share: 'Have you ever considered what would happen if everyone accepted your invitation – perhaps almost your request – that they should have an account at the Trustee Savings Bank?' He reflected wistfully: 'Think back to the days when the periodic visit to the Bank meant something to the depositor. To the days when they looked with pride at the Bank book as the deposits grew from shillings to pounds and so on. There is very little of that now.'

The problems caused by higher turnover were exacerbated by the high prevailing interest rates which allowed the clearing banks and the building societies to offer larger savers far better returns on their capital. Throughout the era of cheap money there had been little incentive for the High Street banks to expand personal banking, but the combination of higher interest rates and office automation in the mid-1950s spurred them into seeking a larger foothold in this neglected part of their market. Like the TSBs, the clearing banks had been developing their branch networks, especially in the fast-growing cities and towns in southern England. Using this existing infrastructure, they began to search for new services to attract private clients. The Midland Bank in 1955 introduced the first gift cheque, bright and cheerfully designed for birthdays, weddings and Christmas. Such initiatives were reflected in a sharp rise in clearing bank deposit account balances, climbing from £2.1 billion to £2.4 billion between 1957 and 1958. Building societies, which offered a well-trodden path to home-ownership at a time when private-sector house-building was on the increase, could not afford to be left out of what showed signs of becoming a race for personal deposits. For those with taxable incomes, there were considerable fiscal advantages in having a mortgage. The total deposits with building societies advanced from £2.1 billion in 1956 to £2.5 billion in 1958. Although special investment departments rates were increased, the TSBs complained bitterly that they were unable to compete, asserting that, despite the income tax concession on ordinary department deposits, 'people transferred their balances in much greater volume to other forms of savings where the interest was better'.

In attempting to manage the economy, Peter Thorneycroft, the Chancellor of the Exchequer, was aware that the increasing fragmentation of financial services made it difficult to maintain a tight monetary stance necessary to defeat inflation. Unable to divine a solution, he appointed a committee in May 1957, chaired by Lord Radcliffe, to review the working of the Monetary and Credit System. The committee immediately embarked upon the first comprehensive review of all Britain's monetary institutions and Treasury policy. Every financial institution was given the opportunity to submit evidence. The TSB Association, led by Sir Kenneth Stewart, seized the opportunity to present a strategy for the future which would give the TSBs a pivotal role in catering for private client business. When putting together its evidence, Sir Kenneth told the Executive Committee in mid-July 'the whole structure of our country had changed: nothing has been done which had made any impression on the large class which had arisen which had a margin over and above their absolute necessities. They needed education in savings and probably a special bank system. The commercial banks were totally unsuited to provide them with the necessary banking facilities and ... the Trustee Savings Banks could undertake this work better than any other organisation.'

Sir Kenneth's bold declaration prompted Charles Lawton of the York Savings Bank to call for a rigorous reappraisal of the philosophy and outlook of the movement in the context of a quickly developing affluent society: 'It was necessary not merely to teach people to save but to teach them to manage their money sensibly.' Well aware of Lawton's extensive knowledge of the individual TSBs, the Association invited him to help prepare the submission to the committee. In framing their evidence, the members of the Executive Committee adopted a very conservative attitude, turning a deaf ear to Lawton's forecast that customers required a greater range of services. 'What the Association wanted from the Radcliffe Committee was approval of the work the Banks were doing and the way they were doing it. They did not want suggestions for altering the conduct of their affairs nor for closer combinations with other saving institutions.' Astonishingly, the Executive Committee was not convinced that interest rates had much effect on either the propensity to save or on existing savers' choice of investments.

While the TSBs were waiting for the Radcliffe Committee to report, the need for change in both policy and presentation became more and more urgent as competition from the clearing banks for personal custom intensified. Following the Cheque Act of 1957 that allowed wages and salaries to be paid by cheque, all the clearing banks reduced their charges for the receipt and payment of cheques in personal current accounts, introducing the so-called 'ICI terms' for weekly wage earners early in 1959. The name derived from the Wilton works of Imperial

Chemical Industries, where the scheme was piloted. Under its terms, customers who kept a minimum of £50 were charged 10 shillings every half year for a maximum of thirty cheques. Responding to this fresh assault, individual TSBs took up Lawton's suggestion by publishing leaflets on personal and family finance. Falkirk Savings Bank led the way, conducting a survey of 12,000 homes of non-savers, which revealed that over 40 per cent would like to save, but 'in

The thrifty Robinsons.

many instances were ignorant of the facilities available'. To provide this information, the Bank published and distributed widely a simple booklet, *How to Live Within Your Means* and the South Eastern Savings Bank had printed a *Budgeting Booklet*, which could be purchased by other TSBs. The budgeting booklet was thought by some bank staff to be so complicated that it required a degree in mathematics to interpret its recommendations. Helpful and informative as such initiatives may have been, other organisations, apart from the National Savings Committee, were addressing the question nationally. The Marriage Guidance Council, for example, produced a popular booklet, *The LSD of Marriage*. The difficulty for the Association, as their advertising agents Sells had discovered, was that it could only encourage and not compel the individual savings banks to adopt literature produced centrally. It took more than a year for a strategy to be agreed before the TSBs' Personal Budgeting Scheme, supported by a set of three pamphlets and the Thrift Family Robinson poster campaign, was launched in December 1958. The literature was market-tested beforehand by the Belfast, Brighton and Falkirk savings banks, all of which were already committed to this approach to savings. In their final form, the pamphlets were well received, attracting a good deal of press comment and being avidly taken away by customers. Unfortunately, like the previous booklets, much of the text was too complicated for the average saver and hard to follow. Archie Hunter later admitted that the campaign was 'too soon, too elaborate'. As a result, it made relatively little impact on non-customers. The Association had warned of the difficulty of promoting the concept of personal budgeting and the long time it would take to achieve results, but the relative failure of the scheme did nothing to instil enthusiasm for central publicity amongst the individual banks.

By the time the Personal Budgeting Scheme was unveiled, the whole concept of national advertising was threatened by the massive promotional campaigns of the clearing banks and the

A still from one of two television cartoon adverts commissioned by
the North West Area Publicity Committee, 1958.

Building Societies' Association, estimated to cost together at least £1 million in the coming six months. The TSB Association's publicity committee immediately sought members' agreement to an increase in its budget for the half year to £50,000. Deeply aggrieved that the clearing banks and the building societies were deliberately attacking the TSBs' customer base, the members, with the memories of the lack-lustre Personal Budgeting Scheme fresh in their minds, clung tenaciously to the time-honoured method of local promotion, unconvinced that a well-orchestrated national campaign using both press and developing commercial television stations would have any real impact. The attitude of the honorary secretary of the Association, Andrew Thomson of the Savings Bank of Glasgow, was typical of those in Scotland and the north where savings banks were more strongly represented: 'Local advertising, which had been very successful, was not always in line with the national advertising which emanated from the south.' As a result of such entrenched opposition, it was decided to refer the matter to the individual TSBs. As might have been expected, there was no general agreement. At the annual meeting in June 1959 at Scarborough, Archie Hunter, the chairman of the Publicity Committee and now actuary of the Liverpool Savings Bank, made an impassioned plea for a national response to the mounting competition which was daily eroding their market share: 'It would be generally accepted that in addition to their old and valued local status, Trustee Savings Banks were recognised also as a national organisation with a national status.' To his dismay, his speech was followed by delegates who refused to raise their sights above their own local concerns for fear that any concessions on national publicity would result in loss of much-cherished independence, advantaging the smallest English TSBs at the expense of those in Scotland and the north.

If individual TSBs were unwilling to sacrifice their independence in publicity, they were likely to be even more resistant to calls from R. G. (Dick) Kirklew of the South-Eastern Savings Bank for the mechanisation and centralisation of all customers' accounts by every TSB. In

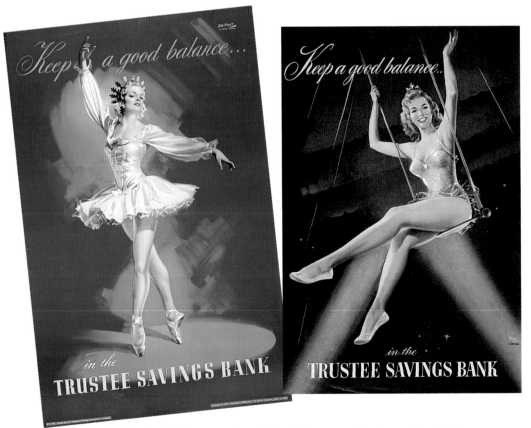

While the TSB's own national advertising was under threat, the NSC
continued the attractive 'Keep a Good Balance' theme.

presenting his controversial and revolutionary proposals, which had the blessing of the National Debt Office and the Inspection Committee, to the Mechanisation Ad Hoc Committee in July 1958, he explained that his Board of Management was convinced that 'in the long run, [this was] the only way in which operating costs could be cut'. The committee was again divided, but was persuaded to launch a radical re-appraisal of the existing manual systems that had been in use for 150 years and to assess experiments in centralisation at the London Savings Bank. At this juncture, the individual savings banks, particularly those in receipt of mutual assistance grants, resisted pressure from the Inspection Committee for the right to sanction the purchase of adding machines. In the meantime, the London Savings Bank was pressing ahead with its centralisation experiments, selecting the IBM Electronic Computer System and standardising procedures. The Ad Hoc Committee was reluctant to endorse the choice of IBM equipment without a thorough comparative review of alternatives, particularly the Powers-Samas Punched Card Accounting System and the Burroughs Sensimatic Series 50. Denis Greenwood of Bolton Savings Bank was called on to undertake this task. During the summer of 1959, representatives of TSBs visited the Post Office Savings Bank and savings banks in Germany, to see systems in operation. At the end of September the Ad Hoc Committee approved a much larger experiment in mechanisation and centralisation at the South Eastern Savings Bank. In Scotland the Research Manager of the Savings Bank of Glasgow, John Lowrie, was given a wide brief to review systems in Europe, Scandinavia and the United States. He concluded that 'there was no valid exit from accounting machines, whether sensitronic or sensimatic and that the effective path lay in the use of the On Line Real Time (OLRT) passbook systems now planned in Sweden and the United States'. OLRT systems allowed transactions to be entered directly into customers' account records held on to a mainframe computer by means of terminals at the counters. Under other 'off-line' systems, transactions were batch processed in a central unit, normally at night. The chief obstacle to OLRT systems, apart from the untried technology, was cost and for the present the only practical route was the 'off-line' system being pioneered by the London & South-Eastern Savings Bank.

Fundamental to meeting the challenge of the now predatory clearing banks was the range of services the TSBs could offer. A rising number of transactions in most accounts necessarily meant that depositors were less interested in earning a return on what were increasingly very short-term investments than on what TSBs could do for them in making personal and family budgets more convenient and flexible. This was true even if deposits were eventually to be transferred into more permanent forms of savings with higher rates of return and a wider range of investment opportunities. Here the TSBs were confronted with a serious dilemma. They had been established to promote saving in an age long before the Welfare State. To many trustees encouraging spending in expectation of income was anathema – yet one of the main platforms of the clearing banks in winning private customers was their increasing willingness to make personal loans available. The withdrawal of credit controls in July 1958 had made it possible for the clearing banks to promote personal loans to assist with the purchase of consumer durables, particularly cars and electrical goods – televisions, washing-machines and refrigerators – that were becoming more and more readily available. As before the Midland Bank were the pioneers with a scheme modelled on Australian and American practice. Lloyds Bank replied with a simpler, less expensive scheme which within a year had advanced over £8 million to almost 50,000 customers. There were voices within the TSB movement calling for the introduction of personal loans, but the Association set its face against such a potentially divisive policy that challenged directly the whole philosophy of thrift. It even refused to consider making standing order facilities available for customers to meet hire-purchase instal-

A TSB draft.

ments. Unable to make progress in this direction, the more forward-looking members pressed the Association to make a start with the less contentious issue of a cheque scheme for all TSB customers which had been made very necessary by the clearing banks' response to the 1957 Cheque Act. The TSBs had already tried to offer customers a more flexible service by tentatively introducing in 1957 TSB travel drafts – a form of travellers' cheque, which could be cashed at any TSB office. This was much more straightforward than the existing arrangements between TSBs for customers' holiday facilities. The drafts were to be processed through the inter-banks' clearing house which had been set up in 1955 by H.L. Westoby, General Manager of the Surrey Savings Bank, to settle inter-bank indebtedness. In the first year 74,000 drafts with a value of £4 million were processed. The principal advocates of TSB cheques were Stanley Kershaw of the Hull Savings Bank and Eric Gilbert of South Shields Savings Bank, both of whom had amongst their depositors a large number of merchant seamen, who were now required by their employers to settle mess bills by cheque rather than the time-honoured method of cash.

Although there was discussion about a cheque scheme throughout 1957 and 1958, nothing was done by the Association until November 1958 when the TSBs in the south of England, unnerved by the mounting tide of competition from the clearing banks, demanded immediate action. They pointed to the growing number of employers who, in contravention of the Truck Act, were keen to pay wages directly into employees' private bank accounts. The Association's problem was the reluctance of the National Debt Office and the Treasury to sanction such an innovation which would bring the TSBs into head-on competition with the clearing banks, despite the fact that the clearing banks were deliberately raiding the traditional market of the savings movement. Spurred into combat, another *ad hoc* committee, chaired by Robert Foster of the London Savings Bank, drafted a scheme in less than two months which provided for the formation of a central clearing division operated by either the National Debt Office or the TSBs themselves. With the endorsement of the Executive Committee, the matter was referred to the National Debt Commissioners and subsequently the Treasury, neither of which were prepared to provide an immediate response. The Scottish TSBs, in June 1959, called for the establishment of a 'remittance request service' believing it would give a limited exposure to

An advertisement for World Thrift Day, 1959.

staff and depositors of a Giro service used in many continental countries and be within the National Debt Office and Treasury regulations. Under this system, any customer could 'transmit money at low cost merely by notifying the clearing organisation that he wished payment to be made from his account'. For example, a depositor, providing he had sufficient funds in his account, would notify a supplier that he wished to make the payment in this way and at the same time instruct his TSB to make the payment. Apart from learning that the proposals were being considered by the Treasury, no progress was made during the summer and autumn. A glimmer of hope came in August with the publication of the findings of the Radcliffe Committee which, among its recommendations, advocated the establishment of such a Giro system in the United Kingdom.

Overall, the TSBs were pleased with the findings of the Radcliffe Committee which paid tribute to the 'significant, although small part' they played in the finances of the country. They were delighted by the broad hint to the National Debt Commissioners that they should adopt a much less rigid policy towards interest rates, by making changes in the rate available on National Savings as one of the indicators of which direction the Treasury wished monetary conditions to move. The sympathetic tenor of the references to National Savings led the TSBs to misinterpret the likely consequences of the report as a whole. At a time when the variety of types of credit available to corporate concerns and individuals was increasing relentlessly, the report concluded that simply restricting the money supply would not prove an effective means of economic management. Hence the need to use interest rates as a mechanism for encouraging or reducing demand. With scant reference to the changes that had occurred in attitudes to private client business since the committee's appointment, there was specific encouragement for the clearing banks to develop this side of their business in competition with the TSBs and building societies. Although the reintroduction of controls was recommended, the committee was unanimous in believing that the credit made available through hire-purchase companies was not excessive and did not have a deleterious effect on the economy. The other cause for concern for the TSBs in the report was a suggestion that local authority borrowing should once again be channelled through the Public Works Loan Board. Nevertheless, the TSBs remained keen to win permission to introduce cheques. Still the Treasury prevaricated, blaming the lack of a decision on the publication of the Radcliffe Report and the general election on 8 October which gave the Conservatives an even larger majority. A meeting at the National Debt Office on 21 October left the TSB representatives with a deep sense of frustration. The Treasury was clearly unwilling to do anything to ruffle the feathers of the powerful clearing bank lobby. After nine months of shadow boxing, all the Commissioners could say was that it might be possible to obtain Treasury approval in a year's time. Their frustration was made all the more intense by the news that the government intended to introduce legislation in the coming session of Parliament allowing wages to be paid by cheque. Unwilling to wait any longer for legislation and wishing to give his staff experience, the chairman of the Savings Bank of Glasgow, Andrew Rintoul, who came from a background in investment management, won permission from the National Debt Office to implement a remittance system using Giro facilities. Local retailers, Glasgow Corporation and other local authorities in the west of Scotland, and public utilities were encouraged to accept payment in this way and local success in the west of Scotland was achieved. National negotiations remained at a standstill.

While the TSBs had been arguing about the best means of tackling competition for their services, there had been complete agreement on the importance of celebrating in 1960 the

A Rush Hour Depository, installed in the
Falkirk & Counties TSB, 1965.

150th Anniversary of the founding of the savings bank at Ruthwell. Plans had been nurtured over almost three years and were announced in February with a series of local events, culminating in the annual meeting of the Association to be held in Aberdeen and the publication of a brief history of the movement by A.R.B. Haldane, deputy chairman of the Edinburgh Savings Bank and chairman of the Inspection Committee. TSBs which had steadfastly refused to contribute to national publicity, willingly subscribed to the cost of the celebrations. As well as representatives of the TSBs, there were delegates at the celebrations in Aberdeen from savings banks in Australia, Belgium, Canada, Denmark, Finland, the Republic of Ireland, Netherlands, New

Zealand, Norway, Sweden, Tasmania, Thailand, and the USA, all of whom reported on the progress of the movement in their countries. The principal guest was the Chancellor of the Exchequer, Heathcoat Amory, who, it was hoped, might announce that the cheque scheme should be implemented. Instead he agreed to abolish limits on the monetary volume of annual deposits in both ordinary and special investment departments and lifted the ceiling on aggregate deposits in ordinary departments to £5,000 and special investment departments to £3,000. Welcome as these announcements were, there was widespread indignation at the Chancellor's failure to comprehend the anxiety of the TSBs in a rapidly changing market for personal saving.

The Rt. Hon. D. Heathcoat Amory, MP,
Chancellor of the Exchequer, 1958–60, and trustee
of the Devon & Exeter Savings Bank.

He had rubbed salt into the wound by telling his audience that the TSBs 'were a success because they were able to keep abreast of the time and adapted themselves to changing conditions'.

Those in the movement who still believed that change was not really necessary took comfort from the fact that with no additional services the numbers of active accounts in ordinary departments exceeded 8 million for the first time in 1960, even though total deposits remained in the doldrums. They could also point at the continued rapid advance of special investment departments with total deposits now over £433 million and 728,000 active accounts. There was delight that in the 150th anniversary year total funds passed the £1,500 million mark. Such enthusiasm, as Sir Kenneth Stewart warned those present, overlooked increasing turnover which, following the raising of the ceiling on aggregate deposits and the Payment of Wages Act in 1960, exceeded £950 million, more than half total funds. Turnover was highest in the ordinary department where it represented almost 85 per cent of the total balance.

Although the TSBs were out-performing the more or less moribund Post Office Savings Bank and sales of National Savings Certificates, the growth of special investment departments could not match the advancing sales of higher yielding defence bonds. Outside the scope of national savings, the TSBs were dwarfed by the meteoric growth of building society deposits which, by 1960, totalled a staggering £3 billion. Like the TSBs, the building societies that now dominated the market for personal saving, were also experiencing a sharp rise in turnover, but on nothing like the same scale and with a much smaller customer base of only 4 million members. Life insurance companies, the other prominent players in the market for personal saving, shared in the sharp advance in business in the late 1950s as more people joined pension schemes or used policies as collateral security for mortgages. Curiously, despite the worries of the Association about competition from the clearing banks, total balances in their current and deposit accounts showed little movement.

To maintain their activities and remain solvent, the TSBs, as a matter of priority, had to prevent any haemorrhage of funds from special investment departments and at the same time persist in the extension of their network in the south of England where there was an increasingly higher proportion of larger incomes. In addition, newer banks, which lacked the resources to cover the administrative costs of escalating turnover, had to continue to be supported. These objectives, clearly understood by Sir Kenneth Stewart, predicated a larger role for the Mutual Assistance Scheme, which expired the following year. This third scheme had been much less successful than its predecessor (which had helped underwrite the construction of a large number of new branches), partly because the amount of 'grants of right' to cover shortfalls in operating costs had risen markedly due to the relentless rise in turnover. There was a suspicion that extravagant development to win market share at any price was being underwritten by the more prudently managed Scottish and northern TSBs, which had reined back their own plans for expansion in systems and mechanisation. In scrutinising the banks which made regular demands on the fund, such as the Bristol Savings Bank, the Association shied away from any suggestions that uneconomic branches should be closed and hoped only that they would 'ultimately be self-supporting'. By 1960 the pace of new branch openings had slowed to a trickle and such investment as there was, was in the refurbishment of existing offices, principally to improve efficiency and reduce operating costs.

Sir Kenneth was conscious that, to stimulate any meaningful development, the funds available to the Mutual Assistance Fund would have to be enlarged by persuading the National Debt Office and the Treasury again to raise interest rates. The Treasury had been down this road before and was broadly sympathetic, on the understanding that the whole increase of 0.05 per cent would once more be made available to the Mutual Assistance Fund, this time to create a revolving capital fund from which all banks would be allowed to borrow free of interest to finance rebuilding or new construction. Each application would have to be vetted by the National Debt Office and the Association, and the applicant would be expected to repay capital to the National Debt Office at the rate of 5 per cent a year. In discussion of this proposal, the Belfast Savings Bank and the Savings Bank of Glasgow voiced their concerns that it 'did not in any way help their position with regard to their diminishing surpluses'. These had been eroded by their contributions to the previous schemes which had allowed the TSB network to be extended in the south of England with the inevitable consequence that the relative standing of the Scottish and Northern Ireland banks in the Association had declined as deposits there had increased. Keenly aware of the growing competition for their services, particularly with the arrival of English building societies in Scottish and Irish high streets, the Scottish and Northern Ireland savings banks wished to retain more of their surplus for their own development purposes.

The Carluke branch of the
Savings Bank of Glasgow, 1965.

Sensitive to these objections, Sir Kenneth explained to the principal contributors to the scheme that no TSB that was permanently in deficit and therefore making regular demands on mutual assistance would be allowed to borrow money for further capital projects. It was also agreed that in the future contributions to the Mutual Assistance Scheme as a whole would be on a declining scale, allowing individual savings banks from 1962 to retain a larger proportion of their surpluses. With these reassurances the fourth scheme was approved for another five years from November 1961.

While these negotiations had been taking place, Robert Foster, the actuary of the London Savings Bank and the driving force behind the plans to introduce cheques, had been contemplating how best to proceed. The press, informed at regular press conferences by the Association, were behind the TSBs but the Treasury was still reluctant to act unless the co-

A savings bank for the sixties: the Bolton Savings Bank head office
after modernisation in 1962.

operation and goodwill of the London clearing banks had been secured. At a meeting with
TSB representatives, F. Keighley, chairman of the Chief Executive Officers Committee of the
London Clearing Banks, was openly hostile, more or less telling the TSBs that they should
mind their own business of collecting savings and ruling out any possibility of admission to the
'walks' method of clearing in London, i.e. the London Clearing House. The clearing banks
were in a strong position to dictate terms since the TSBs were dependent on them to process
credit transfers and for access to the clearing system. The clearing banks insisted that TSB
cheque accounts, if permitted, should be operated on the same terms as clearing bank current
accounts, with no interest available. They also condemned as unfair the £15 a year tax-free
interest available to savings bank depositors. The Association concluded that if cheques were
to be introduced, concessions would have to be made.

There was an urgent need for the TSBs to arrive at an understanding with the clearing banks which would allow deposits made at any clearing bank to be credited to accounts in any TSB – essential for the payment of salaries and wages direct into TSB accounts. As things stood, salary payments by credit transfer, which were becoming increasingly popular, were being directed by the clearing banks' London Clearing House for TSB customers to the Head Office of individual English and Welsh TSBs, where they had then to be sorted and forwarded to branches; whereas payment to clearing bank customers were sent direct to branches. As a result, a TSB customer's account was credited with a salary payment at least a day after a clearing bank's customer. The solution was for the TSBs to join the Credit Clearing Scheme operated by the Committee of London Clearing Bankers. Credit transfers could work in both directions, being used by TSB customers to meet insurance premiums, mortgage and hire-purchase instalments, and other recurrent expenditure. Under the terms of admission to the Credit Clearing Scheme, the TSBs agreed to clear credits to their accounts free of charge, but, to the annoyance of the TSBs, the clearing banks imposed a charge of sixpence for every two transactions to their accounts. In Scotland the position was different as, although the Scottish savings banks were also refused entry to Scottish clearing, the Bank of Scotland assisted by acting as a clearing agent.

After the National Debt Office had been satisfied that the TSBs could afford to finance participation in the credit transfer scheme, a credit transfer centre was established during 1962 in the basement of the Cheapside branch of the London Savings Bank. This was to act as a clearing house for salary credits paid to savings bank customers through the clearing banks and to share premises with the TSBs' own Inter-Bank Clearing Centre previously operated by the Surrey Savings Bank. Within three years the new TSB Clearing Centre had handled over a million transactions worth some £46 million. The clearing bankers had no objection to the TSB joining the Credit Clearing Scheme in the belief that with access to such services the argument for the TSBs introducing cheques would be less compelling, as a Giro system could now be implemented with no difficulty. They hoped to exploit the known disagreement amongst the banks over the introduction of a cheque service. The Savings Bank of Glasgow, still the largest TSB, clung tenaciously to the belief that a Giro service was all that was required, as cheques were 'open to abuse' and 'contrary to the primary objectives of trustee savings banks'. Altogether, fifty-three TSBs supported the introduction of cheques; twenty-five remained undecided. In the knowledge that he spoke for a majority of TSBs, Foster made it clear that there could be no linkage between credit transfers and the introduction of cheques.

Unable to reach agreement with the Committee of London Clearing Banks over the vexed question of the £15 tax concession on ordinary accounts, Sir Kenneth was determined to force the issue, telling a press conference in 1963: 'In the changed social conditions of the 1950s and 1960s, people simply had not time to come to the counter every time they wanted to transmit a sum of money from A to B.' The Treasury remained reluctant to intervene directly for fear of upsetting the clearing banks, but signalled informally that the government would not oppose a private member's Bill should one be introduced. Immediately, Foster persuaded James Hoy, chairman of the TSB Parliamentary Committee and the MP for Leith, and Sir John Arbuthnot, the Committee's secretary and MP for Dover, to sponsor the measure. On the advice of Edward Du Cann, the Economic Secretary of the Treasury, the Association re-approached the Committee of London Clearing Bankers, who, when informed that legislation would be introduced later in the year, were willing to come to an understanding. Although there was some disagreement about the charge for clearing TSB cheques, discussions this time were less

The first TSB cheque.

frosty. The Bill was introduced in the House of Lords in November 1963 by Lord Burden, a vice-president of the Association, and became law the following January. Under its terms the TSBs were allowed to operate from 21 May 1965 non-interest-bearing current accounts, on which customers could draw cheques, providing there was a sufficient balance to cover the payment. Overdrafts were prohibited. Current accounts could not be used for commercial purposes. The TSBs were not to be admitted to the Committee of London Clearing Banks, which was to continue to control cheque clearing. On 21 May 1965, Stanley Kershaw of the Hull Savings Bank, who had been one of the leading advocates of the cheque scheme when it was initially mooted almost a decade before, paid his wife, Mabel, £5 with the first TSB cheque to be drawn. By the end of the TSB year in November, twenty-three banks had adopted the scheme and £600,000 had been transferred to current accounts suggesting demand for this service was not as strong as had been assumed. This apparent failure was due almost certainly to the long delay in getting the scheme off the ground, forcing depositors like the merchant seamen in Hull and South Shields, who needed cheque facilities, to take their custom to the clearing banks long before.

Preoccupation with credit transfer and cheques pushed mechanisation down the Association's agenda, and it was not until February 1961, after nearly eighteen months, that the Ad Hoc Committee on Mechanisation and Centralisation reconvened to consider progress. By then, four savings banks – London, South-Eastern, Falkirk and Bolton – had experimental centralised systems up and running using different equipment. All reported a large initial outlay, but expected large gains in efficiency and productivity. Progress was slow. There were delays in getting permission from the National Debt Office for the new procedures, which involved counter staff preparing duplicate slips to be sent overnight to the posting centre for processing. The size and weight of the computers presented problems in locating and adapting suitable premises. They also proved less reliable than manufacturers claimed. In making these pioneering experiments, these TSBs had a narrow lead on the clearing banks. By now there were altogether twenty-eight savings banks with ninety-eight ledger posting machines.

The widespread support for the 150th anniversary celebrations in 1960 revived the spirits of the Association's publicity committee after the bruising experience of previous years. Totally committed to national advertising to promote the TSBs, the committee invited experts to comment on the existing state of affairs at a conference in Folkestone in March 1961. Leslie Horden, of the North Thames Gas Board and the Institute of Public Relations, told the delegates that the TSBs, to survive in a highly competitive market, must develop a house style for all their literature, advertisements, displays and stationery. W. Motson of the Institute of Practitioners in Advertising went further when he advised that, without national publicity, directed across the age range and income groups, the savings banks were doomed despite local loyalties. He believed that contrary to the opinion of some actuaries and trustees, the TSBs were perceived as being part and parcel of a national movement. Taking this advice to heart, the publicity committee drew up an eight-point agenda for action, which included a house style, a simple symbol more easily recognised than the existing castle keep, the co-ordination of local and national advertising and the employment of a market research organisation to establish 'the markets to which the Banks' advertising should be directed, and the best media to be employed to achieve this end'. A new symbol with the letters TSB in three rings, designed by Sells, was accepted at the end of October even though more than half the savings banks still did not use trustee in their title. More difficult was to secure an adequate budget for the rest of the programme, estimated to cost at least £100,000 a year.

Pressure of other business made it hard to find an opportunity to discuss this perennial problem until the 1962 annual meeting. At the last moment the agenda was changed and the matter shelved. Instead there was a debate about the future of the whole movement, initiated by Sir Kenneth from the chair, arising from his anxieties about continuing support from the Mutual Assistance Scheme for banks that persistently made a loss. Some delegates believed that the existing fragmented structure held loosely together by the Association could stagger on: others such as Sir George Williamson, chairman of the Aberdeen Savings Bank, had no doubt that amalgamations into large groupings were inevitable, with centrally directed publicity and

TSB Association posters, 1964 and 1965; and (RIGHT) the design for
an interior illuminated hanging sign, 1962

computer facilities. Debate or no debate, the omens were not auspicious; contributions towards
the proposed publicity budget were derisory, delaying progress.

A Central Design Service was, however, established in the autumn of 1962 and immediately
issued the new symbol and agreed house style for lettering to all the TSBs. Although this was
well received, there was still disagreement about the direction and utility of national publicity.
Several TSBs remained convinced that local campaigns were as effective and potentially less
expensive. From 1962 the TSBs in the North-West, and Lancashire and Cheshire collaborated
to experiment with regional television advertising, using the theme of family saving. This was
followed at Christmas 1963 by a live television commercial in the Southern Area, featuring
two TSB officials and covering 1.3 million households and fifty-seven TSB offices. Despite a

tiny budget of just £20,000, the Publicity Committee did its best to develop a coherent approach to promotion by producing posters and literature which could be used in local campaigns. The underlying cause of the unwillingness of individual TSBs to subscribe to the national publicity pool was trustees' persistent fear of losing local autonomy reinforced by their continuing success in attracting deposits.

Between 1962 and 1965 even the ordinary departments began to come out of the doldrums with net gains in total deposits, which increased from £913 million to £1,027 million. The number of depositors also grew by almost 1 million to reach 9.5 million. Most striking was the continuing gain in turnover which, by 1965, just exceeded total deposits. As in the previous decade, special investment departments maintained their uninterrupted growth, with total deposits soaring from nearly £434 million in 1960 to almost £994 million in 1965. While some of this expansion could be attributed to inflation, most of it reflected a real growth in savings. There was an equivalent gain in the number of active accounts which almost doubled from 728,336 in 1960 to 1,437,823 in 1965 due almost entirely to higher rates of return. Despite this achievement, there was evidence that the TSBs continued to lose larger depositors to other forms of saving, particularly the building societies.

This expansion of business and the volume of transactions placed great strain, particularly on the staff in the larger TSBs, many of whom were being asked to grapple with the problems of introducing new technology and working practices. Despite the recognition of the National Union of Bank Employees in 1947, the Employers' Council was reluctant to allow any wages claim to go to arbitration. The Union, keen to protect the position of its members, had often been in the position of having to drive a hard bargain with a reluctant Employers' Council to win improvements in conditions of service, occasionally resorting to arbitration. Relations were sometimes strained with the more reactionary trustees and actuaries resenting NUBE's role. Infuriated by the Employers' Council's recalcitrance, NUBE organised an unprecedented series of lightning one-day strikes up and down the country, which had the desired effect of bringing the Employers' Council to the negotiating table. This led, in mid-October 1963, to TSB staff being given the right to go to arbitration if agreement with a savings bank or the Employers' Council could not be reached after six weeks. The Union immediately put this understanding to the test, winning at arbitration in February 1964 a 3.7 per cent rise for clerical staff and parity for clerical staff with those employed by Barclays Bank. Further improvements in conditions of service followed for all grades of savings bank staff including non-clerical workers.

By 1960, although there continued to be more depositors in Scotland per head of population, the Scottish savings banks could no longer claim to have more deposits than any other part of the United Kingdom. With the Scottish economy seriously affected by the inability of her old staple industries of shipbuilding and heavy engineering to compete with emerging competition from Europe and Japan, Scotland's relative position continued to decline throughout the first half of the 1960s. The north-east of England was in much the same position, but here the retreat was less pronounced because the shipbuilding industry had been less reliant on passenger liners and naval tonnage where demand was weakest. The North-Western Area headed the league table in 1965, followed by the Southern Area, the North-Eastern Area; Scotland; and, finally, Northern Ireland. The enthusiasm with which each new record was greeted overlooked the general improvement in wage levels, inflationary pressures, and even more sparkling results from the TSBs' principal competitors for savings. Total funds of the building societies doubled between 1960 and 1966, from £3,000 to £6,000 million. This was due to a complex interaction of factors – continuing growth in demand for home-ownership, a reduction in the need to hold money readily available with the growth in personal credit facilities, and the tax concessions on building society accounts. There were a few actuaries, who, looking beyond the totals at the underlying trends, were convinced of the urgent need for radical change. Regardless of such warnings, even the forthcoming establishment in June 1966 of the Post Office Savings Bank's Investment Account yielding a very competitive 3.75 per cent failed to give rise to any immediate anxiety amongst the majority of trustees. Some more far-sighted banks took action by raising rates of return on special investment departments to 5 per cent for the first time in the history of the movement. By the end of the year most TSBs were forced to pay 5.5 per cent to retain business, even though rising management costs, due to higher turnover, made it difficult for many to do so.

Despite the entrenched opposition to any action that smacked of central direction of the movement, a small group of trustees and actuaries remained determined to investigate and, where possible, implement collective policies likely to improve the efficiency and competitive position of TSBs. The introduction of cheques and the credit transfer schemes would of necessity fuel the inexorable rise in turnover and the number of transactions, which could only be processed cost-effectively through greater use of mechanised systems. Progress had been frustratingly slow; all the early installations had had teething problems and did not entirely match expectations. During 1963 the North-West Area of the Association formed its own committee to investigate the potential of computers without consulting the Association's own committee. The Scottish Area also looked at computational machines in a wider study of counter procedures and accounting methods, which in Glasgow had resulted in the wholesale simplification of branch work practices. When their report was discussed by the Association's committee in November, it was rejected as there was disagreement about the volume of transactions that could be processed and staff attitudes to the new technology. Disappointed, Charles Lawton, chairman of the Mechanisation Sub-Committee, sought a way forward by inviting Denis Greenwood, now of the South-Eastern Savings Bank, to prepare a report on the various 'off-line' computational machines available for savings bank use. At the same meeting, A.J. Miller of the Aberdeen Savings Bank made a more radical proposal when he announced that 'after studying numerous machine systems over a period of thirty years he had not found what he considered to be an ideal system, nevertheless he felt that the latest on-line computer systems, such as the Teleregister system which had been introduced by six American Savings Banks, was perhaps the nearest approach to an ideal system for savings banks'. He readily admitted that such an on-line system was beyond the resources of any one bank, but

The Tabulator at the London TSB's
integrated electronic data
processing unit, 1962.

believed that with the improved telephone system being installed it might be possible for a consortium to make such an investment.

Despite strong objections from Denis Greenwood, still committed to the outmoded bookkeeping machines and who believed 'on-line computer systems were out of the question for the time being', the Savings Bank of Glasgow commissioned a further study into OLRT systems and Alan Scott, John Lowrie's assistant, was sent to the USA for six months to evaluate the experience of the American savings banks where transactions were entered by tellers directly into passbooks, the teller's records, and the mainframe computer at once all in 'real-time'. He reported that the success of OLRT 'may be judged by the fact that all the major American Mutual Savings Banks and, indeed, many of the smaller wealthier ones which have joined together in a co-operative basis, are installing OLRT computers or investigating the feasibility of such systems. Thus of the largest twenty-five savings banks, fifteen have already ordered

OLRT computers.' He explained they had chosen OLRT to improve their competitive edge:

> Updating of passbooks is the area in which OLRT can make the greatest impact since transactions can be entered automatically into the passbooks in about two seconds by the counter machines without the intervention of the teller. All banks installing OLRT have experienced shorter queues, especially at peak times.

All the Scottish TSBs were impressed by this glowing recommendation, except for the Edinburgh Savings Bank which urged caution and a decision from the Mechanisation and Methods Sub-Committee, as it had now become. The Committee was agreed on only one thing – that it could provide information about the competing claims of different systems and manufacturers, but it could not recommend any single policy. Meanwhile, the London Savings Bank requested permission from the National Debt Office to install an advanced off-line IBM system to replace its existing equipment. The National Debt Office asked the Treasury Organisation and Methods Department to evaluate the system and made it clear through the Inspection Committee that approval for expenditure on further computer applications would have to await the outcome of the report. However, the Savings Bank of Glasgow, acting for Aberdeen, Edinburgh, Dundee and Paisley Savings Banks, was given permission to appoint consultants to recommend a suitable system. The consultants were concerned 'at the disparity of operating methods encountered during their investigation, not only between banks but also between offices', suggesting until working practices had been standardised, there was little scope for automation. When such steps had been taken, they recommended the purchase of a Burroughs 2300 mainframe with standard software requiring the minimum of alteration to meet UK standards.

After Treasury criticism of the choice of the IBM system over an untried Honeywell system that would be manufactured in Britain and be available in 1966 had been countered, the Inspection Committee gave the go-ahead to the London proposal. No sooner had this permission been granted in April 1965, than the National Debt Office referred the whole matter of savings banks automation to the newly formed Ministry of Technology. This did not prevent the Mechanisation and Methods Sub-Committee commissioning C.R. Stiles of the small Sunderland Savings Bank to investigate the National Cash Register's on-line system recently installed at the Amsterdam Savings Bank. In the meantime, having evaluated the costs and savings, the Scottish consortium opted for an off-line system on the understanding that an eventual switch to OLRT would be feasible with an upgrade of the mainframe. Sir Thomas Dunlop, chairman of the Savings Bank of Glasgow, and John Lowrie, now acting general manager operations, convinced the Ministry of Technology that a Burroughs system was preferable to either ICL or Honeywell, largely because Burroughs had a rudimentary research and development unit based in Scotland which they were willing to expand to support the implementation. Having won permission, the Savings Bank of Glasgow financed the building and equipping of a computer centre.

Although the Scottish savings banks had flirted with OLRT for some time, it was David Wilson, the chief accountant of the Manchester & Salford Savings Bank who grasped its advantages for savings bank customers. He dismissed off-line solutions as failing to provide the flexibility that would allow transactions to be made at several branches without accounts being overdrawn, prohibited by TSB rules. He was convinced that only on-line systems could make this possible with the immediate updating of passbooks. A shy, acerbic man, he prosecuted his

Olivetti TC 349 terminals installed in branches
as part of the OLRT system.

campaign for an on-line system with missionary zeal and thoroughness. A feasibility study was commissioned by the Manchester & Salford trustees in 1967, which was quickly followed by an invitation to tender for the mainframe computer and terminals. Before the contract was settled, five neighbouring savings banks, lacking the resources to purchase their own installations, asked to participate in the on-line venture and founded the Manchester and District Computer Accounting Project (MADCAP) early in 1968. In May, after tenders from a number of suppliers had been worked through with a fine comb by David Wilson, contracts for terminals were placed with Olivetti and for the mainframe with the newly formed ICL. Since ICL was a

British supplier, neither the Ministry of Technology nor the National Debt Office placed obstacles in the way of MADCAP. Shortly after Manchester & Salford decided to adopt an on-line system, a consortium of savings banks in the West Midlands and South Wales had reached the same conclusion.

The movement quickly polarised between supporters of off-line and OLRT. With the Inspection Committee encouragement for the formation of further consortia covering the

David Wilson, the architect of
the on-line real time system.

whole country, regional groupings began to coalesce in support of the two systems. The on-line approach also found favour in Northern Ireland, and partially in the North-West '8 bank group', which had already come to an agreement for a bureau service provided by the Post Office's National Data Processing Service. The advocates of on-line were opposed by the London Savings Bank servicing the Essex, Cambridge and East Anglia Savings Banks; and a South-Eastern consortium known as SPOTS, comprising the South-Eastern, Surrey, Portsmouth, Oxford and Thames Valley savings banks. Drawing on the experience of Scandinavian savings banks, there was support for the formation of a separate company under the Association's control to manage regional computer centres meeting the needs of the competing consortia. Crucial to further progress, however, was a decision on which system the Association should support. Will Dick of Preston Savings Bank chaired meetings at the close of 1968 which resulted in London Savings Bank offering to allow other savings banks access to its off-line system now installed and Manchester & Salford its OLRT system, but no agreement on the competing claims of either the two systems or different manufacturers. At this juncture, the National Debt Office and Ministry of Technology made it clear that co-operation was a condition of the sanction of any further expenditure on automation. As a result MADCAP and

Will Dick of the Preston Savings Bank.

the West Midlands consortia came together in November 1968 to form the TSB joint computer project under Albert Potter based in ICL's Wilmslow offices on the outskirts of Manchester. As the consultants in Scotland had made clear, an essential prerequisite of automation was standardisation of procedures, particularly common account numbering. This was agreed by the Association with surprisingly little argument and the huge task of renumbering customer accounts for the two consortia began in 1969. This involved printing numbers on to strips of sticky labels, one each for the passbook, the ledger card and the index card. The whole operation nearly came to grief when the glue on the labels jammed the computer printers.

While these tortuous negotiations were being conducted, the Association had been persuaded to examine the feasibility of the TSBs entering the unit trust business. Unit trusts traced their origins in Britain back to 1931 when they were introduced from the United States by W.B. Burton-Baldry. A unit trust simply allows an investor through the purchase of units to have an interest in a range of different securities held on his behalf by the manager. They only became generally popular in the late 1950s, with the relaxation of wartime controls on the equity market and the expanding market for personal saving. By the early 1960s, the TSBs were experiencing a loss of funds from special investment departments to buy unit trusts, which in a period of gathering inflation appeared to offer a better return. There was also a more general movement in favour of wider share ownership. An early advocate of a TSB unit trust was Andrew Rintoul, the chairman of the Savings Bank of Glasgow, who had witnessed the success of the issue in November 1959 of Scotshares, controlled by Scottish Industry Unit Trust (Management) Ltd, which in just four weeks raised over £5.75 million in over-the-counter sales in Scottish high street banks. It was believed that Scottish banks had demonstrated that investors, 'regardless of occupation, status and income', were now keen to look beyond deposit accounts and government securities to other types of investment. Rintoul found an able ally in Viscount Lambert, chairman of the Devon & Exeter Savings Bank, and won support from the financial press. There were those, notably Sir Kenneth Stewart and the authoritative television presenter Richard Dimbleby, who, from the outset, raised the perennial moral concern of encouraging savings bank depositors to invest in fluctuating securities.

After five years of internal debate, the Association's annual meeting in June 1964 authorised a detailed investigation because:

> Existing depositors and the general public were becoming more and more conscious of the effect of inflation on their capital; unit trust companies were attracting considerable sums of money away from the TSB movement; a TSB unit trust would be a useful method of attracting longer term savings; the TSBs were losing their more sophisticated savers and, unless they updated their services, this trend was likely to continue, and a TSB unit trust would be in keeping with the traditions and objectives of the TSB movement – to provide thrift.

A working party was set up, chaired by Harold Young of the South-Eastern Savings Bank. Viscount Lambert, a member of the committee, co-opted A.P.W. (Tim) Simon, joint founder of the Target group of unit trusts and chairman of Unit Trust Services, which administered unit trusts for other companies. He encouraged the TSBs to form their own trust company so that the individual banks would be able to take a share in the profits proportionate to the amount of business they secured. By 1966 a draft scheme had been drawn up. Despite the doubts of some representatives, it was overwhelmingly supported by all the TSBs at the annual meeting in Oban. At that meeting, the 84-year-old Sir Kenneth Stewart, who had done more than anyone to modernise the movement, stood down after twenty years as chairman. He was succeeded by Athelstan Caröe, the chairman of the Liverpool Savings Bank and deputy

Sir Athelstan Caröe,
chairman of the TSB Association.

E. C. C. Evans, President of the Savings Bank Institute, and Sir Kenneth
Stewart, at the opening of the TSB Residential College in 1967.

chairman of the Association. A brilliant linguist, he had played an important part in the reconstruction of the International Thrift Institute into the International Savings Bank Institute in 1963. As the Institute's first president, he was keen that the British TSBs should learn from the experience of those in other countries, particularly North America and continental Europe. It was left to him to secure Treasury approval for the plan.

The reaction of the National Debt Office had initially been cool, suggesting that the TSBs could make use of existing services. This led Charles Lawton of the York Savings Bank to put forward a number of compromises which he hoped might overcome Treasury objections. These were all turned down by the Association's members, who favoured a frank explanation of the reasoning behind the draft scheme. The negotiations during the winter of 1966 proved more straightforward than had been anticipated and to the delight of the movement James Callaghan, the Chancellor of the Exchequer, included the necessary permission in his 1967 budget statement. On 19 July TSB Unit Trust Management Ltd was incorporated as a wholly owned subsidiary of the Association. At Tim Simon's suggestion, the articles of association included the power to transact insurance business. Philip Keens, of the London Savings Bank and a member of the working party who had originally been hostile to the whole idea, was appointed chairman. The other directors were Athelstan Caröe, Willie Dick, chief actuary of Preston Savings Bank, Andrew Archibald, chairman of the County & City of Perth Savings

Bank, and J.D. Campbell, general manager of the Savings Bank of Glasgow, with Freddie Miller, secretary of the Association, as secretary.

Since the Chancellor had made it clear that there could be no government involvement in the Trust Company and the National Debt Office had ruled out a levy on the individual TSBs, the Association put up £100 capital out of its petty cash. Urgent talks were held with the Mercantile & General Reinsurance to borrow £25,000. M & G so liked the venture that instead they invested £100,000 in £1 redeemable preference shares in the Trust Company.

The 'Good for Harry!' TSB Unit Trust advertisement.

Unable to set up its own organisation to issue certificates, deal with sales and purchases and pay dividends, the Trust Company appointed the merchant bankers, J. Henry Schroder Wagg, as fund managers. Unfettered by the Association's hidebound committee structure, the Unit Trust company planned an ambitious launch using a cartoon character called Harry and the slogan *Good for Harry! . . . and good for you.* The purpose was to change investors' perceptions of not only TSBs but of the whole financial system, making them aware that there was room for small investors. The campaign was recognised by the burgeoning unit trust industry as trail-blazing. Riding on the back of this achievement, Brian Brown, the newly appointed marketing manager with only a tiny office, had next to deploy his sales force of just seven to win custom in the teeth of opposition from some individual TSBs; York refused to participate outright and East Anglia would make sales only in response to customer inquiries. To circumvent such institutional obstacles, arrangements were made for the TSB units to be purchased by post and from joint stock banks. The result of the initial sales drive far exceeded the projected £2.5 million, in the first ten days yielding £5.5 million – a record for the industry. By the end of the year, after further extensive promotion and press advertising, £16 million worth of units had been taken up by 60,000 subscribers of whom 75 per cent were TSB depositors. Moreover, the fund had achieved a substantial capital growth of about 40 per cent. A small number of unit-linked life-insurance policies, which enjoyed favourable tax concessions, had also been sold. These involved considerable administrative support that went well beyond that for simple unit trust sales.

This stunning achievement boosted the morale of the TSBs whose fortunes had shown signs of going into reverse. The launch of the Post Office Savings Bank's Investment Account in June 1966 had been a success, attracting £70 million in six months from 200,000 depositors. Building society deposits were continuing to roar ahead. Both the building societies and the Post Office Savings Bank carefully focused their publicity, particularly targeting young people with no family commitments who had larger disposable incomes than ever before. The TSBs had already re-examined their more and more manifestly inadequate collaborative promotional activity at a second publicity conference, held once again at Folkestone in March, which had gone over much the same ground as before. This time, however, a market research report was commissioned from Overmark Sells Ltd – the parent company of the Association's publicity agents. Given the history and social objectives of the movement, the findings, contained in six volumes, were hardly surprising, showing that the typical customer, who now represented a fifth of the adult population of Britain, had left school early, was probably a manual worker, did not own a car, was paid in cash at relatively low rates, and read the popular press. The better-off customers (one-fifth of the total), who accounted for most of the funds of the TSBs, also had an account with a clearing bank and a tenth had building society accounts.

Overwhelmingly, preference for TSB accounts was determined by the convenience of having a branch within walking distance of the home rather than any tax benefit. Only the better-off customers, whose continuing support was vital if the TSBs were to survive, wanted improved services like the newly introduced cheque books. The report also showed that the TSBs were appealing to a steadily ageing population. Although many children had school savings accounts, few of these were now being carried into adult life. As a result, there was a relatively low percentage of depositors in the 18–34 age group in which disposable incomes were known to be high. As worrying was a lack of awareness of TSBs or their services amongst non-customers, most of whom had learned something of the clearing banks and building societies from mass advertising campaigns.

Archie Hunter of Liverpool Savings Bank, chairman of the Publicity Committee, was determined to prevent further erosion of the TSBs' market. Drawing on the experience of the highly successful 'Harry' promotion for the TSB Unit Trust, a new general publicity campaign for all TSBs was carefully planned with the agents, Sells, targeted at the 18–34 age group and featuring a girl called Sally, described as 'A pleasant, wholesome, lively young girl – up-to-date, modern and with it. Nevertheless, a serious thinker, especially when it comes to money – her money. In fact, representative of the day and age AND REPRESENTATIVE OF THE BANK SHE USES – TSB'. For the launch in the spring of 1968, sixteen colour posters were printed, with captions like 'Sally to the big SAVE-IN', 'Sally for a big save in', and 'Sally, the girl who started the Save in Thing'. Despite all the planning, Sally was a flop. Many TSBs claimed they were reluctant to make use of the material for fear of deterring their existing elderly customers. More probably, individual TSBs, after the launch of the TSB Unit Trust, were suspicious of what appeared to be the growing power of the Association and its executives. The majority of TSB staff had been brought up in a culture where aggressive marketing was frowned upon and believed that customers would continue to make use of their services, publicity campaign or no publicity campaign. In the face of, at best, apathy, and, at worst, hostility, the Publicity Committee tried with little success to support the concept behind Sally. The problem was compounded early in 1967 by the publication of a blurred Further Education leaflet by Sells. This was the last straw, touching a raw nerve and caused the publicity committee to transfer the Association's account to J. Walter Thompson Ltd.

One of the factors that contributed to the failure of central publicity in the 1960s was resentment by the staff of the individual TSBs at being asked to compete with the clearing banks and the building societies which offered much better conditions of employment. There had been difficulties in 1966 when the newly established Prices & Incomes Board refused to give permission for an extension in holiday entitlement, which was frozen until June 1967. TSB staff, through their Union, also demanded equivalent conditions to the clearers, in particular a house-purchase loan scheme at favourable rates of interest. Over three-quarters of clearing bank

LEFT
J. Walter Thompson's first TSB campaign, 1969.

OPPOSITE
The *TSB Gazette*'s cartoonist,
on the problems of recruiting suitable
staff in 1967.

staff enjoyed this benefit. The Employers' Council had drawn up a plan costing some £10 million the year before, which had been rejected out of hand by the Treasury and the National Debt Office. Prompted by the Treasury, the TSBs devised a scheme to be met from management expenses, but it became clear that the rate of interest charged to employees by building societies and clearing banks could not be matched and some TSBs would not be able to afford to participate without mutual assistance. Against a background of mounting difficulty in recruiting and retaining suitably qualified and trained staff, the scheme was approved. Well aware that this could be only a holding operation to stem a staffing crisis, the recruitment committee felt unable to do more to improve conditions of service until wider questions concerning the future of the movement as a whole had been settled. The TSB Employers' Council, however, reached an understanding in 1967 with the Union to persuade all the TSBs to adopt common conditions of service for female staff, ironing out many inconsistencies, not least by ensuring that after one year's service, all female staff were entitled to full pension rights.

The house-purchase scheme had been possible only because, towards the end of 1967, the Treasury had finally yielded to pressure and prepared a new Bill which raised the interest paid to the TSBs on ordinary department deposits to 3.65 per cent, increasing the available margin for management expenses. It also replaced the existing now inadequate capital fund set up under the fourth Mutual Assistance Scheme, by giving the National Debt Office powers to lend up to £10 million at current market rates for capital expenditure on property and equipment, particularly computers. At the same time the Mutual Assistance Scheme was renewed for a fifth time with much the same provisions as before. The new Act made no provision for increasing interest paid to depositors in the ordinary departments. From 1966, withdrawals from ordinary departments exceeded deposits on a massively rising turnover which reached £1,500 million in 1968/9 with total deposits stuck at £1,000 million, reflecting the inflationary pressures at work within the economy as a whole. Turnover was bolstered in 1968 by the introduction of TSB cheque cards, making current accounts much more flexible.

'*Don't write us, we'll write you*'

The government was also planning a shake-up of National Savings. A National Giro on the lines recommended by the Radcliffe Committee was established in October 1968. The following year the Post Office Savings Bank was reconstructed as a National Savings Bank, heralded at the time as a third force in British banking. There were also whispers that an incoming Conservative government would outlaw the clearing banks' competition and credit controls which regulated, through the Committee of London Clearing Banks, bank interest rates and terms of loans to customers. Uncertain of their role in what was becoming an even more competitive market for personal financial services, trustees and actuaries were at long last becoming convinced that reforms were imperative. The most immediate, to capture more customers in the 18–34 age-group, was the introduction of a personal loan service to complement cheques and the unit trust. With fast-growing special investment departments, there was no insuperable problem in identifying a source of funds. Urgent decisions still required to be taken about the choice of computer systems. These individual items on the agenda for reform pointed firmly in one direction, greater integration and possible uncoupling from the strict interest-rate regime imposed by the National Debt Office, once considered to be one of the principal selling points of the TSBs. At the 1968 annual meeting of the Association, the chairman floated the idea of a Central Bank, modelled on the experience of TSBs elsewhere in Europe, where such banks had been established 'to advise on investments and to execute orders given by Member branches'. Only later had they gone on to manage central cheque clearance and credit transfers. The main advantage in the view of the chairman of the Association, Athelstan Caröe, was that it would allow the TSBs in the not too distant future greater control over special investment departments. This suggestion was linked to a statement by the Governor of the Bank of England, Sir Leslie O'Brien, that amalgamations into larger groupings were essential, providing better facilities for depositors, better prospects for staff, more economical working and the benefit of modern techniques. Taking this advice to heart the Liverpool & Chester Savings Bank embarked on preliminary discussions and the South-Eastern Savings Bank made overtures to its neighbours.

By the autumn of 1968, there was mounting pressure for a clear statement on the benefits of amalgamation by the Association. When the matter was discussed at the Executive Committee, there were understandable reservations by some members who stood to lose both their independence and their power if large-scale amalgamations came about. There was concern that, if TSBs were amalgamated, they would lose their essentially local character. Apart from agreement that amalgamations had to be voluntary, there was no consensus as to whether to adopt the Governor's advice. By contrast there was support for a Central Bank for TSBs which it was envisaged would provide a secure base to compete with the National Savings Bank's Investment Department and enhance the investment advice that could be provided to customers. There was no doubt that the existing central credit transfer and inter-bank clearing service could provide a nucleus for the creation of a Central Bank. At the annual meeting in 1969, the chairman went further in demanding mergers, local opposition or no, if the TSBs were to survive. He was particularly worried by the irrefutable evidence that the TSBs were losing custom to other financial institutions. In redefining their objectives to meet the competition, J.D. Campbell, the General Manager of the Savings Bank of Glasgow, writing in the *Trustee Savings Bank Gazette*, had already challenged as a fallacy the commonly held assumption that the savings banks had a social role in helping the poor through times of economic crises, and repeating the conclusion of John Bone more than 160 years before that the poor never had sufficient income to save: 'Many trustees and savings bank officials have had, like myself, as part of their "conventional wisdom" the belief that savings banks exist to relieve poverty and to encourage the poor to help themselves ... But the fact is that the savings banks' contribution to the relief of poverty has never been more than minimal. No doubt the banks were instrumental in relieving much distress and hardship but the poor have usually been too poor to use the savings banks.' He accurately identified as the principal customers 'those who were above subsistence level and who had a margin between earnings and the cost of subsistence'. As he intended, the article fuelled the debate about the direction of the movement.

The Treasury had already gone some way to answer the clamour for greater freedom of manoeuvre. A further Act in 1969 made it possible for pensions to be paid to widows and children, now a common provision in most occupational pension schemes. The Act also allowed TSBs to 'undertake any business which is, in the opinion of the Commissioners, calculated to encourage thrift and within the financial capacity of the banks' – a permissive clause open to generous interpretation. Interest rates paid to the banks, but not to depositors, were again nudged forward. At the same time, bowing to pressure from the National Union of Bank Employees, the TSBs followed the clearing banks and began closing on Saturday mornings on the first Saturday in July of that year. However, for many, progress by both the Association and the Treasury was painfully slow and very conservative. Meetings were immensely frustrating, with long delays in agreeing minutes and procedures and regular interruptions from representatives of smaller banks with little or no understanding of the problems of the larger banks. The more adventurous banks took matters into their own hands. The South-Eastern Area set up a committee to examine the possibility of establishing a TSB Building Society, a strategy also urged by Graham Hamilton of Aberdeen Savings Bank. Merger talks continued, resulting in the amalgamation of Edinburgh and Dalkeith in 1969, and terms for the merger of the London and South-Eastern Savings Banks in 1971. To meet the challenge of higher-yielding accounts with building societies and the National Savings Bank, the Savings Bank of Glasgow created a two-tier interest structure in its special investment department; 6.5 per cent at one month's notice and 7.5 per cent at six months. All this disparate activity, illustrating the need for flexibility, still begged the pressing question of central direction. Plans for a Central Bank were held up by the reluctance of the clearing banks to admit the TSBs to the Central Walks Clearing in the City, where all the English clearing was done, until the question of principle had been resolved. The Treasury, while sympathetic with the need for personal loans, believed that 'the proposed step represented a major departure from the traditional role of TSBs and therefore it would need careful and detailed consideration before it was submitted to Ministers'. The TSB Unit Trust, after its excellent start, was flagging along with the rest of the industry due in part to the launch of the government's Save As You Earn (SAYE) scheme announced in the budget. The TSBs, which had first suggested the idea as long ago as 1957, had agreed to co-operate in the scheme. A cause for some optimism was the progress of the TSB joint computer project which in 1969 moved from St Anne's House, Wilmslow, to The Graftons at

Robert Brotherton, recruited to deliver the complete
on-line real time system in 1969.

Altrincham nearby. Robert Brotherton was recruited from English Sewing Cotton as project manager, responsible for delivering the complete on-line system within two years. Following a decision that TSBs should own their own facilities rather than use a bureau service, the eight banks (now in fact nine banks) consortium joined the project in April 1970 committed to building a computer centre at Bootle because all the necessary telephone wires had been installed in the local exchange adjacent to the NDPS facility that served the National Giro Bank.

Any misconceptions that the TSBs may have had that the National Debt Office did not understand their anxieties were totally dispelled by the speech of the Comptroller-General, Italo de Lisle Radice, at the 1970 annual meeting of the Association. He was direct and hard-hitting, telling the representatives that 'the modern phenomenon of ever-accelerating change was affecting the financial and banking world as much as industry, and social habits, and the

Trustee Savings Bank still seemed to be caught hopelessly in the current rather than diverting it to their own benefit'. He then proceeded to review all the areas of most concern, the role of the trustees, a central organisation, the scale of operation, the development of services to the customer, finance and publicity. He concluded with a stern warning: 'At the present time there was a clear trend towards the development of comprehensive banking services. If the Trustee Savings Bank wished to follow this trend, then they would have to become increasingly independent, since governments might see little reason to provide special privileges for financial institutions which were competing in the commercial world.' Such a homily, however well

TSB Unit Trust advertisement for
'Harvest Bonds', from 1970.

# TSB snatches the lion's share.

The importance of National Savings has never been underestimated in this country, especially by The Trustee Savings Banks.

For many years the TSB has interested more people in savings – over 10 million – than any other bank in Britain's high streets.

Now the TSB can add another success. That of contributing more to National Savings than any other single organisation in Britain. It amounts to the record figure of £2,899·6 million.* That's 32·7% of National Savings.

Over 1,500 Trustee Savings Bank branches help ordinary people to help themselves. It's a big help to Britain's finances. And that's straight from the lion's mouth.

*Source: Department of National Savings, June 1971.

**T S B**

# TRUSTEE SAVINGS BANK

meant, was of little avail when, in July, the Committee of London Clearing Banks made it plain that admission to the 'commercial world' was barred. By then the political climate had changed fundamentally with the return of the Conservatives to power at the general election in June committed to a thorough shake-up of the financial system to encourage competition and improve credit terms. The Association was in a quandary: should it openly challenge the clearing banks or continue to seek an understanding? With the government bent on radical overhaul of the banking system, it was evident that, without external scrutiny and direction, it would be impossible for the savings banks to reform themselves. It was perhaps inevitable that in his budget speech in April 1971 Anthony Barber should announce the appointment of a committee to review the entire field of National Savings under the chairmanship of Sir Harry Page, the former City Treasurer of Manchester. At the same time he raised the tax exemption on interest paid on savings bank ordinary accounts to £21 from £15 where it had remained for fifteen years.

The appointment of the Page Committee marked an end of twenty years' struggle by the TSBs to re-establish their separate identity distinct from the National Savings Movement that had played such a vital role during the Second World War and in the immediate post-war years. Although advance was regularly hampered, and at times brought to a standstill by entrenched opposition or local misgivings, there had been real progress: the re-establishment of the Special Investment Departments, the creation of the Savings Bank Institute, the extension of the movement into the south of England, and the launch of the cheque service and, most recently, the Unit Trust. These were considerable achievements for a voluntary movement whose central Association had no power to impose policy. If at times decision-making seemed fragmented and confused, this was simply a reflection of the nature of the movement. Despite all the frustrations, the greatest virtue of the Association was a willingness to explore (if not to act on) any new ideas brought to the attention of the Executive, providing there were enough enthusiastic supporters (not easily disillusioned) to serve on a sub-committee. Its greatest handicap was the difficulty of translating the findings of numerous sub-committees into anything resembling a coherent strategy, which might enjoy majority support. The more far-sighted members of the movement looked to the Page Committee to do this for them.

An aggressive image for 1971.

# CHAPTER EIGHT

# A

# FULLY FLEDGED

# BANK

## *1971–86*

The mood of the country by 1971 had changed markedly from that of twenty years before. The spirit of community and co-operation engendered by the privations of war and the early years of peace had been eroded by calls for greater independence and freedom of expression, particularly from the young. The children born in the baby boom that followed at the start of peacetime reached adolescence in the 1960s and were no longer willing to conform with the conventions of previous generations. They made their point by adopting unconventional dress, new styles of pop music, and of social behaviour. They were enthusiastic supporters of satirical comedy that poked unrestrained fun at politicians, and other Establishment figures, yet they lacked any coherent philosophy. In an age of full employment, what many of them wanted was credit to purchase flats and houses, consumer goods, and the good things of life on an unprecedented scale. The conventional political debate about welfare benefits, health care, and education mattered less than the means to 'do your own thing'. Such ambitions had important political lessons which were to prompt a pruning of the overgrowth of government bureaucracy over the last sixty years. Edward Heath, the leader of the Conservative Party, sensed this change and based his manifesto for the 1970 general election on the withdrawal of government from some areas and the improvement of service in others. The economy was identified as the principal area for the removal of government regulation and involvement in the expectation that a larger measure of free enterprise would make for greater efficiency and more consumer choice. There was no doubt that this approach would have fundamental consequences for the whole financial sector and particularly the National Savings Movement with its close link to government financial policy.

It was not until the Conservatives' first budget in March 1971 that a change was confirmed, when the Chancellor of the Exchequer, Anthony Barber, announced: 'It should be possible to achieve more flexible but still effective arrangements basically by operating on the banks' resources rather than by directly guiding their lending.' This was followed in May by the Bank of England's publication of a consultative document *Competition and Credit Control*, which was adopted by the government in September. Under its terms, all lending restrictions were abolished and the banks were free to compete with one another for deposits. Designed to generate credit for industrial investment, Competition and Credit Control had quite the opposite effect of stimulating a consumer boom as the pent-up expectations of the post-war generation were unleashed. The TSBs and the building societies were deeply disappointed that the Bank of England showed no indication of treating them on equal terms with the clearing banks. It was against this background that the Page Committee on National Savings began their deliberations.

The savings banks had already received fair warning of what might be in store for them from Italo de Lisle Radice, the Comptroller-General of the National Debt Office, in his speech to the 1970 annual meeting – the TSBs could delay no longer in heading off the challenge of

During the early 1970s customers became increasingly concerned
about the effect of rising inflation on their savings. The TSB responded
with reassuring advertisements.

the clearing banks and building societies which were steadily eroding their customer base. Tired of trying to persuade individual TSBs to contribute to the publicity fund, he had called for a mandatory levy of 1s 6d (7.5 pence) for every £1,000 held on deposit. The regions remained unenthusiastic unless the Treasury was willing once again to raise the interest paid to the banks to cover costs. The Treasury, anticipating that the TSBs would have to compete directly with other financial institutions, were agreeable on the understanding that the whole of the additional interest should be used for national publicity. Although there were still voices of dissent, particularly from the Scottish TSBs which believed that the Association's propaganda was weighted in favour of the south of England, the proposal was backed unanimously by the Association's members. At last the Publicity Committee had sufficient funds to launch some semblance of a nationwide campaign, including experimental advertising on Border and Westward Television. As important, for the first time for nearly ninety years, under the terms of the outgoing Labour government's final budget, the interest rate paid to depositors with ordinary departments was lifted by 1 per cent to 3.5 per cent.

Welcome as these improvements were, they were only a start. The Association was besieged with questions, all of which required urgent attention. These ranged from dwindling sales of TSB Unit Trusts, the forthcoming renewal of the Mutual Assistance Scheme, to the difficulty of recruiting a new generation of trustees. The only one where progress was sustained, with the support of the National Debt Office and the Inspection Committee, was in installing computers in the regional centres at Manchester – MADCAP (6 banks), West Midlands-Kidderminster (6 banks), Bootle (8 banks), York (14 banks), Crawley (5 banks), London (3 banks), Glasgow (4 banks), Belfast, and Falkirk. The ICL computers were delivered in February 1971 to MADCAP and the West Midlands. Pilot testing in selected branches began immediately. One of the most radical decisions the project had to take was to agree a uniform passbook that could be updated mechanically. It had to be flexible, of a uniform size and the layout had to allow for any slippage in the printers. At the same time, following the exclusion of the TSBs from the London Clearing Banks' Inter-Bank Computer Bureau, the remit of the TSB joint computer project was extended to provide technical advice and support to the Association.

Directly the appointment of the Page Committee was announced, all other concerns had to take second place to preparing the movement's evidence. From the beginning the Executive Committee led by Athelstan Caröe adopted a cautious approach, unwilling to be trapped by the Page Committee into supporting a radical agenda for reform. The Page Committee was dominated by the private sector. The members, in addition to Sir Harry Page, were Professor R.J. Ball of the London Business School; J.M. Clay of Hambros Bank; James Gulliver of the Argyll Group; Godfrey Heywood, a consulting actuary; and Mrs A.M. Ward-Jackson, the finance director of the John Lewis Partnership, with David Butler of the Treasury as secretary. Responsibility for co-ordinating the Association's evidence was entrusted to Will Dick, the recently retired general manager of the Preston Savings Bank. He worked expeditiously to

Sir Harry Page, Chairman of the Page Committee.

submit a ninety-page document by the end of July 1971, outlining the history of the movement and calling for a series of modest reforms to which there could be no objection from any of the Association's members. These were:

- The ability to provide personal credit, under five headings, namely:
  Personal Loans
  Bridging Loans
  Loans for the payment of Estate Duty
  Temporary Overdrafts on Current Accounts
  Home Loans (mortgages)
- A TSB Central Bank
- A new source of capital for the provision of additional branches
- Wider investment powers in the Special Investment Department

- An increased income tax concession on depositors' interest
- Removal of deposit restrictions
- Relaxation of out-of-date statutory control by the National Debt Office and TSB Inspection Committee
- Wider investment powers for Superannuation Reserve Funds
- A more equitable share of National Savings Committee support
- Better relationships with joint stock banks

In framing these recommendations, the Association saw the future of the TSBs entirely in the context of their original purpose of promoting savings and wise money management for the benefit of the individual and, coincidentally, the community as a whole. Although the need for collective action through the medium of the Association and the possibility of further amalgamations were admitted, there was little discussion of the growth in competition for personal financial services in the last twenty years or of the likely outcome if the Page Committee recommended that the complete apparatus of National Savings should be abolished as anachronistic. The whole tone of the evidence was guarded, failing to capture the spirit of the Conservative government's fundamental reappraisal of the financial sector.

In the meantime, Sir Harry Page and members of the committee had been visiting TSBs to gauge the mood of general managers. The Association was called on to give oral evidence on 13 and 20 September. At the first meeting, the Committee, drawing on the results of discussions with individual TSBs, urged the delegation, led by Caröe, to add flesh to the proposals and to consider much more sweeping changes, such as the merger of the TSBs with the National Savings Bank, and the advantage and disadvantages of the TSBs entering the private sector. At the second meeting, Sir Harry pressed for a response to the proposition that the TSBs might be able to operate more effectively if they became 'companies limited by guarantee', adopting a more or less mutual status – a proposal favoured in Scotland where there was a strong tradition of mutual life insurance companies. Caröe refused to be drawn, choosing to defend the existing system of voluntary trustees as fundamental to the ethos of the movement. On the whole, the delegation was pleased with the outcome, believing that the Committee had only encouraged the Association to consider a wider brief in the expectation that it was as well to ask government for more than was required in the certain knowledge that less would be conceded. Others, including Sir Kenneth Stewart, were not so sure, calling for a contingency plan should the Page Committee recommend the removal of all existing controls. Their suspicions were heightened by the lukewarm reaction of the press to the publication of the Association's evidence in May 1972.

Speaking at the Association's annual meeting the following month, G.A. Downey of the Treasury paid tribute to Sir Kenneth Stewart, who had died on 21 May, and went on to suggest that he had been right to be concerned about the likely outcome of the Page Committee. Impressing on his audience that change was an inevitable consequence, he cautioned the Association to outline a strategy for independent management of the TSBs: 'It could be argued that the further they went along the road to competition with other banks, the stronger became the case for the TSBs to be expected to stand on their own feet financially and to be brought into more equal competition with other banks.'

His theme could almost have been orchestrated to provide an overture for Richard Ellis of the Aberdeen Savings Bank, who followed with an analysis of the role and responsibilities of trustees. Ellis had no doubt that, whatever the circumstances in the future, the general managers (actuaries) and their staff would serve the TSBs well. However, he was less certain if, as presently conceived, trustees could discharge their responsibilities effectively. He dared to raise the difficult questions: to whom were they responsible or for whom did they act? Pointing out that, unlike 'the board of directors of a company, or of a building society, or of a co-operative society, they were not even elected', he concluded that, until the formation of the Special Investment Departments, they were trustees for the Comptroller of the National Debt Office and thereafter in some respects trustees for the depositors. 'But savings bank trustees were not, as were most private trustees, answerable and accountable to the beneficiaries. Therefore, they were not answerable in any strict sense to the depositors. To whom, therefore, were trustees responsible, by what criteria of success, and by whom and on what standards were trustees of a savings bank to be judged? They were trustees for depositors, but they could not be removed if they did not do their job properly.' Ellis spoke for other more progressive trustees and general managers when he stated that the existing arrangements were incompatible with demands for greater autonomy, particularly as the average age of the trustees serving on the Association's Executive Committee was sixty-seven. In some individual savings banks the average was even higher; Huddersfield Savings Bank had no trustee under the age of seventy-five. Having described the problem, however, Ellis was unable to offer any solution other than to exhort banks to recruit younger working trustees. He rejected emphatically any suggestion that trustees should be elected.

The problem of management and authority was well illustrated by the opening of the office of the TSB joint computer project, only a few weeks earlier by the Chancellor of the Exchequer. The project had recently widened its remit to include the management of the North East & Midland consortia (12 banks) which planned a mixture of on-line, off-line and manual systems. Already W.F. Rishton, general manager of the Preston Savings Bank, had warned that the computer consortia that were coming into operation would make it virtually impossible for trustees of individual banks to exercise any effective control over their business. For two years the Association had been working towards a co-ordinated and coherent strategy in the installation of computer systems. Regular meetings were arranged of the chairmen of the eight computer consortia – Scottish, South-Eastern (SPOTS), Liverpool (8 banks) West Midlands, London, Manchester (MADCAP), North-East and Midlands, Belfast and the TSB joint computer project. The Mechanisation and Methods Sub-Committee had been replaced by a Computer and Mechanisation Committee and a Computer Technical Committee with the responsibility of monitoring development. MADCAP and the West Midlands consortia went on-line successfully in 1972, defeating similar on-line initiatives by the clearing banks which failed to deliver effective systems. Unknown to David Wilson, when he committed Manchester & Salford TSB to on-line, the savings bank consortia were ideally suited to such systems. Although they had a large number of accounts, there were neither a great number of transactions not were there many different types of transactions. As it turned out, more than fifty standing order payments per account in a year stretched the system to its limits. The eight banks consortia went on-line in 1974 and the North-East and Midlands the following year.

The decision of these four consortia to place their computers under the management of the joint computer project led to the formation of TSB Computer Services Ltd to own and manage the Altrincham facility as a subsidiary of the Association. Integral to the formation of the subsidiary was the opportunity afforded to make progress in coherent strategic planning for the use of computers throughout the whole movement. There was a feeling that the £10 million made available by the National Debt Office that had been invested so far for computing facilities for the savings banks could have been better deployed if there had been more central direction. In creating a framework for forward planning, there was an urgent need for appraisal of the next generation of new technology giving greater attention to cost-effectiveness, particularly through savings in staff time, rather than 'suitability for a specific task'. Under pressure from the National Debt Office, a Computer Research & Development Unit (CRDU) was established by the Association for this purpose under the direction of Haydn Taylor. Although no final decisions about future strategy could be taken until the Page Report had been published, the members of the Association were determined to put the necessary mechanisms speedily in place. A report on the 'cost-effectiveness and human aspects of computerisation' was commissioned from the University of Durham, the London School of Economics and the Manchester Business School. This established that currently OLRT was more expensive than off-line, but overlooked gains in productivity that could be achieved.

The Association's Executive Committee displayed similar resolution in driving ahead with the formation of the Central TSB Ltd, with encouragement and help from the Bank of England. The Treasury had given the necessary permission by the spring of 1973, and Robert Catt, the chief of the management services division at the Bank of England, was seconded as general manager. His first task was to take over the management of the Clearing Centre from the London Savings Bank. Thereafter accounts would have to be opened by every savings bank, the Association and its subsidiaries, and the Birmingham Municipal Bank to enable the Central Bank to handle their cash balances and make interest payments. After the National Debt Office had agreed that the Central Bank could invest all overnight money, Catt estimated that, when all the savings banks were linked to a common computer network, annual savings of almost £2 million could be achieved. The work of implementation was entrusted to the CRDU, which, lacking the expertise to carry it out, was forced to subcontract it to TSB Computer Services Ltd. Although admission to the Committee of London Clearing Banks had still to be negotiated, the establishment of the Central Bank allowed the TSBs to enter the City as bankers for the first time. The Central Bank was ready to take over credit clearing in June 1973 and within a month had achieved a profit of £8,000. Catt and the chairman of the Central Bank, Philip Keens, immediately sought permission from the Bank of England to begin formal negotiations with the Committee of London Clearing Banks with a view to extending the scope of the Central Bank's clearing services. These discussions were interrupted by the publication of the findings of the Page Committee in June 1973.

In the two years since the Page Committee had been appointed, the market for personal banking had been transformed by the Competition and Credit Control policy and the high levels of inflation it helped fuel. The response of all the clearing banks to Competition and Credit Control had been to enlarge even further their fast-growing personal customer services, winning new business, particularly through the medium of interest-bearing deposit accounts. They complemented growth in deposit-taking by using their greater freedom to expand personal loan facilities out of all recognition, with almost no restrictions on use. With inflation

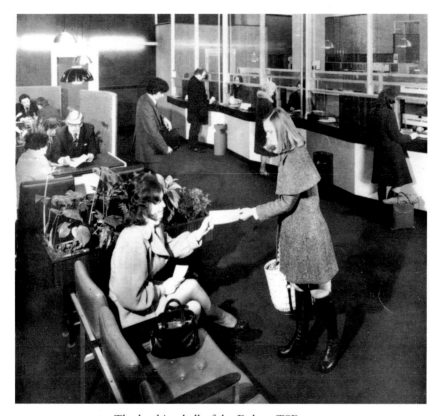

The banking hall of the Bolton TSB, 1973.

roaring ahead, more and more personal customers began to see the advantage of buying consumer goods on credit in the certain knowledge that prices would rise in the near future. Such a pattern of behaviour made a nonsense of the savings institutions' rhetoric of deferred spending or saving for spending. 'What is the good of saving, when the pound you save today will be worth less in a year's time, and probably much less in ten years' time?' The TSBs thus believed that they had no alternative but to reaffirm their belief that saving was in the interests of not just national economies, but the whole world monetary order. Sir Athelstan Carôe (recently knighted) declared boldly in 1972: 'Without personal savings there could be no personal freedom. Everyone would be beholden to the Welfare State for their comfort and support.' However, there were some who continued to question whether, in a more commercial environment, the TSBs really wanted everyone's savings. Tom Bryans of the Belfast TSB pointed out that ordinary accounts with large numbers of transactions and small balances could result only in substantial losses, even when OLRT systems had been installed as in Northern Ireland.

For the savings institutions it was difficult to achieve a clear picture of underlying trends, because wage inflation combined with more freely available credit and higher interest rates to raise turnover and end of year balances substantially. Shares subscribed in building societies soared from £2.8 billion in 1970 to £5.8 billion in 1973; withdrawals advanced rapidly from £1.9 billion to £4.5 billion. Total share capital climbed from £9.7 billion to just over £16 billion, lacking any direct connection with the increasing popularity of home-ownership, which was also seen as a powerful hedge against inflation. The performance of the TSBs was less spectacular. Deposits in ordinary departments rose from £1.8 billion in 1970/1 to nearly £3 billion in 1973/4, barely keeping in front of withdrawals. Balances advanced steadily, from £1.1 billion to £1.4 billion in the ordinary department and from £1.5 billion to over £2 billion in the special investment department. These gains, helped by an increase in the tax concession on ordinary account interest to £40 in 1973, were heralded as evidence of the continuing importance of TSBs, especially as they represented a far stronger performance than other components of national savings.

Well aware of changes in the market for personal finance, the mechanism for government borrowing in a less regulated financial environment, and in the social purpose of savings, the Page Report outlined an agenda for change far more radical than even the most far-sighted general managers and trustees would dared have believed. At the heart of the Report were two well-substantiated assumptions that there were now cheaper ways for government to finance its borrowing requirements than drawing on National Savings and that government-encouraged deposits in the TSBs and the National Savings Bank were not particularly effective methods for combating inflation. These two central arguments represented a major shift in Treasury thinking which, since 1950, had taken for granted that 'deferred spending', in the form of deposits with TSBs and the Post Office Savings Bank, was a strong weapon in defeating inflation. Questioning whether there was any longer a moral imperative to save, the Report suggested that there were more appropriate means of long-term saving than National Savings, particularly in a period of high inflation, such as unit trusts and life assurance. In general, the Committee concluded that the market for personal finance was changing so fast that there was no case for retaining the present structure of National Savings. Having cleared the ground, the Report gave pride of place to the TSBs, the most successful component of National Savings since 1945. It came as no surprise that the Committee considered the Association's evidence 'to be directed specifically to a modest set of requirements which they considered to be capable of early achievement, rather than a blueprint for the long-term future of the trustee savings bank system'. However, from 'other proposals, mainly of an unofficial character, which arose

The dealing desk at Central TSB.

from within the trustee savings bank organisation or from outside bodies', the Committee were convinced that the movement was deeply divided between 'the old reluctance to rationalise their areas except in a piecemeal and haphazard fashion; the pattern of amateur and paternalistic management; and the new chequing accounts, unit trusts and computerisation'.

In keeping with the clear signals that had been given to the TSBs since 1971, that fundamental change was inevitable, the Committee had no sympathy with the 'old'. Recognising that the TSBs had become almost indistinguishable from commercial banks, the Committee could see no reason for the government to continue to guarantee their funds. It was recommended that over a transitional period, 'the trustee savings banks should become banking organisations similar in most respects to the clearing banks, except that they will be mutual and non-profit making, and will confine their activities to the operation of personal accounts'. The TSBs would be allowed to offer the full range of personal banking services, including personal loans and, appropriate to their new status, change their names to People's Mutual Banks or Trustee Mutual Banks. Although the Committee formed the view that the banks' principal area of activity should be personal or family banking, it was appreciated that a demarcation line would be impossible to impose and, therefore, any legislative framework should not exclude 'any profitable business in this area'. In line with the argument that there were cheaper ways for government to raise funds, the banks were no longer to be required to invest funds in ordinary departments in the Fund for Banks for Savings, which was to be wound up and the assets handed over to the banks to manage.

Crucial to the proposals was a strong Central Bank, taking over not just central cheque-clearing but all the functions of the Association and the Inspection Committee which was also to be dissolved. In addition, the Central Bank would be responsible for all staff matters, regional and local organisation, branch development, the use of computers, the management of the unit trust, and the supervision of personal credit facilities. The Report recommended that the seventy-odd existing TSBs should be rationalised into between sixteen and twenty regional banks. The Committee had difficulty in deciding how the TSBs' senior management was to be recruited 'in an organisation that will not have shareholders in the ordinary way'. Pursuing the idea of mutual status, it was suggested that the model of building societies could be adopted for the savings banks, whereby 'paid part-time and full-time trustees' would be elected by the depositors. Conscious that to function autonomously, the TSBs would need reserves at least as large as those of the building societies, the Committee proposed that some of the surpluses paid into the Consolidated Fund over the previous twenty years be repaid to make up the balance. Since the TSBs would no longer be required to invest ordinary department funds with the government, they were to cease to be considered part of the National Savings Movement. Although the Report urged that transition to the new system should be rapid, the details of the timetable, which would involve legislation, were left vague – a matter for government and the Treasury.

Directly the Report was published, copies were distributed for consideration by TSB Association Regional Committees. Encouraged by the Chancellor of the Exchequer, Anthony Barber, an extraordinary general meeting was arranged for 25 July 1973 to be addressed by Sir Harry Page himself. As might have been expected from the Report, his speech was direct, challenging the TSBs to seize the opportunity of becoming the 'third force' in banking with the interests of depositors at heart. Demolishing the myth of the government guarantee of deposits and local knowledge, he drew attention to the Report's recommendations for regional amalgamations and the streamlining of national organisations around the Central Bank. He was under no illusion that readjustment would be difficult and at times painful, but was convinced this was no cause for delay as time was not on the side of the TSBs; 'competition from the clearing banks, building societies, Unit Trusts, and even money shops, was rapidly becoming more intense'. His subsequent questioning served only to highlight the difficulties. There was suspicion of central direction and of amalgamation, particularly from smaller banks. After Sir Harry had left the meeting, Sir Athelstan explained that he had been informed by the Treasury that the report was a 'package deal', although some elements were negotiable. Anxious to conduct discussions with the Treasury with the full support of all the TSBs, Sir Athelstan called for the results of the regional consultations. The reports revealed deep divisions. In Scotland five of the larger banks – Edinburgh, Glasgow, Aberdeen, Perth and Stirling – wholeheartedly accepted the recommendations, while fifteen were less than keen for any negotiations to begin without further consideration. The North-East and the North-West Areas broadly accepted the proposals, but disagreed on points of detail. The Southern Area, led by Philip Keens, was the most enthusiastic, believing that 'if the banks could not improve their position by managing their own portfolio, they ought not to be in business'. There was unanimous opposition to the change of name to Trustee Mutual Bank. The meeting agreed that the immediate priority was the formation of 'a strong central organising and co-ordinating mechanism', which would devise a blueprint for amalgamation. The meeting concluded by appointing a committee to handle negotiations with the Treasury, comprising Sir Athelstan Caröe, Philip Keens, Andrew Archibald, James Campbell, L. Barber, and Freddie Miller, the recently re-designated Secretary-General of the Association.

As might have been expected, the Negotiating Committee immediately encountered difficulties in attempting to define the relationship between a strong central board and the new regional banks. This was a perennial problem that had bedevilled the operations of the Association throughout its ninety-year life. Understandably, the Negotiating Committee, representing the Association, felt unable to reach a decision until the views of general managers were known. Again, the Areas were asked to express an opinion. Led by the North-West, three favoured the formation of a Full-Time Page Co-ordinating Working Party with representatives from each area. Armed with these views, three weeks' intensive review of the Report was arranged in November 1973 at a hotel at Burnham Beeches in Buckinghamshire. The Working Party was chaired by Tommy Bryans, general manager of the Belfast Savings Bank, and included Philip Charlton, general manager of the Chester, Wrexham & North Wales Savings Bank; Graham Hamilton, general manager of the Aberdeen Savings Bank; John H. Hill, general manager of the Sheffield Savings Bank; J.H. Philpot, secretary of the TSB Employers' Council; J.R. Ryan, general manager of the Bristol Savings Bank; and Ken Cherrett, assistant secretary of the Association. They were asked to investigate four courses of action for implementing the Page recommendations:

○ far fewer autonomous banks with a relatively powerless central board, similar in construction and composition to the existing Association;

○ a smaller number of banks, all offering identical services, with a national invest-ment policy and controlled by a central board elected by the individual banks;

○ a single national TSB with a number of subsidiary regional groupings with little autonomy, operating within policy and budgetary frameworks articulated by the main board – a similar structure to the clearing banks;

○ any alternative options.

The Working Party was given until early December to complete its report so that a final decision could be reached in time for an announcement to be included in the Chancellor's spring budget statement. During the two weeks of robust discussion, a fourth form of structure was developed – federal decentralisation or Structure D, a federation of eight to ten independent regional banks with nominated trustees and general managers all represented on a strong Central Board responsible for articulating overall strategy. This form of organisation, it was argued, would allow the regional banks to develop services to suit the needs of their local customers in the context of national policy objectives. The gist of the discussion was reported to the half-yearly meeting in October 1973, which confirmed the appointment of the Full-Time Page Co-ordinating Working Party and approved the timetable. The subsequent debate gave little cause for optimism. The Scottish TSBs were fiercely opposed to the 'One Bank' concept and supported the creation of several regional banks. They wished to strike a balance between central control and regional autonomy, which would allow individual savings banks to maintain local loyalties. Bowing to the inevitable , the supporters of the 'One Bank' explained that what was at issue was not the existence of regional banks but the nature of their relationship with the Centre. There were some trustees, such as Canon J.R. Smith of Bury TSB, representing a vocal minority in the movement, who remained unconvinced that the Page recommendations had anything to offer the small saver. He and his fellow clergyman, Canon J.C. Longbottom of Warrington TSB, so infuriated the chairman, Sir Athelstan Caröe, with their opposition that he quoted the famous lines from Tennyson's 'Charge of the Light Brigade' – 'Cannons to the left of him, cannons to the right of him, volleyed and thundered'. Aware that discussion at an Association meeting with Canon Smith, who had once claimed to have buried people more alive than the delegate trustees, would spell the doom of the Page Report, Sir Athelstan cleverly side-stepped the question of a debate. Pleading lack of time he postponed discussion until after the Negotiating Committee met the Treasury in early January 1974.

By then the whole British banking and financial community was in turmoil, shaken by the worst financial disaster since the collapse of the City of Glasgow Bank in 1878 or the Barings crisis of 1890. One unforeseen consequence of the Competition and Credit Control Policy, in addition to boosting consumer spending, had been a property boom on a scale unprecedented for a century. The principal actors were secondary banks who committed the cardinal sin in banking of borrowing short and lending long on property at inflated values. The property market turned down sharply in the late autumn of 1973 and slumped when it became apparent that the trade unions were determined to defeat the Conservative government's prices and incomes policy. Worse was to come when the Arab oil-producing countries retaliated against the Israeli victory in the October War by restricting supplies and raising prices. Seizing the opportunity to win a substantial improvement in pay and conditions, the miners began an overtime ban. Interest rates were raised to 13 per cent and the Bank of England took steps to reduce credit, the final trigger for a financial crisis, causing the collapse of two secondary banks – London & County Securities and Cedar Holdings – in November 1973. In its role as lender of last resort the Bank of England stepped in to shore up the financial system, preventing panic from turning to rout through the launch of the 'lifeboat' with contributions from all the

London and Scottish clearing banks. By March 1974 the lifeboat was standing by twenty-one banks and had advanced over £400 million. There was no prospect of immediate recovery following the narrow victory of the Labour Party in the general election the month before. Having promised a strong financial hand on the tiller, Harold Wilson and the new Chancellor of the Exchequer, Denis Healey, took the easier course of conceding the miners' demands. In these stormy economic conditions, the beleaguered financial community was buffeted by mounting seas, bringing increased demands on the lifeboat rescue service which by the end of the year had made over £1 billion available. This gigantic sum represented two-fifths of the capital and reserves of all the clearing banks combined. The largest single advance was made to the hire-purchase finance house, United Dominions Trust. The scale of the crisis convinced both the Treasury and the Bank of England that urgent action had to be taken to improve supervision of the banking sector and this was given formal expression in the 1976 Banking Act.

As the drama was being played out at the Bank of England, the TSB Association and its members were embroiled in a seemingly endless series of discussions, going over and over the same ground to the frustration of the Treasury officials whose attention was riveted by far larger considerations. The debate was conducted by the Association's Negotiating and Page Co-ordinating Committees through a series of working parties with specific briefs, such as finance, services, staff, bank/branch inspection, and taxation. The most heated arguments were in the Restructuring Working Party over the question of rationalising the number of banks to between fifteen and twenty, and in the Co-ordinating Committee itself over the structure and function of the Central Board. These related issues were as much to do with the ambitions of the participants and the relative position of the resultant groupings in the new pecking order, as they were to do with the interests of the customers. Some general managers tried to pre-empt the outcome by taking the initiative in putting mergers together, with little reference to central advice. By April 1974, Philip Charlton and John Hill as members of the Restructuring Working Party were at the end of their tether because of the lack of progress in the regional restructuring sub-committee. Their main cause for concern was the failure of local negotiations to consult the National Union of Bank Employees whose members would be most exposed in any mergers. Sir Athelstan responded with a clear statement that any amalgamation would require the approval, not only of the National Debt Office, but also the Association's Executive Committee. Fortified, the Restructuring Working Party returned to its task. Progress was frustrating; some TSBs refused even to acknowledge the need for amalgamation and the resulting gains in managerial efficiency. Even where amalgamation was accepted, discussions between banks were often bitter with swiftly changing alliances. By mid-July it had been agreed that the target should be fifteen banks, but details of the mergers still remained uncertain. There had as yet been no final decision about the Central Board – although opinion seemed to favour Structure D.

The change of government prevented the Chancellor of the Exchequer from making a statement in his budget, but towards the end of April 1974 the new Labour Paymaster-General, Edmund Dell, was asked to come to an early decision about the implementation of the Page Report. Although the philosophy of the Report was diametrically opposed to that of the Labour Party, the government announced in July that it had accepted its findings in principle, making political capital out of the movement's service to small savers. The Treasury immediately informed the TSB Association that there was one over-riding condition: that every TSB had to agree to amalgamate before the Bill implementing the Page Report was published the following year – termed Day X. Despite this warning, several TSBs, particularly those in the Midlands, vacillated, waiting to see the details of the national plan. John Hill was adamant that, unless there was central direction, it would be impossible to achieve a satisfactory resolution in time. Philip Keens, chairman of the London & South-Eastern TSB, stole a march on the other regions by announcing in August the formation of the South-East TSB which would begin trading in November 1975. Despite Hill's misgivings, nearly all the TSBs were committed to a restructuring plan by the end of October 1974, although many boundary disputes remained to be adjudicated. There were other issues to be settled. Timetables had to be set for winding

In 1975 Gordon Jackson featured in the first of a series of highly
successful press and television advertisements for the TSBs.
This advertisement features the new logo.

up of the Fund for Banks for Savings and for creating a reserve fund which, in the light of the secondary banking collapse, was to be in the region of 10 per cent – three times as large as first envisaged. A method for the selection of trustees had to be agreed and arrangements made to phase out the ordinary department. Throughout the closing months of 1974 and into 1975, the working parties were engaged in feverish activity to sort out all the complex details involved in the transformation of the movement into a fully fledged clearing bank.

Preparatory to the formation of a Central Board, a Steering Committee composed of the general managers designate of the seventeen emerging regional banks was formed in February, taking over all the functions of the Page Co-ordinating Working Party and General Purposes Committee of the TSB Association. Even this decision had not been straightforward, requiring the consent of each Area. Some, like the North-East, would have preferred an unwieldy committee with equal representation of general managers and trustees. After heated debate, there was a tentative understanding that the Central Board, when appointed, would comprise the chairmen and general managers of the regional banks. The general managers designate were appointed by the regional banks without central consultation. Apart from overseeing the details of the negotiations and the time-consuming task of scrutinising the draft Bill, the

With the increasing popularity of travel,
the TSBs were keen to promote
their travel drafts.

Steering Committee was concerned to prepare the staff for the cultural shock of the commercial world. The consultancy firm, Urwick Orr & Partners, was brought in to implement a management-by-objectives programme which had been under discussion for some time. Integral to changing attitudes was the streamlining and standardisation of the TSB's corporate image. The TSB logo was re-designed in a more striking style and a new cheque book introduced. Experiments were also conducted in the use of on-line real-time self-service cash dispensers operated by plastic bank cards. The most pressing matter was the choice of both a chairman and chief general manager, with sufficient stamina and vision to pilot the TSB through the difficult period of transition.

The obvious person to become chairman was Philip Keens with his experience in London and nationally with the Unit Trusts. However, his abrasive thrusting style was not to the liking of Sir Athelstan and the Scots suspected Keens intended to shift the focus of TSB to the south of England. As a result he was passed over in favour of Andrew Rintoul, an investment manager and sometime chairman of the Savings Bank of Glasgow. Although he was a compromise candidate, he was greatly favoured by the Scottish TSBs and those which had little faith in handing their freedom over to London executives. The first choice as general manager had been Denis Greenwood of the London TSB. A long-standing sceptic, he had recently been converted to on-line real time and was preparing to take London into TSB Computer Services Ltd. Staff from London had been sent to Altrincham to learn the system and plan implementation. Sadly, Greenwood died suddenly before his appointment could be confirmed and Tom Bryans of the Belfast Savings Bank was chosen as a replacement candidate, with Freddie Miller as his deputy. They were to find their room for manoeuvre circumscribed by the local ambitions of the general managers and chairmen of all the constituent banks and the number of committees and working parties that still remained in being. A good example was the difficulty in harmonising computing strategies. When equipment came up for renewal in the near future, there was the potential for introducing a single system at least in England and Wales, but the opportunity had passed with Denis Greenwood's death. London Savings Bank abandoned its plans to go on-line real time and Bryans's own on-line consortium of Northern Ireland TSBs, using Burroughs computers, refused to join the larger Altrincham-based consortia with ICL machines. The Scottish banks, serviced through the Savings Bank of Glasgow, remained committed to their Burroughs off-line system as still being more cost-effective than available OLRT systems. Unable to secure a single national system, the chairman of TSB Computer Services Ltd, speaking at the Association annual meeting in May 1975, 'did so with heavy heart because the Movement was so split in its approach to computers'. He cautioned that clearing banks, taking advantage of on-line technology, were 'lining up to give TSBs a run for their money'. Well aware of this challenge, the four consortia using Altrincham and the South-West off-line consortium, were determined to press ahead with a replacement system based on a single computer centre at Wythenshawe to meet all their needs.

The TSB Bill was published on 20 November 1975, granting the banks powers to operate with equivalent services to the commercial banks. The Central Board was charged to give 'general and specific direction to the member banks and provide common services'. It was to comprise representatives of each bank over a certain size, three co-opted members, and the Chief General Manager and Deputy Chief General Manager *ex officio*. As intended by Page, it acquired the regulatory and supervisory powers previously exercised by the Inspection Committee and the National Debt Commissioners. It was responsible for creating and managing reserves in line with Bank of England requirements and could levy contributions from members to cover expenditure.

Most of the existing accounts were to be renamed in 1976/7: cheque accounts were to stay, ordinary department accounts were to become savings accounts, special investment department accounts were to become investment accounts, and a new fixed-term bond similar to a National Savings Certificate was to be introduced. Under the terms of the legislation, somewhere in the region of 25 per cent of the trustees in future were expected to be elected by depositors and remunerated for their work. All existing trustees were to retire at the age of seventy-five and any of those newly elected at seventy. As they had wished, the TSBs were given a ten-year transitional period before they became fully independent on 21 November 1986 – Day Y. Over this time the Fund for Banks for Savings would be progressively repaid to the TSBs to be invested as they saw fit.

At the same time as the Bill was published in November, the final structure of the seventeen new regional banks was unveiled. The new structure had been agreed for almost a year, with four exceptions. Bolton, Liverpool and Wigan TSBs had remained undecided and North Staffs TSB steadfastly refused to enter into any negotiations. In the event, North Staffs TSB was the only bank not to become part of the new regional structure, which was:

TSB of South-East: a merger of Essex, London & South Eastern, Oxford, Portsmouth, Surrey, Thames Valley

TSB Yorkshire & Lincoln: a merger of Huddersfield, Hull, Leeds, Lincoln, Sheffield, York

TSB North-West Central: a merger of Ashton-under-Lyne, Bury, Derby, Leigh, Manchester, Stockport, Warrington

TSB of Eastern England: a merger of Cambridge, East Anglia, East Midlands, Northampton

TSB of Mid-Lancashire & Merseyside: a merger of Bolton, Liverpool, Ormskirk, Wigan

South-West TSB: a merger of Bristol, Devon & Exeter, Plymouth, Somerset & Wiltshire, Wessex.

TSB of Leicester & Nottingham: a merger of Leicester, Nottingham

TSB North-East: a merger of Northumberland & Durham, Sunderland

TSB of Lancashire & Cumbria: a merger of Blackburn, Chorley, Cumbria, Preston

TSB of the Midlands: a merger of Coventry, Walsall, Wolverhampton

TSB of Wales & Borders: a merger of Chester, Wrexham & North Wales, South Wales East & Monmouthshire, South-West Wales, West Midlands

West of Scotland TSB: a merger of Campbeltown, Glasgow, Paisley

TSB Tayside & Central Scotland: a merger of Arbroath, Cupar, Fife, Dundee, Falkirk, Kirkcaldy, Laurencekirk, Montrose, Newburgh, Perth, Stirling

TSB South of Scotland: a merger of Border Counties, Dunfermline, Edinburgh, South of Scotland

Aberdeen Savings Bank: a merger of Aberdeen, Inverness

TSB of N. Ireland: a merger of Belfast, Enniskillen

TSB of the Channel Islands: a merger of Jersey, Guernsey

The Birmingham Municipal Bank, which had been party to all the negotiations, announced that it would join TSB of the Midlands during 1976. The Greenock Provident Bank and the Dumfries Savings Bank in western Scotland, which had continued to operate under the 1816 legislation, declared their intention of joining the West of Scotland TSB.

The Bill reached the statute book in the spring of 1976 and on 10 May the Central Board Designate met for the first time. One of its early actions was to extend the common account numbering system to all the English and Welsh TSBs to avoid confusion, and also to propose standards on the variety of computing and accounting systems in operation. By September, the Central Board had appropriated a realistic budget of £1.3 million for national publicity, using the theme 'TSB Family' to drive home to depositors the changes that had taken place in the movement. Adapting to the new structure was not without its difficulties. In September, Councillor Hargreaves of the Birmingham Municipal Bank launched a blistering attack on the recently established Personnel Division which he criticised for being bureaucratic and inflexible in assessing branch performance. The work of the Central Board was conducted against a background of a rapid deterioration in the economy, with soaring inflation and rising wage rates. Harold Wilson had resigned unexpectedly in March 1976 and was replaced as Prime Minister by James Callaghan. The April budget, which was portrayed as broadly neutral but in fact was not anything of the kind, failed to win support. The economy continued to spiral downward, the pound came under heavy pressure and interest rates were raised to record levels. As part of a tough package to reduce inflation, bank lending was severely curtailed and large cuts announced in future government expenditure. The National Savings Bank promptly raised its rates with the permission of the Treasury, who failed to consult the TSB – leading to

*An advertisement illustrating the new structure of the TSBs, 1976.*

# Frankly, we're all over the place.

in Aberdeen (and Northern Scotland)

in Tayside and Central Scotland

in the West of Scotland

in the South of Scotland

in the North East

in Lancashire and Cumbria

in Yorkshire and Lincoln

in the North West

in the South East

in Leicester and Nottingham

in Birmingham

in the Midlands

in Eastern England

in Wales and Border Counties

The TSB has almost 1650 branches, organised in eighteen local regions.

Wherever you are, you'll find a TSB that offers the same friendly comprehensive banking service that you've come to expect.

If you've never experienced our service, why not drop in? You're sure to find a branch nearby.

in North Staffordshire

in the South West

**TSB**

"It's the bank for me"

Post to: Marketing Dept., TSB of Yorkshire & Lincoln, FREEPOST, 308 Tadcaster Road, York Y01 1YL. (No stamp necessary)

Dear TSB, Which is my nearest branch?

Name _____

(BLOCK CAPITALS, PLEASE)

Address _____

in Northern Ireland

and in the Channel Islands.

S20

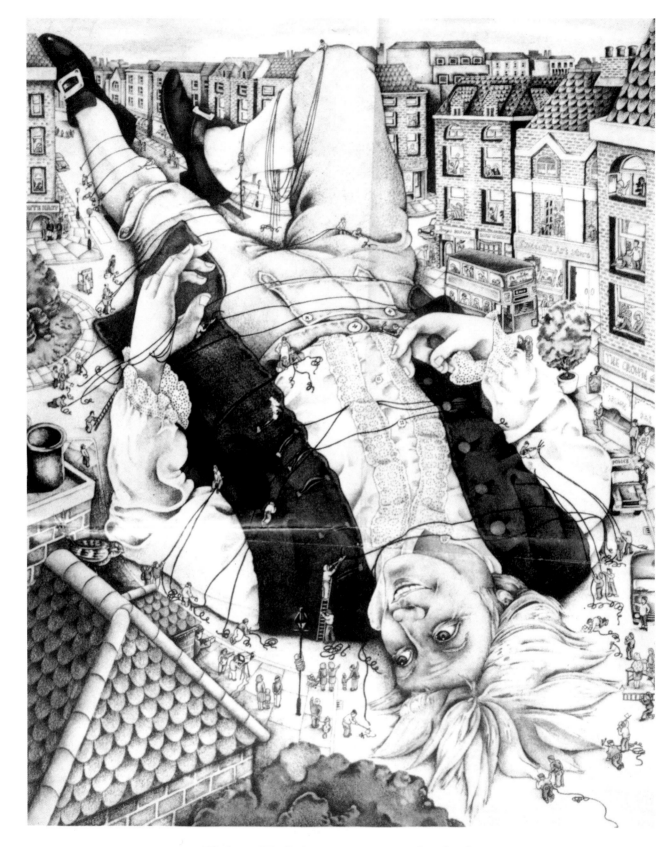

## Today, a High Street giant is unleashed.

The giant "third force in banking" is now freed from previous regulations. From today, the TSB offers a full personal banking service.

The time is right.

The Trustee Savings Banks have national coverage, with branches in and around almost every High Street in the land.

Over 11 million accounts are now handled in the 1,658 branches, one for every five people in Britain. Cheque Accounts, Savings Plans, Investment Accounts, Unit Trusts, plus all the services you expect from your bank.

And from today, personal loans and overdrafts.

The TSB has much to offer. But then from giants you do expect great things.

**TRUSTEE SAVINGS BANKS**
Central Board, PO Box 99, 3 Gracechurch Street, London EC3P 3BX.

accusations from the TSBs that the National Savings Bank had been offered higher rates of interest on their deposits in the Fund for Banks for Savings. One of the victims of this credit squeeze was the introduction of TSB personal loans due to be launched in November with a nationwide promotional campaign, using the slogan 'The Giant Awakes'. The economy began to show signs of picking up in 1977, allowing personal loans finally to be introduced in August of that year.

The TSB depositors, appreciative of the friendly service of their banks, remained loyal throughout this upheaval in the organisation of their banks. Deposits and turnover in the ordinary and special investment departments (shortly to be renamed) continued to grow, partly reflecting high wage inflation. At the end of the first year of operation of the new accounts, the TSB had total assets of £3.1 billion, invested mostly in gilt-edged securities and local authority stock. This was insignificant when compared with the more than £30 billion held by the building societies with well over a third of the population as customers. In managing their much smaller enterprise with fast approaching freedom from Treasury participation, the Central Board became very concerned about the failure of new approaches to management style filtering far down the group. During May 1977 the board resolved unanimously that the whole organisation had to become more profit oriented, but at the same time keeping faith with their original social purpose: 'Without profits the Bank would not be able to create the reserves necessary to preserve the funds of their depositors nor the reserves necessary to maintain a modern banking facility.' In keeping with this maxim, the Central Board was encouraged to put its own house in order by defining its statutory duties, its method of operation, and size. The Government Price Commission reinforced this criticism by questioning the suitability of the federal structure, which made it almost impossible for the TSBs to react decisively or speedily to events.

A proposal for the formation of an executive committee was dismissed, but there was general agreement that the Central Board should concern itself less with detail and more with policy, and that the role of the general managers' committee should be enhanced. Failure to respond decisively to the call for action was hardly surprising. Most of the members of the Central Board were chairmen of regional banks which they had put together after a hard-won fight and, as a result, had a vested interest in preventing the Centre interfering in their activities. Those recruited to the central administration found the lack of authority deeply frustrating. A consensus could be achieved only after intense time-consuming lobbying of all the constituent banks. One way to achieve a more coherent commercial approach would have been for the TSB to have received a massive transfusion of new blood through an alliance with a private sector finance house. Two big American banks – Citibank, through its UK subsidiary Citicorp,

A proof of the stillborn 'Giant Awakes' promotion, 1977.

and Chemical Bank – contemplated a bid for the TSBs but were dissuaded by their labyrinthine structure, uncertainty of ownership, and their relationship with the Treasury.

One area where there was agreement was in the need for a TSB credit card to complement the developing loan services. Earlier proposals to introduce a TSB credit card had been rejected by the Association's Executive Committee for legal reasons and like other such initiatives because it represented a radical departure from the TSB's traditional aim of promoting thrift and self-sufficiency. In 1976 the Central Board agreed that a credit card facility would fill a gap in TSB service as a vehicle for lending small amounts. It was decided that TSBs could not exclude themselves from this important market and would wish to be closely linked with plastic card developments generally. Having examined whether TSB should launch a card system on its own, together with three different proposals from Access and two from Barclaycard, the Central Executive recommended that TSB should have its own card, becoming a principal member of VISA, with Barclaycard undertaking the processing function, at least initially. In late 1977, the Central Board agreed that this represented the most speedy yet secure entry for

The launch of TSB Trustcard, 1979.

TSB into the credit card market. To allay some fears, the card was to be marketed as a payments card, rather than emphasising the credit card aspects, and incorporating a cheque guarantee card facility.

TSB Trustcard Ltd was formed as a subsidiary company, with Peter Paisley, a trustee of the West of Scotland TSB, as chairman and Ken Cherrett as director and general manager. In addition to handling the relationship with Barclaycard and the marketing of the card, the company was to act as the legal entity and manage the funding of the card outstandings with the individual TSBs. A press conference was held in January 1978 and the card launched in November through a carefully organised 'mail-shot'. Despite the complexities of writing, under the signatures of the General Managers of the seventeen regional TSBs, to over 1 million cheque card customers, the operation was almost flawless and the response rate a staggering 25 per cent. The card base grew rapidly and of equal importance, the marketing stance led to Trustcard having a much lower bad debt experience than was usual with other banks' products. The successful launch of Trustcard, combined with its subsequent sound track-record, both silenced the critics of TSB's entry into the credit card market and helped ensure that the TSBs were able to provide a full range of personal banking services.

While efforts were being made to extend the services and sharpen the management profile of the TSBs, it emerged that the 1976 Act was full of loopholes and ambiguities. The TSBs had no powers to secure loans against mortgages and criteria for investment were ill defined. Under pressure from the TSB Central Board, the government hurriedly put matters right with a further Act passed in 1978. By the time these adjustments had been made, the regulation of the market for personal financial services was being re-assessed by the Bank of England in the wake of the secondary banking crisis and in the light of the EEC Directive on Credit Institutions. The directive required all member countries to have equivalent mechanisms in place for authorising all deposit-taking institutions by 1985. A new Banking Act was passed in 1979, giving the Bank of England, for the first time, formal powers to regulate the banking system and defining prudential criteria for two distinct categories of licensed institutions: fully fledged 'banks' and 'deposit takers' which did not offer a sufficient range of financial services to qualify for bank status. The criteria were drawn deliberately wide to allow the Bank of England as much discretion as possible in policing the system. Immediately the Act was passed, the Bank of England opened discussions with financial institutions to establish appropriate ratios that took due account of the nature of differing types of assets and risks.

The faltering Labour government of James Callaghan was swept from office in the May general election, which brought Margaret Thatcher and the Conservatives to power. Mrs Thatcher had articulated and extended the 'free market' philosophy that had characterised the thinking of the early years of the Heath government. In fashioning policy towards the financial system, the new government sought to encourage competition within the framework of tight Bank of England supervision. The first signal of this change in direction was a loosening of the straitjacket of the clearing banks' liquidity ratios, thus allowing them to move into mortgage-lending in direct competition with the building societies. The TSBs responded to this challenge to their market by broadening their lending base through the introduction of commercial loans on a trial basis in 1979 and entering the mortgage market itself in June. Within a year the *Sunday Times* judged that the TSBs had the most competitive home-loan scheme of any of the five clearing banks.

At a time when 45 per cent of the adult population still did not have bank accounts, Tom

'It's the bank for me' promotion, part of the TSBs' effort to broaden
their base, 1978.

Bryans, the TSB chief general manager, had no doubt that the change in the legal and political environment demanded a telescoping of the relaxed ten-year timetable for independence if the TSBs were not to be left out in the scramble for depositors. He called for yet further legislation that would enable the TSBs to win Bank of England recognition as a fully fledged bank within three years, and envisaged the extension of the provision of the 1976 Act for the election of a quarter of trustees by depositors, to all trustees – allowing for 'independent mutual status'. Andrew Rintoul and his Central Executive did not need to be reminded that mutual status would not of itself secure recognition as a bank rather than simply as a deposit taker under the 1979 Act, there had to be further structural change, not least because there was an ever-present danger that the bank would dissolve into its constituent parts. To address this problem, a restructuring committee was formed in the summer of 1979 chaired by David Thorn, who had been recruited from outside the TSBs and held the post of general manager finance in the Central executive. The committee comprised members of the Central Board, members of the Central Board legal staff and representatives of Lazards, the merchant bank advisers to the TSB. Its brief was to devise an organisational framework that would be acceptable to the constituent banks, win Bank of England and Treasury approval and, above all, provide a secure platform to meet growing competition for personal financial services. Philip Charlton, general manager of TSB of Wales & Borders, had no doubt that the movement faced a stark alternative: 'participate or perish – compete or retreat'. This was easier said than done.

The restructuring committee had no difficulty in agreeing that it was imperative for the TSB not only to have a single corporate identity, but also an integrated standard range of products as well as a single national rate of interest on the various accounts and levels of deposit. Adopting this strategy demanded a unified national computing network linking all banks together with consequent savings in costs and improvements in customer services. TSB Computer Services Ltd at Altrincham was making progress. Agreement had been reached to switch from both ICL mainframe and Olivetti terminals to a Univac mainframe with Burroughs terminals and work had begun on the new computer centre at Wythenshawe. The equipment was installed towards the close of 1979 and went on-line during the summer of the following year. At this stage the network did not include the South East, North Staffs and the Scottish TSBs. A common on-line computer system needed to be paralleled by a rapid strengthening of the balance sheet through the expansion of commercial lending to provide an additional outlet for depositors' funds no longer invested with the Commissioners of the National Debt, in direct competition with the clearing banks. There was agreement that for the time being no new branches should be opened. It was recognised that it would be very hard to achieve the required volume of commercial business within the tight timetable imposed by the legislation and the Conservative government's free-market philosophy. The solution was clearly for the TSBs to buy financial concerns with complementary portfolios. It would have been possible simply to add new businesses as wholly owned subsidiaries of the Central Board, like the Trust Company, but there were considerable VAT disadvantages deriving directly from the Group's federal structure. This was compounded by the urgent necessity of enlarging the TSB's presence in the south-east of England that had bedevilled the Association for over fifty years. With the creation of the Central Board, the Mutual Assistance Fund had lapsed, resulting in the rapid accumulation of reserves by regional banks in Scotland and the north of England. By the end of 1980 the reserves of West of Scotland TSB had climbed to £32 million and those of the South of Scotland to £13.6 million.

The sole mechanism for the release of funds by one region in support of another was through the highly charged atmosphere of the Central Board itself, a system more dependent on personal relationships than national policy objectives. David Thorn had little difficulty in persuading his fellow executives at the Central Board that only a single corporate structure could safeguard the future of the TSBs, yet it proved as impossible to gain unanimous approval for such a plan as it had six years earlier. The South-East, South-West, West of Scotland, Aberdeen, Northern Ireland and Channel Islands TSBs refused point-blank from widely different perspectives to countenance any change. Lord Coleridge, speaking for the South-West TSB, summed up one strand in the opposition: 'The present constitution has passed the test of time, depositors like dealing with regionally based institutions. There is a case for depositors knowing that they can turn to local trustees who are not part of the professional management of the bank.' When the first vote was taken in August 1979, only one member of the Central Board was in favour.

The reorganisation committee was forced to re-examine ways the existing structure could be reinforced. The chief obstacle was the lack of accountability of the Central Board. It was not even technically accountable to the TSBs and simply presenting annual accounts to the Registrar of Friendly Societies was hardly likely to satisfy the Bank of England. At a lengthy meeting of the Central Board in September, there was agreement that it was essential to have a 'wider body of people' to whom the Central Board would be responsible. The question of mutuality was again raised, but discounted, as it was difficult to 'derive a form of mutual ownership for bank customers'. The Scottish banks were disturbed by the refusal to take mutuality seriously. The West of Scotland TSB went so far as to secure the opinion of John Murray (later Lord Dervaird), QC, as to the ownership of the bank. He reported that, in his view, the TSBs were owned by their depositors. Undeterred by this development, the argument within the TSBs as a whole again polarised around a group structure with the Central Board owning all the subsidiaries, with the tax advantage that implied, and the preservation of the existing structure with its trustees and well-defined social objectives. When a resolution seemed almost out of reach, Thorn restated the case for a group structure which he believed was not incompatible with local initiative within broadly defined national policy. Finally, there was grudging agreement for the restructuring committee to produce a blueprint for a holding company. Despite this decision, matters remained unresolved, and the Central Board was deeply divided between those who favoured 'a companies' structure [seeing] federation as a system under which collective decision-making was undertaken in a representative forum', and those who favoured 'the statutory corporation structure [regarding] the main function of federation as the preservation of ultimate independence of action of the Banks'. By April 1980 there were tentative signs that the holding company form was gaining support with two legislative safeguards – the preservation of a clear majority of TSB-appointed representatives on the Central Board and a 75 per cent majority of members to alter standing orders. Press comment was also encouraging, suggesting that the TSBs were beginning to match the big four 'service for service', with a much less extensive branch network. However, the six banks that had initially objected to the single bank structure maintained their opposition, preventing discussions with the Treasury about a timetable for further legislation and bringing forward Day Y, in addition to holding up Bank of England recognition under the 1979 Banking Act.

While the Central Board was groping for a solution, Andrew Rintoul's five-year term of office as chairman of the Central Board expired. After an exhaustive search for a replacement who could command the respect of the Treasury, the Bank of England and the City in the uncharted waters that lay ahead, the Central Board chose Sir John Read, former sales director of the Ford Motor Company and, until recently, chairman of EMI, the record and electrical group. By the time he joined the TSB there were over 3 million cheque account holders, £6,000 million on deposit, and 1,640 branches. With his experience of senior management in the private sector, Sir John was quick to recognise that the deep divisions in the Central Board, amounting at times to personal animosity, urgently needed to be resolved if the TSBs were to have any chance of becoming a 'third force' in British banking. His attention was, however, diverted by the culmination of negotiations initiated in 1978 for the purchase of United Dominions Trust, the finance and hire-purchase company which had been the chief casualty of the secondary banking crisis in 1973.

UDT enjoyed a wide reputation for the quality of its personal hire-purchase business, but, like other secondary banking houses, had sown the seeds of its destruction by entering the unknown territory of the London property market. Although UDT had received the lion's share of the support from the lifeboat funds, the assets had been nursed under the careful chairmanship of Len Mather, previously chief general manager of Midland Bank. The impact of the high interest rates imposed by the incoming Conservative Chancellor of the Exchequer, Geoffrey Howe, in 1979 had driven UDT back to unprofitability, because the bulk of its advances were at fixed levels of interest. The TSBs seemed an ideal partner, as Mather later reflected: 'We needed a big brother because of our shortage of capital and vulnerability to increases in the cost of money.' The TSB Central Board executives were equally keen, because UDT, with its reliable consumer credit portfolio, provided an excellent means of strengthening the Group's balance sheet quickly and at an equitable price. Bryans declared bluntly, 'We need UDT and its management.' Others, particularly the Aberdeen and West of Scotland TSBs, did not agree with Bryans and were deeply concerned that the proposed deal was far too costly. Sir John refused to be diverted and continued negotiations.

With the whole future structure and legal framework of the Group still unresolved, the Central Board had recently established Trustee Savings Banks (Holdings) Ltd as a vehicle for such acquisitions. The TSBs opened the batting with an offer from TSB (Holdings) Ltd for the whole of UDT's remaining business. The Treasury rejected this proposal on the grounds that the TSBs lacked sufficient management expertise to run such a diverse business alongside its own banking operations. After protracted negotiations, it was agreed with Treasury and Bank of England approval, that the TSBs should pump £58 million into UDT's consumer credit business in exchange for a 75 per cent stake with an option over the remaining 25 per cent in the future. UDT's non-finance business was to be split off into a new company named Endeavour. Within three months of the announcement of the merger in August 1980, a rival bid was launched by Lloyds & Scottish, the consumer credit and finance house, owned jointly by Lloyds Bank and the Royal Bank of Scotland. Lloyds & Scottish had already acquired the remnant of Cedar Holdings, whose collapse in December 1973 had triggered the secondary banking crisis. Lloyds & Scottish offered £106 million for the whole of UDT. Sir John Read and Tom Bryans immediately won permission from the Treasury to join battle, despite the

Philip Keens, the first chairman of the
Trust Company, 1967–1979.

original misgivings. With the line of attack clear, the TSBs responded with a cash offer of £116 million supported by Mather and the UDT board. The Central Board let it be known that the TSBs were a determined opponent with a deep pocket. The paymasters of Lloyds & Scottish had no desire to be drawn into a war of attrition and withdrew. The City institutions, however, remained cautious, refusing to sign acceptances for their preference shares and forcing the Central Board to extend its offer until March 1981. The acquisition of UDT not only provided considerable support for the TSBs' fledgling consumer loan business, but also brought an infusion of experienced loan managers. Used to a very different corporate culture, some of their new recruits found it difficult to adjust. Derek Stevens, who moved from being finance director of UDT to being the Central Board's general manager/finance, found the TSB structure unfamiliar and frustrating: 'I found that what one thought of as subsidiaries were regarded as laws unto themselves. It was very much a rule-by-committee environment.' Equally, TSB executives, who moved in the opposite direction into UDT, found the ways of the City just as foreign and sometimes incompatible with their outlook.

Following the acquisition of UDT its insurance services division was transferred to the

TSB Trust Company's Offices at Keens House, Andover,
opened in 1978.

Trust Company, which itself had been transformed. Sales of unit trusts and life insurance had grown rapidly after the appointment of the first seven sales representatives – 'the Magnificent Seven' as they were nicknamed in 1973. In the autumn of the following year, the company moved out of central London to White Bear House at Andover. Within three years, net sums insured had reached £80 million and the members of the sales team were each writing £3,000–£4,000 worth of new business every month. To cope with the volume of business, a much larger office – named Keens House after the company's chairman, Philip Keens – was planned at another location in Andover; work on which began in June 1977. A month later, the Trust

Company celebrated its tenth birthday with the launch of a new TSB Income Unit Trust, the revamping of the monthly savings plan as the Unit Link Harvest Savings Plan, and the introduction of a convertible insurance and mortgage protection scheme. These extensions to the product range were accompanied by a decision to adopt an integrated database system, TONIC (TSB On-Line Integrated Computer), which, it was hoped, would help to reduce the growing mass of paper. The TSB Trust Company joined the premier league of the top ten United Kingdom trusts in 1978 with funds of £76.8 million; marked towards the end of the year by the formation of the TSB Gilt Fund and the TSB Gilt Fund (Jersey). The success of these issues underlined the need for greater management depth, including the appointment of an actuary to assess risks more accurately. Philip Keens stood down as chairman in March 1979 and was replaced by Senator Reg Jeune of Jersey. He at once took steps to improve the structure of the administration of the company before any further expansion. He soon found himself swept along by the tide of events as the TSBs responded to the changing market for personal finance following the Conservative victory in the polls. The decision by the Central Board to enter the home loans business in June 1979 was underpinned by a revolutionary (at the time) 'index-linked' home insurance plan. So fast was the pace of change that the decision was taken to abandon TONIC (which it was anticipated would not be working efficiently for at least two years) and replace it with the off-shelf industry-standard PALM (Personalised Automated Life Management) system, using the Rediffusion network.

The unmapped territory of the new decade persuaded the board of the Trust Company to bring the management of its funds invested mainly in the United Kingdom securities in-house. Their management was switched from outside managers to a new subsidiary, TSB Investment Management Ltd, in March 1981. This change coincided with the inauguration of low-cost endowment and with-profits endowment life insurance as collateral security for TSB mortgages. During the year the second and final phase of Keens House was opened to accommodate the ever-increasing numbers of staff. The next priority was the construction of a computer centre on an adjoining site, completed in 1982. The year before, an effort had been made to broaden the base of the unit trust business, which had become very reliant on insurance-linked contracts, through the introduction of two direct trusts: the TSB American Unit Trust and the TSB Pacific Unit Trust. During 1982, three more direct trusts were added to the portfolio. This welter of activity in creating a broad basis of ancillary personal financial services fundamental to gaining recognition from the Bank of England under the 1979 Banking Act would be to no avail as long as the central question of the future structure of the bank remained unresolved. Once the acquisition of UDT had been concluded, Sir John could devote his energies to finding some basis for achieving an understanding between the warring factions on the Central Board.

Instead of attempting to negotiate at a national level, Sir John carried the argument into the regional boardrooms. Sensing that a single national bank was beyond his grasp, he con-

The Wythenshawe computer centre.

centrated on securing agreement for the merger of all the regional banks in England and Wales into one bank and all those in Scotland into another, with separate TSBs in Northern Ireland and the Channel Islands. These regional banks were to operate in close co-operation with the Central Bank and the Central Board. As before, negotiations were tense, particularly in Scotland, where the West of Scotland TSB considered the formation of a Scottish Central Board with similar powers to the English Board but still within the Group. This proposal failed to win wider support. Integral to the process of amalgamation was the implementation of a single on-line system with capacity to service the whole movement managed by TSB Computer Services Ltd from the new Wythenshawe computer centre. As a sop to the South-East, a second centre was to be opened somewhere near London. After a long search, a site was chosen in 1981 at Milton Keynes which would enable all the TSBs in England and Wales to go on-line using a single system within four years. It was the decision of the TSB of South-East to join the consortia serviced by TSB Computer Services Ltd more than anything else that persuaded the smaller uncommitted banks. North Staffs was told bluntly that continued refusal to collaborate would debar them from access to the OLRT system. Details of the amalgamations themselves had been more or less settled by the spring of 1982, still leaving the wider question of the final organisational form of the TSB to be decided.

By now the restructuring committee were convinced that the only appropriate structure was as some form of company under the Companies Act with the depositors acquiring the status of shareholders. With the territorial wranglings gradually receding, the Central Board approached the Treasury during 1982 to seek the necessary legislation. Bryans had hoped that it would be possible to convert the TSBs into a company limited by guarantee with the type of mutual status envisaged by Page. Such a route was beset with difficulties because, with the Central Board owning the assets of the whole group, there was no identifiable institution to act as guarantor. Instead, the Central Board had opted during 1980 on a nine to seven vote for the creation of a statutory corporation on the pattern of a nationalised industry. This decision had been greeted with dismay by some trustees and general managers, especially those in Scotland who demanded a meeting with the Treasury. This had been refused and in a subsequent vote only the Scottish TSBs supported mutuality. A keen advocate of the TSBs becoming a statutory corporation was Philip Charlton who moved during 1982 from TSB of Wales and Borders to be Deputy General Manager of TSB.

The Conservative government, committed to a policy of privatisation and far less State intervention in commerce and industry, had refused to discuss any strategy other than flotation on the grounds that they failed to address the crucial problems of accountability and the long-term funding of the TSB as a fully fledged bank under the terms of the 1979 Act. Numerous attempts had been made to devise structures that preserved an element of mutuality within public limited company status, but these again foundered on the rock of accountability and corporate funding. When the merger plans were finally made public in August 1982, Sir John predicted that within three years the TSB would become a publicly quoted company with several subsidiaries – functioning just like any other commercial bank. He, publicly, regretted the renunciation of mutuality and placed the blame firmly at the door of the government and the Treasury. However, there were those who doubted if he had presented the case for mutuality forcefully enough to Ministers. Sir Harry Page was critical, warning that, however wide the shareholding at flotation, the TSB would soon fall into the hands of the financial institutions. Such an analysis begged the very large question of precisely how the shares were to be allocated. The TSBs had been founded for the benefit of their depositors, but the depositors had no legal claim to the trust's assets beyond the balances in their accounts. On the other hand, the government had no interest in the bank's properties and reserves.

Shortly after it became known that the TSBs would be floated, Tom Bryans, deeply disappointed, stood down as chief general manager and was succeeded by his deputy, Philip Charlton. Charlton believed passionately that the TSBs could succeed in the competitive world for personal financial services that was unfolding in the early 1980s only by adopting flexible structures that preserved the best of the past, but allowed room for manoeuvre in the future. His immediate priority was to push through the merger plan; treading a fine line between establishing the authority of the Central Board and preserving local and regional characteristics.

Following the example of the clearing banks, regional advisory boards, composed largely of former trustees, were to be established to provide continuity essential to maintaining customer loyalties that, once lost, could not easily be regained.

Following the government's public support of the flotation of the TSBs in February 1983, Sir John Read gave an undertaking that the Scottish TSBs would operate in a distinct manner within the Group. With this assurance, the first merger became effective in May, when the four Scottish TSBs joined forces in TSB Scotland with headquarters in Edinburgh. Richard Ellis, chairman designate of the new bank, engaged the consultants Price Waterhouse to determine the location of the head office. They recommended Glasgow and at a stormy meeting at Perth this was agreed; but at a later date the chairman, encouraged by the new general manager, Ian Macdonald, reversed this decision and Edinburgh was chosen. The Conservatives, under Mrs Thatcher, inflicted a crushing defeat on the Labour party at the polls in June, confirming the free-market economic policy that had been the touchstone of her first administration. In November, the ten banks in England and Wales amalgamated to form TSB England & Wales with headquarters in London. The subsidiary companies operated by TSB Holdings Ltd, TSB Trustcard, TSB Trust Company, and UDT became the property of the constituent banks. At the end of the year, Sir John could declare that the TSB now had a standard range of products and a unified schedule of interest rates in place throughout the United Kingdom in the way in which the restructuring committee had envisaged. The harmonisation of services was made less difficult in England and Wales by the introduction of the single on-line real-time computer system based at Wythenshawe, with computer centres there and at Milton Keynes. In Scotland the situation was similarly simplified by the conversion of the Burroughs system to OLRT, with the incorporation of Aberdeen Savings Bank which had remained committed to manual systems.

Meanwhile, the executives in the Central Board had been working hard with their legal and financial advisers, stockbrokers, and the Treasury Solicitors Department, to draft the necessary enabling legislation and a prospectus for potential shareholders. The scale of these undertakings soon demanded the complete attention of all the executives on the Central Board. After the amalgamations were completed, the restructuring committee, renamed the strategic planning group, assumed overall control. It was chaired by Sir John Read and included Philip Charlton – the only old TSB hand – his deputy, David Thorn, the company secretary Peter Rowland, and Derek Stevens handling finance. As well as preparing the documentation, the strategic planning group also began investigating the likely level of interest in the flotation amongst investors. It was calculated that there might be a 10 per cent uptake from the existing 6 million customers, with a further 600,000 private investors – some 1.2 million shareholders. This was an enormous total – three times greater than that for any existing quoted company or for an issue of government stock. No receiving bank or company registrar, or even the Bank of England, had experience of managing an exercise of such proportions. It was eventually decided that the only practical ways of servicing such a vast number of shareholders was to use a group of receiving banks and registrars.

The scale and complexity of these new negotiations, coupled with the increasing executive power of the Central Board, demanded new London offices for the TSBs. In May 1984, the Central Board left the offices in Copthall Avenue and moved to Milk Street on the edge of the City, around the corner from the Guildhall. These offices had originally been occupied by Keyser Ullman, the issuing house and merchant bank that had collapsed almost as spectacularly as UDT during the secondary banking crisis. The Group did not just need more space; it also needed to build an effective promotional and marketing team to persuade depositors, who had never owned shares in any company, to become investors at flotation. Group communications were strengthened in an effort to assert the authority of the Central Board over the individual banks, particularly TSB Scotland, in preparation for the share issue sometime early in 1986. This timetable was soon accelerated.

In early September 1984, Sir John Read called on the new Chancellor of the Exchequer, Nigel Lawson, to explain the planned flotation and outline the shape of the proposed legislation. The Chancellor indicated that Parliamentary time could be found, providing the TSB gave a firm pledge to enlist more than 1 million shareholders. Before the end of the month, Ian Stewart, the Economic Secretary of the Treasury, told the TSBs that space could be found in the legislative timetable in the coming session of Parliament. A White Paper would be published in December and the Bill introduced before Christmas. The Central Board could not afford such an opportunity to slip from their grasp. The Central Strategic Planning Group set to work expeditiously to prepare for the unveiling of the plan. Crucial to the acceptance of the scheme was the appointment of consultants to advise on the mechanism of securing the promised number of investors. It took little time to select Dewe Rogerson, who were helping mastermind the privatisation of British Telecom. The notable success of the BT flotation in November 1984, with its 2.3 million applications, made the planned number of shareholders for the TSB seem attainable, although nobody pretended that the two concerns had much in common.

On schedule, the White Paper and the Bill were published in December 1984. The White Paper outlined the background to the proposed legislation, stating categorically that the TSBs belonged neither to the government, the trustees nor depositors. It explained that the only way the new holding company TSB Group plc could be made accountable was by flotation. All the regional banks and operating companies were to be subsidiaries of TSB Group. Included in the White Paper was a letter from Sir John Read in which he took care to emphasise that the change of status did not mean that the TSB was abandoning its past – 'our traditions as a personal bank, proud of our achievements in the communities which we were established to serve'. It was for this reason, he declared, that the Central Board were seeking as wide a share-ownership as possible by giving priority to all customers with open accounts on the day before the announcement.

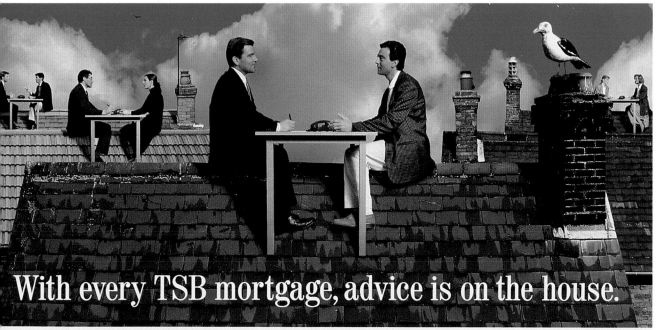

The bank that likes to say yes.

Advertisement highlighting TSB's achievements designed to prepare
the public for flotation, 1985.

The Bill was simple, straightforward and largely non-controversial, commanding all-party support. Despite the strong reservations of many Scottish trustees, particularly those in the west of Scotland, that their local identity within the community and their healthy reserves, built out of prudent management, would be deployed elsewhere when the Bill reached the statute book, it progressed with little comment through the House of Commons. In the Lords, an unhappy coincidence in March 1985 of a lengthy debate on local authority finance and a state banquet for Kenneth Kaunda, the President of Zambia, attended by many Conservative peers at Windsor Castle left the government benches denuded for the third reading of the Bill. Lord Taylor of Gryfe, a Scottish Social Democrat peer, who was convinced that TSB Scotland was being betrayed in the cause of a national bank, led an effective attack that defeated the Bill. Sir John Read and the Central Board were stunned, but could elicit no practical support from the Treasury, which professed other preoccupations. Stung into action by Treasury reluctance, Sir John and Richard Ellis, now the chairman of TSB Scotland, reassured Lord Taylor, and subsequently Lord Grimond, Baroness Elliot of Harwood, and other Scottish peers that the independence of TSB Scotland was guaranteed and that there would be no redundancies. The peers were satisfied when the TSBs offered always to register the new company in Scotland and to hold the annual meetings there. TSB Scotland would continue to function as an independently managed Scottish bank within the Group and there would be no redundancies. Lord Jacques, reviving an idea originally put forward by TSB Scotland, also inserted a clause in the Bill that provided for a proportion of the equity of the bank to be owned by regional charitable foundations 'to promote an on-going programme of financial support for socially worthwhile activities'. The Central Board had little choice but to comply with these amendments, and the legislation became law without further mishap in July 1985. Its provisions became effective in September, with Day Y — flotation or independence day fixed for February 1986 — ten months earlier than originally envisaged. The following month, fifteen years after the implementation of the first OLRT system, the whole of TSB England and Wales went on-line, an achievement that no other clearing bank was yet able to match.

Regardless of the hold-up in the House of Lords, the strategic planning group had worked

Boys at St Hilda's East Community Centre in east London, which is
funded with the help of a TSB Foundation grant.

hard to have the mechanism for the share issue in place. TSB Holdings became a public limited company in October and the following month advertisements promoting the launch appeared on television. Everything seemed to be progressing smoothly when, in November 1985, Lord Davidson ruled in the Court of Session in Edinburgh that the Treasury had no powers to vest the assets of TSB Scotland in the new company. He pronounced that TSB Scotland and, therefore by implication, TSBs elsewhere in the United Kingdom were unincorporated associations whose assets belonged to their depositors. The action had been brought by the Scottish Depositors Association formed in 1984 to challenge the legality of the flotation and led by

James Ross, a retired civil servant in the Scottish Office. His cause for complaint, as a long-standing customer, was as much the failure of the TSBs to consult their depositors about future directions as it was against flotation itself. The Association, having failed to secure a meeting on its terms with Ian Macdonald, chief general manager of TSB Scotland, invoked TSB rules to call the first special general meeting of TSB Scotland in August 1985 in an effort to remove five of the trustees under the terms of the 1976 Act. Ian Macdonald had quite correctly

James Ross, chairman of the Scottish Depositors Association,
formed in 1984 to challenge the legality of the flotation.

indicated a willingness to meet members of the Association as individual depositors, but not as representatives of a pressure group that had no authority to speak for depositors as a whole. He had to tread warily as there were trustees and senior staff in Scotland, including his own chairman, Richard Ellis, with reservations about the whole flotation process. According to the rules, only depositors with a minimum balance of £100 invested for a year qualified for tickets of admission, which had to be obtained in advance of the meeting, and only trustees and ticketholders could be admitted. As a result a number of TSB officials, the press and depositors lacking the appropriate qualifications were excluded. At the meeting the motion from the

Scottish Depositors Association was resoundingly defeated, leading to accusations that it had been packed with employees who were also depositors.

The Association used the occasion of the special general meeting to hold their own gathering, at which James Ross was elected chairman, and to make their views known to the press, chiefly that the TSBs should adopt mutual status as recommended by Page. Unaware of either the context or the antecedents of the objections to flotation in Scotland, Dewe Rogerson wrote a critical report of the way the meeting was handled, suggesting that there were opponents to change within the Bank. This was leaked to the press, fuelling the controversy. When the Scottish National Party obtained a copy of the Counsel's Opinion given by John Murray in 1979 suggesting that the TSBs belonged to their depositors, the Association brought the action in the Court of Session against the government, which resulted in Lord Davidson's judgements in November 1985. Realising that Day Y would have to be postponed until the legal position was clarified, the Central Board sought urgently to establish the veracity of Lord Davidson's conclusion in the High Court in England.

In the meantime, the Revd Dr John Vincent, a Methodist minister in Sheffield, and his wife, Grace, had established a TSB Depositors' Association in England and Wales on the Scottish model. Dr Vincent stood firmly for the original principles of the founders of the savings banks movement that they existed to promote thrift amongst the poorer sections of society and not to provide the same range of services as the clearing banks. Cheered by the outcome of the Scottish case, the Vincents began to initiate proceedings in England, but costs were prohibitive. In an effort to heal the breach and achieve a decisive judgement, the TSB Central Board agreed to meet all the costs. At the same time, an appeal was lodged against Lord Davidson's judgement and a similar offer to meet costs made to James Ross. In a crowded courtroom and under the eyes of the media, the Inner House of the Court of Session unanimously threw out Lord Davidson's judgement in March 1986 and a month later the Chancery Division of the High Court ruled that depositors were entitled to the cash in their accounts but had no interest in any other assets. However, since the matter was of intense public concern, it was recommended that the two cases should be combined and reviewed in a final appeal to the House of Lords.

The publicity surrounding both these court proceedings had stirred up all the old arguments and tensions about the role and function of the TSB that dated back for at least a century. Although the TSB had been successful in gaining a share of the market in the battle for personal savings in the 1980s, many older investors were confused and concerned by the pace of change and at what they regarded as the loss of the old caring image of the savings banks. James Ross and the Vincents were inundated with letters, voicing such anxieties. Sensitive to such criticisms of the new face of the TSBs, Philip Charlton, whose career had been spent entirely in the service of the savings banks, met the Vincents secretly at their home, with Ron Tilbury, a retired vice-chairman of the TSB Central Board. The discussion conducted from opposing positions went over the ground that had been hotly debated at many meetings of the old TSB Association: how far were the savings banks to act as commercial banks for the benefit of their larger depositors and how far were they to act as philanthropic organisations, extolling the virtue of saving in a society where there were temptations to spend on every side. As so often in the past, there was no agreement, but this time there could be no turning back as, since the Page Report, the government was no longer willing to provide through the savings banks at least a guaranteed home for the savings of small depositors.

In July 1986, after considering a mass of evidence, the House of Lords upheld the findings of the High Court and the Inner House of the Court of Session that the depositors had no claim on the assets of the bank. Eleven days later, the Chancellor of the Exchequer, Nigel Lawson, told the House of Commons that vesting would now take place, leaving the way open for flotation in September, just two months earlier than envisaged in the 1976 Act.

The events of the past fifteen years had been traumatic for the savings banks, reflecting the upheaval in the whole market for personal financial services following the introduction of Competition and Credit Control in 1971. The conclusion of the Page Committee, that the government could finance its borrowing requirements more cheaply than through National Savings and that promoting saving was not an effective mechanism for combating inflation, forced the pace of change. Once the findings became Treasury policy, there was no alternative for the TSBs but to move closer towards the status of a commercial bank.

# CHAPTER NINE

# TSB GROUP PLC:

## A PROCESS OF

## REORGANISATION

### *1986–93*

Directly the Chancellor of the Exchequer set the date for flotation in September 1986, two months ahead of the massive British Gas flotation, the TSB's publicity and promotional machinery had to be hurriedly restarted. Throughout the nine months of the court proceedings, the TSBs had consciously maintained a low profile in case the Depositors' Associations sought to make capital of their successful delaying tactics. The time had not been wasted. A comprehensive critical path had been carefully mapped out for the launch based on detailed market research which showed that a remarkable one adult in five was interested in buying shares. This target population had been defined as the TSB's own staff, its customers, the share-buying public, their professional advisers and the financial institutions. Although TSB staff were prevented by law from promoting and advising on the sale of shares in the bank, their loyalty and enthusiasm were vital to the success of the issue. A well-developed staff communications programme was in place by the summer of 1986, supported by videos, newsletters and regular visits to branches by Philip Charlton. Directly anyone registered an interest in participating in the flotation, they received regular mailings and eventually an application form from the TSB Share Information Office (SIO) managed by Group staff. Modelled on British Telecom's use of Telecom Tan during its privatisation two years earlier, the SIO was equipped to handle the expected hundreds of thousands of calls from individuals inquiring about the TSB and the flotation. The financial institutions and the press were to be kept informed by briefings and a programme of meetings arranged by Lazards and Rowe & Pitman, the TSB stockbrokers. Already Rowe & Pitman had appointed sixteen provincial stockbrokers to act as regional co-ordinators for the launch and to host a TSB senior management roadshow designed to drive home the message in local financial communities.

The whole launch was to be given a clear visual identity through the simple image of a

Raising bowlers at the official announcement of the flotation with,
from left to right, Nick Verey of stockbrokers Rowe & Pitman, Sir
John Nott of merchant bankers Lazard Brothers, Sir John Read and
Philip Charlton, August 1986.

bowler hat. Presenting a comical caricature of a 'City gent', the 'bowlers are back' theme quickly caught the public imagination, confirming that if anyone, regardless of sex, colour or occupation, could wear a bowler hat, they could also own shares. This initial assault through the media was followed up by 'Now It's Your Turn To Say YES', 'It Won't be Long Now', and 'Don't Leave it Too Late To Say YES'. Such was the interest, that the SIO was inundated with inquiries, overwhelmingly from customers with specific questions about the launch. Extra staff had to be brought in to handle telephone calls and mailings. All advertisements and promotional material were vetted by a Copy Clearance Committee to ensure not only that it complied with the law but also that it was consistent with the overall launch strategy. Since many of those who registered an interest had never owned shares, information packs included a booklet, published by the Stock Exchange, *An Introduction to Buying and Selling Shares*, first used in the British Telecom flotation. The mass mailings to customers and staff were handled by Vernons Pools, who had the experience and technology to deal with an operation on this scale. Fleets of vans were used to deliver literature to the branches. The complex logistics were controlled from Milk Street and progress monitored against the timetable each week.

No sooner had the flotation begun to regain momentum than Lords Keith and Templeman published their judgement in the House of Lords of the appeal which stated explicitly that TSB belonged to the State, subject to the depositors' contractual rights. There was a storm of protest from Labour MPs, who denounced the government for giving away to speculators the Group's estimated £1 billion of reserves. Accused of hasty action in giving the launch the green light before the legal position was clear, Treasury ministers and officials tried to draw a distinction between assets belonging to the Crown, the State and the government. Despite the criticism, Conservative ministers remained determined to clear up the anomaly of TSB's ownership which sat unhappily with their concept of a self-regulating financial market. Sir Patrick Mayhew, the Solicitor-General, stated that 'although Lord Templeman had ruled that the TSB assets belonged to the State, it did not follow that they accrued to the Exchequer'.

Sir John Read, chairman of the TSB
at the time of flotation.

In mid-August the government gave an undertaking that the maximum shareholding in the TSB Group was to be restricted to 5 per cent in the first five years and 15 per cent thereafter. Foreign investors in the flotation were to be discouraged by requiring them to make payment in sterling, in cheques drawn on a British bank. Later in the month, TSB announced it had formed four regional charities, the TSB Foundations, that were to receive 1 per cent of profits averaged over three years annually, to be spent on local causes, keeping faith with the Group's origins. The formal campaign started at the end of the holiday period on 27 August – six weeks before flotation – with the publication of the *Pathfinder*, a prospectus containing a comprehensive review of the TSB Group, but without the share price and profits forecast. Immediately the TSB roadshow went into action on a ten-day tour of fifteen provincial centres to present the

Philip Charlton, the TSB's first
group chief executive.

TSB flotation publicity, 1986; and (OPPOSITE) processing share application forms.

Group to packed audiences. The share price of £1 for each 25 pence share was announced on 12 September – Impact Day – marked by the release of 10,000 TSB balloons in the City by the unfamiliarly bowler-hatted senior managers. Half the price was payable at once and half a year later. So intense was the interest that branches throughout the country were thronged all day with people seeking advice, filling in application forms and transferring funds to buy shares. It was evident that the bowler hat and the television advertising were making an impact far beyond the expectations of TSB management. As well as a flood of priority applications from staff and customers, applications poured in from customers of other banks. To prevent public attention flagging in the crucial final fortnight, the press office worked hard to exploit any news item relating to the Group in the national and local newspapers, sending out numerous press releases. When the offer closed at 10.00 a.m. on 24 September, over 5 million applications had been received for £11.2 billion worth of shares – eight times the value of shares on offer.

The week before the offer closed, TSB were aware that a final register of at least 3 million shareholders was likely. This presented a serious practical problem as, at the time, there was no computer capable of handling any larger register. Whatever happened, the total number of shareholders could not be allowed to exceed 3 million. However, Sir John Read was pressed by the Treasury to issue as many shares as possible in small parcels to private shareholders. Even after excluding the 145 institutional applications for more than 3 million shares, a ballot was still inevitable to reduce the number of unpreferred applications by some 50 per cent. There were complaints that the method of putting applications in batches of receipts and the system

The first day of dealing in TSB shares, 10 October 1986.

of balloting by removing alternate batches of applications resulted in the rejection of many family groups. Given the time scale and the lack of technology, there was no other practical alternative.

It was possible that many private shareholders would simply sell their allocation immediately trading began on 10 October. In the event only 650,000 shareholders sold their stake in the first three months after flotation, confirming the market surveys conducted during the campaign, which suggested that most applicants regarded TSB as a serious long-term investment. These were largely customers who believed the TSB was their bank. By the end of January 1987, TSB had 2.45 million shareholders, of whom 94 per cent held 600 shares or less. This was a notable achievement – a share issue that had broken every record and raised £1,273 million for TSB.

The total cost of the campaign came to £86 million: £60 million in marketing, underwriting and legal costs, and £26 million to the High Street banks to meet the cost of processing applications. Although management had made every effort to contain costs, negotiating a special underwriting deal and ensuring that publicity kept within budget, there were those who remained sceptical of the need to incur such a large bill and the wisdom of the strategy adopted by TSB, encouraged by the Treasury and the Conservative government. An editorial in the *Financial Times* on the day after the offer closed, under the headline 'Easy Money for the

TSB', roundly condemned the sequence of events since the House of Lords' judgement in July. It suggested that the government should have waited until the judgement was published and then itself privatised TSB for a price close to the £900 million of tangible net assets, using the proceeds to cut taxes. The *Financial Times* was dubious about the methods used to attract such a large number of shareholders with no adequate explanation of the attendant risks. The editorial concluded prophetically:

> More seriously the TSB, which was over-capitalised even in advance of the flotation, has now become bloated with nearly three times as much as it needs for its normal business. To make effective use of all this extra money before the protective layers that have been erected against a hostile takeover bid are dismantled, the TSB will be forced into a spending spree over the next five years. And that could lead to further inflation in the prices of insurance brokers and estate agents, if those are to be targets of the TSB's attentions, and may stretch too far for the capacity of the incumbent management.

There was a good deal of truth in this onslaught. The structure of the Group, representing all the compromises that had to be made since the publication of the Page Report in 1974, was unwieldy. The board had twenty-six members, many of whom represented regional or factional interests. With such a large board, most decisions had, inevitably, to be taken by a small policy committee. Underneath the main board were nine principal subsidiary companies with overlapping and competing responsibilities. To meet some of the problems within the Group highlighted by the *Financial Times*, senior executives with experience of commercial banking had been either recruited or promoted: Leslie Priestley came in from Barclays as Director and Chief General Manager of TSB England & Wales plc, and Don McCrickard, who had come from the British arm of American Express some time before, was appointed Managing Director of TSB Commercial Holdings Ltd. Throughout the campaign, Sir John had been adamant that he had no intention of being panicked into spending the TSB cash pile. Derek Stevens, the Finance Director, declared: 'If we bought something tomorrow, we'd probably pay too much and have trouble integrating it into the business. We want to buy well-managed businesses because we don't have a surfeit of good managers in the TSB.'

Despite all the distractions of the launch and the related legal proceedings, TSB had remained in constant touch with its customers, whose loyalty was fundamental to future success in the open market. The TSB tradition of service to its depositors was captured by the successful advertising slogan: 'The Bank that likes to say YES'. The general managers met regularly to report progress to Philip Charlton, the Group chief executive, who tried to establish his authority over the ambitions of the individual companies. The introduction of new products was discussed with the fashionable objective of offering an integrated financial service, from banking to house purchase facilities. TSB Scotland made a start during 1986 with the acquisition of the Glasgow-based estate agents, Slater, Hogg & Howison. In England and Wales, efforts were made to reposition branches at strategic points in High Streets and to build a portfolio of corporate client business without sacrificing the quality of the Group's lending. The pace of investment in new technology quickened, particularly in the increased installation of automatic teller machines or 'speedbanks'. In July the Group announced the expenditure of £4.6 million to link its cash dispensers to the joint network of Midland and National Westminster Banks, giving customers access to 4,000 additional cash-disposal machines. New products included TSB European and TSB British Growth Unit Trusts, and Mortgage Express, a centrally processed first mortgage facility made available through insurance company intermediaries. Profits for the year were ahead of forecast at £205 million, up over 20 per cent on 1985. The future for TSB as a commercial bank, albeit small in comparison to the big four, seemed assured. However, the market for financial services was changing rapidly. The flotation of TSB had been a small component in the much wider policy of the Conservative government of deregulation to ensure that London retained its position as the world's leading financial centre.

Immediately after the Conservatives' 1983 general election victory, plans to reform the Stock Exchange and financial markets had been announced. This was followed, after a hurried period of consultation, by the passing of the Financial Services Act in 1986. The Stock Exchange reforms abolished stockbrokers' fixed commission, allowed stockbrokers and jobbers to belong to the same firm, made it possible for banks and other financial institutions to buy stockbroking and jobbing firms, and opened the London Stock Exchange to foreign firms. These reforms came into effect in the much-heralded 'Big Bang' of 27 October 1986. The Financial Services Act established a new regulatory body in 1987, the Securities & Investment Board (SIB) with oversight of a number of new Self-Regulatory Organisations (SROs). The new regulations issued by the SIB were labyrinthine in their complexity and subject to regular revision as time went by. Although clearing banks continued to be supervised by the Bank of England, they were also required now to report to the SRO responsible for their other services; for instance, for investment management to the Investment Management Regulatory Organisation (IMRO) and for securities operations to the Securities Association.

At the same time, wider powers were given in separate legislation to TSB's chief competitors, the building societies. This abolished the building societies' cartel, forcing them to compete with one another for savings and mortgage business. They were also allowed to provide customers with much the same range of services as High Street banks, such as money transmissions, cheque accounts, investment services, and insurance, and to own estate agencies and undertake conveyancing. A new Banking Act was passed in 1987 to tighten up bank supervision by the Bank of England in the wake of the Johnson Matthey collapse in 1984.

As with nearly all the reforms of Margaret Thatcher's government, deregulation meant that the cost of policing the markets fell to the industry. The Financial Services Act not only added to the costs of the banks and other financial institutions in maintaining the various regulatory bodies, it also required them to seek permission from their clients to act on their behalf; and to explain if they were providing independent advice or simply selling own-brand product. To help branches deal with the increased flow of correspondence with customers, a project was initiated to automate back offices allowing routine letters to be generated automatically. With a budget of £100 million the system was completed in a very tight timetable of eighteen months and was in advance of TSB's competitors. At the time it was believed that deregulation would encourage banks and building societies to become financial supermarkets, offering customers an integrated service, from current account to share purchase and mortgage facilities. Its immediate consequence, as in the early 1970s at the time of Competition and Credit Control, was an explosion in competition for corporate and personal credit with too little regard sometimes for either underlying securities or ability to repay, fuelling a massive housing and property boom.

In these changed conditions, and under intense pressure from the press, Sir John Read and his team were convinced that they had to use some of their cash endowment to keep in the race. At the end of June 1987, TSB made an agreed offer of £220 million for Target, the country's fourth largest unit-linked life office and which had been contemplating a Stock Exchange listing. Ostensibly, it seemed a good match. TSB's life business had been built up largely on its existing customer base, chiefly socio-economic group C, whereas Target operated in the premium end of the market in socio-economic groups A and B. One of Target's joint founders, A.P.W. Simon, had advised in the establishment of TSB Trust Company. As part of the formal understanding, Sir John Read agreed that the management was to be left undisturbed and independent, with J.K. Stone as Managing Director. Some commentators reckoned that TSB were paying too high a price for a business without proper investigation of the liabilities.

TSB interim results released towards the end of June 1987 suggested that, although profits were increasing as they should have been with the huge injection of cash at flotation, returns from banking were sluggish due to rapidly rising costs. The news increased the pressure on Sir John to make an imaginative investment. In mid-July, TSB made a hostile bid of £282 million for Hogg Robinson, the insurance broking and travel agency group, which also owned a network of estate agencies. The plan was to retain the travel and estate agencies, which would have given TSB a High Street presence in southern England, and sell the insurance business. Rejected by the Hogg Robinson board as derisory, the offer failed to win any support amongst their shareholders. After the success of the launch the year before, TSB suddenly, in view of the media and financial commentators, seemed unable to do anything right. The TSB personal equity plan (PEP), introduced at the end of July as the 'People's PEP' for the small saver, was written off by the press as 'not a plan for the small investor to say yes to'. At the end of August, within days of the second instalment on the TSB shares being paid, the Banking Insurance & Finance Union made a blistering attack on TSB's proposed reduction in staffing levels, conditions of service and pay, calling for an immediate overtime ban.

In October 1987 came the news that the City had been anticipating. TSB, advised by the merchant bankers Lazards, was negotiating a big purchase – the take-over of the merchant bankers Hill Samuel, which was in trouble owing to a shortage of capital to support its investment business. After a decade of difficulties in the 1970s, Hill Samuel was now reported to have a highly sophisticated corporate finance service, specialising in trade finance, lending on property for development, and management buy-outs, along with interests in fund management, personal investment, insurance, unit trusts, and stockbroking. In July, following the collapse of take-over talks with the Union Bank of Switzerland, the chief executive, Christopher Castleman, had resigned and since then the Australian financiers, Larry Adler and Kerry Packer, had acquired control of almost 30 per cent of the shares. The future of the bank had become more uncertain during September, when the head of corporate finance and his deputy had been summarily dismissed for trying to sell themselves and their department to Barclay de Zöete Wedd (BZW), the successful merchant banking arm of Barclays. Later in the month an improbable bid was made by the advertising agents, Saatchi & Saatchi. As originally proposed, TSB would buy the Hill Samuel investment management, life insurance and unit trust operations, and BZW the corporate finance department. Wood MacKenzie, the stockbroking and securities firm, purchased the year before, was to be sold; initially to an American investor, but eventually to County NatWest. In the event, BZW withdrew and, within two days, TSB made an agreed offer of 810 pence per share, valuing Hill Samuel at £777 million. Almost immediately, TSB purchased Adler's and Packer's stake in the company. Before the terms of the bid could be put to TSB shareholders, the world financial markets crashed. In London on 'Black Monday', 19 October, over 10 per cent was wiped off the value of shares. The price of TSB shares tumbled by 13 pence to 133 pence. By close of business on Wednesday the *Financial Times* ordinary share index was down 21 per cent on the week. Concerted international action rallied the markets on Thursday, leaving financial institutions relieved, but with their confidence badly bruised by the experience. Hill Samuel's shares finished the week at 770 pence, 40 pence lower than the offer price. For TSB's large number of small shareholders, with little experience of investment in equities and rules of corporate behaviour, this massive readjustment in share prices gave the clear impression that their board was paying over the odds for Hill Samuel.

The TSB Extraordinary General Meeting to approve the purchase of Hill Samuel was held on 2 November at Methodist Central Hall, Westminster, just ten days after the close of this catastrophic week. The TSB management, failing to grasp what a deep impression the crisis had made on the popular mind, expected that, with a majority of favourable votes in their hands, the meeting would be a formality – it was anything but. The meeting lasted for six and a half hours, with regular interruptions from smaller shareholders complaining that 'the board had no right to "throw away" needlessly shareholders' cash by proceeding with the bid at 810 pence'. Sir John was accused of using the proxy votes 'to steam-roller the issue'. He was saved from a vote of no confidence only by the intervention of Peter Rowland, the Company Secretary, who ruled the motion was not allowed under the articles of association. After several adjournments, the take-over was approved by 177 million votes to 12.32 million. As with

Target, Hill Samuel became an independently managed subsidiary of TSB Group plc. Three of its directors, Sir Robert Clark, David Davies and D.C. Mootham, joined the Group board, making it even more unwieldy and factionalised with now thirty members. In his chairman's statement, published in January 1988, Sir John Read remained convinced of the correctness of the decision to buy Hill Samuel: 'The rationale behind the acquisition and the strategic fit of the two groups is as sound now as it was when the offer was first made. The decision to proceed with the acquisition despite the subsequent fall in stock markets round the world was based on the fundamental benefits to be gained from the investment in the longer term.' While recognising that TSB had little option under the terms of the take-over rules than to proceed with the deal, the financial community, mostly with the benefit of hindsight, was less convinced. Many commentators believed that TSB should have renegotiated the price, pleading the events of 'Black Monday' as extenuating circumstances. This, however, would have had the attendant risk of further reducing the value of TSB's 29 per cent investment in Hill Samuel purchased from Adler and Packer at 810 pence per share.

Hard on the heels of this damaging experience came the publication at the beginning of December 1987 of the findings of the House of Commons Public Accounts Committee inquiry into the flotation. Despite the reassurances from Sir Peter Middleton, the permanent secretary at the Treasury, the Committee had no doubt that Parliament had not been given sufficient evidence on which to base the decision about who should benefit from the proceeds. This news was followed by rumours of a boardroom split over the timing of Sir John's retirement, due when he reached the age of seventy the following year. The continuing poor press fuelled criticism of the Group's management, which even the good results for the year failed to meet. In January 1988, the Lex column of the *Financial Times* told readers that TSB was 'more interested in spending money than boosting shareholders' returns'. The acid test, it was claimed, of 'whether the TSB remains a dull investment or becomes a high-flying financial services company' would be how successfully and quickly Hill Samuel was integrated with the Group. The announcement late in February that Sir Nicholas Goodison, the chairman of the Stock Exchange, would succeed Sir John at the close of the year was greeted by some commentators with a similar lack of enthusiasm. His appointment was dismissed by one columnist as a missed opportunity on the grounds that what TSB needed was someone skilled in selling financial services. Such opinions overlooked the structural problems of the Group, legacies of the intensely political atmosphere that had characterised the TSB Association from its foundation, and Sir Nicholas's experience of directing fundamental change in his previous post.

During April 1988, tentative steps were taken by Sir John Read to reorganise the Group's banking business in England and Wales into two divisions, leaving Scotland, Northern Ireland and the Channel Islands undisturbed for the time being. These were retail and personal banking and corporate banking. Don McCrickard became banking chief executive, with oversight of the whole of the Group's banking business. Two separate activities, insurance and investment

services, were to be brought together to manage the unit trusts, life assurance, and pensions of TSB, Hill Samuel, and Target, with David Thorn as chief executive. A final subsidiary division was to care for TSB's commercial holdings. Despite these well-publicised reforms, the press remained relentless in attacking the Group's record since flotation, accusing the management of squandering the proceeds on highly priced acquisitions and of failing to take advantage of its strong balance sheet and extensive customer base.

Later in the spring of 1988, it was decided to improve branch access to customer information by installing an updated Unisys computer system with a total of 7,500 terminals in 1,650 branches. As a result TSB, still the only bank with an 'On-Line-Real-Time' system, would have a significant advantage over its competitors in selling its range of financial products. At the same time, as an experiment, TSB Scotland attempted to extend its customer base to socio-economic groups A and B through the 'Elect' package, which included interest-bearing cheque accounts. These initiatives with an emphasis on retailing marked a turning point in the external perception of the Group, reinforced in the autumn by far more pro-active public statements by McCrickard which sought to explain TSB's distinctive approach: 'The bank sees its 1,650 branches as "sales channels" through which different services can be directed to individual customers.' He defended the purchase of Hill Samuel as an excellent vehicle for improving TSB's loan book, now approaching £1.7 billion. Further structural reforms followed when in October a unified treasury was formed in Hill Samuel to handle the Group's activities in the wholesale money markets, particularly foreign exchange dealing, sterling and off-balance sheet instruments. During the year, TSB had raised £335 million using these innovative instruments, including £135 million in mortgage-backed investments to take some of the £2 billion committed by Mortgage Express off the balance sheet.

Sir Nicholas Goodison, who had joined the Board in April, took over as chairman in January 1989 on the retirement of Sir John Read. At the same time, David Davies stood down as chief executive of Hill Samuel. Sir Nicholas immediately set about reform of the structure and management. TSB Scotland and TSB Northern Ireland were brought together with TSB England & Wales under Don McCrickard and renamed TSB Bank. The board was slimmed right down with the resignation of twelve directors. At the same time Sir Nicholas demolished the complex structure of regional boards – a vestige of the compromises that had preceded flotation. Hill Samuel sold its share registry subsidiary to Barclays Bank. At the annual meeting in March, Sir Nicholas gave warning of difficult times ahead, raising the question among outside observers that market share, rather than sound assessment, had driven the Group's corporate lending. Peter Ellwood, chief executive of Barclaycard, was appointed as chief executive of retail banking. The interim figures published in June were grim, showing a sharp

Sir Nicholas Goodison, chairman of TSB
standing by a clock presented by York Savings Bank.

advance in costs and a downturn in earnings per share. The press was now scathing in its condemnation, but missed the large-scale reorganisation that was under way. In July, Leslie Priestley and David Cobbold, head of the new unified treasury, left. Special task forces were set up to review every aspect of the business. There were few surprises in the findings which concentrated on the unnecessarily high operating costs caused by the highly fragmented structure inherited from the past. TSB announced substantial job losses in November 1989 and

Brian Brown who laid the foundations of the success
of the TSB Trust Company.

a restructuring of branch organisation and management. In all, staff members were reduced by 5,500 as a result of this exercise. The head office was to be drastically slimmed and the number of regions cut from seven to three.

The 1989 results when they were published in January were disappointing; exceptional provision, of £125 million, was made to cover the cost of restructuring the bank and a further £76 million was provided for likely losses incurred on past swap contracts with local authorities which had recently been ruled *ultra vires* by the courts. At this time Don McCrickard succeeded Philip Charlton as group chief executive and Philip Charlton became one of the deputy chairmen. The annual report held out little prospect of any significant recovery in 1990. The City was taken aback by the size of the provisions, which were typical only of clearers with exposure to Third World countries. Sir Nicholas earned applause for his 'unflinching presentation' of TSB's problems. More bad news followed with the announcement in May

1990 that Target, a victim of poor controls, was in serious trouble. It was put up for sale at a price of £53 million, £167 million less than TSB paid for it just three years earlier. The Group's interim results published in June were a little more encouraging, with a 6.7 per cent rise in profits, but the bad debt provision had climbed from £26 million to £83 million, reflecting the severity of the developing recession. This slight improvement suggested that reconstruction was beginning to bear fruit. Further changes were made in the senior management. In October, David Thorn retired early and was replaced as head of insurance and investment services by Hugh Freedberg, chief executive of the Mortgage Corporation. As a result, Brian Brown, the long-standing chief executive of TSB Trust Company, also retired early in February 1991. A month earlier, Derek Stevens resigned as Finance Director and joined British Airways in a similar capacity. He was replaced by Dolf Mootham from Hill Samuel. Target was sold in the same month at a knockdown price to Equity & Law, forcing TSB to make provision of £80 million in its accounts to cover the loss.

No sooner had the Group extricated itself from this ill-considered investment than even more serious problems became apparent at Hill Samuel. At the height of the boom, Hill Samuel had expanded its loan book and branch network, accepting risks, particularly in the property market, which in the cold light of recession looked very doubtful. The chief executive, Hamish Donaldson, and Ted Emerson, the head of commercial banking, resigned in March. Hugh Freedberg became chief executive of Hill Samuel and other senior managers were replaced. The new team worked at breakneck speed to identify the scale of Hill Samuel's exposure, revealing bad debts of a colossal £344 million. Simultaneously, TSB had been searching for a buyer for Mortgage Express, which had also run into serious trouble resulting from the rapid deterioration of the housing market and rising interest rates. Eventually, in April when no purchaser could be found, TSB closed the operation for new business – a decision 'unprecedented in the industry', but not wholly unexpected. Early in May, the profitable TSB Northern Ireland was sold to Allied Irish Banks for £111 million. Sir David Plastow, chairman and chief executive of Vickers, was appointed deputy chairman to replace the two previous deputy chairmen, Sir Ian Fraser and Sir Robert Clark, who had retired two months before. At the annual meeting in March the chairman issued a public profits warning. In the days before the publication of the interim results in June 1991, TSB carefully prepared the financial community for an appalling first half. The loss of £150 million resulting from the profound problems at Hill Samuel exceeded the City's worst fears. There were calls for Sir Nicholas's resignation, even though he had nothing to do with the purchase of Hill Samuel and had been appointed expressly to effect badly needed change.

The full year results showed a return to profitability in the second half as the charge for bad and doubtful debts fell. Acknowledging that 1991 had been a very difficult year for banks, Sir Nicholas was able to look forward with more confidence to the future.

1992 was a year of further change. On the retirement of Dolf Mootham, John Burns joined the Group as Finance Director after a long career at National Westminster Bank. The head office of the retail bank moved to new premises in the heart of Birmingham. In a bold move, TSB's lead in the selling of insurance products to bank customers was further extended through the integration of its banking and insurance operations under common management. The outstanding 49 per cent of TSB Channel Islands was acquired, providing a platform for the development of the business both in the islands and as an offshore centre for customers on the mainland.

The Birmingham Head Office of TSB retail bank, opened in 1992.

Sir Nicholas had been planning to create closer links between the Group head office and its largest business, TSB Retail Banking & Insurance, for some time. In August Don McCrickard resigned as Group Chief Executive. He was succeeded by Peter Ellwood who was also appointed Chief Executive of TSB Bank. John Elbourne, who had been recruited a year earlier from Legal & General to head TSB's insurance operations, became Chief Operating Officer of the retail bank and insurance businesses and joined the Group board. By the end of the year Sir Nicholas was able to say that after a comprehensive process of change, leading to this final fusion of the management of the Group and bank, the Group now had a strong team with the necessary expertise and experience to carry it forward.

Further sales had taken place, including the motor dealership of Swan National, as the Group became increasingly focused on the development of its core banking and insurance business under the name of TSB. Although there was no formal 'for sale' notice outside any of the businesses, it was accepted that if a purchaser came along with a realistic offer for any of the non-core business, it would be seriously considered. As part of this strategy the Hill Samuel branch network was subsumed under the TSB name and Hill Samuel itself returned to providing

Peter Ellwood, group chief executive in 1993.

merchant banking facilities on a fee and relationship basis to middle-size enterprise. Setting realistic profits targets, the Group was determined to build on the loyalty of TSB customers and shareholders, despite the problems since flotation, to expand its services to private clients and small businesses.

Having drawn a line under the mistakes that were made in the heady days of the late 1980s, the TSB was returning to what it knows best: personal banking and insurance for people of all ages and from all walks of life – keeping alive the ideals and vision of the founder of the savings movement almost two centuries ago.

# TABLES OF BALANCES, DEPOSITS AND WITHDRAWALS

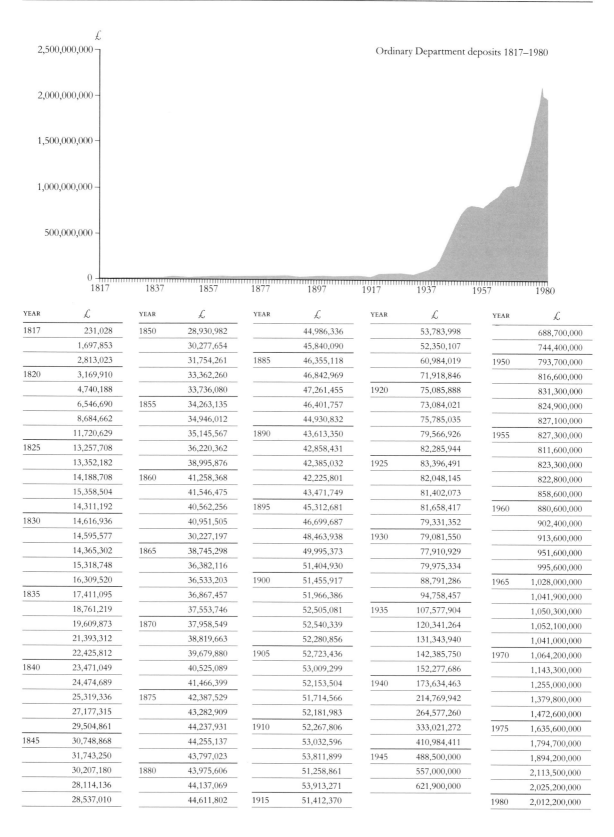

Ordinary Department deposits 1817–1980

| YEAR | £ | YEAR | £ | YEAR | £ | YEAR | £ | YEAR | £ |
|---|---|---|---|---|---|---|---|---|---|
| 1817 | 231,028 | 1850 | 28,930,982 | | 44,986,336 | | 53,783,998 | | 688,700,000 |
| | 1,697,853 | | 30,277,654 | | 45,840,090 | | 52,350,107 | | 744,400,000 |
| | 2,813,023 | | 31,754,261 | 1885 | 46,355,118 | | 60,984,019 | 1950 | 793,700,000 |
| 1820 | 3,169,910 | | 33,362,260 | | 46,842,969 | | 71,918,846 | | 816,600,000 |
| | 4,740,188 | | 33,736,080 | | 47,261,455 | 1920 | 75,085,888 | | 831,300,000 |
| | 6,546,690 | 1855 | 34,263,135 | | 46,401,757 | | 73,084,021 | | 824,900,000 |
| | 8,684,662 | | 34,946,012 | | 44,930,832 | | 75,785,035 | | 827,100,000 |
| | 11,720,629 | | 35,145,567 | 1890 | 43,613,350 | | 79,566,926 | 1955 | 827,300,000 |
| 1825 | 13,257,708 | | 36,220,362 | | 42,858,431 | | 82,285,944 | | 811,600,000 |
| | 13,352,182 | | 38,995,876 | | 42,385,032 | 1925 | 83,396,491 | | 823,300,000 |
| | 14,188,708 | 1860 | 41,258,368 | | 42,225,801 | | 82,048,145 | | 822,800,000 |
| | 15,358,504 | | 41,546,475 | | 43,471,749 | | 81,402,073 | | 858,600,000 |
| | 14,311,192 | | 40,562,256 | 1895 | 45,312,681 | | 81,658,417 | 1960 | 880,600,000 |
| 1830 | 14,616,936 | | 40,951,505 | | 46,699,687 | | 79,331,352 | | 902,400,000 |
| | 14,595,577 | | 30,227,197 | | 48,463,938 | 1930 | 79,081,550 | | 913,600,000 |
| | 14,365,302 | 1865 | 38,745,298 | | 49,995,373 | | 77,910,929 | | 951,600,000 |
| | 15,318,748 | | 36,382,116 | | 51,404,930 | | 79,975,334 | | 995,600,000 |
| | 16,309,520 | | 36,533,203 | 1900 | 51,455,917 | | 88,791,286 | 1965 | 1,028,000,000 |
| 1835 | 17,411,095 | | 36,867,457 | | 51,966,386 | | 94,758,457 | | 1,041,900,000 |
| | 18,761,219 | | 37,553,746 | | 52,505,081 | 1935 | 107,577,904 | | 1,050,300,000 |
| | 19,609,873 | 1870 | 37,958,549 | | 52,540,339 | | 120,341,264 | | 1,052,100,000 |
| | 21,393,312 | | 38,819,663 | | 52,280,856 | | 131,343,940 | | 1,041,000,000 |
| | 22,425,812 | | 39,679,880 | 1905 | 52,723,436 | | 142,385,750 | 1970 | 1,064,200,000 |
| 1840 | 23,471,049 | | 40,525,089 | | 53,009,299 | | 152,277,686 | | 1,143,300,000 |
| | 24,474,689 | | 41,466,399 | | 52,153,504 | 1940 | 173,634,463 | | 1,255,000,000 |
| | 25,319,336 | 1875 | 42,387,529 | | 51,714,566 | | 214,769,942 | | 1,379,800,000 |
| | 27,177,315 | | 43,282,909 | | 52,181,983 | | 264,577,260 | | 1,472,600,000 |
| | 29,504,861 | | 44,237,931 | 1910 | 52,267,806 | | 333,021,272 | 1975 | 1,635,600,000 |
| 1845 | 30,748,868 | | 44,255,137 | | 53,032,596 | | 410,984,411 | | 1,794,700,000 |
| | 31,743,250 | | 43,797,023 | | 53,811,899 | 1945 | 488,500,000 | | 1,894,200,000 |
| | 30,207,180 | 1880 | 43,975,606 | | 51,258,861 | | 557,000,000 | | 2,113,500,000 |
| | 28,114,136 | | 44,137,069 | | 53,913,271 | | 621,900,000 | | 2,025,200,000 |
| | 28,537,010 | | 44,611,802 | 1915 | 51,412,370 | | | 1980 | 2,012,200,000 |

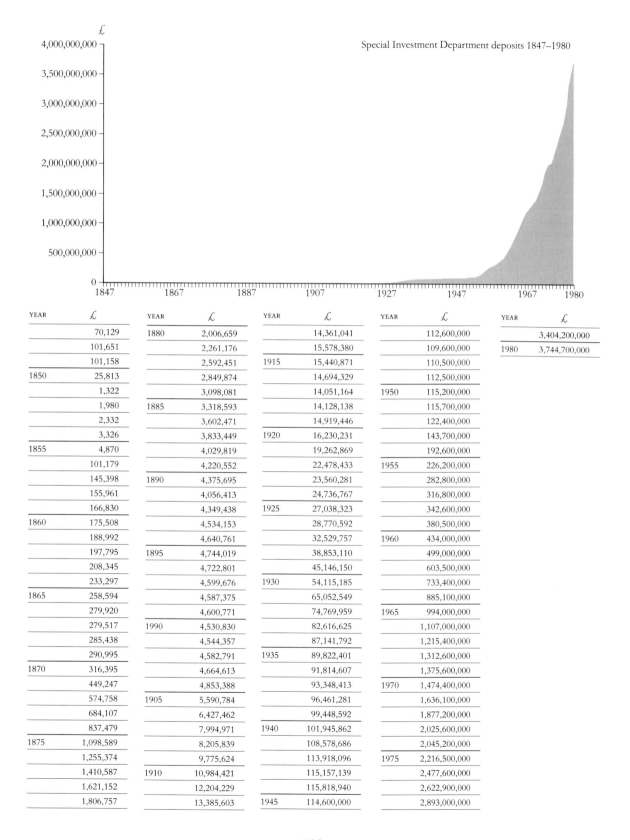

Special Investment Department deposits 1847–1980

| YEAR | £ | YEAR | £ | YEAR | £ | YEAR | £ | YEAR | £ |
|---|---|---|---|---|---|---|---|---|---|
|  | 70,129 | 1880 | 2,006,659 |  | 14,361,041 |  | 112,600,000 |  | 3,404,200,000 |
|  | 101,651 |  | 2,261,176 |  | 15,578,380 |  | 109,600,000 | 1980 | 3,744,700,000 |
|  | 101,158 |  | 2,592,451 | 1915 | 15,440,871 |  | 110,500,000 |  |  |
| 1850 | 25,813 |  | 2,849,874 |  | 14,694,329 |  | 112,500,000 |  |  |
|  | 1,322 |  | 3,098,081 |  | 14,051,164 | 1950 | 115,200,000 |  |  |
|  | 1,980 | 1885 | 3,318,593 |  | 14,128,138 |  | 115,700,000 |  |  |
|  | 2,332 |  | 3,602,471 |  | 14,919,446 |  | 122,400,000 |  |  |
|  | 3,326 |  | 3,833,449 | 1920 | 16,230,231 |  | 143,700,000 |  |  |
| 1855 | 4,870 |  | 4,029,819 |  | 19,262,869 |  | 192,600,000 |  |  |
|  | 101,179 |  | 4,220,552 |  | 22,478,433 | 1955 | 226,200,000 |  |  |
|  | 145,398 | 1890 | 4,375,695 |  | 23,560,281 |  | 282,800,000 |  |  |
|  | 155,961 |  | 4,056,413 |  | 24,736,767 |  | 316,800,000 |  |  |
|  | 166,830 |  | 4,349,438 | 1925 | 27,038,323 |  | 342,600,000 |  |  |
| 1860 | 175,508 |  | 4,534,153 |  | 28,770,592 |  | 380,500,000 |  |  |
|  | 188,992 |  | 4,640,761 |  | 32,529,757 | 1960 | 434,000,000 |  |  |
|  | 197,795 | 1895 | 4,744,019 |  | 38,853,110 |  | 499,000,000 |  |  |
|  | 208,345 |  | 4,722,801 |  | 45,146,150 |  | 603,500,000 |  |  |
|  | 233,297 |  | 4,599,676 | 1930 | 54,115,185 |  | 733,400,000 |  |  |
| 1865 | 258,594 |  | 4,587,375 |  | 65,052,549 |  | 885,100,000 |  |  |
|  | 279,920 |  | 4,600,771 |  | 74,769,959 | 1965 | 994,000,000 |  |  |
|  | 279,517 | 1990 | 4,530,830 |  | 82,616,625 |  | 1,107,000,000 |  |  |
|  | 285,438 |  | 4,544,357 |  | 87,141,792 |  | 1,215,400,000 |  |  |
|  | 290,995 |  | 4,582,791 | 1935 | 89,822,401 |  | 1,312,600,000 |  |  |
| 1870 | 316,395 |  | 4,664,613 |  | 91,814,607 |  | 1,375,600,000 |  |  |
|  | 449,247 |  | 4,853,388 |  | 93,348,413 | 1970 | 1,474,400,000 |  |  |
|  | 574,758 | 1905 | 5,590,784 |  | 96,461,281 |  | 1,636,100,000 |  |  |
|  | 684,107 |  | 6,427,462 |  | 99,448,592 |  | 1,877,200,000 |  |  |
|  | 837,479 |  | 7,994,971 | 1940 | 101,945,862 |  | 2,025,600,000 |  |  |
| 1875 | 1,098,589 |  | 8,205,839 |  | 108,578,686 |  | 2,045,200,000 |  |  |
|  | 1,255,374 |  | 9,775,624 |  | 113,918,096 | 1975 | 2,216,500,000 |  |  |
|  | 1,410,587 | 1910 | 10,984,421 |  | 115,157,139 |  | 2,477,600,000 |  |  |
|  | 1,621,152 |  | 12,204,229 |  | 115,818,940 |  | 2,622,900,000 |  |  |
|  | 1,806,757 |  | 13,385,603 | 1945 | 114,600,000 |  | 2,893,000,000 |  |  |

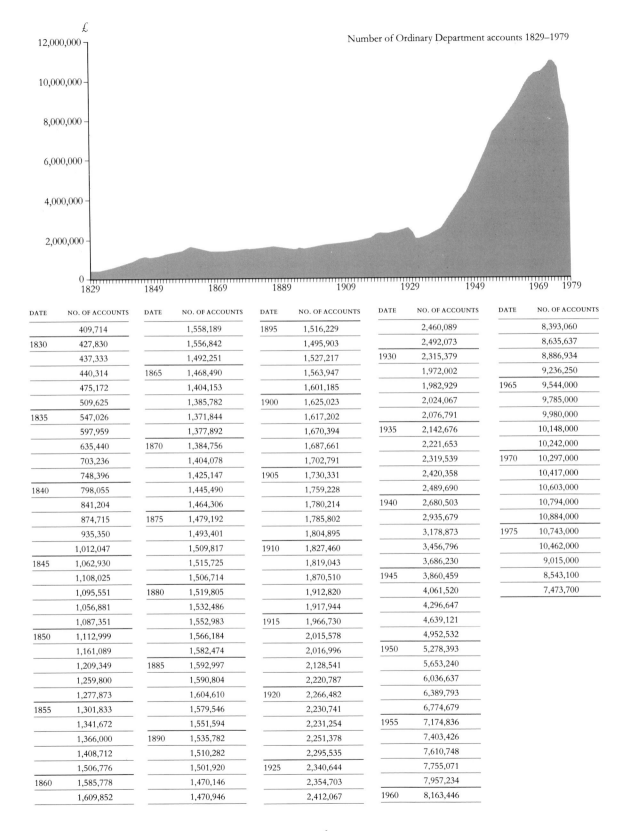

Number of Ordinary Department accounts 1829–1979

| DATE | NO. OF ACCOUNTS | DATE | NO. OF ACCOUNTS | DATE | NO. OF ACCOUNTS | DATE | NO. OF ACCOUNTS | DATE | NO. OF ACCOUNTS |
|------|-----------------|------|-----------------|------|-----------------|------|-----------------|------|-----------------|
|      | 409,714         |      | 1,558,189       | 1895 | 1,516,229       |      | 2,460,089       |      | 8,393,060       |
| 1830 | 427,830         |      | 1,556,842       |      | 1,495,903       |      | 2,492,073       |      | 8,635,637       |
|      | 437,333         |      | 1,492,251       |      | 1,527,217       | 1930 | 2,315,379       |      | 8,886,934       |
|      | 440,314         | 1865 | 1,468,490       |      | 1,563,947       |      | 1,972,002       |      | 9,236,250       |
|      | 475,172         |      | 1,404,153       |      | 1,601,185       |      | 1,982,929       | 1965 | 9,544,000       |
|      | 509,625         |      | 1,385,782       | 1900 | 1,625,023       |      | 2,024,067       |      | 9,785,000       |
| 1835 | 547,026         |      | 1,371,844       |      | 1,617,202       |      | 2,076,791       |      | 9,980,000       |
|      | 597,959         |      | 1,377,892       |      | 1,670,394       | 1935 | 2,142,676       |      | 10,148,000      |
|      | 635,440         | 1870 | 1,384,756       |      | 1,687,661       |      | 2,221,653       |      | 10,242,000      |
|      | 703,236         |      | 1,404,078       |      | 1,702,791       |      | 2,319,539       | 1970 | 10,297,000      |
|      | 748,396         |      | 1,425,147       | 1905 | 1,730,331       |      | 2,420,358       |      | 10,417,000      |
| 1840 | 798,055         |      | 1,445,490       |      | 1,759,228       |      | 2,489,690       |      | 10,603,000      |
|      | 841,204         |      | 1,464,306       |      | 1,780,214       | 1940 | 2,680,503       |      | 10,794,000      |
|      | 874,715         | 1875 | 1,479,192       |      | 1,785,802       |      | 2,935,679       |      | 10,884,000      |
|      | 935,350         |      | 1,493,401       |      | 1,804,895       |      | 3,178,873       | 1975 | 10,743,000      |
|      | 1,012,047       |      | 1,509,817       | 1910 | 1,827,460       |      | 3,456,796       |      | 10,462,000      |
| 1845 | 1,062,930       |      | 1,515,725       |      | 1,819,043       |      | 3,686,230       |      | 9,015,000       |
|      | 1,108,025       |      | 1,506,714       |      | 1,870,510       | 1945 | 3,860,459       |      | 8,543,100       |
|      | 1,095,551       | 1880 | 1,519,805       |      | 1,912,820       |      | 4,061,520       |      | 7,473,700       |
|      | 1,056,881       |      | 1,532,486       |      | 1,917,944       |      | 4,296,647       |      |                 |
|      | 1,087,351       |      | 1,552,983       | 1915 | 1,966,730       |      | 4,639,121       |      |                 |
| 1850 | 1,112,999       |      | 1,566,184       |      | 2,015,578       |      | 4,952,532       |      |                 |
|      | 1,161,089       |      | 1,582,474       |      | 2,016,996       | 1950 | 5,278,393       |      |                 |
|      | 1,209,349       | 1885 | 1,592,997       |      | 2,128,541       |      | 5,653,240       |      |                 |
|      | 1,259,800       |      | 1,590,804       |      | 2,220,787       |      | 6,036,637       |      |                 |
|      | 1,277,873       |      | 1,604,610       | 1920 | 2,266,482       |      | 6,389,793       |      |                 |
| 1855 | 1,301,833       |      | 1,579,546       |      | 2,230,741       |      | 6,774,679       |      |                 |
|      | 1,341,672       |      | 1,551,594       |      | 2,231,254       | 1955 | 7,174,836       |      |                 |
|      | 1,366,000       | 1890 | 1,535,782       |      | 2,251,378       |      | 7,403,426       |      |                 |
|      | 1,408,712       |      | 1,510,282       |      | 2,295,535       |      | 7,610,748       |      |                 |
|      | 1,506,776       |      | 1,501,920       | 1925 | 2,340,644       |      | 7,755,071       |      |                 |
| 1860 | 1,585,778       |      | 1,470,146       |      | 2,354,703       |      | 7,957,234       |      |                 |
|      | 1,609,852       |      | 1,470,946       |      | 2,412,067       | 1960 | 8,163,446       |      |                 |

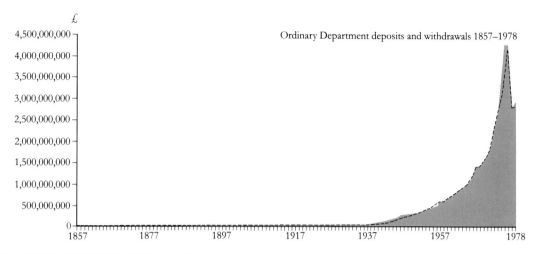

Ordinary Department deposits and withdrawals 1857–1978

| DATE | DEPOSITS | WITHDRAWALS | DATE | DEPOSITS | WITHDRAWALS | DATE | DEPOSITS | WITHDRAWALS | DATE | DEPOSITS | WITHDRAWALS |
|---|---|---|---|---|---|---|---|---|---|---|---|
|  | 7,581,415 | 8,375,095 | 1890 | 9,564,407 | 12,126,400 |  | 35,635,000 | 33,703,000 |  | 491,900,000 | 532,800,000 |
|  | 7,901,925 | 7,839,903 |  | 9,253,470 | 11,089,693 |  | 35,687,000 | 34,887,000 |  | 591,700,000 | 605,100,000 |
|  | 9,021,907 | 7,335,349 |  | 9,141,200 | 10,678,094 | 1925 | 38,662,000 | 39,519,000 |  | 596,400,000 | 602,000,000 |
| 1860 | 9,478,585 | 8,258,421 |  | 9,098,129 | 10,284,612 |  | 33,755,000 | 37,065,000 |  | 665,300,000 | 668,200,000 |
|  | 8,764,870 | 9,627,589 |  | 10,354,449 | 10,177,039 |  | 36,736,000 | 39,304,000 | 1960 | 710,900,000 | 691,100,000 |
|  | 8,136,630 | 10,195,629 | 1895 | 11,802,500 | 10,339,646 |  | 38,810,000 | 40,475,000 |  | 764,900,000 | 761,900,000 |
|  | 8,248,702 | 8,906,642 |  | 12,024,129 | 11,764,179 |  | 39,266,000 | 43,413,000 |  | 823,800,000 | 830,100,000 |
|  | 8,174,679 | 10,781,829 |  | 12,015,556 | 11,415,156 | 1930 | 39,368,000 | 41,487,000 |  | 892,100,000 | 885,800,000 |
| 1865 | 7,684,637 | 9,557,072 |  | 12,244,176 | 11,917,209 |  | 39,317,000 | 42,359,200 |  | 972,900,000 | 950,400,000 |
|  | 7,225,809 | 10,652,993 |  | 12,737,645 | 12,569,951 |  | 42,017,000 | 41,799,000 | 1965 | 1,085,400,000 | 1,069,700,000 |
|  | 7,260,831 | 8,160,060 | 1900 | 12,247,672 | 13,448,957 |  | 50,401,000 | 43,634,000 |  | 1,206,000,000 | 1,186,600,000 |
|  | 7,411,203 | 8,076,918 |  | 12,489,513 | 13,251,630 |  | 49,422,000 | 45,661,000 |  | 1,377,700,000 | 1,417,900,000 |
|  | 7,667,735 | 7,857,091 |  | 12,805,185 | 13,559,498 | 1935 | 51,971,000 | 41,568,000 |  | 1,405,500,000 | 1,410,700,000 |
| 1870 | 7,571,667 | 8,167,783 |  | 12,712,802 | 13,981,749 |  | 56,557,000 | 46,510,000 |  | 1,502,400,000 | 1,521,600,000 |
|  | 8,038,022 | 8,150,513 |  | 12,560,322 | 14,120,730 |  | 61,073,000 | 53,077,000 | 1970 | 1,635,700,000 | 1,666,200,000 |
|  | 8,562,971 | 3,386,184 | 1905 | 13,218,125 | 14,083,437 |  | ★ |  |  | 1,855,600,000 | 1,827,300,000 |
|  | 8,788,385 | 9,071,244 |  | 13,408,810 | 14,442,412 |  | 70,200,000 | 61,500,000 |  | 2,235,300,000 | 2,211,300,000 |
|  | 9,066,674 | 9,216,325 |  | 12,116,951 | 15,280,492 | 1940 | ★ |  |  | 2,687,300,000 | 2,603,000,000 |
| 1875 | 9,295,515 | 9,509,219 |  | 12,294,640 | 15,023,970 |  | 116,700,000 | 71,900,000 |  | 3,466,700,000 | 2,929,700,000 |
|  | 9,203,879 | 9,537,695 |  | 13,749,384 | 14,583,524 |  | 128,600,000 | 78,900,000 | 1975 | 4,234,600,000 | 3,346,600,000 |
|  | 9,363,631 | 9,655,135 | 1910 | 13,722,062 | 14,940,695 |  | 154,300,000 | 90,900,000 |  | 4,217,800,000 | 4,143,300,000 |
|  | 9,158,628 | 10,365,597 |  | 14,284,386 | 14,836,964 |  | 184,900,000 | 117,700,000 |  | 2,775,600,000 | 2,723,600,000 |
|  | 8,915,772 | 10,659,756 |  | 14,752,145 | 15,310,017 | 1945 | 217,100,000 | 160,400,000 |  | 2,781,400,000 | 2,911,500,000 |
| 1880 | 9,008,315 | 10,076,557 |  | 15,291,856 | 16,197,000 |  | 261,800,000 | 208,100,000 |  |  |  |
|  | 9,227,816 | 10,210,640 |  | 14,749,101 | 16,424,292 |  | 279,000,000 | 227,900,000 |  |  |  |
|  | 9,640,544 | 10,327,794 | 1915 | 17,779,269 | 21,640,292 |  | 285,000,000 | 242,600,000 |  |  |  |
|  | 9,592,038 | 10,388,710 |  | ★ |  |  | 298,700,000 | 267,600,000 |  |  |  |
|  | 10,003,541 | 10,343,374 |  | ★ |  | 1950 | 325,900,000 | 309,900,000 |  |  |  |
| 1885 | 9,805,707 | 10,507,289 |  | 30,115,000 | 22,800,000 |  | 312,200,000 | 295,400,000 |  |  |  |
|  | 10,023,683 | 10,772,153 |  | 40,452,000 | 31,086,000 |  | 358,800,000 | 353,600,000 |  |  |  |
|  | 9,876,561 | 10,708,602 | 1920 | 40,595,000 | 39,522,000 |  | 381,400,000 | 400,400,000 |  |  |  |
|  | 9,796,307 | 11,910,579 |  | 32,955,000 | 36,733,000 |  | 403,000,000 | 431,300,000 |  |  |  |
|  | 9,557,931 | 11,949,504 |  | 36,101,000 | 35,142,000 | 1955 | 450,500,000 | 462,300,000 |  |  |  |

★ Data not available due to wartime conditions

# MAPS SHOWING DISTRIBUTION OF SAVINGS BANKS

Savings Banks
certified under
the Act of 1817
in England
and Wales
by end of 1819

Trustee
Savings Banks
offices, 1860

Principal Offices
of Trustee
Savings Banks
in 1904

Principal Offices
of Trustee
Savings Banks
in 1944

The information above is based on maps
in *A History of Savings Banks* by H. Oliver Horne (OUP, 1947).

# FURTHER READING

A vast amount has been written about the Trustee Savings Banks. Short histories of scores of the old banks have appeared in print since the late nineteenth century, written by bank officials or local historians. The savings banks themselves published a great deal of information on their activities, most notably in *The Trustee Savings Bank Gazette* and *The Trustee Savings Bank Yearbook*, published by the TSB Association from 1931 and 1934 respectively, in the reports of the TSB Inspection Committee (from 1892), the *Journal of Savings Bank Institute* (from 1948), and in the annual reports of individual banks. The TSB Institute held annual vocational schools from 1951, and published the addresses and lectures given on all aspects of savings bank business.

There are many government publications, in the form of Annual Returns and official reports dealing with all aspects of savings banks and other elements of the thrift movement since the early nineteenth century. The most important are referred to in the text. Thrift and the savings banks were favourite subjects for essayists and social commentators throughout the period covered by this book.

The progress of and controversies surrounding the savings banks were reported widely in the local and national press. Apart from published literature, the savings bank movement has left behind a large archive, including, from individual banks, minutes of meetings of trustees, customer ledgers, and correspondence, and the records of the TSB Association. In England and Wales, this archive is still being transferred to local authority record offices and most of the material is still unlisted. In Scotland there are four regional TSB archive centres and a comprehensive catalogue has been prepared which is available, along with other lists, in the reading room of the Historical Manuscripts Commission in London.

BLACKABY, F.T. (ed.), *British Economic Policy 1960–1974*, Cambridge, 1978

BROWN, ARCHIBALD, *The Romance of the Savings Banks*, London, 1898

BURDETT, SIR FRANCIS (ed.), *Annals of Banks for Savings*, London, 1818

CAMPBELL, J.D., *The Savings Bank of Glasgow*, Glasgow, 1988

COLLINS, MICHAEL, *Money and Banking in the UK: A History*, Beckenham, 1988

FRASER, DEREK, *The Evolution of the British Welfare State*, London, 1984

GOSDEN, P.H.J.H., *The Friendly Societies in England 1815–1875*, London, 1961

GOSDEN, P.H.J.H., *Self Help*, London, 1973

HALDANE, A.R.B., *One Hundred and Fifty Years of Trustee Savings Banks*, TSBA, 1960

HALL, SOPHY, *Dr Duncan of Ruthwell*, 1910

HARRISON, BRIAN, *Drink and the Victorians: The Temperance Question in England 1815–1931*, London, 1973

HEBDEN, C. DONALD, *Trustee Savings Bank of Yorkshire and Lincoln*, York, 1981

HOLMES, A.R. & GREEN, EDWIN, *Midland: 150 years of banking business*, London, 1986

HORNE, H. OLIVER, *A History of Savings Banks*, Oxford, 1947

JOHNSON, PAUL, *Saving and Spending: The Working-Class Economy in Britain, 1870–1939*, Oxford, 1985

McCREARY, ALF, *By All Accounts: A History of Trustee Savings Banks in Northern Ireland*, Antrim, 1991

SMILES, SAMUEL, *Self-Help*, London, 1859

SMILES, SAMUEL, *Thrift*, London, 1875

TIDD PRATT, JOHN, *The History of Savings Banks in England, Wales and Ireland*, London, 1830

# INDEX

NOTE Titles and ranks are generally the highest mentioned in the text